AF323305

THE CONCEPT OF CONTRACTION IN GIORDANO BRUNO'S PHILOSOPHY

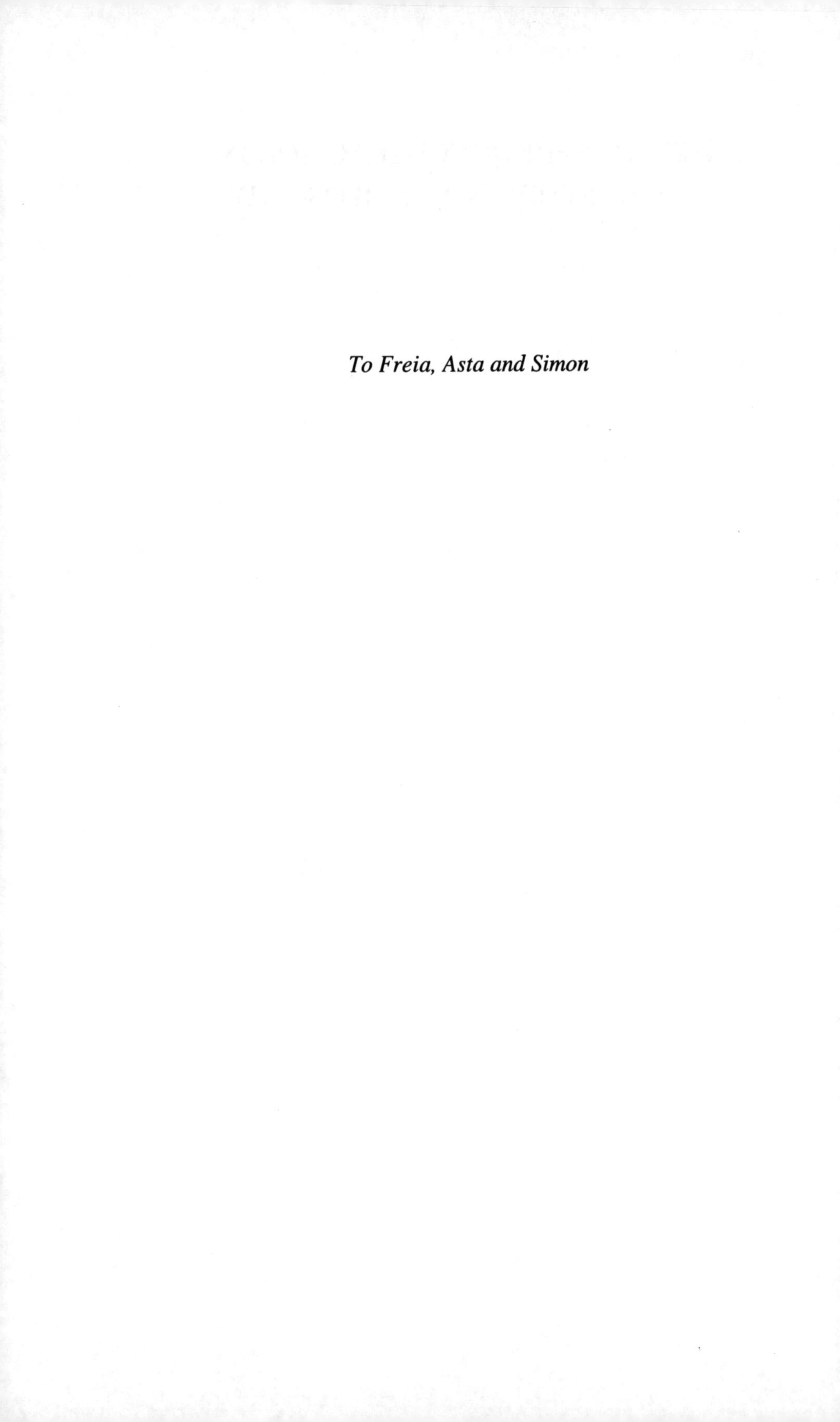

To Freia, Asta and Simon

The Concept of Contraction in Giordano Bruno's Philosophy

LEO CATANA
The University of Copenhagen, Denmark

ASHGATE

Published by
Ashgate Publishing Limited
Gower House
Croft Road
Aldershot
Hants GU11 3HR
England

Ashgate Publishing Company
Suite 420
101 Cherry Street
Burlington, VT 05401-4405
USA

Ashgate website: http://www.ashgate.com

British Library Cataloguing in Publication Data
Catana, Leo
    The concept of contraction in Giordano Bruno's philosophy
    1.Bruno, Giordano, 1548-1600
    I.Title
    195

Library of Congress Cataloging-in-Publication Data
Catana, Leo.
  The concept of contraction in Giordano Bruno's philosophy / Leo Catana.
      p. cm.
  Includes bibliographical references and indexes.
  ISBN 0-7546-5261-0 (hardcover : alk. paper)
  1. Bruno, Giordano, 1548-1600. I. Title.

B783.Z7C38 2005
195—dc22

2005007950

ISBN-10: 0 7546 5261 0

Printed and bound by Athenaeum Press, Ltd.,
Gateshead, Tyne & Wear.

Contents

Acknowledgements

The research for this book has been carried out in two stages. The first goes back to my PhD on Giordano Bruno, submitted to the University of London in 2002. The second stage has been carried out during my present employment at the Department of Philosophy, University of Copenhagen, which has allowed me to research more fully the reception of the *Liber de causis* in the Renaissance. Carl Henrik Koch, lecturer in the History of Early Modern Philosophy at this department, has supported my endeavour throughout. I should like to thank him for his support.

Among the staff in the Italian Department, University College London, I should like to express my gratitude to the late Giovanni Aquilecchia, with whom I had important conversations about Bruno in the early days. He sadly died in 2001. My largest debt is, however, to Dilwyn Knox. I have benefited from his knowledge of Renaissance philosophy, and I owe many of my references to him. His precise, well-informed and challenging criticism of my early drafts has been a continuous inspiration.

I should also like to thank Leen Spruit and Jill Kraye for their constructive criticism, which has been important in the final research for this publication. Likewise, Cristina d'Ancona Costa kindly brought to my notice more recent studies of the *Liber de causis*, for which I owe her thanks.

Several other persons have been helpful, and I should like to state my gratitude to all of them: Pasquale Arfè, Luca Bianchi, Salvatore Camporeale, Eugenio Canone, Stephen Clucas, Carlotta Dionisotti, Germana Ernst, Hillary Gatti, Guido Giglioni, Delfina Giovannozzi, Kristian Jensen, Lucy McGuinness, Stephen Pigney and Jonathan Rolls. Finally, I should like to thank the staff in the Warburg Institute in London, and Heidi Hein in the Institut für Cusanus-Forschung in Trier.

Abbreviations

B&C	*Bruniana & Campanelliana.*
BOeuC	Giordano Bruno, *Oeuvres complètes*, general eds Y. Hersant and N. Ordine, vol. 1-. Les Belles Lettres: Paris, 1993-.
BOL	Giordano Bruno, *Opera latine conscripta*, eds F. Fiorentino, F. Tocco, H. Vitelli, V. Imbriani and C. M. Tallarigo, 3 vols in 8 pts. Morano and Le Monnier: Naples and Florence, 1879-1891. (Anastatic reprint: Stuttgart, Bad Cannstatt, 1961-1962.)
BOM	Giordano Bruno, *Opere magiche*, general ed. M. Ciliberto, eds, tr. and notes by S. Bassi and E. Scapparone, N. Tirinnanzi, intro. M. Ciliberto. Adelphi: Milan, 2000.
CHLGEMP	*The Cambridge history of later Greek and early medieval philosophy*, ed. A. H. Armstrong. Cambridge University Press: Cambridge, 1967.
CHLMP	*The Cambridge history of later medieval philosophy. From the rediscovery of Aristotle to the disintegration of scholasticism 1100-1600*, eds N. Kretzmann, A. Kenny and J. Pinborg. Cambridge University Press: Cambridge, 1982.
CHRP	*The Cambridge history of Renaissance philosophy*, general ed. C. B. Schmitt, eds Q. Skinner, E. Kessler and J. Kraye. Cambridge University Press: Cambridge, 1988.
COO	Nicholas of Cusa, *Opera omnia*, eds E. Hoffmann, R. Klibansky et al., vol. 1-. F. Meiner: Leipzig and Hamburg, 1932-.
DS	*Dictionnaire de spiritualité, ascétique et mystique, doctrine et histoire*, ed M. Viller et al., vol. 1-. Beauchesne: Paris, 1937-.
GCFI	*Giornale critico della filosofia italiana.*
JWCI	*Journal of the Warburg and Courtauld Institutes.*
MFCG	*Mitteilungen und Forschungsbeiträge der Cusanus-Gesellschaft.*
NRL	*Nouvelles de la République des Lettres.*
PG	*Patrologiae cursus completus, series graeca*, ed. J. P. Migne, 162 vols. Paris, 1857-1912.
PL	*Patrologiae cursus completus, series (latina) prima*, ed. J. P. Migne, 221 vols. Paris, 1844-1864.
RCSF	*Rivista critica di storia della filosofia.*
REP	*Routledge encyclopedia of philosophy*, general ed. E. Craig. 10 vols. Routledge: London and New York, 1998.

Citations

In quotations from fifteenth- and sixteenth-century Latin texts, I have expanded abbreviations, changed "&" to "et", "u" to "v" and *vice versa* to distinguish respectively vocalic and consonantal "u", omitted accents, and changed "j" uniformly to "i". Otherwise I have retained the orthography and punctuation of the editions I have used. I have modernised the capitalisation and accents in quotations from Greek. All translations into English are mine, unless otherwise indicated. A number immediately following a full stop denotes a line number, e.g. p. 277.73 denotes line 73 of page 277 and §29.2-3 denotes lines 2-3 in paragraph or section 29.

All Biblical references are to the Vulgate; where the numbering in the Vulgate and King James' translation differ, I have included references to the latter in brackets. Unless something else is stated, references to Plotinus' *Enneads* are to the Greek text edited by Henry and Schwyzer (entitled *Opera*), as cited in the Index of Primary Sources. References to classical authors are to standard texts, as given in the Index of Primary Sources.

Introduction

The aim of this book is twofold. The first is to explain the concept of *contractio*, or contraction, in the philosophy of Giordano Bruno (1548-1600).[1] The second is to discuss its sources. The interpretations of contraction in Bruno's writings are ontological and noetic, and Bruno develops these two interpretations in parallel. Through his doctrine of contraction, Bruno endeavoured to explain the relationship of God to his Creation in a way that conformed with his pantheism. Moreover, for Bruno, the metaphysical structure defined through contraction determines the means by which the human soul can ascend to the One, for, as he states, noetic ascent is a reversed descent.[2] The first part of the book deals with contraction in its ontological and noetic interpretations in Bruno's Latin and Italian works. The second part deals with the sources of contraction.

From the nineteenth century to present day the doctrine of contraction presented by Nicholas of Cusa, also called Nikolaus Krebs or Nikolaus Khrypffs (1401-1464), has been seen as Bruno's only source of the notion in its ontological sense. Through this concept Cusanus had explained the relationship of God to his Creation in a way that agreed with Christian theology. Bruno picked up this notion from Cusanus, it has been argued, but reinterpreted it in keeping with his pantheism.[3] I shall argue instead that Cusanus' and Bruno's interpretations of contraction derive from late medieval and Renaissance interpretations of the *Liber de causis*. In particular, I shall examine the commentary on the *Liber de causis* by Giles of Rome, also called Aegidio Romano or Aegidio Colonna (ca. 1243-1316), and its possible contribution to Bruno's idea of contraction. This possibility has been ignored in Bruno studies.

The term contraction had been applied in scholastic commentaries on the *Liber de causis*, a work falsely attributed to Aristotle.[4] The *Liber de causis* draws, among other sources, on the *Elements of theology* of Proclus (ca. 412-485). The treatise expounds a hierarchy of causes ultimately depending on one cause, God. Although pagan and Neoplatonic in origin, it was susceptible to Christian interpretations. In scholastic commentaries on the *Liber de causis*, 'contraction' was employed in various ways in theories of individuation within this hierarchy of causes, in

---

[1]   For the various meanings of 'contraction' in classical Latin, see p. 91 below.

[2]   BRUNO, *Sigillus* ii 10, ii 22, pp. 202.19-203.14, 213.21-23. This point is also made in BRUNO, *De umbris* §34.2-7, p. 34; *Causa* v, pp. 291, 297; *Spaccio* iii 2, p. 415; *De magia naturali* §6.1-23, pp. 168-170 (= *BOL*, vol. 3, pp. 401.25-402.21).

[3]   CLEMENS, *Giordano Bruno*, p. 143; MANCINI, *La sfera infinita*, p. 67; MIGNINI, 'La dottrina dell'individuo in Cusano e in Bruno', p. 348.

[4]   For Aquinas' attribution, see COSTA, '"Philosophus in libro *De causis*"', pp. 611-612. For other attributions among other scholastic philosophers before Aquinas, see ibid., pp. 633-644.

keeping with commentators' philosophical inclination. The *Liber de causis*, and to some extent its medieval scholastic commentaries, remained popular in Renaissance philosophy, also among figures traditionally interpreted as Platonic or Neoplatonic in orientation, for instance Cusanus, Giovanni Pico della Mirandola (1463-1494) and Marsilio Ficino (1433-1499). Recently Leen Spruit has conjectured that Bruno was familiar with the commentary on the *Liber de causis* composed by Thomas Aquinas (ca. 1225-1274).[5] Nevertheless, the fortune of the *Liber de causis* and its scholastic commentaries has not yet been studied in the context of Renaissance philosophy. The following discussion of contraction in Bruno's philosophy will, I hope, remedy this omission.

Bruno's criticism of Aristotelian natural philosophy is well known.[6] It is widely agreed that Bruno integrated Neoplatonic elements in his philosophy in order to articulate an alternative, and it has typically been assumed that Ficino's Latin translation of Plotinus in 1492 was decisive in this respect. Although this translation was important to Bruno's philosophy, I shall point out that the *Liber de causis* had infused a Neoplatonic strain into scholastic philosophy, and that Bruno's alternative to Aristotelian natural philosophy to a considerable extent built on this tradition.

The second important sense in which Bruno uses the term 'contraction' is, for lack of a better word, 'noetic'. Frances Yates' astrological-magical interpretation gave rise to a renewed interest in Bruno's early mnemonic works. However, she, and those following her interpretation, saw Ficino's astrological and magical works as the chief source of Bruno's philosophy.[7] This line of interpretation identified Bruno's noetic notion of contraction with what was perceived as Ficino's theory of noetic ascent, that is, Ficino's theory of a physiologically induced contraction ultimately induced by astral influence.[8] I shall argue instead that Bruno's noetic interpretation of contraction derives from his epistemology, particularly his theory of memory, both of which had strong Neoplatonic connotations. Even though Bruno knew and used Ficino's notion of a physiologically induced contraction, he did not regard it as self-sufficient, but

---

[5] SPRUIT, *Il problema*, p. 27. See also ibid., pp. 47 nn. 21 and 22, 109 n. 28, 111 n. 37, 144 n. 132, 283 n. 14, 307 n. 106, 309 n. 113, 313 n. 128. Spruit does not, however, consider Giles' commentary on the *Liber de causis* as a possible source for Bruno. Studies on Bruno's Aristotelian background do not examine the influence of the *Liber de causis* on his thought; see BLUM, *Aristoteles*; PAPULI, 'Qualche osservazione', pp. 201-228.

[6] For this criticism, see pp. 30-35, 132-134 below.

[7] For this interpretation applied to Bruno's early mnemonic works, especially *De umbris* and the *Sigillus*, see YATES, *Giordano Bruno and the Hermetic tradition*, pp. 190-204, 205-206, 209, 271-273, 307-308; *The art of memory*, pp. 53, 198-201, 204, 208-213, 220-221, 246-255, 287-288, 290. Yates claimed that Bruno's *De umbris* "was in line" with Camillo's memory theatre (ibid., p. 204), which Yates claims was strongly influenced by Ficino's magic as presented in his *De vita* (ibid., pp. 154-159).

[8] INGEGNO, *Cosmologia*, pp. 251-256; *La sommersa nave*, pp. 89-93; *Regia pazzia*, pp. 133-136; MANCINI, *La sfera infinita*, pp. 67-70.

subordinated it to his idea of noetic ascent, conforming with his theory of descent, that is, of contraction in the ontological sense.

PART ONE
BRUNO'S CONCEPT OF CONTRACTION

Chapter 1

Methods Facilitating
Noetic Ascent

Bruno on heroic ascent

I shall introduce Bruno's unified idea of descent and noetic ascent, articulated through his concept of contraction, as he presented it in the *Sigillus sigillorum*, which he published in London in 1583 as part of the *Ars reminiscendi*.[1] Bruno discusses ontology in this work, but the practice of noetic ascent — or, to be more precise, the mind's movement from the manifold to unity — is the real purpose of the *Sigillus*: "We want to treat these matters [descent from the One] not because we think that this is the place for considering the nature of these matters but so that we may teach how to examine, meditate upon and produce unity in every multiplicity and identity in every diversity."[2]

Immediately after this quotation, Bruno presents the so-called 'fifteen contractions' (i 35-49), that is, the fifteen methods facilitating noetic ascent, which are the subject of this chapter. In the sentence introducing these fifteen contractions, he states that "a manifold power originates in the multiple contraction."[3] Just as there are several ways to ascend, there are several intellectual virtues and hence several *contractiones* leading the soul from multiplicity to unity, depending on the mode of noetic ascent. Such an interpretation agrees with a passage in the *Spaccio*, where the interlocutor Saulino explains to earthly Sofia that even though influence from higher ontological realms is the same for everyone, it is approached differently by different people, depending on their different intellectual qualities.[4]

Traditionally, noetic ascent presupposed a hierarchically ordered universe. Bruno's Copernicanism, however, entailed a physically homogenous universe. What did that mean to his theories of noetic ascent? Is Bruno, one may ask, inconsistent on this score? Or can it be argued that he worked out an ontology,

---

[1]   AQUILECCHIA, 'Bruno, Giordano', p. 657; BASSI, 'Editoria e filosofia', pp. 437-458, especially pp. 439-440, 454-458.

[2]   BRUNO, *Sigillus* i 34, p. 180.7-10: "Haec non quia de istarum rerum natura hic considerandi locus habeatur, tractasse volumus, at vero ut in omni multitudine unitatem, in omni diversitate identitatem tentare, meditari et efficere doceamus."

[3]   Ibid., i 35, p. 180.21-23: "Ex proxime dictorum consideratione delitescit, quemadmodum multiplex a multiplici contractione virtus exoriatur."

[4]   BRUNO, *Spaccio* ii 1, p. 191. See also BRUNO, *Furori* ii 1, pp. 325-327.

characterised by hierarchically ordered ontological realms, which were consistent with his cosmology?[5] I shall leave aside this problem related to his cosmology, and restrict my analysis to his use of the concept of contraction within his unified idea of ontological descent and noetic ascent.

I shall discuss Bruno's sources for his doctrine of noetic ascent in the second half of the book. In this chapter I shall summarise Bruno's fifteen contractions, bringing out the connections with some key concepts in Bruno's psychology and with his unorthodox doctrine of noetic ascent. In the *Eroici furori* Bruno refers explicitly to the fifteen contractions in his *Sigillus*, which, he says, some practise in a "shameful manner", others "in a heroic manner".[6] I shall ask, therefore, which forms Bruno considers "shameful", which "heroic".

The fifteen contractions in the *Sigillus sigillorum*

The fifteen contractions are as follows:

(i) Contraction produced by solitude

The kind of solitude which stems from living in a secluded manner may induce a contemplative and inventive state of mind.[7] Pythagoras, Zoroaster, Moses, Jesus Christ, Ramon Lull (1235-1315) and Theophrast Paracelsus (1493-1541) are examples of this contemplative contraction, according to Bruno.[8] Bruno was

---

[5]   For discussions of this problem, see SPRUIT, *Il problema*, pp. 300-316; 'Giordano Bruno and astrology', pp. 242-249.

[6]   BRUNO, *Furori* ii 1, p. 327: "De quali alcune vituperosa, altre eroicamente fanno che non s'apprenda téma di morte, non si soffrisca dolor di corpo, non si sentano impedimenti di piaceri". On the same page of the *Furori* Bruno mentions the contractions "nel libro *De' trenta sigilli*" ("in the book *On thirty seals*"). Bruno probably means the *Sigillus*, since it is there, and not in the *Triginta sigilli*, that he discusses the fifteen forms of contraction (BRUNO, *Sigillus* i 35-49, pp. 180.19-193.5). The title of the *Explicatio* (BRUNO, *Explicatio*, p. 73), covering the *Triginta sigilli* as well as the *Explicatio*, indicates that the *Sigillus* is "added" to the *Triginta* and the *Explicatio* (ibid., p. 73; "*Explicatio triginta sigillorum ... Quibus adiectus est Sigillus sigillorum*").

[7]   BRUNO, *Sigillus* i 35, p. 180.21-26.

[8]   Ibid., i 35, pp. 180.26-181.16. In the Renaissance the ideas attributed to Pythagoras and Zoroaster were believed to part of an ancient theology; see WALKER, *Ancient theology*, pp. 1, 2, 11, 13, 19-22, 26, 34-35, 39, 49-50, 54-56, 72-73, 78, 81-82, 85, 87, 100, 102-103, 110, 118, 125, 143-146. See also CELENZA, 'Pythagoras in the Renaissance', pp. 667-711; *Piety and Pythagoras*. For Ficino as a possible source for this first contraction in Bruno's *Sigillus*, see STURLESE, 'Le fonti', p. 141. In Ch. 5, pp. 101-102 below, I shall discuss Sturlese's identifications of the sources for these fifteen contractions. In this section, however, I shall also mention her identifications. For discussions of this first contraction, see also TOCCO, *Le opere*, p. 77; RICCI, *Giordano Bruno*, pp. 229-230; CILIBERTO, *La ruota del tempo*, pp. 84-85.

convinced, here and elsewhere, that potentially creative seclusion can be abused by those who have the possibility to live a contemplative life, e.g. the monks: "But among them you will find that many have secluded themselves from the conduct of everyday affairs in order to escape human toil and concerns, seduced by the love of sloth and gluttony; only very few have done so from a desire for virtue so that they can pursue goodness and truth".[9]

Several scholars have suggested that in the *Spaccio* Bruno criticised the Protestant doctrine of justification by faith (*iustitia sola fide*), and the alleged sloth, *ocio*, accompanying it.[10] But on this particular occasion in the *Sigillus*, Bruno's attack on monastic idleness had a precedent not only in the widely known criticisms of the religious life, including monastic life, by Desiderius Erasmus (1466/1469-1536), but also in the Protestant John Calvin (1509-1564), whose ideas Bruno had encountered while he was in Geneva during June and July 1579, and those of many others besides.[11] On Augustine's authority, Calvin held that monasteries should be free from idleness, but Calvin remarked that in his day the opposite was the case. He asked ironically what would become of the so-called "contemplative life" which some monks claimed made them equal to angels, if that idleness were taken away.[12]

(ii) Contraction produced by restricting imagination to a place

The imagination, says Bruno, is sometimes contracted to a particular place, making someone indifferent to distances near and far. Examples are those people who go to a steep and narrow summit and stand there upright on one foot. Even more startling are those suffering from melancholy who wander along

---

[9] BRUNO, *Sigillus* i 35, p. 181.16-20: "Sed ex iis plurimos, ut humanum laborem et curas fugerent, ocii et gulae amore illectos, perpaucos vero virtutis amore, ut bonitatem et veritatem persequerentur, invenies se a negociosorum conversatione sevocasse". For this passage, see ORDINE, 'Introduction', pp. XC-XCII. For Bruno's social and religious criticism, see RICCI, *Giordano Bruno*, pp. 230-232; ORDINE, 'Introduction', pp. XCIII-CXV. In the quotation above from the *Sigillus*, Bruno is probably alluding above all to contemporary religions; see RICCI, *Giordano Bruno*, pp. 77-79.

[10] For the theme of sloth, see BRUNO, *Spaccio* iii 1, p. 365, *et passim*. On grace and salvation in the thoughts of Luther and Bruno, see INGEGNO, *La sommersa nave*, especially pp. 11-20; CILIBERTO, *Giordano Bruno*, pp. 128-169.

[11] For Bruno's criticism of sloth, see BRUNO, *Sigillus* i 35, pp. 181.22-182.11. For Bruno's stay in Geneva, see FIRPO, *Processo*, p. 160; RICCI, *Giordano Bruno*, pp. 128-137. For the date of Bruno's stay there, see ibid., p. 129. For Bruno on Calvin, see FIRPO, *Processo*, pp. 28, 65, 177, 249, 251, 292.

[12] CALVIN, *Institutio religionis christianae* IV xiii 10, col. 932: "Augustinus fortiter contendit, non licere monachis de alieno otiosis vivere. Tale exemplum suo tempore exstitisse negat bene constituti monasterii. Nostri praecipuam sanctimoniae suae partem in otio collocant. Nam si otium illis tollas, ubi erit illa contemplativa vita, qua se alios omnes excellere et ad angelos propius accedere gloriantur?"

precipices.[13] Who Bruno has in mind in these examples is not altogether clear. Is he perhaps alluding to episodes in saints' lives? The posture of standing on one foot on top of a mountain might, for instance, be an imitation of Christ on the cross or the Transfiguration. Be this as it may, this is the first of the fifteen contractions concerning humours. I shall return to the humours below.

(iii) Contraction of the horizon into the centre

Some religious men, endowed with unusual mental sight, are able to intuit what is going on in distant places. This ability Bruno describes as a "contraction of the horizon into the centre".[14] This image has not yet been explained in the literature on Bruno, and it is very puzzling. What does it mean?

Let me first consider the term 'horizon'. There are two meanings of the term in this passage. First, it can denote the human soul existing on the boundary of the sensible and the intelligible worlds. Second, 'horizon' can symbolise the hypostasis Soul in the Neoplatonic system of emanation. Bruno may, however, be combining both meanings in his account of the third contraction.

In *De magia naturali* Bruno explains that the human soul is not spatially confined to the body.[15] This comment probably derives from the soul-body theory of Plotinus (ca. 205-270), according to whom the soul ensouls the body without being confined to it spatially. In that sense the body is in the soul, not *vice versa*.[16] The soul, Bruno continues in *De magia naturali*, thus stretches "throughout the horizon", that is, beyond the sensible world perceivable by the corporeal sense organs, upwards through the hierarchy of hypostases. This transcendent aspiration of the soul means, Bruno explains, that the soul can not only obtain cognition of that which it can comprehend though corporeal sense organs, but also of that which is imperceptible to the senses. The soul can thus also obtain cognition of

---

[13] BRUNO, *Sigillus* i 36, p. 182.13-18: "Contractione imaginationis ad situm, per indifferentiam distantis atque proximi conceptam, nonnullos vidimus in alto arctoque culmine se se exagitasse, rectosque unico innixos pede in aëre constitisse; idemque atque magis per imprudentiam, atra bile laborantibus, per alta praecipitia obambulantibus accidisse." For the doctrine of the four humours, see SIRAISI, *Medieval and early Renaissance medicine*, pp. 104-109. For this second contraction, see also TOCCO, *Le opere*, p. 78.

[14] BRUNO, *Sigillus* i 37, p. 182.20-24: "Contractione quadam horizontis in centrum (de qua forte alias) a quibusdam religiose affectis maximo loci intervallo seposita per eam animi vim, quae corporeis non est adstricta terminis, veluti intelligentiarum obtutu potitis, reddita sunt ad sensum non fallentem perspicua." Examples are provided ibid., i 37, pp. 182.24-183.7. For Ficino as a possible source for this third contraction, see STURLESE, 'Le fonti', pp. 141-142. On this particular occasion Sturlese does not, however, indicate any source for the expressions 'horizon' and 'centre'. TOCCO, *Le opere*, p. 78, describes this third contraction, but ignores the Neoplatonic sources that I point out over the pages below.

[15] BRUNO, *De magia naturali* §16.6-7, p. 188 (= *BOL*, vol. 3, p. 409.16-17). The same idea comes up in BRUNO, *Causa* ii, pp. 121-125.

[16] For Plotinus' soul-body theory, see BLUMENTHAL, *Plotinus' psychology*, pp. 9-19.

that with which it "has contracted" "any use, participation and communion", that is, we may assume, higher ontological realms than that of the perceptible world.[17] When Bruno speaks of a "contraction of the horizon into the centre" in this third contraction in the *Sigillus*, he may be referring to this or a similar idea.

The second possible meaning of 'horizon' — that is, the hypostasis Soul — has at least two possible sources. Plotinus says that the hypostasis Mind appears to the individual human soul just as the sun rises over the horizon. When Bruno speaks of a "contraction of the horizon into the centre", he may be alluding to that image as it appears in Ficino's translation.[18] Another and more likely source for the expression 'horizon' is the *Liber de causis*, in which the hypostasis Soul — which is dependent upon Mind — is said to exist "on the horizon of eternity from below and above time".[19] In the *Eroici furori* Bruno may employ this expression from the *Liber de causis* to explain how the human soul, which, like the hypostasis Soul, exists on the frontier, the 'horizon' of the intelligible and the sensible worlds.[20] In

---

17   BRUNO, *De magia naturali* §16.6-10, p. 188 (= *BOL*, vol. 3, p. 409.16-20): "Hinc manifestum est animam plus se diffundere extra corpus, per totum horizontem suae naturae. Hinc accidit ut non solum sua membra cognoscat, sed etiam omnia cum quibus aliquem usum et participationem et communionem contraxit." 'Horizon' is used similarly in BRUNO, *De immenso* i 1, p. 202.16-19: "[homo] in confinio aeternitatis atque temporis, inter archetypum et exemplatum, intelligibilem inter sensibilemque mundum positus, utriusque particeps substantiae, extremorum quodammodo interstitium, in horizonte naturae constitutus." The description of man, i.e. his soul, as existing on the boundary of the eternal and the temporal worlds, is parallel to that of the hypostasis Soul in PSEUDO-ARISTOTLE, *Liber de causis* ii 22, ed. Pattin, p. 138. The expression "in horizonte naturae" used of the human soul in *De immenso* is parallel with the description of the hypostasis Soul in PSEUDO-ARISTOTLE, *Liber de causis* viii(ix) 84, p. 156. Both passages from the *Liber de causis* are quoted on p. 11 n. 19 below.

18   PLOTINUS V v [32] 8.3-7, which reads in Ficino's translation, p. 527.13-18: "quapropter non decet prosequi [Mind], sed potius requiescere, donec nobis effulgeat, ita nos ad id spectaculum praeparantibus, sicut et oculus ortum solis expectat, cui sol ipse ex orizonte resurgens, et ut poetae aiunt, [']ex Oceano exhibet se spectandum[']." By "poeta" he probably alludes to HOMER, *Iliad* vii.421-422.

19   PSEUDO-ARISTOTLE, *Liber de causis* ii 22, ed. Pattin, p. 138: "Esse vero quod est post aeternitatem et supra tempus est anima, quoniam est in horizonte aeternitatis inferius et supra tempus." See also ibid., viii(ix) 84, p. 156: "Et intelligentia quidem comprehendit generata et naturam et horizontem naturae scilicet animam, nam ipsa est supra naturam." For the date of the *Liber de causis*, see pp. 103-104 below.

20   BRUNO, *Furori* i 4, p. 189: "come il raggio del sole il quale quindi tocca la terra et è gionto a cose inferiori et oscure che illustra, vivifica et accende, indi è gionto a l'elemento del fuoco, cioè a la stella da cui procede, ha principio, è diffuso, et in cui ha propria et originale sussistenza: cossì l'anima ch'è nell'orizonte della natura corporea et incorporea, ha con che s'inalze alle cose superiori, et inchine a cose inferiori." For this passage, see SARAUW, *Der Einfluss Plotins*, pp. 36-37, where PLOTINUS IV iii [27] 12.1-5 is pointed out as a source. It reads in Ficino's translation, p. 381.24-30: "Hominum vero animae ipsorum simulachra tanquam Dionysii prospicientes in speculo, illic extiterunt desuper properantes, neque tamen a principio suo intellectuque disiunctae ["intellectus" is translated from "νοῦς"]. Neque enim una cum intellectu descenderunt,

his commentary on the *Liber de causis*, Giles had stressed this image of Soul, though without connecting it with 'centre', as Bruno does in this third contraction.[21] It should be added that the two possible sources, Plotinus and the *Liber de causis*, are not mutually exclusive. Bruno may be consciously adapting both.

What, then, does Bruno mean by 'centre'? What is it that the soul approaches? Rita Sturlese has interpreted the term *centrum* in another context as the *sensus communis*, which unites the sense data from the five senses.[22] However, this interpretation would not in itself explain the use of 'centre' in the third contraction, since the cognition achieved transcends the reach of the senses.[23] Another possibility, not pointed out by Sturlese in relation to this contraction, is that 'centre' denotes a Neoplatonic hypostasis. Only a few pages before this third contraction in the *Sigillus*, Bruno explains that the hypostasis Mind (*mens*) gives shape to the seed from the centre, thus forming the mass of the universe.[24] Hence, through the third contraction in the *Sigillus*, Bruno may explain that through the human soul's ascent to the Ideas in Mind, it becomes able to comprehend things without reference to time and beyond the reach of the senses, due to the soul's participation in Mind. Bruno, in short, reduces what might appear to be the supernatural cognition of some "religious zealots" to a metaphysical system.

There is one possible source for this meaning of 'centre'. In Plotinus' theory on the human soul's ascent towards Mind, he speaks of one centre, the human soul, being united with another centre, Mind. Bruno may have picked up the expression 'centre' from Ficino's translation and commentary.[25] In Plotinus' theology, this

---

sed pervenerunt quidem usque ad terram: at interim caput earum extat etiam super coelum." PSEUDO-ARISTOTLE, *Liber de causis* ii 22, ed. Pattin, p. 138, quoted p. 11 n. 19 above, is an alternative source, which is ignored in SARAUW, *Der Einfluss Plotins*, pp. 36-37, and GRANADA in his note to BRUNO, *Furori* ii 4, p. 188 n. 53.

[21] E.g. GILES, *Super authorem De causis, Alpharabium* ii, fol. 7ᵛ, lines 16-37.

[22] STURLESE, 'Le fonti', pp. 112-113, refers the use of 'centrum' in BRUNO, *Sigillus* i 18, p. 165.17-21, to FICINO, *Theologia platonica* vii 2, vol. 1, pp. 263, 265-266, where the expression is used synonymously with *sensus communis*. This meaning of 'centrum' may also, perhaps ultimately, derive from Alexander of Aphrodisias; see SINNIGE, 'Metaphysical and personal religion in Plotinus', pp. 149-150.

[23] BRUNO, *Sigillus* i 37, pp. 182.24-183.7.

[24] Ibid., i 31, p. 174.12-15: "Mens enim, quae universi molem exagitat, est quae a centro semen figurat, tam mirabilibus ordinibus in suam hypostasim educit". For 'centre' as an expression of the absolute, or God, see also BRUNO, *Camoeracensis*, pp. 68.27-69.5; *Infinito* i, p. 85.

[25] PLOTINUS VI ix [9] 10.13-17, which reads in Ficino's translation, p. 769.34-41: "Tunc sane neque proprie videt, neque tanquam videns ipse discernit, neque duo quaedam imaginatur: sed animus tunc tanquam factus iam alius, neque ipse ulterius, neque sui duntaxat illuc se confert, eique se dedit, factusque totus illius, evadit protinus unum tanquam centrum [τό κέντρον] cum centro coniungens." See also FICINO, *In Plotinum* VI ix [9] 11, p. 769.48-51: "Animus ergo cum ipso principio rerum uno tunc demum unitur arctissime, quando ipse potissimum in se fit unum: id autem efficitur, quando exutus multitudinem [multitudine] quae ad imaginationem, rationem, intelligentiam

image was used on several occasions to illustrate how man — that is, the contemplative philosopher — can achieve mystical union with his first origin, the ineffable One, by travelling noetically through the hypostases Soul and Mind.[26]

Bruno's statement that the third contraction occurs when the soul contracts from the 'horizon' into the 'centre' could mean, then, that the individual soul turns from its nature towards the Ideas in Mind, that is, the 'centre'. In another context Bruno uses a similar image. The five senses, he says, have their centre in the human soul, the *sensus communis*, from where the human soul ascends to a second centre, God.[27] Further, again in keeping with Neoplatonic metaphysics, Ficino says that God is the only 'centre' of everything, and that the emanations Mind, Soul, nature and matter form concentric circles around that centre.[28] None of these sources, however, completely fits Bruno's image in the third contraction, and they all require further clarification of the Platonic or Neoplatonic epistemology involved. I shall return to this issue in Chapters 3 and 4.

(iv) Contraction producing divine dreams, visions and revelations

Through the soul's "contraction" on, or attentiveness towards, the image of a thing to be understood, the human soul may expose itself to "divine dreams, visions and revelations".[29] Although this idea seems to open up the possibility of a supernatural agent transmitting knowledge to a sleeping human, this may not be Bruno's intention, since he qualifies the idea by adding that "to the one who truly

---

pertinet, evadit sola sua unitas, atque hac ipsa per amatorium affectum fruitur unitate divina, centrum ita suum cum centro copulans universi." For this metaphor of the 'centre' as the "point" from which emanation occurs in Plotinus, see ARMSTRONG, *Intelligible universe*, p. 60; SINNIGE, 'Metaphysical and personal religion in Plotinus', pp. 147-148, 150-151, 153.

[26] For the ascent of the soul, see PLOTINUS VI ix [8] 1-11 (= tr. Ficino, pp. 756.27-771.19). The image of the One as a 'centre' with which another 'centre', the human soul, may unite, also appears ibid., V i [10] 11.11 (= tr. Ficino, p. 492.22). For similar uses of 'centre' to express mystical union with the One, see ibid., VI viii [39] 18.8, 9, 10, 11 (= tr. Ficino, p. 752.52, 54, 55). For the One as a 'centre' from which multiplicity derives, see ibid., VI v [23] 5.1-23 (= tr. Ficino, pp. 663.41-664.12).

[27] BRUNO, *Lampas* §74.1-16, pp. 1036-1038 (= *BOL*, vol. 3, p. 50.4-19): "Figurabatur circulo, qui tum circa proprium centrum, tum circa alium secundum totum movebatur, ad denotandum duplicem intelligendi rationem illi tribui — ut Platonicis est satis vulgare: altera, qua vertit se circa seipsum, altera circa Deum. [Bruno explains the first 'centre':] Quemadmodum omnes sensus particulares ad sensum communem — quemadmodum ad unum centrum — referuntur et reducuntur". However, here Bruno speaks of the human soul moving in a circle around a centre, not towards it. This image may derive from PLOTINUS VI ix [9] 8.1-8 (= tr. Ficino, p. 76[6].29-41).

[28] FICINO, *De amore* II iii, p. 147.17-19: "Centrum unum omnium deus est, circuli quatuor circa deum, mens, anima, natura, materia." See also FICINO, *In Plotinum* VI ix [9] 8, p. 760.17-28.

[29] BRUNO, *Sigillus* i 38, p. 183.8-11: "Contractione intentionis in rei cognoscendae speciem, divinis insomnis, visionibus et revelationibus exponitur animus".

strives, nothing is difficult [to comprehend]".[30] Iamblichus' *De mysteriis Aegyptorum* may be a source. There Iamblichus says that the soul disposes of a double road to knowledge, one dependent on the body, another independent of the body. In sleep, the soul can pursue the latter, since then it is free from the bonds of the body and can comprehend the intelligible world.[31] In the *Eroici furori* Bruno says explicitly that Iamblichus' idea of contemplation independent of the body is the model of the fifteen contractions in the *Sigillus*.[32] Could it be that Bruno, in this fourth contraction, regards the human soul's attentiveness, stimulating the soul to experience "divine dreams, visions and revelations", as such a form of contemplation? I cannot say so definitively, but I think it is very probable.

In the fifth to the ninth contraction Bruno moves on to psychological issues, dealing with the role of various emotions in noetic ascent.

(v) Contraction produced by faith

A mental tension produced by faith can empower the soul to affect physical things.[33] Bruno, ironically, illustrates this with mountains being moved by faith, an obvious allusion to Matthew 21.21-22: "Jesus answered and said unto them, Verily I say unto you, If ye have faith, and doubt not, ye shall not only do this which is done to the fig tree, but also if ye shall say unto this mountain, Be thou removed, and be thou cast into the sea; it shall be done. And all things, whatsoever ye shall ask in prayer, believing, ye shall receive."[34] In the Bible, the mountain is moved by Jesus because the disciples have faith in him. In Bruno's fifth contraction faith cures the body and, Bruno adds ironically we may assume, moves mountains. No supernatural agent is needed.[35] Events caused by faith, as the mountain being moved by faith, occur, Bruno says, when a 'passive principle' is found together with an 'active principle'.[36] By 'passive principle' he may mean the object towards which faith is directed, e.g. a mountain, and by 'active

---

[30] Ibid., i 38, p. 183.11: "ipsi quippe vere intendenti nihil est difficile."

[31] IAMBLICHUS, *De mysteriis Aegyptorum, Chaldaeorum, Assyriorum*, tr. Ficino, fol. b5^v, line 37 to fol. b6^r, line 8 (= IAMBLICHUS, *De mysteriis Aegyptorum*, ed. des Places, iii 3, p. 101).

[32] BRUNO, *Furori* ii 1, p. 327: "È tanta la virtù della contemplazione (come nota Iamblico) che accade tal volta non solo che l'anima ripose da gli atti inferiori, ma et oltre lascie il corpo a fatto. Il che non voglio intendere altrimente che in tante maniere quali sono esplicate nel libro *De' trenta sigilli*, dove son prodotti tanti modi di contrazzione." By "*De' trenta sigilli*" Bruno means the *Sigillus*. See p. 8 n. 6 above.

[33] BRUNO, *Sigillus* i 39, pp. 183.12-184.7.

[34] Secundum Mattheum 21.21-22.

[35] As we shall see in Ch. 4, in 1624 the French philosopher, scientist and theologian Marin Mersenne (1588-1648) wrote, precisely in connection with the fifteen contractions advanced in the *Sigillus*, that Bruno "does not believe at all in the Christian faith". See MERSENNE, *L'impiété des déistes* i 10, pp. 232-234, as quoted on p. 99 n. 53 below. For Mersenne's strong rejection of Bruno's treatment of faith in this paragraph of the *Sigillus*, see BUCCOLINI, '*Contractiones* in Bruno', pp. 504, 509, 514, 517.

[36] BRUNO, *Sigillus* i 39, p. 183.15-17.

principle' he may mean the subject who directs faith towards that object.[37] Bruno adds in this fifth contraction that psychological affects — such as faith, fear, desire, hope, joy and sadness — are decisive to the efficacy of magicians' and doctors' work. Accordingly, Bruno denies that witchcraft (*artificiosae fascinationes*) and medical incantations (*medicae adiurationes*) work by virtue of anything supernatural.[38]

Although Bruno only deals briefly with magic in these fifteen contractions, namely in this fifth contraction, it should be noted that he does dedicate two important pages to the theme of magic in the *Sigillus* ii 5, where it is treated as one of the guides (*rectores*) to noetic ascent.[39] It may be true that the object in the *Sigillus* ii 5 is magic, but his discussion of various forms of magic may also be intended as a defence against potential accusations for the heterodox equation of the Christian practice of faith with magic, even base magic, which may take place in the passage in question. One kind of magic, Bruno maintains there, eradicates reason through faith and credulity, which brings about an unworthy contraction of the human mind, so that reason is "mortified" and the mind dragged down to something ontologically lower by an imagination disturbed by faith. Another kind of magic produces a praiseworthy kind of contraction, building on "regulated faith", enabling the human being to make his senses acute and strong, and, on that basis, to ascend gradually to the higher parts of the soul, ultimately to contemplate the universals.[40]

---

[37] BRUNO, *Theses de magia* §93.2-5, p. 394 (= *BOL*, vol. 3, p. 489.25-28). This parallel passage in the *Theses de magia* is pointed out by TIRINNANZI in BRUNO, *Le ombre delle idee*, etc., tr. N. Tirinnanzi (Milan 1997), p. 384 n. 190.

[38] BRUNO, *Sigillus* i 39, pp. 183.17-184.5.

[39] For Bruno's theory of magic in the *Sigillus*, see ibid., ii 5, pp. 197.25-199.17.

[40] Ibid., ii 5, pp. 197.26-199.1: "Quid de magia, quae cum media mathesi fere in eadem ab extremis physicis atque metaphysicis aequidistantia consistit? Haecque duplicis est generis: altera, quae vel per credulitatem et fidei vim, vel per alias non laudabiles contractionis species sensum mortificat, quo propria ratio per aliquod extrinsecum penitus absorbeatur, ut natura melior in alicuius deterioris imaginem transformetur ... ; altera vero est, quae per regulatam fidem et alias laudandas contractionis species tantum abest ut sensus perturbatione quandoque utatur, ut eumdem claudicantem fulciat, errantem corrigat, imbecillem et obtusum roboret et acuat. Haec cum norit, daemonis magni (qui amor est) virtute, animam per spiritum corpori copulari, magisque separatam divinamque vim spiritui per animam, et universalia omnia omnibus per media plura vel pauciora adnecti et concatenari, cumque non lateat geminam esse animam, superiorem videlicet magisque intellectualem quae in se ipsa pulchrum effingit, et inferiorem quae in alio, primam ad superiorem, secundam ad inferiorem et vulgarem Venerem referri, illamque gemini Cupidinis matrem esse, in quorum utroque naturae sensus consistit, qui per se vita dicitur, hunc in naturalibus omnibus contemplatur; ab isto etenim sensu est appetitus in partibus corporum et praecipuis mundi membris, puta magnis animalibus atque Diis, ut ad locum suum illa se conferant, et haec vitales circuitus peragant." For the two kinds of faith and the two kinds of magic to which they are related, see SPRUIT, '*Magia*', p. 149.

Outside the *Sigillus* Bruno distinguishes between theological and philosophical faith in a way which seems parallel to the distinction in *Sigillus* ii 5 between credulity (one sort of faith, possibly corresponding to theological faith), and rationally controlled belief (a second sort of faith possibly corresponding to philosophical faith). Theological faith, Bruno says, is firm belief obtained through first principles, which are given by a superior intelligence, i.e. God, but which are not comprehensible to human reason. Philosophical faith, on the other hand, is firm belief in that which is manifest to human senses and reason, and whose appearance depends on first principles.[41] How does this fit into the pages on magic in the *Sigillus* ii 5? It would make sense to assume that the contraction of the mind undertaken through a "regulated faith" enables man to comprehend the intelligible realm, and that it corresponds to philosophical faith; faith would then be "regulated" by the hierarchy of being, through which the soul ascends. This assumption may find support in *De la causa, principio et uno*, published in London in 1584, where Bruno asserts that, for someone who "does not believe", "contemplation" and noetic "ascent" will be impossible.[42]

Bruno uses the orthodox Neoplatonic distinction between the two Venuses in an unorthodox context, namely to explain the two kinds of magic and the corresponding two forms of faith. Following Plato's *Symposium*, Plotinus had correlated to the two-fold soul two kinds of desire, namely heavenly Aphrodite, characteristic of the higher part of the soul, and vulgar Aphrodite, characteristic of the lower part of the soul.[43] The higher part of the soul, symbolised by heavenly Aphrodite, enables humans to comprehend the eternal Ideas.[44] The Greek Aphrodite, used by Plotinus, corresponds to the Latin Venus, or the Italian *Venere*. In the Renaissance, Ficino had embraced the metaphor of the two Venuses and had made it a prominent metaphor in his Neoplatonism, symbolising two distinct human desires. Heavenly Venus stands for the desire for the Ideas in Mind, existing free of matter. Vulgar Venus, on the other hand, stands for the soul's desire for the sensible beauty produced by generation and multiplicity in matter.[45] Hence, in the thought of Ficino, the metaphor came to denote a distinction

---

[41]   BRUNO, *Summa*, pp. 71.20-72.3, 126.19-25; *Lampas* §246.12-27, pp. 1232-1234 (= *BOL*, vol. 3, p. 143.1-16). For the distinction in Bruno, see SPRUIT, *Il problema*, pp. 92-96.

[42]   BRUNO, *Causa* iv, p. 253: "Possete quindi montar al concetto, non dico del summo et ottimo principio, escluso della nostra considerazione, ma de l'anima del mondo, come è atto di tutto e potenza di tutto, et è tutta in tutto: onde al fine (dato che sieno innumerabili individui) ogni cosa è uno; et il conoscere questa unità è il scopo e termine di tutte le filosofie e contemplazioni naturali: lasciando ne' sua termini la più alta contemplazione, che ascende sopra la natura, la quale a chi non crede, è impossibile e nulla." For the date of publication, see AQUILECCHIA, 'Bruno, Giordano', p. 658.

[43]   PLOTINUS VI ix [9] 9.1-60 (= tr. Ficino, pp. 767.45-769.4). Plotinus derived the myth of the two Venuses from PLATO, *Symposium* 180D3-E5.

[44]   PLOTINUS III v [50] 2.1-3.38 (= tr. Ficino, pp. 292.63-294.45).

[45]   FICINO, *De amore* II vii, pp. 153-155. See also ibid., VI v, VI vii-viii, pp. 205.7-12, 208-212. For Ficino's use of the metaphor, see PANOFSKY, *Studies in iconology*, pp. 141-144.

between intellectual and sensual desire. Other philosophers in the Renaissance influenced by Neoplatonism took up the metaphor.[46]

Bruno integrates the Neoplatonic idea of the two Venuses into his personal idea of noetic ascent and his criticism of contemporary religious institutions, that is, against orthodox Christianity. Elaborating on the kind of magic produced through "regulated faith", i.e. the rationally controlled powers of the soul, he says, picking up on the metaphor of the two Venuses, that the human soul is twofold. In order to ascend noetically, the higher soul should desire and ascend towards celestial Venus.[47] Contraction, understood as the soul's desire for the celestial Venus is, then, an intrinsic concept of Bruno's concept of a pantheistic religion in which faith and revelation are replaced by the individual's rational understanding of, and wonder at, the divine.[48]

(vi) Contraction produced by filial piety

Similarly, filial affection (*pietas erga patrem*), may bring about a certain concentration of the mind. The mute son of Croesus, for instance, moved by filial affection, uttered words he was believed never to have heard before. But one should not believe, Bruno notes, that the son of Croesus was able to speak words never heard before. Rather, Bruno explains, one should imagine that the son of Croesus had previously heard those words, and that filial affection made him recall them.[49]

(vii) Contraction produced by fear

Fear of natural dangers, such as snakes, can produce a fearful state of mind in which words uttered in the dangerous situation are imprinted so powerfully in the fearful person that it may be possible for him or her to recall them years later. Bruno claimed to have had this experience as a child. He was scared by a snake, which his father drove away using vehemently angry words. When Bruno later recalled the words shouted by his father, his parents were indeed surprised. This, Bruno asserts, indicates how a so-called miraculous event, in which men speak in

---

[46] LANDINO, *Disputationes camaldulenses* iii, pp. 125-126; PICO, *Commento* ii 10-13, pp. 498-504; DIACETTO, *I tre libri d'amore* iii 2, pp. 108-110. For the use of the metaphor of the two Venuses in Renaissance thought and art, see PANOFSKY, *Studies in iconology*, pp. 141-144, 147-148, 152-155, 167-168; CHASTEL, *Art et humanisme*, pp. 269-272; WIND, *Pagan mysteries in the Renaissance*, pp. 113-151. However, the application of the metaphor in BRUNO, *Sigillus* ii 5, pp. 197.26-199.1, as quoted on p. 15 n. 40 above, has not been described in these studies.

[47] BRUNO, *Sigillus* ii 5, pp. 197.26-199.1, as quoted on p. 15 n. 40 above.

[48] This meaning of contraction is not described in GRUNEWALD, *Die Religionsphilosophie*, pp. 135-142. There, however, Bruno's stance in regard to faith and reason in his Italian dialogues is described in parallel to this treatment of contraction in the *Sigillus*.

[49] BRUNO, *Sigillus* i 40, p. 184.8-20. For Ficino as a possible source to this passage, see STURLESE, 'Le fonti', p. 142.

an extraordinary manner, is not caused by the intrusion of a foreign spirit, but caused naturally. Bruno explains fear as a phenomenon with natural causes and effects, thus refuting a supernatural line of interpretation typically evoked in traditional religious explanations.[50]

(viii) Contraction of spiritus produced by fear

Another possible outcome of fear is that the *spiritus* becomes tense and is driven towards the "castle of the heart" and other internal parts. (By the Latin term *spiritus*, as it is used here and in the following, I mean the vapour, derived from the finer blood, that acted as an intermediary between body and soul. The term 'spirit' and cognates elsewhere in this book do not concern *spiritus*.) The psychological effect described in the eighth contraction may in turn cause physiological change, for good or worse. It may, for example, cure the scared person.[51] In a sound and robust soul, however, fear will not have such effects. Pythagoras is one example.[52] In the *Eroici furori* Bruno mentions the fifteen contractions in passing and condemns contraction caused by fear of death as to be disdained.[53] He does not, however, speak explicitly about fear of death during his discussion of the fifteen contractions in the *Sigillus*, only about fear in general, but the discussion of fear in the seventh and the eighth contraction may imply fear of death. In other works Bruno explains that there is no reason to fear death, since the form and matter of which a human being is composed are permanent principles and do not dissolve on death.[54] Lastly, in the *Spaccio*, a dialogue about religious reform, Bruno complains that fear of death tyrannises his contemporaries. We may assume that he means the Christian idea of the soul's afterlife and the resulting fear of life after death.[55] Fear is not wholly rejected by Bruno. It must, however, be joined with prudence in order to be acceptable, not with cowardice and desperation.[56]

---

[50] BRUNO, *Sigillus* i 41, pp. 184.21-185.18.

[51] Ibid., i 42, pp. 185.19-186.14. For Ficino as a possible source for this eighth contraction, see STURLESE, 'Le fonti', pp. 142-143. As already mentioned above, I shall discuss Sturlese's identifications of the sources for these fifteen contractions in Ch. 5, pp. 101-102 below. For an explanation of the term *spiritus* in Ficino's thought, see pp. 91-94 below.

[52] BRUNO, *Sigillus* i 42, pp. 185.24-186.27.

[53] BRUNO, *Furori* ii 1, p. 327, as quoted on p. 8 n. 6 above.

[54] BRUNO, *Causa* ii, pp. 139-141; *Cena* v, p. 257.

[55] BRUNO, *Spaccio* ii 3, p. 317: "Ecco qua, o Sofia, la più degna et onorata ricetta per rimediar alla tristizia e dolor che apporta la matura etade, et all'importuno terror de la morte che da l'ora che abbiamo uso di sensi suol tiranneggiar il spirto de gli animanti."

[56] Ibid., iii 3, p. 471: "Provediamo ora a la Lepre, la qual voglio che sia stata tipo del timore per la Contemplazion de la morte. Et anco per quanto si può de la Speranza, e Confidenza, la quale è contraria al Timore: perché in certo modo l'una e l'altra son virtudi, o almeno materia di quelle, se son figlie della Considerazione e serveno a la Prudenza: ma il vano Timore, Codardiggia, e Desperazione, vadano insieme con la

(ix) Contraction produced by an intensity of desire

Desire for a certain physical feature may effectuate the physical state desired. One example Bruno gives is that of a pregnant woman, who can imprint on the foetus the characteristics she desires most.[57]

(x) Contraction produced by restriction of number of sense organs used

Because we shut our eyes during sleep, we experience certain mental images more clearly. Similarly, if we restrict the number of sense organs applied (*numerum contractio*), we use the remaining senses more acutely than if we had used all our senses.[58]

(xi) Contraction produced by melancholy

From the tension of the mind produced by black bile (also mentioned in the second contraction) originate disturbed fantasies and lustful states of mind in some men. By eating special food it is possible to induce certain physiological forms of *spiritus* and thereby certain erotic fantasies, which the practitioners erroneously hold to be real.[59] Even though Bruno regards this form of contraction as despicable, he does not completely reject melancholy from his theory of noetic ascent. "More noble souls" who manage to contemplate the divine can, Bruno concludes in this contraction, be assisted by melancholy. However, this is not due to their *spiritus*, but to their superior intellect. Similarly, those who fail to undertake such contemplation do so because of their intellectual incapacity.[60] Hence, in itself melancholy is insufficient to provide noetic ascent, although it can provide a starting point of contemplation if well balanced. This is the second time Bruno uses the term 'contraction' in connection with the theory of humours. The following contraction also concerns the humours.

    Lepre a basso a caggionare il vero inferno et Orco de le pene a gli animi stupidi et ignoranti."

[57] BRUNO, *Sigillus* i 43, p. 186.15-22. For Ficino as a possible source for this ninth contraction, see STURLESE, 'Le fonti', p. 143.

[58] BRUNO, *Sigillus* i 44, pp. 186.23-187.14. For Ficino as a possible source for this tenth contraction, see STURLESE, 'Le fonti', pp. 143-144.

[59] BRUNO, *Sigillus* i 45, pp. 187.15-189.14. For Ficino as a possible source for this eleventh contraction, see STURLESE, 'Le fonti', p. 144.

[60] BRUNO, *Sigillus* i 45, p. 189.6-14: "Plane enim constat, haec nobilioribus animis ingeniisque felicioribus et actum imaginationis supra phantasticum obiectum reflectere potentibus esse impossibilia. Haec etenim (sicut et altera proxime referenda) non ex temperatioris melancholiae divinioribus ingeniis subserviente materia, supra quam per cogitationis fortitudinem attolluntur, sed per quandam ratiocinii imbecillitatem in gremium materiae crassioris immersi supprimuntur."

(xii) Contraction produced by starvation

A similar kind of melancholic state of mind turns up from the precepts of some of "our not very ingenious apocalyptics". Self-inflicted hunger, which produces a "Saturnine complexion" ('complexion' understood in the technical sense, i.e. the balance of humours determining the character of a person), and self-flagellation, producing ecstasy and leading the soul's attention towards "the death of some Adonis", generates a melancholic spirit (in the sense of soul) inwardly.[61] In this passage Bruno is clearly alluding sardonically to extreme forms of Christian asceticism. Apart from Ficino, to whom I shall return below, Bruno may here be alluding to the meditations endorsed in the *Exercitia spiritualia* of the Spanish founder of the order of Jesuits, St Ignatius Loyola (1491-1556).[62] In his *Exercitia spiritualia*, Loyola recommends that during meditation on Hell, one should eat less and torment one's body with pain, for instance, by self-flagellation.[63] Moreover, the meditations of Loyola were arranged around the life and death of Christ, which is possibly what Bruno alludes to with the words "the death of some Adonis": The meditations of the first week were dedicated to sins; the second to the life of Christ; the third to the passion of Christ; and the fourth to the resurrection and ascension of Christ.[64]

---

[61]   Ibid., i 46, pp. 189.15-190.5: "Iam ad non magis ingeniosos apocalypticos nostros respiciamus, qui cum eiusdem pessime olentis melancholiae specie laborent, fine tamen per libidinis diversitatem differunt; hoc maxime detestamur, quandoquidem interim stulti non propriam modo, sed et aliorum ignorantum et asinorum (quibus prophetae atque revelatores pietatis apparent) turpissimam stultitiam enutriunt. Hi mage naturale nutrimentum contemnentes postquam in maciem et vitiose Saturniam complexionem fuerint adacti, quibusdam (ad phantasiam perturbandam) aptissimis praeviis (quas pias credunt) meditationibus ipsi faventem noctis umbram potiti, tristitiam quandam subeunt, ubi flagris lenius caedendo sese, ab internis calorem ad partes exteriores evocant, ut hoc interius mage remisso amplius in spiritu melancholicus tepor intendatur, et ut nulla ad extasim contrectandam desit occasio, animi excogitationem ad alicuius Adonidis mortem adpellentes". On this passage, see RICCI, *Giordano Bruno*, pp. 232-233. CLEMENS, *Giordano Bruno*, p. 177, asserts that in BRUNO, *Sigillus* i 46, p. 190.14-18 we find an allusion to Francis of Assisi. For 'complexion' in the passage quoted, see SIRAISI, *Medieval and early Renaissance medicine*, pp. 101-104.

[62]   The text went through a complex editorial process, involving many corrections and several translations. The vernacular version in Spanish was finished already around 1541. A Latin version was printed in Rome in 1548, translated by Andrè de Frusius. The Spanish version was often regarded as the official version. See IPARRAGUIRRE, 'I. Vie et oeuvre', cols 1270-1272.

[63]   LOYOLA, *Exercicios espirituales*, p. 48: "La 3.ª castigar la carne, es á saber, dándole dolor sensible, el qual se da trayendo cilicios, ó sogas, ó barras de hierro sobre las carnes, flagelándose, ó llagándose, y otras maneras de asperezas." ("The third way is to chastise the flesh, to wit, by putting it to sensible pain, which is inflicted by wearing hair-shirts, or cords, or iron chains on the bare flesh, by scourging oneself, or wounding oneself, and by other modes of austerities." Tr. J. Rickaby.)

[64]   Ibid., p. 4. See also CORSANO, *Il pensiero*, pp. 81-82, who identifies the Franciscans' passion for Christ on the cross as the target of Bruno's irony. In BRUNO, *De monade* v,

There may, however, be other sources than Loyola. Self-flagellation was a widespread practice among Christians, used, among other things, to imitate the suffering of Christ.[65] And, again, the choice of Christ as a figure to meditate on in a spiritual exercise is hardly surprising, given the epoch we are dealing with. Bruno's criticism probably, therefore, aims at a much wider religious culture than that of Jesuits.

(xiii) Contraction producing levitation

In persons of eminent contemplative capacity, such as Aquinas, it is possible to unite in the soul the animal, sensitive and natural *spiritus*.[66] Here *spiritus animalis sensitivus atque motivus* presumably refers to animal spirit in its various capacities rather than to the traditional threefold distinction of animal, natural and vital spirits. Elsewhere Bruno speaks of *spiritus sensitivi et motivi* flowing through the nerves.[67] This suggests that *spiritus sensitivi et motivi* correspond to the animal spirits in that, according to the standard theory of the humours, natural spirits were transmitted through the system of veins, vital spirits through the arterial system, and animal spirits through the nervous system.[68] Thereby, Bruno continues, the body floats in the air — not because of a miracle, but because of the power of Aquinas' soul. The rapture of St Paul may be assigned to the same cause, Bruno adds.[69] We cannot, however, completely rule out the possibility that Bruno is ironic here, since Aquinas was notoriously corpulent.[70]

Aquinas was well known for his powers of concentration, which were so great that he was sometimes taken by rapture intellectually.[71] However, Bruno may be referring to a legend, ignored so far in the literature on Bruno, according to which Aquinas was seen in levitation whilst praying in the chapel of Saint Nicholas in

---

p. 387.20, "Adonai" is cited as a Hebrew name for God. In the Christian liturgy the term is applied especially to the Second Person of the Trinity, Christ.

[65] BERTAUD, 'Discipline', cols 1304-1309.

[66] BRUNO, *Sigillus* i 47, p. 190.22-25: "hic [Aquinas] enim cum collectis animi viribus in imaginatum coelum raperetur, adeo in unum spiritus animalis sensitivus atque motivus est collectus, ut corpus a terra in aerem vacuum tolleretur". WALKER, 'The astral body', p. 120, and *Spiritual and demonic magic*, p. 5 n. 4, points out that Ficino and Avicenna followed Galen, and others, and divided *spiritus* into three kinds, namely, natural, vital and animal *spiritus*. For *spiritus* in Ficino's *De vita*, see WALKER, 'The astral body', p. 124 n. 1; *Spiritual and demonic magic*, p. 5 n. 4.

[67] BRUNO, *Libri physicorum aristotelis explanati*, p. 381.22.

[68] E.g. FICINO, *In Timaeum* lxxx, p. 1479.43-60.

[69] BRUNO, *Sigillus* i 47, pp. 190.25-191.5. St Paul's *raptus* is depicted in Actus apostolorum 9.1-12. See also ibid., 22.5-16; 26.12-18. The flight up into heaven, to which also Mersenne refers (*L'impiété des déistes* i 10, p. 234), is described in 2 Ad Corinthios 12.1-4. For Ficino as a possible source for the thirteenth contraction, see STURLESE, 'Le fonti', p. 144.

[70] WEISHEIPL, *Friar Thomas d'Aquino*, p. 17.

[71] Ibid., pp. 137, 235-236, 244, 300-301. For Aquinas *in spiritu rapitur*, see ibid., p. 236.

Naples.[72] Given Bruno's association with Naples, and his familiarity with Aquinas, he probably knew this legend.[73] Is this the legend Bruno refers to? It says nothing about contemplation, but about prayer. Furthermore, the story suggests that it was Christ, to whom Aquinas was praying and who spoke to Aquinas in response, who levitated Aquinas, and not Aquinas' own contemplative powers. According to Ingegno, Bruno offers a naturalistic explanation of Aquinas' levitation, which may otherwise have been explained through supernatural interference.[74] Is this a plausible interpretation?

To begin with, Bruno's and Ficino's accounts of St Paul's levitation differ. Ficino insists that the rational powers of the individual are insufficient to bring about a rapture like that of St Paul; faith, hope and grace must also be present.[75] Here, as in the case of faith, which is able to move mountains without divine intervention, Bruno apparently assigns powers to the human being which are assigned to God in the Christian tradition, implying a devaluation of divine supernatural intervention. This agrees with Ingegno's interpretation.

(xiv) Contraction produced by malnutrition

This detestable contraction is produced by deliberately eating in such a way as to disturb a person's natural complexion (again understood in the sense of humoral balance). People deliberately upsetting their natural balance of humours in this way can become demented and possessed (*amentes atque fanatici*), either because of a change in their own spirit or through the intrusion of an external spirit. In this

---

[72]   TORRELL, *Saint Thomas Aquinas*, pp. 285-286. This story is not considered in INGEGNO, 'Nota sul *Sigillus sigillorum* del Bruno', p. 366; *Cosmologia*, pp. 253-254; CILIBERTO, *Giordano Bruno*, p. 46.

[73]   For Bruno's associations with Naples, see RICCI, *Giordano Bruno*, pp. 32-105. For the importance of Aquinas' philosophy to Bruno, see references p. 107 n. 25 below.

[74]   INGEGNO, 'Nota sul *Sigillus sigillorum* del Bruno', p. 366; *Cosmologia*, pp. 253-254, where Ingegno observes that Bruno's treatment of Aquinas' levitation is "puramente naturale". See also RICCI, *Giordano Bruno*, pp. 70-71, who, like, Ingegno, observes that Bruno refuses to explain Aquinas' levitation as a miracle but, instead presents it as the result of natural causes.

[75]   FICINO, *In Epistolas Pauli* prooemium, p. 425.29-31: "Quoniam vero nec ipsa mentis contemplatio propriis viribus intelligentiae ad divina pervenire potest. In hac nobis iterum tres quidam gradus, quasi coeli tres constituendi, seu potius a Deo per Paulum petendi, videntur. Fides, spes, charitas." For the role of grace in this text of Ficino, see VASOLI, 'Considerazioni sul *De raptu Pauli* di Marsilio Ficino', pp. 383-385, 397-398. Pico may refer, critically, to Ficino's interpretation of St Paul's rapture in PICO, *Commento* iii 4, p. 530: "E delle cagioni di questa separazione [soul separated from body in the ecstasy of St Paul] molte cose vi sarebbono a dire, le quali nel commento nostro sopra el *convivio* di Platone diffusamente diremo, però che da altri, che io abbia letto, non è ancora detto a sufficienzia." CUSANUS, *De docta ignorantia* iii 11, pp. 152.25-153.4, states that through faith (in Christ) it is possible to ascend to the third heaven.

way the simple-minded can appear wise and the credulous seem contemplative.[76]
To illustrate this point Bruno mentions a monk from Brescia who through
contraction in this way seemed suddenly to have turned into a prophet, a great
theologian and well versed in every language. His brother monks had imprisoned
him, because they attributed these powers to an evil force. But Bruno cured him.
By means of a potion made of a polyp sucker blended with the juice of crushed
polypody (a fern), he cured the monk, who thereafter reverted to being the ass that
he had always been.[77] Once again there is a suspicion that Bruno is ridiculing
Christian beliefs, notably in this case, the glossolalia described in Acts, and
proposing that supposedly miraculous events of this kind should be attributed to
natural causes.

(xv) Contraction practised by philosophers

Lastly, Bruno mentions the praiseworthy concentration of the soul, characteristic
of philosophers. He mentions two philosophers — Anaxarchus and Polemon —
and a Christian saint — Saint Lawrence — as examples of people who were able
to ignore physical pain because they had separated, 'contracted', their souls from
their bodies.[78]

Heroic practice in the fifteen contractions and its theory

In these fifteen contractions we have seen Bruno's views on a variety of physical
and psychological circumstances which he thinks relevant to noetic ascent. Some
of these circumstances overlap with religion, such as his treatment of faith, fear
and other emotions in the fifth to the eighth contractions, others with medicine,
such as his comments on melancholy in the eleventh, twelfth and fourteenth
contractions. Two features recur in his remarks on these various types of noetic
ascent. The first is his tendency to explain them by means of natural processes,
that is, without recourse to a supernatural agent. The second is his insistence that
the human mind can be autonomous.

---

[76]   Bruno, *Sigillus* i 48, p. 191.6-24.

[77]   Ibid., i 48, pp. 191.24-192.5: "et monachus Brixiae, me praesente ipsumque curante, qui
       hac arte [of Saturnine temperament enhanced by melancholic humours] repente
       propheta, magnus theologus et linguarum omnium peritus videbatur effectus, ipse, cum
       monachorum tantam sapientiam ad malum principium referentum consilio fuisset in
       cacerem detrusus, virtute acetabuli cum polypodii contusi succo temperati, humoribus
       melancholicis atque spiritu evacuatis, talis, qualis semper extiterat, asinus apparuit."
       This monk may, according to Ricci, *Giordano Bruno*, pp. 119-120, have been someone
       that Bruno actually met in Brescia.

[78]   Bruno, *Sigillus* i 49, pp. 192.6-193.5. He may refer to his fifteenth contraction in
       Bruno, *Furori* ii 1, p. 327, as quoted on p. 8 n. 6 above. For Ficino as a possible source
       for this fifteenth contraction, see Sturlese, 'Le fonti', pp. 145, 158-159; Ricci,
       Giordano Bruno, p. 234.

Which of the contractions are heroic? Bruno disdains traditional religious interpretations in terms of emotions, in particular faith, as in the contractions five to eight. And in the second, the eleventh, the twelfth and the fourteenth contractions he strongly criticises the attempt to ascend noetically through inducing melancholy artificially. The thirteenth contraction, about Aquinas' powers of concentration, is dubious. The third, "contraction of the horizon into the centre", and the fourth contraction, about intellectual concentration, which is described very briefly, are presented without any overt criticism. The first contraction, about solitude, is described very positively. But only the fifteenth contraction (contraction of philosophers) is explicitly praised. Hence the solitary, contemplative philosopher's endeavour is ideal, or "heroic", to use Bruno's word.

This account of the various forms of noetic ascent agrees with Bruno's theoretical comments in a passage entitled 'On the fivefold and simple degree of ascent', included immediately before his discussion of the fifteen contractions.[79] First, in this theoretical discussion, as for the fifteen contractions, Bruno regards ascent achieved through the exercise of intellect as the only valid form of ascent. Ascent achieved through the emotions — treated with disdain in the fifth to the eighth contractions — and an imbalance of humoral fluids — fiercely criticised in the eleventh, the twelfth and the fourteenth contractions — are not considered at all in this theoretical discussion. Second, Bruno clearly has in mind Plotinus' account of the human soul's ascent to the One.[80] As we have seen in the third contraction, this theory of Plotinus may well be among the direct or indirect sources.

The soul's noetic ascent corresponds objectively to the ontological structure of the intelligible universe, which means in this context that noetic ascent passes through four stages before reaching the One, namely sensation (*sensus*), imagination (*imaginatio*), reason (*ratio*) and mind (*intellectus*). The first stage is sensation, which by means of sense organs initiates the soul's cognition.[81] The second stage is imagination, which considers the sense data transmitted by the sense organs and, in addition, discursive thought in the soul.[82] The third stage is reason, which examines the content of imagination discursively.[83] The fourth stage is mind, which is when the soul leaps from discursive reasoning into intuitive

---

[79] BRUNO, *Sigillus* i 31, p. 172.14-15: "De quintuplici et simplici progressione gradu." The theoretical account is given ibid., i 31-34, pp. 172.16-180.18.

[80] Plotinus is mentioned by name ibid., i 32, i 33, pp. 175.22, 178.7. Moreover, ibid., i 33, p. 175.22-24, whose context is noetic ascent, reads: "Plotinus ... si non ex toto, magna tamen ex parte nobis consentire videtur".

[81] Ibid., i 31, p. 173.2-4. Sensation, the first stage of noetic ascent, is treated ibid., i 31, pp. 172.16-174.20.

[82] For this twofold function of imagination, see ibid., i 31, i 32, pp. 173.4-6, 174.22-175.3. For Plotinus as a source for Bruno's idea of the twofold function of imagination, see pp. 73-74 below. For imagination as the second stage in Bruno's account of noetic ascent, see BRUNO, *Sigillus* i 32, pp. 174.21-177.4.

[83] Ibid., i 31, p. 173.6-7. For reason as the third stage, see ibid., i 33, pp 177.5-178.26.

comprehension of the hypostasis Mind.[84] The fifth and last stage is ecstasy and union with the One.[85]

This line of interpretation agrees with the fact that Plotinus himself had used the verb 'I contract' (in Greek συστέλλω, translated into Latin by Ficino with the verb *contraho*) to describe the individual human soul's ascent towards the intelligible world:

But when it [the individual human soul] shines in itself, so to speak, by its inclination towards the things which are alien from this place [that is, alien from the bodily world], then it is contracted into the whole, and it neither exists in act, nor, again, does it perish.[86]

This usage of Plotinus may well be an important source to Bruno's concept of contraction in its noetic sense — a usage which is also consistent with Bruno's explicit mentioning of Plotinus as a source to the fifteen contractions.[87]

The double contraction

Bruno explains the philosopher's ascent to unity in his *Eroici furori* and, even more conspicuously, in his mnemonic works. Of particular interest is his *Sigillus*. Having set out the fifteen contractions in the first part, he returns to the theme of contraction in the second part. On one occasion he ties contraction as a noetic concept to contraction as an ontological concept, stating that these two concepts denote opposite movements on the ladder of nature. Contraction in the ontological sense is movement from unity to multiplicity, whereas contraction in the noetic sense is a movement from sensible multiplicity to intelligible unity. The following passage outlines how Bruno conceives of the philosopher's movement from multiplicity to unity, praised in the course of the fifteen contractions:

There is then a double contraction. The first contraction is one by which absolute form becomes form of this or that in this or that entity, in the same way as light [*lux*], which is, as it were, first in itself and then, subsequently [*postea*], by a certain progression of this and that becomes the light [*lumen*] in this or that (without, however, ever emitting anything from its substance and without detracting from its own integrity). The second contraction is that by which inferior nature, through a certain disposition of agreement and consent, a multiplicity participating by virtue of an impulse that is

---

84 Ibid., i 31, i 34, pp. 173.7-29, 178.27-179.16.

85 Ibid., i 34, pp. 179.17-180.6.

86 PLOTINUS VI iv [22] 16.45-47, trans. Ficino, p. 659.54-56: "Sed cum ipsa velut in se refulget, nutu quodam ad illa quae hinc sunt aliena, tunc ad totum iam contrahitur, neque existit actu, neque etiam interit." This passage is ignored in TOCCO, *Le opere*, p. 363.

87 See the references p. 24 n. 80 above.

sometimes natural, at others conceptual, is collected together and collects many participating entities into one. The first contraction is whereby absolute and infinite form is determined through essence to this and that matter; the second contraction is whereby infinite and indeterminate matter is determined through number to this or that form.[88]

This quotation needs some explanation. The idea explained at the end of the quotation is that there are two indeterminate principles, namely form and matter. Form is indeterminate inasmuch as matter is the principle that individuates form, and matter is indeterminate potentiality that becomes individuated through form. Both matter and form are characterised by infinity. The idea that number individuates infinite and indeterminate matter may be derived from the Neoplatonic theory of causation produced by means of numbers.[89]

The analogy for the first contraction of forms — the light (*lux*) intrinsic to a light-giving source remaining undiminished even though it issues light (*lumen*) — derives from a Neoplatonic doctrine, namely that the One does not diminish on account of its 'flowing out', its emanation. This is the Neoplatonic doctrine of 'undiminished giving'.[90] Bruno mentions this idea elsewhere in the *Sigillus*, stating that this is the light which "spreads from the sun through everything as its image".[91] In the Renaissance, Ficino had also used this distinction between the light intrinsic to a source (*lux*) and the light that it emits (*lumen*) to illustrate the

---

[88]   BRUNO, *Sigillus* ii 22, p. 214.6-19: "Duplici ergo existente contractione: altera, qua absoluta forma fit huius illiusque in hoc et in illo forma, sicut lux, quae est primo velut in se ipsa, postea progressu quodam huius efficitur atque illius in hoc et in illo lumen, (dum tamen de sua substantia nihil emittat et a propria integritate non deficiat); altera contractio est, qua inferior natura per quamdam assensus et obedientiae habitudinem, tum naturali tum notionali adpulsu et multitudo particeps colligitur, et multa participantia colligit in unum. Prima contractio est, qua per essentiam infinita et absoluta forma finitur ad hanc et ad illam materiam; secunda est, qua per numerum infinita et indeterminata materia ad hanc illamque formam terminatur." (I have deleted a comma after "efficitur atque illius".) For a discussion of this passage, see SPRUIT, *Il problema*, pp. 148-149, 157-158; MANCINI, *La sfera*, pp. 67-70. STURLESE, 'Le fonti', p. 150, cites FICINO, *Theologia platonica* viii 16, vol. 1, pp. 329.30-330.11, as the source for lines 15-19 ("Prima contractio est ... formam terminatur") of the above quotation of Bruno. Ficino does not, however, mention the term *contractio* or its cognates in that passage.

[89]   For this role of numbers, see also BRUNO, *Sigillus* ii 22, pp. 214.26-215.5. For the Neoplatonic theory of causation produced by means of numbers, see O'MEARA, *Pythagoras revived*, pp. 62-66.

[90]   WALLIS, *Neoplatonism*, p. 62; DODDS' note in PROCLUS, *Elements of theology*, p. 214; GERSH, ΚΙΝΗΣΙΣ ΑΚΙΝΗΤΟΣ, p. 28.

[91]   BRUNO, *Sigillus* ii 7, p. 200.6-8: "Est lumen intimius, quo sol per se lucet, a quo genere differens habetur lumen, quod inde velut imago solis per omnia manat."

Neoplatonic theory of emanation.[92] He may well have been Bruno's immediate source.

Bruno elaborates on the analogy of absolute form (*forma absoluta*) and light (*lux*) a few pages before the above quotation from the *Sigillus*. Absolute form, he says in the passage on form, "is the absolute form of being" which communicates itself to all forms. It "gives being (*esse*) to all things" and is the "giver of forms".[93] The last expression had been used by Albert the Great (1193-1280) in his account of Stoic and Platonic theories of the origin of Ideas, as well as by Arabic philosophers as an equivalent for the Active Intellect.[94] Bruno concludes in the *Sigillus*: "This universal form of being [i.e. absolute form] is infinite light, which bears the same relation to the forms of everything that the form of essential light bears to the forms of participated light (*lux*), light (*lumen*) and colour."[95] So, absolute form is like light (*lux*), as it is intrinsically in the light producing body, existing in itself and for itself. When communicated to matter, this essential *lux* becomes the participating form of *lux* — light and colours (*lumen* and *color*) in things. Here Bruno draws on a standard Neoplatonic distinction, elaborated most authoritatively by Proclus, between unparticipated, participated and participating

---

[92] FICINO, *In Timaeum* x, p. 1442.5-10. See also FICINO, *Liber de lumine* ii, p. 977.1-3; *In Plotinum* II i [40] 7, p. 93.27-31. For the light metaphor in Ficino's philosophy, see SCHEUERMANN-PEILICKE, *Licht und Liebe*, pp. 61-258.

[93] BRUNO, *Sigillus* ii 10, pp. 202.20-203.5: "Est una prima forma, per se et a se subsistens, simplex, impartibilis, essentiae, formationis et subsistentiae omnis principium, indiminuibiliter omnibus se com[m]unicans, in qua omnis forma, quae com[m]unicatur, est aeterna et una; ipsa enim est absoluta essendi forma et dans omnibus esse, unde et pater formarumque dator appellatur, ita ut non sit forma membrorum partiumque mundi vel universi totius, sed formae universi et partium ipsius absoluta forma. Estque forma infinita, quia est ita omne esse, ut non ad hoc et ad illud esse finiatur, ad hanc vel ad illam materiam vel subiectum contrahatur, sicut ex opposito infinita dicitur materia, quae non hoc vel illo esse per formam terminetur." The Italian equivalent of the Latin expression 'dator formarum' also features in BRUNO, *Causa* iii, p. 189: "Questo vuole il Nolano: che è uno intelletto che dà l'essere [a] ogni cosa, chiamato da Pitagorici et il Timeo 'datore de le forme'; una anima e principio formale che si fa et informa ogni cosa, chiamata da medesmi 'fonte de le forme'; una materia della quale vien fatta e formata ogni cosa, chiamata di tutti 'ricetto de le forme'."

[94] The expression 'datore de le forme' is translated from the Latin "dator formarum", which probably derives from PLATO, *Timaeus* 28A6-B1. A Latin translation of a phrase in that passage of the *Timaeus* reads in the translation of Calcidius (fourth century AD): "Operi porro fortunam dat opifex suus" (PLATO, *Timaeus* 28A, tr. Calcidius, p. 20.22). See also ALBERT, *De causis et processu universitatis a prima causa* I i 3 (Stoics), I iv 1 (Plato), pp. 8.21-22, 8.34, 43.4, 43.63. It had also been used by Arabic philosophers, such as Avicenna (980-1037) and Averroes (1126-1198); see SPRUIT, 'Motivi peripatetici', pp. 393-396; *Il problema*, p. 109.

[95] BRUNO, *Sigillus* ii 10, p. 203.10-13: "Haec forma universalis essendi est lux infinita, se habens ad omnium formas, sicut forma lucis essentialis ad lucis participativae, luminum et colorum formas."

being, corresponding to transcendent Idea, immanent Idea and the material particulars.[96]

In the quotation Bruno also explains the second contraction of inferior nature from multiplicity to unity. In relation to this process he speaks of inferior nature and multiplicity being united "through a certain disposition of agreement and consent", taking place "by virtue of an impulse that is sometimes natural, at others conceptual". His meaning is not entirely clear, but I shall make two suggestions which do not necessarily exclude one another. First, by the terms 'inferior nature' and "multiplicity" Bruno may be thinking relatively of any inferior hypostasis in the Neoplatonic scheme of emanation; the more multiple a hypostasis is, the more inferior it is. Matter is the lowest level in this scheme and it generates more multiplicity than at any other ontological level. Bruno seems, then, to suggest that matter has an intrinsic and active potency to cause some kind of unity, and that this process takes place "by virtue of an impulse that is sometimes natural". Here he may be hinting at an idea developed in *De la causa*, according to which the two principles of matter and the World Soul reciprocally determine each other to produce individual things.[97] Second, the expression "conceptual impulse" may also mean that human contemplation is able to gather the multiplicity of the sensible world into unity.[98] This last interpretation fits with Bruno's ideas about experience of unity in the intelligible realm, the heroic method of ascending noetically according to his account of the fifteen contractions.

In the following chapter I shall deal with contraction in the ontological sense, and then, in Chapter 3 and 4, I shall focus on the noetic sense of the term. By 'noetic', it may be best to state here once and for all, I mean 'mystical' in the sense that it can be applied to the *philosophies* of Plotinus, Proclus and other Neoplatonists. Philosophy can lead the soul from the multiplicity of the perceptible world to the intelligible realm, preparing it, perhaps, for an ultimate step that will take it out of itself in ecstasy to enjoy union with an absolute unity (however that may be conceived). I shall use the terms 'noetic' and 'mystical' and their cognates in this sense.[99]

---

[96] WALLIS, *Neoplatonism*, p. 126.

[97] BRUNO, *Causa* ii, p. 147, as quoted on p. 36 n. 48 below. Ciliberto noted the similarity between the principles of individuation in the *Sigillus* and *De la causa*; see CILIBERTO, *Giordano Bruno*, pp. 36-39; 'Introduction', pp. XXVI-XXVII. Ciliberto did not, however, point out contraction as a common component.

[98] In one instance Bruno uses "adpulsus" in this noetic sense, see BRUNO, *Explicatio*, p. 133.14-19: "Primus praecipuusque pictor est phantastica virtus, praecipuus primusque poëta est in cogitativae virtutis adpulsu, vel connatus vel inditus noviter quidam enthusiasmus, quo vel divino vel huic simili quodam afflatu ad convenienter aliquid praesentandum excogitatum concitantur."

[99] O'MEARA, *Plotinus*, pp. 106-108, comments that we should not see mysticism as the antithesis of rationality.

Chapter 2

Contraction as an Ontological Concept

Bruno's discussion of ontological contraction

In Bruno's philosophy, contraction in the ontological sense is used in his theory of individuation to describe how a universal, infinite and singular substance relates to the individual entities dependent upon it.[1] The term is also applied in a special case in his philosophical description of human beings, who are ensouled like the rest of nature, though in a particular way.[2] The concept of contraction has often been mentioned and paraphrased in accounts of Bruno's theory of individuation, but it has not yet, in my view, received the attention it deserves in itself.[3] By paying attention to how Bruno describes the individuation of individual entities through contraction, we can clarify some important ideas in Bruno's philosophy and in particular his interpretation of nature as a living and divine being.

We find 'contraction' employed in the ontological sense in many of his writings, but his treatment of the concept in the *Sigillus* and *De la causa*, published in London in 1583 and 1584 respectively, are of particular interest. *De la causa* offers Bruno's most detailed account of contraction and for this reason I shall chiefly base my account of contraction on it. Bruno's comments in the *Sigillus*, written shortly before *De la causa*, though less specific, complement his

---

[1]   Bruno, *De umbris* §§29.2-4, 63.2-6, 92.12-17, 94.2-9, 234.14-17, pp. 32, 52, 69, 69-70, 193; *Sigillus* ii 10, ii 18, ii 22, pp. 203.1-5, 209.11-14, 213.14-214.19; *Causa* epist., ii, iii, iv, pp. 21, 147, 187, 233, 243, 247; *Spaccio* epist., iii 2, pp. 23-25, 427; *Furori* i 4, p. 167; *Lampas* §419.15-22, p. 1452 (= *BOL*, vol. 3, p. 245.16-24); *Acrotismus*, pp. 93.19-94.3, 94.18-95.3, 148.19-149.3; *De principiis* §77, p. 684.3-7 (= *BOL*, vol. 3, p. 553.1-8); *De minimo* I 4, I 9, pp. 145.28-29, 169.21-22; *De immenso* i 1, v 12, viii 6, pp. 205.1-4, 156.10-17, 303.6-8; *De compositione* I i 4, p. 100.12-17; *Summa*, pp. 15.8-12, 21.7-12, 73.3-8, 95.18-19, 108.5-11.

[2]   Bruno, *De umbris* §61.5-8, p. 51; *Cabala* ii, pp. 95-97; *Lampas* §408.13-23, pp. 1434-1436 (= *BOL*, vol. 3, pp. 238.22-239.6); *De minimo* V ii 3, p. 193.3-7.

[3]   Clemens, *Giordano Bruno*, pp. 9, 17-18, 143; Huber, *Einheit*, p. 50; Ingegno, 'Nota sul *Sigillus sigillorum* del Bruno', p. 362; *Cosmologia*, pp. 247-248; *Regia pazzia*, pp. 135-136; Védrine, *La conception*, pp. 74, 274; 'L'influence', pp. 216-217, 219; Papuli, 'Qualche osservazione', p. 204; Blum, *Aristoteles*, pp. 58, 66, 68-71, 73, 78-79; Spruit, *Il problema*, pp. 147-149, 157-158, 203; Ciliberto, 'Introduction', p. XXIX; Calcagno, *Giordano Bruno*, pp. 31-32; Mancini, *La sfera infinita*, pp. 67, 134, 146-147; Canone, *Il dorso e il grembo dell'eterno*, pp. 71-73.

treatment in *De la causa* nicely. Metaphysics is not Bruno's main concern in the *Sigillus*. The various metaphysical comments in the *Sigillus*, including that of contraction as a theory of individuation, are sketchy and subordinated to the main purpose, the epistemological aspects of noetic ascent.[4] Together the *Sigillus* and *De la causa* present a more or less coherent theory, one that enables us to interpret most of Bruno's references to contraction in other works. In what follows, then, I shall base my account of contraction mainly on *De la causa*, where the metaphysical context of contraction is clearly set out, and include the *Sigillus* when it elucidates the metaphysical themes raised in *De la causa*.

The metaphysical context of contraction

Bruno's theory of individuation is probably Aristotelian in origin, though it also adopts elements from non-Aristotelian philosophies. For instance, Bruno's concern about the respective roles of matter and form in the process of individuation derives from the terminology and problems characteristic of Aristotelian philosophy. But Bruno also adopts Platonic and Neoplatonic ideas. This is not to deny that classical and Renaissance Neoplatonism included many elements of Aristotelian philosophy, notably for present purposes the doctrine of matter as potency. But blurred though it may sometimes be, the distinction between Aristotelian and Neoplatonic ideas in Bruno's philosophy is usually quite evident and important. These originally Platonic and Neoplatonic elements were used by Bruno in his formulations of a unity underlying and determining the multiplicity of nature, in keeping with his inclination towards pantheism.

The fundamental philosophical problem in *De la causa* is that of substance, and the concept of contraction is strictly connected to it. Bruno's discussion of substance is directed against various philosophers — Aristotelian, Platonic and otherwise — who present matter as a formless, passive potentiality, analogous to the timber used by a carpenter to realise his ideas.[5] Bruno's main target is, however, Aristotle's concept of substance, which leads, he claims, to unsatisfactory consequences in two branches of philosophy, namely, ethics, on the one hand, and metaphysics on the other.

---

[4]   Metaphysical themes are primarily dealt with in the following passages; BRUNO, *Sigillus* i 14-16, pp. 164.9-165.7: descent and ascent from and to the One (*prima mens*), Mind (*intellectus*), and nature; i 32-34, pp. 174.22-180.18: Plotinus' metaphysics and epistemology (Plotinus is mentioned at i 32, i 33, pp. 175.22, 178.7); ii 3, pp. 195.17-196.25: using the art of memory, one should unite oneself with the *anima mundi*; ii 11, pp. 203.15-204.4: absolute form descends; ii 22, pp. 212.14-215.20: on contraction as descent and ascent. For BRUNO, *Sigillus* i 14-16, see SPRUIT, *Il problema*, pp. 285-286. For *Sigillus* i 32-34, see STURLESE, 'Le fonti', pp. 138-141. For *Sigillus* ii 3, see ibid., pp. 145-146. For *Sigillus* ii 22, see ibid., pp. 150, 160.

[5]   For the comparison, see BRUNO, *Causa* iii, p. 173. For the concept of matter in *De la causa*, see VÉDRINE, *La conception*, pp. 273-288; BLUM, *Aristoteles*, pp. 66-75; SPRUIT, *Il problema*, pp. 46 n. 17, 166-185, 291-292.

Aristotle distinguishes primary from secondary substances. A primary substance is an individual entity, an individual horse for instance, which can be a subject of predication, e.g. "white", but never itself be predicated of anything else.[6] A secondary substance is the essence or definable form represented by the species or genus to which the primary substance belongs, e.g. that of 'horse'.[7] In the sublunary sphere we find corporeal substances. A corporeal substance is an individual entity composed of matter and form. Matter is the principle of individuation.[8] Form is immanent in such an entity, not transcendent.[9] The unity of form and matter produces an individual substance.[10] A corporeal substance's form is the immanent principle of its change, and it determines which species the substance belongs to. Therefore, all members of the same species share the same form. Form is the cause of being of a corporeal substance composed of matter and form.[11] This Aristotelian theory of substance is the aim of Bruno's criticism.[12]

In the case of human beings this means, Aristotle maintains, that the substance of the individual is the individual soul imparting life to the body. As such, the human soul was the *entelecheia* or 'act' of the body.[13] The soul is the form, or as scholastics would call it, 'substantial form', of the individual human being, considered as a substance, whereas its body is the matter of it.[14] Consequently, Bruno points out, human beings are fearful of death, since it dissolves the body, the material part of the individual human being as a substance, and leaves its soul without the component it requires to make up a substance.[15] One of the implicit aims of *De la causa* is to console mankind by working out an alternative notion of

---

[6] ARISTOTLE, *Categories* v 2ᵃ11-14; *Metaphysics* V viii 1017ᵇ13-14. This definition also features ibid., VII xiii 1038ᵇ15-16. For Aristotle's concept of substance, see GUTHRIE, *A history of Greek philosophy*, vol. 6, pp. 203-222.

[7] ARISTOTLE, *Categories* v 2ᵃ14-19.

[8] ARISTOTLE, *Metaphysics* VII i-iv 1028ᵃ10-1030ᵇ13.

[9] Ibid., VII xi 1037ᵃ29-30.

[10] Ibid., VII iv 1030ᵃ3-6.

[11] Ibid., VII xvii 1041ᵃ9-1041ᵇ28; VIII ii 1043ᵃ2-26. For Aristotle's concept of being, see OWENS, *The doctrine of being in the Aristotelian 'Metaphysics'*. For Aristotle's idea about form giving being and its further development in Aquinas, see OWENS, 'Thomas Aquinas (b. ca. 1225; d. 1274)', pp. 176-177.

[12] For Bruno's report of Aristotle's view, see BRUNO, *Causa* ii, iii, iv, pp. 141, 191, 219. For Bruno's report of, and criticism of, the Peripatetic view that matter is like a woman, i.e. passive, whereas form is like a man, i.e. active, see ibid., iv, pp. 219-231, 265. For the source of this simile, see ARISTOTLE, *Physics* I ix 192ᵃ13-25. For Bruno's report of Aristotle's ideas of matter as formless, and other philosopher's similar ideas, see BRUNO, *Causa* iii, pp. 173-179.

[13] ARISTOTLE, *De anima* ii 1 412ᵃ27-28. For Bruno's report of this view, see BRUNO, *Causa* iii, pp. 185-187.

[14] ARISTOTLE, *Metaphysics* VII xi 1037ᵃ5-7.

[15] BRUNO, *Causa* ii, pp. 139-141: "Dicono [Aristotelians] quello esser veramente omo che resulta dalla composizione; quello essere veramente anima che è o perfezzione et atto di corpo vivente, o pur cosa che resulta da certa simmetria di complessione e membri; onde non è maraviglia se fanno tanto, e prendeno tanto spavento per la morte e dissoluzione: come quelli a'quali è imminente la iattura de l'essere."

the origin and nature of the human soul in order to eliminate this fear of death.[16] This is an important ethical and theological implication in *De la causa*, but one that *De la causa* does not treat in detail. Bruno deals with it instead in his discussion of the fifteen contractions in the *Sigillus*, in the *Cabala*, and in the *Spaccio*, a dialogue about religious reform.[17] The *Sigillus* and the *Spaccio* present the epistemological and ethical consequences of the metaphysical considerations of substance.

The overall metaphysical problem in Aristotle's conception of substance is, Bruno maintains in *De la causa*, that substances individuated according to Aristotle's scheme are subject to dissolution, and, accordingly are not eternal and permanent, which, Bruno argues, substance — that is, Aristotle's concept of primary substance — should be.[18] Aristotle, Bruno says, conceives of substance as something 'accidental', in the sense that it has a corruptible and dependent existence, rather than being a self-subsistent entity.[19] Here Bruno presumably addresses Aristotle's notion of primary substances. For instance, as the oak tree grows and finally decays, the oak tree as a substance dissolves. When Bruno claims that Aristotle conceives of substance as something accidental, and asserts that this is self-contradictory, he refers to Aristotle's contrast between substance and accidence.[20] Bruno notes the following problem. When Aristotle explains corporeal substances as unities of form and matter, the latter being accidental, he also, implicitly conceives of the former as accidental, which conflicts with Aristotle's own ideas about the difference between substance and accidence.

Bruno, for a long time, he tells us through his mouthpiece Teofilo, adhered to the solution to this problem of substance proposed by the Greek materialists Democritus and the Epicureans. They held that only body existed, that matter is substance, and that forms are nothing but "certain accidental dispositions of matter", a solution which agrees better with nature than the position of Aristotle, Teofilo says.[21] However, Bruno eventually rejected this materialistic conception, since it implies that matter would be able to individuate itself, which Bruno thinks is untenable. There must be, then, two types of substance, both being principles,

---

[16]   For "consolation", see ibid., ii, pp. 139-141. For the "terror" of fear of death, see BRUNO, *Spaccio* ii 3, p. 317: "importuno terror de la morte". Elsewhere, Bruno similarly states that with his philosophy fear of death can be overcome, see BRUNO, *Cena* iii, pp. 171-173; *Infinito*, epist., p. 55; *De immenso* i 1, p. 201.3-6.

[17]   For Bruno's theories on the immortality of the human soul and on metempsychosis, see SPRUIT, 'Motivi peripatetici', pp. 371-373, 383; GRANADA's note to BRUNO, *Furori* arg., p. 42 n. 71.

[18]   BRUNO, *Causa* epist., iii, pp. 17-19, 189.

[19]   Ibid., iii, pp. 185-189.

[20]   E.g. ARISTOTLE, *Categories* v 2ª27-2ᵇ6.

[21]   BRUNO, *Causa* iii, p. 169: "Democrito dumque e gli Epicurei, i quali quel che non è corpo dicono esser nulla, per conseguenza vogliono la materia sola essere la sustanza de le cose ... Questi medesmi ... vogliono le forme non essere altro che certe accidentali disposizioni de la materia: et io molto tempo son stato assai aderente a questo parere, solo per questo, che ha fondamenti più corrispondenti alla natura che quei di Aristotele".

namely, one which forms, another which is formed. The first is form, the second is matter.[22]

It may seem at first sight as if Bruno has returned to Aristotle's position. This is not the case, Bruno does not define form as Aristotle had done. By form he does not mean a secondary substance, that is, a specific species, contracted with matter and rendered an individual substance, but the World Soul.[23] The World Soul is a universal principle which endows individuating forms to the infinite matter of the entire infinite universe, but without itself becoming limited to individuated entities. It therefore remains unaffected by the decay of individual entities.[24] Thereby Bruno ensues that form, the one principle of universal substance, is eternal and permanent.[25] Furthermore, Bruno does not conceive of matter as Aristotle did. First, Bruno ranks matter equal to form, that is, to the World Soul,

---

[22]   Ibid., iii, p. 169: "ma dopo aver più maturamente considerato, avendo risguardo a più cose, troviamo che è necessario conoscere nella natura doi geni di sustanza, l'uno che è forma, e l'altro che è materia; perché è necessario che sia un atto sustanzialissimo, nel quale è la potenza attiva di tutto; et ancora una potenza et un soggetto, nel quale non sia minor potenza passiva di tutto: in quello è potestà di fare, in questo è potestà di esser fatto."

[23]   Ibid., iii, pp. 169-171. For the World Soul as the formal principle, see also ibid., epist., ii, pp. 13, 137. For the World Soul in Bruno's philosophy, in particular in his *De la causa*, see VÉDRINE, *La conception*, pp. 140, 198-201, 203, 282, 286-288, 301-305; MICHEL, 'Renaissance cosmologies', pp. 95-100; SPRUIT, *Il problema*, pp. 185-205. For the World Soul in the Platonic tradition, see MOREAU, *L'âme du monde*, especially pp. 43-55. For the World Soul in Plotinus, see ARMSTRONG, 'Plotinus', pp. 250-258; BLUMENTHAL, *Plotinus' psychology*, pp. 27-28. The concept of the World Soul also played a significant role in twelfth-century Platonism, transmitted by Macrobius (fl. c. 400 AD), Calcidius, Virgil and some Church Fathers, as described in GREGORY, 'The Platonic inheritance', pp. 54-80. In the Italian Renaissance the World Soul was equated with the Holy Spirit by some Platonic or Neoplatonic philosophers, for instance Steuco; see WALKER, *The ancient theology*, pp. 37-41, especially p. 38 n. 5. Bruno reduced the Holy Spirit to the World Soul from a philosophical point of view, as explained in AQUILECCHIA, 'Introduzione', pp. XXXIV-XXXVI. The Stoics too adopted the doctrine of the World Soul, though Renaissance thinkers often interpreted classical Stoic references to it as evidence that an author was in fact a Neoplatonist, Pythagorean or whatever. One Stoic reference understood in this way is Virgil's *Aeneid* vi.726-727: "totamque infusa per arctus, mens agitat molem, et toto se corpore miscet", cited in BRUNO, *Causa* ii, p. 115. On this occasion Bruno interprets Virgil's words as Pythagorean (ibid., ii, p. 115). Similarly, in BRUNO, *Acrotismus*, p. 177.10-12: "... Pythagoricis Deus sit infinitus spiritus omnia penetrans, comprehendens atque vivificans". This interpretation may partly derive from the fact that Ficino thought that Virgil was a Platonist, hence indirectly a Pythagorean; see FICINO, *In Plotinum* II i [40] 3, in Ficino, *Opera* (Basel 1576), p. 1597.31-50, especially lines 36-39: "Rectius admodum Platonicus ille Maro [Virgil] iudicauisse videtur. Cum enim dixisset: 'Omnia spiritus intus alit ... Totamque infusa per artus mens agitat molem.'"

[24]   For the World Soul animating the entire infinite universe, see BRUNO, *Causa* v, p. 285. For the World Soul as spatially unlimited, see ibid., ii, pp. 149-151.

[25]   Ibid., iii, p. 189.

since matter too is a permanent and eternal principle.[26] Second, he takes great care to formulate the respective roles of matter and form in a way which does not reduce matter to passive potentiality formed by the World Soul, but prefers, instead, to assign to matter active potentiality too.[27] This seems, however, inconsistent with Bruno's recognition of the necessity of two kinds of substance, form and matter, of which matter is passive.[28]

This interpretation of substance has profound theological consequences. Bruno assumed the traditional view that there is one and only one ultimate cause for the entire universe, the First Cause.[29] This First Cause is God.[30] Aristotle had distinguished the terms 'beginning' (in Greek ἀρχή; in Latin *principium*) from 'cause' (in Greek αἰτία; in Latin *causa*). A beginning is the first thing from which something either exists or comes into being or becomes known. E.g. a point is the beginning of a line. A cause is that whose presence results in the existence of something. There are four kinds of causes, namely, efficient, material, formal and final causes. A hand drawing a line, for instance, is the efficient cause of the line.[31] According to Bruno, the cause and beginning of the universe do not coincide, for, as he explains, a beginning does not have to be a cause. For instance, a point is not the cause of a line, although a point is the beginning (*principium*) of a line.[32] A principle (*principium*) remains in the effect (as, for instance, matter and form or the elements remain in the object that they constitute, in a conventional sense); a cause is extrinsic.[33] And this applies to the universe too. Matter is eternal and permanent, and matter, Bruno says, gives being to the forms and both remain intrinsic to the things that derive from their composition. In that sense matter is the beginning, the principle, of the universe.[34] Since matter has this role, Bruno calls it

---

[26] Ibid., iii, pp. 189-191. See also ibid., iv, pp. 265-267; *Cena* v, p. 259; *Spaccio* epist., p. 21.

[27] BRUNO, *Causa* epist., iv, pp. 23, 237-239, 251-265.

[28] Ibid., iii, p. 169, as quoted on p. 33 n. 22 above. AQUILECCHIA, 'Introduzione', pp. XIV-XVI, discusses this problem in Bruno's *De la causa*.

[29] BRUNO, *Causa* ii, pp. 101-111.

[30] Ibid., ii, p. 111: "Diciamo Dio prima causa, in quanto che le cose tutte son da lui distinte come lo effetto da l'efficiente, la cosa prodotta dal producente." In AQUINAS, *Summa theologiae* 1a, qu. 44, art. 1, vol. 4, pp. 455-457, the discussion about God had similarly articulated the traditional characteristic of God as First Cause.

[31] ARISTOTLE, *Metaphysics* V i-ii 1012^{b}34-1014^{a}25.

[32] BRUNO, *Causa* ii, p. 111. The example of a point as the beginning of a line may derive from ARISTOTLE, *Metaphysics* V i 1012^{b}34-1013^{a}4, or from AQUINAS, *Summa theologiae* 1a, qu. 33, art. 1, resp., vol. 4, p. 358.

[33] BRUNO, *Causa* ii, pp. 111-113.

[34] Ibid., iii, pp. 189-191: "Noi veggiamo che tutte le forme naturali cessano dalla materia, e novamente vegnono nella materia: onde par realmente nessuna cosa esser costante, ferma, eterna e degna di aver esistimazione di principio, eccetto che la materia; oltre che le forme non hanno l'essere senza la materia, in quella si generano e corrompono, dal seno di quella esceno, et in quello si accogliono: però la materia la qual sempre rimane medesima e feconda, deve aver la principal prerogativa d'essere conosciuta sol

"divine".[35] The role of matter as giving being to the forms contrasts with Aristotle's conception of matter. He had held the problematic view that matter is principle of individuation, but, at the same time, in itself non-being.[36] Bruno's view, that matter is not pure potentiality and not *prope nihil* in that it contains forms potentially rather than in act, and that matter gives being to forms, can be seen as an effort to overcome this problem.[37] Bruno identifies the (efficient) cause of the universe with Mind, the first and principal faculty of the World Soul, which is immanent in the infinite universe, and which is the formal principle of the universal substance.[38] What we should think of when we say 'God', according to these passages in *De la causa*, is not, then, a transcendent God who is the first cause and principle of the universe, but the infinite, animate universe itself. However, Bruno's general position regarding the relationship between God and the universe is problematic.[39]

This is the metaphysical context of Bruno's concept of contraction. In the following two sections I shall describe how contraction played a significant role in Bruno's conception of the universe.

The World Soul

We are told in the *Sigillus* that the World Soul is full of seminal reasons, causing generation in nature. Bruno attributes this doctrine explicitly to Plotinus, presumably *Enneads* IV iv [28] 12.[40] In *De la causa* Bruno mentions seminal reasons too.[41] However, in the *Sigillus* and in *De la causa*, Bruno describes the World Soul very differently from Plotinus.

Plotinus' doctrine of seminal reasons in the World Soul derived from Stoic cosmology, where those seminal reasons were defined as agents of the World Soul, causing organic harmony in the sensible world.[42] The Stoics conceived the

---

principio substanziale". For matter as the principle of being in the thought of Bruno, see BLUM, *Aristoteles*, pp. 62-66.

35 For matter as principle and divine, see BRUNO, *Causa* iii, p. 191. For matter as divine, see also ibid., epist., iii, pp. 17, 193; *Spaccio* iii 2, p. 415.

36 ARISTOTLE, *Metaphysics* VII i-iv 1028ª10-1030ᵇ13.

37 For an exposition of Bruno's discussion of this problem, see BLUM, *Aristoteles*, pp. 62-66, 69, 73.

38 BRUNO, *Causa* ii, p. 113: "Or quanto alla causa effettrice, dico l'efficiente fisico universale essere l'intelletto universale, che è la prima e principal facultà de l'anima del mondo, la quale è forma universale di quello." See also ibid., ii, p. 121: "Or per venire a li principii constitutivi de le cose, prima raggionarò de la forma per esser medesma in certo modo con la già detta causa efficiente: per che l'intelletto che è una potenza de l'anima del mondo, è stato detto efficiente prossimo di tutte cose naturali."

39 Cf. BRUNO, *Spaccio* i 3, pp. 169-171; *Infinito* i, p. 87; *Summa*, p. 88.16-24.

40 BRUNO, *Sigillus* ii 3, p. 196.9-14. For Plotinus' notion of seminal reasons, see WALLIS, *Neoplatonism*, pp. 25, 68.

41 BRUNO, *Causa* ii, pp. 115-117.

42 WALLIS, *Neoplatonism*, p. 25; GRAESER, *Plotinus and the Stoics*, pp. 41-43.

World Soul as the highest deity in the universe and its active principle — the passive counterpart was matter. These two principles were mutually dependent and unified in a corporeal thing.[43] Plotinus accepted the idea of seminal reasons in the World Soul, but, unlike the Stoics, he did not regard the World Soul as the highest deity, nor did he regard it as material and spatial.[44] Instead, Plotinus placed the World Soul on the lowest level of the intelligible world, as the second emanation, dependent upon the first emanation, Mind, which in turn is dependent upon the One.[45] Consequently, the seminal reasons were not material, contrary to the Stoics.

Bruno only refers to the Stoics twice in *De la causa*, though not directly to their idea of seminal reasons, and he does not refer to them in the *Sigillus* in regard to this theme either.[46] Therefore it is difficult to claim that Bruno's conception of seminal reasons derives from that of the Stoics, even though Bruno's general tendency towards materialism makes it easy to conjecture that in regard to seminal reasons he was more in line with the Stoic materialistic view than that of Plotinus.[47]

This conception of the World Soul, the formal principle of the universal substance, is one of two theoretical components in Bruno's theory of individuation. The other is matter, to which I shall return below. Before I do so, however, we must examine Bruno's interpretation of ontological contraction, a key concept in his theory of individuation. Bruno's concept of contraction presupposes mutual dependency between form and matter:

> Furthermore, this form [World Soul] is defined and determined by matter, because, having in itself the capacity of constituting particulars of innumerable species, it becomes contracted and constitutes an individual. And, on the other hand, the potency of indeterminate matter, which can receive any form whatsoever, becomes restricted to a species. So one is the cause of making the other definite and determinate.[48]

---

[43] For the Stoic concept of the World Soul, see SAMBURSKY, *Physics of the Stoics*, pp. 21-48; BLOOS, *Probleme der Stoischen Physik*, pp. 52-89; HAHM, *The origins of Stoic cosmology*, pp. 140-146, 157-174; LAPIDGE, 'Stoic cosmology', pp. 167-176.

[44] PLOTINUS IV vii [2] 3.14-35 (= tr. Ficino, p. 458.16-48).

[45] PLOTINUS V v [32] 9.7-38 (= tr. Ficino, p. 528.4-54). For Plotinus' concept of the World Soul, see ARMSTRONG, 'Plotinus', pp. 250-258; BLUMENTHAL, '*Nous* and Soul in Plotinus: some problems of demarcation', pp. 203-219.

[46] BRUNO mentions the Stoics in *Causa* iii, pp. 169, 203. The context of the first reference is the Stoics' view that forms are nothing but accidental dispositions of matter. The second reference regards the Stoics' idea that matter has a sensible as well as an intelligible aspect.

[47] See the considerations about possible influence from Stoic physics and cosmology in GRANADA, 'Giordano Bruno y la stoa', especially pp. 127-131, 136-145.

[48] BRUNO, *Causa* ii, p. 147: "Oltre, questa forma è definita e determinata per la materia, per che avendo in sé facilità di constituir particolari, di specie innumerabili, viene a contraersi a constituir uno individuo; e da l'altro canto la potenza della materia indeterminata, la quale può ricevere qualsivoglia forma, viene a terminarsi ad una

Here the interdependency is between "indeterminate matter" and the World Soul. In the *Sigillus* Bruno similarly defines individuation through a double contraction (*duplex contractio*) characterised by an interdependency between indeterminate matter (*indeterminata materia*) and absolute form (*absoluta forma*).[49] The latter is synonymous with the World Soul.[50] In the *Sigillus*, Bruno similarly states that the World Soul's animation of matter by forms is influenced by the complexion of matter (*pro conditione materiae*).[51]

Since individuation involves a dialectical relationship between matter and form, and since matter thus affects the outcome of a process of individuation, individual entities within the same species display individual differences. If matter, on the other hand, were regarded as passive potentiality given essence by form, then the problem would arise why there are differences between members of the same species. Bruno avoids this problem by assigning to matter a power of individuating form.

The doctrine of form and matter co-determining particulars is Neoplatonic in origin. I shall return to it in detail later. Here I shall introduce it briefly. The dependency of the World Soul on matter, proposed in the above quotation from *De la causa*, seems to contradict Plotinus' conception of corporeal matter as absolute potency and dependent upon the World Soul.[52] But Plotinus is inconsistent on this point, for on other occasions, such as *Enneads* VI iv-v, he also assigns to matter the power of individuating form, contrary to his principle that matter is pure potentiality. The idea that matter, according to some modern interpreters, has the power of individuating form is explained through the doctrine

---

specie: tanto che l'una è causa della definizione e determinazione de l'altra." See also ibid., epist., p. 15: "Si vede ... come [la forma, i.e. anima del mondo] definisce e termina la materia, come è definita e terminata da quella [i.e. matter]."

[49] BRUNO, *Sigillus* ii 10, ii 22, pp. 203.1-5, 213.14-214.19. The phrase *duplex contractio* appears ibid., ii 22, p. 214.6-7. The Latin term *indeterminatum* is used about matter in BRUNO, *Causa* iv, p. 219. For the formulation of a "double contraction" in the *Sigillus*, see BRUNO, *Sigillus* ii 22, p. 214.6-19, as quoted on p. 26 n. 88 above. This dialectical relationship between matter and form is similarly expressed through contraction in BRUNO, *De immenso* i 1, v 12, pp. 205.1-4, 156.10-17. The description of a "double contraction" in BRUNO, *Sigillus* ii 22, p. 214.6-7, has been observed in INGEGNO, 'Nota sul *Sigillus sigillorum* del Bruno', p. 362. However, Ingegno does not suggest a source.

[50] BRUNO, *Causa* iii, p. 189, as quoted on p. 27 n. 93 above. The World Soul is called "principio formale" ibid., epist., ii, pp. 13, 137, so by "anima" ibid., iii, p. 189, Bruno refers to the World Soul, which is, as he says there, the equivalent of "datore de le forme". "Forma absoluta" is identified with "dator formarum" in BRUNO, *Sigillus* ii 10, p. 202.20-26. For "dator formarum", see p. 27 nn. 93, 94 above.

[51] BRUNO, *Sigillus* ii 3, p. 196.15-19: "Unde cum anima ubique praesens existat, illaque tota et in toto et in quacumque parte tota, ideo pro conditione materiae in quacumque re etiam exigua et abscisa mundum, nedum mundi simulacrum valeas intueri, ut non temere omnia in omnibus dicere cum Anaxagora possimus."

[52] PLOTINUS IV vii [2] 3.14-35 (= tr. Ficino, p. 458.16-48).

of reception according to the capacity of the recipient.[53] This doctrine does not necessarily concern solely matter. Several passages seem to leave the possibility open that it occurs throughout the Neoplatonic system. The doctrine was taken up by Proclus, it later featured in the *Liber de causis*, and it was embraced in Giles' commentary on the latter work, in particular in relation to matter. To anticipate my argument, this doctrine in the *Liber de causis*, and maybe even Giles' application of the doctrine to matter, is probably among the source to Bruno's notion of contraction in the ontological sense.[54]

But let us return to the quotation from *De la causa*. By using the concept of contraction in this manner, Bruno achieves two important things. First, the formal principle of universal substance, the World Soul, is present in all entities in the infinite universe through its contraction with matter. This is a vital element in Bruno's doctrine of universal animation, which he has Dickson proclaiming is a metaphysical novelty.[55] Although the doctrine was new to Dickson, and probably to some Aristotelians too, it was not new to pagan and Renaissance Platonists. Second, insisting on the dialectical relationship between matter and the World Soul, and assigning to matter the ability to contract forms from the World Soul, he uses the term 'contraction' to promote his view of matter as alive. The World Soul is ubiquitous in the infinite universe, but the contraction into individuals depends upon the "capacity" of the recipient, that is, of matter, to receive, or rather allure, forms from the World Soul.[56] Bruno holds, then, that there is a double contraction

---

[53] For the formulation "reception according to the capacity of the recipient", see ARMSTRONG, *Intelligible universe*, p. 60. In O'MEARA, *Structures hiérarchiques*, pp. 56-61, 68, it has been asserted that this doctrine implies a causal dualism between Ideas and bodies, or matter, suggesting that individuation is caused not only by Ideas, but also by matter or bodies which receive Ideas. O'Meara's interpretation has been questioned in LEE, 'The doctrine of reception', p. 85, on the ground that it "appears to undermine ... the theory as theory of eidetic causation, insofar as the dualism suggests that matter has a positively specifiable nature which is causally independent both on the *eide* and of psychical activity." For his alternative monistic interpretation, according to which matter does not have the potency proposed by O'Meara, see ibid., pp. 86-97. Lee claims that the doctrine of reception according to the capacity of the recipient is inconsistent with Plotinus' notion of matter as impassible and deprived of qualities (ibid., pp. 90-96). In BLUMETHAL, 'Did Plotinus believe in Ideas of individuals', pp. 61-80, Plotinus' problematic accounts of the *species differentiae* in relation to individual human beings is related to the general metaphysical question about the power of matter to individuate, later discussed by O'Meara and Lee. For matter in this context, see ibid., pp. 70, 74, 78.

[54] For Giles' treatment of this idea, see pp. 129-131 below.

[55] BRUNO, *Causa* ii, p. 127: "*Dicsono.* Mi par udir cosa molto nova: volete forse che non sola la forma de l'universo, ma tutte quante le forme di cose naturali siano anima? *Teofilo.* Sì."

[56] For the doctrine of reception according to the capacity of the recipient in Bruno, see BRUNO, *De umbris* §63.2-6, p. 52: "Intellectus primus lucis amphitrites, ita lucem suam effundit ab intimis ad externa, et ab extraemis attrahit, ut quidlibet ab ipso pro capacitate possit omnia contrahere, et quaelibet ad ipsum pro facultate per ipsius luminis viam tendere." See also BRUNO, *Sigillus* i 32, p. 176.27-29; *Cena* iii, pp. 159-161; *Causa* v, p. 283; *Infinito* i, p. 85; *Spaccio* iii 2, p. 415; *Furori* i 4, p. 157. The presence of this

involved in individuation, where the forms of the World Soul contribute with one aspect of this double contraction, and where the "capacity" of matter contributes to the other aspect.

Bruno's interpretation of contraction, where matter individuates form, was in conflict with the article 46 in the Condemnation of 1277.[57] It is yet unclear what that meant to Bruno. In the next section I shall explore further the idea of the capacity of the recipient, matter, in order to explain contraction as produced by matter.

Matter

The dialectical relationship between form and matter in Bruno's theory of individuation faces him with the task of explaining how matter can play an active role in the process of individuation and is not simply passive and formless. In what sense is matter alive? How does matter "contract" forms? And what is the "capacity" of matter?

Bruno's point of departure is the traditional Aristotelian interpretation of matter, according to which matter is pure, passive potentiality. Matter, Aristotle held, was the principle of individuation, and was determined into a substance when contracted with form. Form defined the essence of the compound matter and form.[58] The notion of matter implied in this conception of substance is the major point of criticism in Bruno's thoughts about matter. As pointed out, Bruno abandons the notion of individual substances, advanced by Aristotle, and argues, instead, for one single, immanent and universal substance with two principles, one formal and one material. In what follows, matter denotes Bruno's material principle of the universal substance. A second distinctive feature of Bruno's concept of matter is that unlike Aristotle he assigns active potentiality to matter, thereby accounting for matter's contraction of forms.[59]

---

doctrine in Bruno's ontology is not described in VÉDRINE, *La conception*, pp. 273-288; BLUM, *Aristoteles*, pp. 54-75. It is, however, touched upon briefly in SPRUIT, *Il problema*, pp. 46 n. 17, 172-173.

[57] Among the 219 condemned errors in the Condemnation of 1277 we find the one mentioned in article 46, as cited in *Chartularium Universitatis Parisiensis*, vol. 1, p. 546: "Quod, sicut ex materia non potest aliquid fieri sine agente, ita nec ex agente potest aliquid fieri sine materia; et, quod Deus non est causa efficiens, nisi respectu ejus quod habet esse in potentia materie." For the Condemnation of this article in 1277, see MARENBON, *Later medieval philosophy*, p. 73. For the Condemnation in the Renaissance, see MAHONEY, 'Reverberations', pp. 902-930.

[58] For Aristotle's conception of matter, see pp. 30-31 above.

[59] BRUNO, *Causa* iii, p. 193: "Ma prima vorrei saper se per la grande unione, che ha questa anima del mondo e forma universale con la materia, si potesse patire quell'altro modo e maniera di filosofare, di quei che non separano l'atto dalla raggion della materia, e la intendeno cosa divina: e non pura et informe talmente, che lei medesma non si forme e vesta." See also ibid., epist., iii, iv, pp. 17, 239, 249-251; *Sigillus* ii 22, p. 214.17-19.

As mentioned in the preceding section, the doctrine of reception according to the capacity of the recipient is central to Bruno's conception of matter's ability to contract forms. Preceding from this starting point, three characteristics of Bruno's notion of matter are to be considered in this section. First, the sources of Bruno's notion of matter. Second, contraction produced by matter by virtue of its active participation in the individuation of particulars. Third, the cosmological role of contraction produced by matter.

(i) Sources for Bruno's concept of matter

Bruno develops his idea of matter from Plotinus' *Enneads* II iv-v.[60] But he does so partly on the basis of Ficino's commentary on *Enneads* II iv 11, where Ficino discusses the conception of matter and extension found in Averroes (Mohammed ibn Rushd; 1126-1198).[61] Ficino's possible role as an intermediary for, or at least

---

[60] Plotinus' concept of matter has been debated frequently over the last decades. The debate — in which the studies by O'Brien, Schwyzer and Corrigan, all listed below, are central — has dealt with the following question in relation to the *Enneads*. Is matter generated or ungenerated? If it is, it is an integral part of emanation. If not, matter alone is not among the products which derive from the One. O'Brien defends the first position, Schwyzer the second, Corrigan holds that there are three kinds of generation of matter in the *Enneads*. See O'BRIEN, 'Plotinus on evil. A study of matter and the soul in Plotinus' conception of human evil', pp. 68-110; SCHWYZER, 'Zu Plotin's Deutung der sogenannten platonischen Materie', pp. 271-280 (criticising the preceding article by O'Brien); O'BRIEN, 'Plotinus and the Gnostics on the generation of matter', pp. 108-119; CORRIGAN, 'Is there more than one generation of matter in the *Enneads*?', pp. 167-181; NARBONNE, 'Plotin et le problème de la génération de la matière; à propos d'un article récent', pp. 3-31 (criticising Corrigan as above); CORRIGAN, 'On the generation of matter in the *Enneads*. A reply', pp. 17-24 (replying Narbonne); O'BRIEN, 'J.-M. Narbonne on Plotinus and the generation of matter: two corrections', pp. 25-27 (replying to Narbonne's criticism and presentation of O'Brien's positions); O'BRIEN, *Plotinus on the origin of matter*, pp. 11-88 (discussing Schwyzer's and Corrigan's interpretations); NARBONNE, 'Introduction', in PLOTINUS, *Les deux matières*, pp. 47-270; O'BRIEN, *Théodicée plotinienne. Théodicée gnostique*, pp. 61-68 (discussing, among other things, Schwyzer's interpretation of Plotinus' concept of matter). Independently of this debate there are also two recent studies of Plotinus' concept of matter: WAGNER, 'Plotinus' idealism and the problem of matter in *Enneads* vi.4 & 5', pp. 57-83; NIKULIN, 'Intelligible matter in Plotinus', pp. 85-93, 104-108.

[61] BRUNO, *Causa* iv, p. 237. Bruno brings Averroes into the discussion of intelligible matter and extension ibid., iv, pp. 249-251. FICINO, *In Plotinum* II i [40] 1, II iv [12] 11, pp. 86.32-33, 154.37-38, attributed to Averroes the view that extension occurs without matter in the superlunary region. For Ficino's idea of matter, see VITALE, 'Sul concetto di materia nella *Theologia platonica* di Marsilio Ficino', pp. 337-369; KODERA, 'Narcissus, divine gazes and bloody mirrors: The concept of matter in Ficino', pp. 285-306.

as influential source for, Bruno's use of Averroes in this particular context, has been ignored in Bruno studies.[62]

Plotinus distinguishes corporeal from intelligible matter. Corporeal matter, he states in relation to the soul of each individual human being, is "the cause of the soul's weakness and vice: it is then itself evil before soul and is primary evil."[63] Alluding to Plato's metaphor of the human soul as a winged charioteer in the *Phaedrus*, Plotinus exhorts us to avoid corporeal matter so as to make the soul virtuous, "winged and perfect".[64] Apart from this condemnatory view on corporeal matter in relation to ethics, Plotinus also states that this sort of matter is non-being and the same thing as privation.[65]

Intelligible matter is discussed in the *Enneads* II iv 1-5. Contrary to his views on corporeal matter, Plotinus does not condemn intelligible matter, but approves it for being shaped by higher entities, ultimately the One, much like the World Soul is shaped by Mind.[66] Intelligible matter and corporeal matter are both principles of indeterminacy within their respective realms, but intelligible matter is not insubstantial, like corporeal matter, nor is it evil.[67] Hence there is a great difference between the two. Finally, intelligible matter exists in the intelligible world as a model imitated by corporeal matter in the sensible world.[68] Ficino kept the two ideas of matter apart.[69]

In the Middle Ages Avicebron, also known as Avencebrol, whose Arabic name was Salomon ibn Gabirol (1020-1070), and David of Dinant (fl. c. 1200) had conflated these two ideas, corporeal matter (matter as potentiality) with intelligible matter (intelligible matter as a principle of indeterminacy in the intelligible

---

[62] TOCCO, *Le fonti*, pp. 527-529; CORSANO, *Il pensiero*, pp. 140-142, 144-145; PAPULI, *Qualche osservazione*, p. 209; BLUM, *Aristoteles*, pp. 30-31, 71; STURLESE, '"Averroè quantumque arabo"', pp. 321-324.

[63] PLOTINUS I viii [51] 14.49-50, tr. A. H. Armstrong, Loeb ed. (= tr. Ficino, pp. 81.67-82.2). For matter as evil, see RIST, 'Plotinus on matter and evil', pp. 154-166; O'BRIEN, 'Plotinus on matter and evil', pp. 171, 175-177.

[64] PLOTINUS I viii [51] 14.20, tr. A. H. Armstrong (= tr. Ficino, p. 81.25). For the metaphor of the "winged soul", see PLATO, *Phaedrus* 246A3-D2.

[65] PLOTINUS II iv [12] 16.1-27 (= tr. Ficino, pp. 169.37-170.11). See also PLOTINUS II v [25] 4.1-5.36 (= tr. Ficino, pp. 175.33-176.46). For matter as non-being, see WALLIS, *Neoplatonism*, pp. 48-49. For generation of matter, see references on p. 40 n. 60 above.

[66] PLOTINUS II iv [12] 3.1-8 (= tr. Ficino, p. 160.32-44). For intelligible matter in Plotinus, see NARBONNE, in PLOTINUS, *Les deux matières*, pp. 47-134; WALLIS, *Neoplatonism*, pp. 66-67; O'BRIEN, *Plotinus on the origin of matter*, pp. 22-25; NIKULIN, 'Intelligible matter in Plotinus', pp. 85-93, 104-108; RIST, 'The indefinite dyad and intelligible matter in Plotinus', pp. 99-107.

[67] PLOTINUS II iv [12] 5.12-39, II iv [12] 15.14-37, II v [25] 3.1-14 (= tr. Ficino, pp. 161.47-162.20, 169.1-36, 174.34-60).

[68] PLOTINUS II iv [12] 3.1-4.20 (= tr. Ficino, pp. 160.32-161.26). For the relationship between the two worlds in this respect, and the relation between intelligible matter and Mind, see ARMSTRONG, *Intelligible universe*, pp. 65-68.

[69] FICINO, *In Plotinum* II i [40] 1, p. 86.33-35. And for Proclus, see WALLIS, *Neoplatonism*, pp. 148-149.

world).[70] Aquinas rejected the fusion of corporeal and intelligible matter by means of the distinction of essence and existence (to which we shall return later).[71] In *De la causa*, by contrast, Bruno praises explicitly Avicebron and David of Dinant for their views.[72] He similarly says that those nourished by Aristotle's doctrine have not understood the concept of matter as it is understood among those "others", probably a reference to Avicebron and David of Dinant, who have "praised matter greatly" and "scandalised" "some theologians", Aquinas among others we can assume. These critics (of David and Avicebron) do not, Bruno continues, understand that these thinkers who praise matter greatly conflate matter in the intelligible with matter in the sensible worlds.[73]

The essential point is, then, that all potentiality — active as well as passive — is matter, and this applies to both corporeal and intelligible entities. This is the

---

[70] For Avicebron on matter, see BRUNNER, 'Matière chez Avicebron', pp. 261-279, especially p. 267. For David of Dinant on matter, see MACCAGNOLO, 'David of Dinant', pp. 435-436, 439-440. For a comparison between the thought of Dinant and Stoic physics, see LAPIDGE, 'The Stoic inheritance', p. 106.

[71] GILSON, *Aquinas*, pp. 176-177; WIPPEL, 'Essence and existence', pp. 394-396.

[72] BRUNO refers to Avicebron in his *Causa* iii, iv, pp. 169, 191, 233 (explicitly to Avicebron's *Fons vitae* ibid., iii, p. 169) and to David of Dinant (ibid., epist., iv, pp. 17, 267). He also refers to Avicebron's *Fons vitae* and to David of Dinant in *De vinculis* §77.35-47, pp. 518-520 (= *BOL*, vol. 3, p. 696.1-13). For Bruno's indebtedness to Avicebron's ideas, see WITTMANN, 'Giordano Brunos Beziehungen zu Avencebrol', pp. 148-151. According to Wittmann, Bruno probably knew Avicebron's ideas indirectly from Aquinas' unfavourable reports (ibid., p. 151). For Aquinas' report of, and stance towards, Avicebron's philosophy, see WITTMANN, *Die Stellung des h. Thomas von Aquin zu Avencebrol*, pp. 33-77. Avicebron's *Fons vitae* was not printed in the Renaissance. But the library at St Victor held a manuscript and Bruno might have read it during his stay in Paris (VÉDRINE, *La conception*, p. 278 n. 33). David of Dinant's books were ordered to be burnt in 1210 (MACCAGNOLO, 'David of Dinant', p. 429) but were probably known indirectly through Albert's and Aquinas' reports. These reports are listed in THÉRY, *Autour de décret de 1210*, pp. 151-155. However, Théry does not clarify when Albert and Aquinas explicitly refer to David's name, which actually happens a very few times in the reports indicated by Théry. Moreover, Théry does not distinguish direct quotations from indirect quotations, probably because he did not dispose of any of David's survived manuscripts, discovered by Birkenmajer in 1933 and edited by Kurdzialek in 1963. Hence, Théry's list of quotations should be read with caution. For Bruno's use of David of Dinant, see TOCCO, *Le fonti*, pp. 530-531.

[73] BRUNO, *Causa* iii, pp. 213-215: "Conchiudendo dumque vedete quanta sia l'eccellenza della potenza la quale se vi piace chiamarla raggione di materia, che non hanno penetrato i filosofi volgari, la possete senza detraere alla divinità trattar più altamente, che Platone nella sua *Politica* et il Timeo. Costoro per averno troppo alzata la raggione della materia son stati scandalosi ad alcuni teologi. Questo è accaduto o perché quelli non si son bene dechiarati, o perché questi non hanno bene inteso, perché sempre prendeno il significato della materia secondo che è soggetto di cose naturali solamente, come nodriti nelle sentenze d'Aristotele; e non considerano [the critics of David and Avicebron] che la materia è tale appresso gli altri, che è comune al mondo intelligibile e sensibile, come essi dicono, prendendo il significato secondo una equivocazione analoga."

reason why Bruno refutes the traditional description of matter as *prope nihil*.[74] In *De la causa* Bruno's point of departure, however, in relation to the distinction corporeal versus intelligible matter is not Avicebron or David of Dinant, but Plotinus' *Enneads* II iv, cited by Bruno as Plotinus' book *De la materia*, an Italian translation of the Latin title given by Ficino to Plotinus' treatise.[75] From this book of Plotinus and Ficino's commentary on it Bruno takes the idea of corporeal matter as an imitation of intelligible matter but ignores Plotinus' distinction between the two.[76] In general terms Plotinus' treatise lent itself to Bruno's purposes, i.e. to explain the formative principles of the universe as immanent rather than transcendent.

Bruno rephrases Plotinus' argument for the existence of intelligible matter as follows. Since the sensible world is an imitation of the intelligible world, and since the sensible world contains composites of matter and form, then the intelligible world too must comprise forms and matter, the latter being non-corporeal, intelligible matter.[77] Hence form and matter in the intelligible world are a "duplicate of the Aristotelian sense-world", in Armstrong's account of Plotinus' doctrine.[78] Even though Bruno paraphrases Ficino's Latin translation of Plotinus' *Enneads*, he does not, as mentioned, here or over the subsequent pages, retain the distinction between the two kinds of matter which is maintained in Ficino's translation. Ficino opens his comment on *Enneads* II iv by stating that "in Chapter

---

74   Ibid., iv, p. 251. For Bruno's rejection of the expression *prope nihil* in regard to matter, see SPRUIT, *Il problema*, pp. 174-175.

75   BRUNO, *Causa* iv, p. 237. See the title of PLOTINUS II iv [12], in tr. Ficino, p. 159.32-33. See also FICINO, *In Plotinum* II iv [12], p. 148.32. The title of Plotinus' *Enneads* II iv [12], given by his pupil and editor Porphyry, was Περὶ τῶν δύο ὑλῶν (*On the two matters*). See ARMSTRONG, 'Introductory note', in the Loeb edition of Plotinus (Cambridge, Mass., 1966), vol. 2, p. 104.

76   For Bruno's idea of intelligible matter, see VÉDRINE, *La conception*, pp. 277-281; PAPI, *Antropologia*, pp. 80-81; SPRUIT, *Il problema*, p. 171.

77   BRUNO, *Causa* iv, p. 237: "Plotino ancora dice nel libro *De la materia*, che 'se nel mondo intelligibile è moltitudine e pluralità di specie, è necessario che vi sia qualche cosa comune, oltre la proprietà e differenza di ciascuna di quelle. Quello che è comune tien luogo di materia, quello che è proprio e fa distinzione, tien luogo di forma'. Gionge che 'se questo [i.e. the sensible world] è a imitazion di quello [i.e. the intelligible world], la composizion di questo è a imitazion di quello'". Bruno is translating freely from PLOTINUS II iv [12] 4.2-9, in Ficino's translation, pp. 160.64-161.7: "Profecto si plures ibi [intelligible world] sunt species, commune quiddam in ipsis esse necessarium est: rursusque proprium quoad [1492 ed.: 'quo'] aliud ab alio distinguatur. Hoc utique proprium atque haec separans differentia, forma certe est propria. Quod si illic est forma, est insuper et formatum, circa quod differentia est. Subest itaque materia quae illam accipiat formam, perpetuoque subiectum. Praeterea si intelligibilis illic mundus existit: hic vero noster illius est imitatio, atque componitur ex materia: illic quoque oportet esse materiam." Bruno is closer to Ficino's translation than to Ficino's commentary on this passage. Cf. FICINO, *In Plotinum* II iv [12] 4, p. 150.28-29: "Sic itaque mundus corporeus superioris imago est, incorporeum mundum referens velut exemplar: si multiformis referatur ad multiformem, si materia haec referatur ad illam."

78   ARMSTRONG, *Intelligible universe*, p. 66.

four [i.e. *Enneads* II iv 4] Plotinus demonstrates that in the intelligible world there exists something similar to matter in some way."[79] Ficino repeats the ontological distinction between the two kinds of matter, hinted at by the expression "similar to matter", when he writes that just as the sensible world comprises (immanent) forms and matter, so too the intelligible world includes forms (the Ideas) and matter of some kind.[80] Immediately after he quotes from Plotinus' book *De la materia*, Bruno refutes the distinction between the two kinds of matter. Teofilo, refuting Plotinus explicitly, argues that there is only one matter, not two.[81] Consequently Bruno refrains from speaking of two kinds of matters over the next pages in *De la causa*, but only of one.

Having elided the distinction between the two kinds of matter, Bruno applies Plotinus' idea of intelligible matter to corporeal and incorporeal entities. Bruno thus agrees with Plotinus on the existence of a material substrate in order to account for the differentiation in the corporeal world.[82] However, the next thing Bruno does is to claim that "one is matter, one is the potency by which all that exists, exists in act; and with no less reason it [this single matter] is appropriate in incorporeal substances as in corporeal ones".[83]

(ii) Contraction produced by matter

It is in this context that Bruno now introduces the notion of contraction. Matter, together with the World Soul, contracts itself in the course of individuation, partly into corporeal dimensional bodies, partly into non-corporeal and non-dimensional entities.[84] Contracted entities exist in different ways. Incorporeal entities exist as

---

[79] FICINO, *In Plotinum* II iv [12] 4, p. 150.10: "In capite quarto probat in mundo intellectuali esse nonnihil materiae quodam modo simile."

[80] Ibid., II iv [12] 4, p. 150.28-29, as quoted on p. 43 n. 77 above. For PLOTINUS II iv [12] 4, see NARBONNE, in PLOTINUS, *Les deux matières*, pp. 74-79, 319-320.

[81] BRUNO, *Causa* iv, p. 237: "E benché dichi che tutta quella moltitudine conviene in uno ente impartibile e fuor di qualsivoglia dimensione, quello dirò essere la materia, nel quale si uniscono tante forme". Also ibid., iv, p. 239. Here and elsewhere Teofilo is the loyal spokesman of Bruno's philosophy; see ibid., v, p. 317: "Teofilo, fidel relatore della nolana filosofia."

[82] Ibid., iv, p. 237: "Per il che il mondo superiore non solamente deve esser stimato per tutto indivisibile, ma anco per alcune sue condizioni divisibile e distinto; la cui divisione e distinzione non può esser capita senza qualche soggetta materia." For the probable source, see PLOTINUS II iv [12] 4.2-9, tr. Ficino, pp. 160.64-161.7, as quoted on p. 43 n. 77 above.

[83] BRUNO, *Causa* iv, p. 239: "una sia la materia, una la potenza per la quale tutto quel che è, è in atto; e non con minor raggione conviene alle sustanza incorporee, che alle corporali".

[84] Ibid., iv, p. 243: "*Dicsono.* Alcuni, quantumque concedano essere materia nelle cose incorporee, la intendono però secondo una raggione molto diversa. *Teofilo.* Sia quantosivoglia diversità secondo la raggion propria per la quale l'una [i.e. 'sensible matter'] descende a l'esser corporale e l'altra [i.e. 'intelligible matter'] non, l'una riceve qualità sensibili e l'altra non, e non par che possa essere raggione comune a quella

eternal actualisations of one potentiality in matter, and they are therefore incorruptible. Corporeal entities, on the other hand, change. They are actualisations of potentialities occurring over time.[85] It is in this process of individuation that the World Soul also participates, as mentioned above, and it is here that matter receives forms according to its capacity to receive.

The important role attributed to matter in Bruno's theory of individuation is reflected in his thoughts about the source of actualisation. There is no change in the intelligible world, Plotinus asserts. And intelligible matter is all things at once and does not change into anything.[86] Therefore, in the intelligible world form and matter are "one nature", although they may be distinguished conceptually as two different aspects.[87] Commenting on this passage, Ficino wrote that "in the incorporeal world, matter is the essence and nature of form: for form is the being and act of matter."[88] Plotinus' and Ficino's comments have a striking similarity with Bruno's concept of universal matter. The possibility that they were his source is corroborated by Bruno's quotation of Plotinus on just this point.[89] Bruno maintains that matter is the source of what is in act and takes up a feature of Plotinus' intelligible matter, namely the idea that in intelligible matter many forms are united in an undifferentiated unity.[90] Plotinus had said this specifically about

---

materia a cui ripugna la quantità et esser suggetto delle qualitadi che hanno l'essere nelle demensioni, e la natura a cui non ripugna l'una né l'altra: anzi l'una e l'altra è una medesima; e che (come è più volte detto) tutta la differenza depende dalla contrazzione a l'essere corporea e non essere corporea: come nell'essere animale ogni sensitivo è uno; ma contraendo quel geno a certe specie, ripugna a l'uomo l'essere leone, et a questo animale d'esser quell'altro." See also ibid., iv., p. 233. For a discussion of 'dimension' in the fourth dialogue of *De la causa*, see BLUM, *Aristoteles*, pp. 30-31; SPRUIT, *Il problema*, pp. 172-173. Although BLUM, *Aristoteles*, pp. 66, 68-71, 73, 78-79, discusses the metaphysical context of contraction in *De la causa* very well, and even though he mentions the concept of contraction, he does not discuss it in detail.

[85] BRUNO, *Causa* iv, p. 241.

[86] PLOTINUS II iv [12] 3.13-14 (= tr. Ficino, p. 160.54-56).

[87] PLOTINUS II v [25] 3.8-19, tr. A. H. Armstrong (= tr. Ficino, p. 174.50-64).

[88] FICINO, *In Plotinum* II v [25] 3, p. 171.29-31: "In mundo autem incorporeo materia quidem est essentia et natura formae: forma vero est esse actusque materiae. Rursum materia nec ad formam in potentia ibi est, neque potentia est ad formam: sed est potius ipsa potentia formae: forma vero non est actus aliquis in materia sive potentia, sed ipse potius potentiae actus."

[89] BRUNO, *Causa* iv, p. 251: "Costui [Plotinus] facendo differenza tra la materia di cose superiori et inferiori, dice che quella è insieme tutto; et essendo che possiede tutto, non ha in che mutarsi".

[90] For the idea that matter is the source of what is in act; see ibid., iv, p. 263: "sono [le forme] nel seno della materia; che dumque? ella è fonte de la attualità". See also ibid., iv, p. 259: "Tutti dumque per modo di separazione vogliono le cose essere da la materia, e non per modo di apposizione e recepzione: dumque si de' più tosto dire che [la materia] contiene le forme e che le includa, che pensare che ne sia vòta e le escluda." Bruno here refers to the opinion of the Pythagoreans, Anaxagoras, Democritus, mentioned ibid., iv, p. 257. Lastly, Bruno attributes to Plotinus the idea that matter is an active principle, see ibid., iv, pp. 249-251: "Per il qual senso si vede che la materia le [le

intelligible matter,[91] but Bruno applies this to his unified concept of matter. By doing so Bruno makes the forms or Ideas innate to matter.

(iii) The cosmological role of contraction produced by matter

Over the last pages we have seen how Bruno interprets contraction as involving a reciprocal relationship between form, i.e. the World Soul, and matter, as he understood these terms. One last aspect of contraction and matter has to be considered. Bruno not only works out an alternative concept of matter, he also redefines its cosmological role. When Bruno states in *De la causa* that matter provides the extension of particulars, he follows Averroes.[92] By doing so Bruno contradicts Plotinus who argued that matter is without extension in itself, and that dimensions as well as qualities are imposed by form.[93] Even though Bruno agrees with Averroes that matter comprises extension, against the opinion of Plotinus, he does not agree with Averroes when it comes to the question of the materiality of the superlunary sphere. In *De substantia orbis* Averroes had followed Aristotle and claimed that the heavens do not comprise any of the four elements of the sublunary region, implying that materiality had to be denied in the heavens.[94] Ficino criticises Averroes for assigning dimension to the heavens without also assigning matter.[95] According to Plotinus, Ficino reports, dimension and quality are ontologically simultaneous.[96] Hence it is impossible to speak of a superlunary region without materiality.

Bruno voices a similar criticism of Averroes and complains that he had followed the Aristotelians in their conception of dimension as separable from matter.[97] Bruno holds, even more than Ficino, that the universe is homogenous,

---

 forme] manda come da sé, e non le riceve come di fuora. Questo in parte intese ancor Plotino, prencipe nella setta di Platone." For the idea that in intelligible matter many forms are united in an undifferentiated unity; see ibid., iv, p. 237: "quello dirò essere la materia, nel quale si uniscono tante forme".

[91] PLOTINUS II iv [12] 3.9-16 (= tr. Ficino, p. 160.46-61).

[92] BRUNO, *Causa* iv, pp. 249-251: "Dice lui [Averroes] che la materia ne l'essenzia sua comprende le dimensioni interminate: volendo accennare che quelle pervegnono a terminarsi, ora con questa figura e dimensioni, ora con quella e quell'altra, quelle e quell'altre, secondo il cangiar di forme naturali. Per il qual senso si vede che la materia le [forme] manda come da sé, e non le riceve come di fuora." For Averroes on this point, see STURLESE, "'Averroè quantumque arabo'", p. 323.

[93] Cf. PLOTINUS II iv [12] 11.12-19 (= tr. Ficino, p. 165.37-46).

[94] HYMAN, 'Introduction', pp. 29-32.

[95] FICINO, *In Plotinum* II i [40] 1, p. 86.32-33: "Neque licet alicui, more Averrois, dimensiones in caelo sine materia ponere."

[96] Ibid., II iv [12] 11, p. 154.43-44: "ac producto spatio protenditur in ea [materia] simul et qualitas".

[97] BRUNO, *Causa* iv, p. 249: "è consueto modo di parlare di Peripatetici ancora, che dicono tutti l'atto dimensionale e tutte forme naturali uscire e venir fuori dalla potenza de la materia. Questo intende in parte Averroe ... Dice lui che la materia ne l'essenzia sua comprende le dimensioni interminate".

and, partly due to his notion that matter comprises extension, he assigns extension — infinite extension — to the heavens and therefore to the entire universe.[98] Also in line with Plotinus and Ficino (with some qualifications that need not detain us here), Bruno denies the Aristotelian division between sublunary and superlunary regions, thus opening up the theoretical possibility of having his unified concept of matter operating in both regions, which are, in fact, one infinite universe, according to Bruno.[99] Given Bruno's idea about the materiality of the superlunary sphere, he claims the capacity of the universe, i.e. infinite matter, is infinite — a capacity which, as we have seen, individuates particulars together with the World Soul through contraction.[100]

Coincidence of opposites

Ficino's Latin translation of Plotinus in 1492 and its several reprints in the sixteenth century provided Bruno with a new conceptual framework, e.g. the Plotinian idea of intelligible matter. This Neoplatonic notion, and indeed Bruno's own revision of it, gave him a component which was foreign to scholasticism and to Cusanus' medieval Platonism.[101] Admittedly Avicebron and David of Dinant had spoken about 'universal matter' long before Ficino's translation of Plotinus and Bruno knew these sources through scholastic refutations of them. But it was, I believe, Plotinus who proved decisive. Bruno seeks to formulate an original interpretation of the universe by, on the one hand, conflating the Neoplatonic concepts of intelligible and sensible matter and, on the other, expressing this unified concept of matter and its several important corollaries in various philosophical contexts through the notion of contraction. Although Bruno's philosophy is completely different from the orthodox Christian intentions of Cusanus, Bruno strove to adapt Cusanus' principle of coincidence to his own pantheistic philosophy.[102] In this section we shall see how that relates to Bruno's concept of contraction.

---

[98]   Ibid., v, pp. 273-277.

[99]   BRUNO, *Infinito* v, p. 361.

[100]   Ibid., i, p. 85: "Per che deve esser frustrata la capacità infinita, defraudata la possibilità de infiniti mondi che possono essere, pregiudicata la eccellenza della divina imagine, che deverebe più risplendere in un specchio incontratto, e secondo il suo modo di essere, infinito, imenso?" See also BRUNO, *Cena* iii, v, pp. 161, 239.

[101]   For the uses of Platonic and Neoplatonic components in the philosophies of Ficino and Cusanus respectively, see GARIN, 'Cusano e i platonici del quattrocento', pp. 75-96.

[102]   Bruno mentions Cusanus in relation to the principle of coincidence of opposites. See BRUNO, *Causa* v, p. 301. The principle is described ibid., v, pp. 299-307. Bruno's indebtedness to Cusanus on this occasion has been noted in BLUM, *Aristoteles*, p. 92. For a discussion of Bruno's use of this passage in Cusanus, see BÖNKER-VALLON, 'La matematica', pp. 68, 77. BRUNO, *Causa*, v, pp. 302-303, uses Cusanus' illustrations of the principle of coincidence of opposites. They are taken from CUSANUS, *De docta ignorantia* i 13, p. 26. The same figure is used in BRUNO, *De minimo* I 4, p. 148. Moreover, Bruno uses an illustration in *De umbris* and *De minimo* similar to the one in

Cusanus had followed a traditional idea and claimed that potentiality and actuality are identical in God, which means that in Him all potentialities are actualised simultaneously. In the universe, on the other hand, all potentialities cannot be actualised simultaneously, since that would conflict with the principle of contradiction, saying that it is impossible for two contradictory attributes to exist in one subject at the same time and in the same respect.[103] For instance, one leaf of an oak tree cannot be green and yellow at the same time and at the same place, but will be green at one time, during spring time, and yellow at another time, during autumn. No such limitation applies to God, who realises all his potentialities simultaneously. Cusanus formulates this idea about God by stating that in God the greatest (*maximum*) coincides with the smallest (*minimum*).[104]

Bruno adopts Cusanus' idea that the principle of the universe, which is God according to Cusanus, is characterised by a coincidence of opposites. But Bruno specifies that matter, not God, is the principle in which contraries coincide.[105] Here Bruno applies his unified concept of matter, arrived at through Plotinus' treatise on matter, to Cusanus' idea of coincidence of opposites. Whereas contractions from matter, here understood as a substrate, into corporeal entities exist in successive order, in an "unfolded" manner, matter as substrate exists *per se* in one eternal moment of pure actuality, in an "enfolded" manner.[106] Plotinus had applied two

---

CUSANUS, *De beryllo* §§9, 10, 19, pp. 11-13, 22-24, though without mentioning Cusanus explicitly; see BRUNO, *De umbris* §52, p. 44; *De minimo* I 4, p. 147. For the use of Cusanus in BRUNO, *De umbris* §§52-53, pp. 43-45, see STURLESE, 'Niccolò Cusano', pp. 953-957.

[103] For the principle of contradiction, see ARISTOTLE, *Metaphysics* IV iii 1005^{b}19-20.

[104] CUSANUS, *De docta ignorantia* i 2, p. 7.3-12. For the principle of coincidence of opposites in Cusanus, see MORAN, 'Pantheism', pp. 143-145; BEIERWALTES, 'Deus oppositio oppositorum', pp. 175-185.

[105] For the principle, see BRUNO, *Causa* iii, p. 205: "Or contempla il primo et ottimo principio, il quale è tutto quel che può essere; e lui medesimo non sarebe tutto, se non potesse essere tutto: in lui dumque l'atto e la potenza son la medesima cosa." Cf. Bruno's comment on matter ibid., iv, pp. 243-245: "*Teofilo*. ... Quella materia per essere attualmente tutto quel che può essere, ha tutte le misure, ha tutte le specie di figure e di dimensioni; e perché le have tutte, non ne ha nessuna, perché quello che è tante cose diverse, bisogna che non sia alcuna di quelle particolari. Conviene a quello che è tutto, che escluda ogni essere particolare. *Dicsono*. Vuoi dumque che la materia sia atto? vuoi ancora che la materia nelle cose incorporee coincida con l'atto? *Teofilo*. Come il posser essere coincide con l'essere." For the principle of coincidence of opposites in nature, see also ibid., v, pp. 299-311, 315.

[106] Ibid., iv, p. 251: "Costui [PLOTINUS II iv [12] 3.9-14 (= tr. Ficino, p. 160.46-56, as quoted p. 49 n. 107 below)] facendo differenza tra la materia di cose superiori et inferiori, dice che quella [intelligible matter] è insieme tutto; et essendo che possiede tutto, non ha in che mutarsi: ma questa [sensible matter] con certa vicissitudine per le parti, si fa tutto; et a tempi e tempi, si fa cosa e cosa, però sempre sotto diversità, alterazione e moto. Cossì dumque mai è informe quella [intelligible] materia, come né anco questa [sensible], benché differentemente quella e questa: quella [intelligible] ne l'istante de l'eternità, questa [sensible] ne gl'istanti del tempo; quella insieme, questa successivamente; quella [intelligible] esplicatamente, questa complicatamente; quella

similar descriptions to sensible and intelligible matter respectively, saying that sensible matter exists in successive order and intelligible matter in eternal actuality.[107] Bruno applies these two descriptions to his unified concept of matter.

Matter as substrate exists, Bruno continues, as an undifferentiated unity of such actualisations prior to its contractions into particular entities, whether corporeal or incorporeal ones.[108] This means that matter, still in the sense of material substrate, exists in pure actuality and is therefore everything simultaneously. Hence opposites coincide in it.[109] Thus far Bruno confirms Cusanus' idea of coinciding opposites in the principle of the universe. But, importantly, Bruno applies this idea within a very different metaphysical structure, in which matter is the principle characterised by coinciding opposites, not God, thereby accommodating Cusanus' idea to his pantheism.

---

come molti, questa come uno; quella per ciascuno e cosa per cosa, questa come tutto et ogni cosa." The terminology *complicatio-explicatio* is also applied in Bruno's *Sigillus*, see BRUNO, *Sigillus* i 42, ii 3, ii 22, pp. 186.1, 196.24, 215.4.

[107] PLOTINUS II iv [12] 3.9-14 (= tr. Ficino, p. 160.46-56): "Item materia corum quae gignuntur aliam semper et aliam habet speciem. Sempiternorum vero materia eadem semper possidet idem. Ferme vero haec apud nos materia contra se habet, atque illa. Haec enim per partes et alterne fit omnia, in singulisque temporibus singula: ideoque nihil usquam permanet, dum alia ab aliis extruduntur. Iccirco nihil semper est idem. In superis autem materia simul est cuncta. Cumque iam cuncta possideat, non habet omnino in quod valeat permutari."

[108] BRUNO, *Causa* iv, pp. 233-237, especially p. 237.

[109] Ibid., iv, pp. 243-245, especially p. 245: "Quella materia per essere attualmente tutto quel che può essere, ha tutte le misure, ha tutte le specie di figure e di dimensioni".

Chapter 3
Contraction and Noesis

What is contraction produced by noetic ascent?

In the Latin mnemonic works, especially in the *Sigillus* and *De umbris*, and in his Italian dialogue *Eroici furori* Bruno applies the term 'contraction' within a theory of noetic ascent.[1] On these occasions 'contraction' is applied within Bruno's theory of noetic ascent as a descent in reverse, that is, the intellect's movement from multiplicity to unity.[2] This is what I shall mean by 'contraction' in a noetic sense. Bruno's treatment of 'contraction' in this sense reflects scholastic and Neoplatonic sources.

This sense of contraction must be distinguished from three other senses, which I shall mention briefly here before exploring contraction in the noetic sense. First, in the mnemonic works 'contraction' denotes a logical notion, namely, an attribution, i.e. a 'contraction', or specific application, we might say, of one or more predicates to a subject.[3] Second, 'contraction' is employed to describe methods of, or circumstances conductive to, noetic ascent, notably in the fifteen contractions in the *Sigillus*, where, for instance, solitude is one method Bruno

---

[1] BRUÑO, *De umbris* §§54.6-8, 55.9-12, 84.11-12, pp. 47, 48, 63; *Sigillus* ii 22, pp. 213.21-214.19; *De compositione* I i 13, p. 119.3-15; *De magia naturali* §16.6-10, p. 188 (= *BOL*, vol. 3, p. 409.16-20); *Lampas* §243.14-17, p. 1230 (= *BOL*, vol. 3, p. 141.12-15); *De monade* iii, p. 356.20-27; *De minimo* I 4, p. 146.20-24; *Furori* i 3, i 4, ii 1, ii 3, pp. 137, 159, 327, 421. Contraction in this noetic sense has received scant attention; see NELSON, *Renaissance theory of love*, pp. 186, 188; SPRUIT, *Il problema*, pp. 147-149, 157-158; STURLESE, 'Per un'interpretazione', pp. 963-964.

[2] See p. 1 n. 2 above.

[3] BRUNO, *De umbris* §§100.2-6, 180.1-5, pp. 73, 131; *Triginta sigilli*, pp. 90.5-7, 105.30-106.10; *Explicatio*, p. 139.8-11; *De lampade combinatoria* I ix, p. 280.20-25; *De lampade venatoria*, pp. 58.8-18, 75.12-15. For a plausible source for this use of 'contraction' in logic, see LULL, *Lectura artis* xi, pp. 426-428. This source has not been noted in studies on Bruno's use of Lull; it is ignored in YATES, *The art of memory*, pp. 175-196, 206-208, 214, 218-220, 226, 244; *Giordano Bruno and the Hermetic tradition*, pp. 96, 195, 206, 27, 324; VASOLI, 'Immagini', pp. 352, 353, 356-365, 374, 376-378, 384, 403-408; 'Umanesimo e simbologia', pp. 254-258, 260-268, 272, 289-292, 294, 304; ROSSI, *Clavis universalis*, pp. 131-154. Blum does not deal with contraction in the logical sense, but he does discuss Bruno's postulated isomorphy between structures in human thought, as expressed in logic, and ontological structures; see BLUM, *Aristoteles*, pp. 22-23, 26-28. For Bruno's interest in Lull's art of combination in this context, see ibid., pp. 23-24.

describes among others.[4] As we have seen in Chapter 1, Bruno has strong reservations about several of the methods of noetic ascent described in the fifteen contractions, which he consequently dismisses as false. Although the various methods of contraction described in these fifteen contractions differ from contraction in the noetic sense, it should be recalled that they do overlap in some instances. An example is the solitary, contemplative philosopher's noetic ascent, which, in the practice prescribed in the fifteen contractions and in the theoretical account of it which precedes these fifteen contractions, contains significant elements from Plotinus' Neoplatonism. In this and the next chapters we shall see how Bruno analyses this practice of the philosopher. Third, 'contraction' is used in a physiological sense to denote a physiologically induced contraction of *spiritus*. Once again, there is an overlap in meaning. The physiological concept of 'contraction' is related to 'contraction' as a noetic concept, as we shall see in Chapter 5, but the two meanings of 'contraction' are conceptually distinct. In Chapter 5 we shall see how these two meanings relate to each other.

To turn to contraction in the strictly noetic sense. We have seen that Bruno identifies the ontological meaning of contraction through a fairly consistent conceptual framework, involving key concepts like form and matter. We might expect him to do the same in regard to his noetic interpretation of contraction. This is not, unfortunately, the case. Whereas contraction in the ontological sense is a fairly well-defined, technical term inherited, as we shall see in Chapter 6, from the scholastic tradition, contraction in the noetic sense is not a well-established philosophical usage. Bruno never defines what he means by the term.

Even though Bruno's use of contraction in this sense is without the idiomatic stability and repetitiousness which often characterises terminology of long-standing philosophical traditions, it is not an arbitrary and meaningless concept. Bruno, as already indicated, often uses it to describe various aspects of the intellect's movement from plurality to unity. In this chapter I shall set out the philosophical description of man to which contraction in the noetic interpretation is tied (pp. 52-54). Then I shall analyse Bruno's explanation of contraction in the noetic sense in his *Sigillus* (pp. 54-61). As we shall see, his treatment of 'contraction' in this context is coloured by scholastic concepts, in particular his notion of intention. This notion is also, however, interpreted by Bruno in a Neoplatonic manner, allowing him to insert it into his account of intelligibles understood as extramental and intramental realities. In the next section I shall move on to his use of 'contraction' in the *Eroici furori*, where the notion of intention remains important (pp. 61-64). Lastly, I shall turn to Bruno's criticism of noesis induced physiologically by melancholy, in particular its consequences for love poetry and theology (pp. 64-68).

---

[4]   The fifteen contractions, summarised in Chapter 1, are in BRUNO, *Sigillus* i 35-49, pp. 180.19-193.5. Solitude is treated ibid., i 35, pp. 180.20-182.11.

Philosophical anthropology and contraction by noetic ascent

In the preceding chapter we have seen how Bruno integrates some of Plotinus' ideas about emanation into his ontology, though in a revised form which fits into his pantheistic orientation. Plotinus' philosophical conception of man is determined by his theory of the three hypostases, the One, Mind and Soul.[5] Bruno similarly formulates various aspects of his philosophical description of man with an eye on Plotinus' philosophical anthropology. His stance towards Plotinus' conception of man is characterised by different but not necessarily contradicting tendencies. On the one hand he affirms Plotinus' view of man, for instance in *De umbris*, where he says cryptically that, according to Plotinus, man is first of all Idea, thereafter soul, and lastly — that is insofar as he is a corporeal being — not man at all.[6] What did Bruno mean by affirming the allegedly Plotinian idea that man is primarily Idea and secondly soul?

Bruno's fifteen contractions in the *Sigillus* display a parallel reservation in regard to the body, such as melancholic humours, in Bruno's final judgement over the proper method of noetic ascent.[7] Melancholy may provide an initial stimulus for noetic ascent according to Bruno, as we shall see in Chapter 5, but it has to be completed by reason and intellect. These reservations of Bruno resemble, for instance, Plotinus' warning against subjecting the soul to the affections of the body, which will block the soul's ascent.[8] On the other hand, Bruno also maintains that the individual human being is individuated through its contraction of formal and material components, that is, of body and soul, and he regards corporeal complexion as decisive, for the better or worse, for the kind of contemplation which, if any, an individual is able to undertake.[9] This idea was also implied in Plotinus' philosophy through the doctrine of reception according to the capacity of the recipient, but he did not emphasise it as strongly as Bruno, and did not link it to an individual's complexion.[10]

---

[5]   PLOTINUS V i [10] 10.1-10 (= tr. Ficino, p. 491.16-31).

[6]   BRUNO, *De umbris* §61.2-8, p. 51: "Ideam primum hominem, animam secundum, tertium vero quasi iam non hominem dixit Plotinus, ubi de ratione multitudinis idearum edisserit. Dependet secundus a primo, tertius a secundo, dum per ordinationem, contractionem, et compositionem, ordinatur ad physicam subsistentiam. Pro metaphysico igitur conceptu tertius ascendat in secundum, secundus in primum." As pointed out by Sturlese in her note to BRUNO, *De umbris* §61.2-8, p. 51, the source is FICINO, *In Plotinum* VI vii [38] 5, p. 697.36-38: "Quae quidem idea primus homo est: anima vero ita sicut dixi se habens est homo secundus: tertius vero homo est et quasi iam non homo, animal compositum ex corpore nostro simul atque vita quadam huic infusa ab anima praecedente".

[7]   For Bruno's criticism of noetic ascent through melancholic humours, see his eleventh, twelfth and fourteenth contractions, summarised on pp. 19-21, 22-23 above.

[8]   PLOTINUS IV vii [2] 10.7-16 (= tr. Ficino, p. 464.28-43).

[9]   BRUNO, *Lampas* §408.10-18, pp. 1434-1436 (= *BOL*, vol. 3, pp. 238.19-239.1).

[10]   PLOTINUS VI iv [22] 3.1-10 (= tr. Ficino, p. 646.35-50). For this adaptation of the doctrine to human individuals, see BLUMENTHAL, 'Soul, World-Soul and individual soul in Plotinus', p. 60; LEE, 'The doctrine of reception', pp. 87-90. For the ontological

Another aspect of Bruno's reference to Plotinus' idea of man relates to Plotinus' thoughts about the ontological status of the human soul. Although Plotinus is not clear on this point, there are several passages allowing the interpretation (the one preferred by most modern scholars) that the World Soul and individual human souls are both dependent upon the hypostasis Soul.[11] This means, in turn, that individual souls are not dependent upon the World Soul.[12] There is, according to Plotinus, a parallel between the World Soul and the individual soul: just as the World Soul transcends the cosmos, the human soul transcends the body.[13]

According to Plotinus, the individual human soul animates an individual human body.[14] This does not mean, however, that the human soul is located in and confined to the human body in a spatial sense, nor, on the other hand, that the ascent of the human soul requires a separation from the body, but rather an inner detachment from the body, that is, its sensory information and mental images. The human soul pertains to both the sensible and the intelligible worlds.[15] Bruno affirms this equal state of the individual human soul, and of the World Soul, stating that their relation to the body, or the universe, is similar to the helmsman's relation to the ship. He is part of the ship as far as he goes with it when he steers it, but he also exists independently of the ship and is free to leave it.[16]

Bruno applies 'contraction' in his philosophical anthropology. He affirms an idea which he attributes to Plotinus, namely that the human being is created with "light-bearing" eyes and other senses, so that he has an instrument through which

---

     implications of this principle, see references to the modern discussion of this doctrine of Plotinus on p. 38 n. 53 above.

[11] E.g. PLOTINUS IV ix [8] 4.1-26 (= tr. Ficino, p. 479.46-19). This passage leaves it open whether the source of many individual souls is the World Soul, or the hypostasis Soul, in which case the World Soul could also originate from the hypostasis Soul. Blumenthal argues convincingly that Soul and World Soul are distinct in Plotinus, and that there are therefore three kinds of soul in Plotinus: the hypostasis Soul, the World Soul, and individual souls; see BLUMENTHAL, 'Soul, World-Soul, and individual soul in Plotinus', pp. 57-58. Cf. RIST, *Plotinus: The road to reality*, p. 113, who asserts that the hypostasis Soul and the World Soul are identical. For Bruno and the problematic relationship of World Soul and individual soul, see SPRUIT, *Il problema*, pp. 204-205.

[12] For Plotinus on the relationship between the individual human soul and the World Soul, see BLUMENTHAL, 'Soul, World-Soul, and individual soul in Plotinus', pp. 58-63; *Plotinus' psychology*, pp. 14-15, 27-30; WALLIS, *Neoplatonism*, pp. 69-70, 126; GRAESER, *Plotinus and the Stoics*, pp. 30-31.

[13] PLOTINUS IV iii [27] 9.1-50, IV vii [2] 13.8-20 (= tr. Ficino, pp. 378.44-379.50, 466.48-467.3).

[14] On the descent of the soul, see RIST, *Plotinus: the road to reality*, pp. 112-129.

[15] PLOTINUS IV vii [2] 13.1-20, V i [10] 10.1-31 (= tr. Ficino, pp. 466.37-467.3, 49[1].16-62). For Plotinus on the soul's descent into the body, see BLUMENTHAL, *Plotinus' psychology*, pp. 2-6. For Plotinus' theory on the relation between soul and body, see ibid., pp. 10-19.

[16] BRUNO, *Causa* ii, pp. 121-125. For Plotinus' view on the analogy soul-body and ship-helmsman, see BLUMENTHAL, *Plotinus' psychology*, pp. 17-18.

he may "contract something through the kindred light", which is communicated from the intelligible world.[17] Hereby Bruno may refer to the idea in Plotinus that the hypostasis Soul emits Ideas animating the sensible world through the World Soul, and that the sensible universe, thus animated, can be perceived, or 'contracted', though our senses. When Bruno says "kindred light" and not simply "light", understood in the physical sense, he may indicate that the light perceived through the senses is parallel, hence "kindred", to the light experienced by the higher part of the soul contemplating Ideas emanated from Soul, which, together with the Ideas, emits a light which can only be experienced by the higher part of the soul. This is the background for Bruno's use of contraction in his description of noetic ascent.

Abstraction and intention

In the *Sigillus*, 'contraction' is listed as one of the "witnesses" of the One, that is, as a way of understanding something about the One by perceiving its effects, or vestiges, in nature.[18] Having suggested in poetic terms how form and matter are individuated into sensible particulars, Bruno explains contraction, in the noetic sense, as follows:

> Just as the one single, true intelligible entity descends to us by becoming concrete, so we must ascend to it through abstraction. For this is what we

---

[17] BRUNO, *De umbris* §54.6-8, p. 47: "'Luciferos' — inquit Plotinus — 'in facie Deus oculos fabricavit, caeterisque sensibus adhibuit instrumenta, ut inde tum naturaliter servarentur, tum etiam cognata luce aliquid contraherent'. Quibus sane verbis manifestat aliquid esse praecipuum, quod de mundo intelligibili ad ipsos pertineat." The source to the expression "light-bearing eyes" is, according to the editor, PLOTINUS VI vii [38] 1, tr. Ficino, p. 692.16-26: "Cum ipse Deus, vel saltem Deus aliquis animas in generationem demitteret, luciferos in facie oculos fabricavit, et instrumenta caetera reliquis adhibuit sensibus, praevidens videlicet, ita demum animal posse servari, si antevideat audiatque singula, et denique tangat: atque ita alia quidem fugiat, alia prosequatur." For Bruno's interpretation of the expression "luciferi oculi", see TOCCO, *Le opere*, p. 335 n. 1.

[18] For 'contraction' as one of the four witnesses (*testes*), see BRUNO, *Sigillus* ii 22, p. 212.14-17. For the perceptible vestiges of contraction in nature, see ibid., ii 22, p. 213.14-17. For 'vestige' in Bruno's philosophy, see also BRUNO, *De umbris* §§22.4-11, 23.2-8, 25.7-11, 29.7-8, 52.14-15, 70.3-4, 97.2-4, pp. 26, 27, 28-29, 32, 44, 55, 71; *Cantus* iii 1, p. 235.25-27; *Sigillus* i 28, pp. 169.27-170.6; *Cena* i, p. 51; *Causa* ii, pp. 103-107; *Infinito* epist., p. 45; *Spaccio* iii 2, p. 415; *Furori* ii 4, ii 5, pp. 457, 465; *Lampas* §64.14-23, p. 1022 (= *BOL*, vol. 3, p. 43.7-15); *Theses de magia* §21.2-4, p. 340 (= *BOL*, vol. 3, p. 462.28-30); *De minimo* I 4, p. 149.3-5; *De compositione* i 1, i 2, pp. 94.12-18, 98.1-7; *De vinculis* §63.2-8, pp. 492-494 (= *BOL*, vol. 3, p. 684.17-23). For 'vestige' in Bruno's thought, see SPRUIT, *Il problema*, pp. 60-61, 209, 265. For the philosophical background of 'vestige' in Renaissance philosophy, see WIND, *Pagan mysteries in the Renaissance*, pp. 42 n. 25, 241-255.

are attempting to do when we collect infinite individuals into species, innumerable species into many intermediary genera, these into ten or twelve *determinata*, and these finally into a supreme, analogous one of all things. We do this in order that, through these intentions [*intentiones*], as if following a contraction in reverse, we may contract [*contrahamus*] multiple being and an infinity of parts into specific and generic being, and this into being in the most universal genus, and this [finally] into a being or essence absolutely. In this way we contract the posterior into the prior, the effects into causes, then the partial causes into common causes, and the closest and immediate causes into the more distant and intermediate causes, and these second causes into first causes, and these many [first] causes into one cause.[19]

In the quotation contraction is explained through two concepts, abstraction (*abstractio*) and intention (*intentio*). The following two sections explain these terms in more detail.

(i) Abstraction through "ten or twelve determinata*"*

Bruno's explanation of contraction through noetic ascent as abstraction is fairly straightforward at first sight. Just as the One descends to particulars through the hierarchy of genera and species, it is intellectually possible to reverse the process and ascend towards the One, from where all genera originate.[20] What Bruno means by "ten or twelve *determinata*", we may assume *determinata genera*, is puzzling.

A parallel passage in *De la causa*, published only a year after the *Sigillus*, supports the assumption that on pp. 54-55 above Bruno is referring to the

---

[19] BRUNO, *Sigillus* ii 22, pp. 213.21-214.6: "Sic enim per concretionem intelligibile unum et verum ad nos descendit, quemadmodum necessarium est nos ad ipsum per abstractionem ascendere. Id quidem tentamus, cum infinita individua in species, innumerabiles species in plurima genera media, haecque in determinata decem vel duodecim, et ipsa in unum analogum supremum omnium colligimus, ut per ipsas intentiones quasi oppositam contractionem prosequentes, esse multiplex et infinitum particulare in esse specificum et genericum, et hoc ad esse in genere maxime universali, idque ad esse simpliciter sive essentiam contrahamus, sicut posterius in prius, effectus in causas, has partiales in communes, illasque proximas et immediatas ad remotiores atque mediatas, easque secundas ad primas, ipsasque plures ad unam." For *contrahere* used similarly to describe noetic ascent to the One, see BRUNO, *De minimo* I 4, p. 146.20-24: "Siquidem quanto altior ille/ Incumbit, lumen magis intenditque superne,/ Hoc operae precium est ut plus se colligat, atque/ Discutiens numerum in monadem se invertat, et ipsam/ Sic eat in monadem, ut hanc in se contrahat idem."

[20] BRUNO, *De umbris* §28.9-11, p. 31, noetic ascent is described as a movement from many individuals to many species, and from there to one genus. In her note to this passage, Sturlese points out this resembles the description of noetic ascent in Bruno, *Sigillus* ii 22, p. 213.23-27. But there are differences. One is that Bruno does not include the ten or twelve *determinata* in *De umbris*. Another that whereas ascent terminates at one "genus" in *De umbris*, it terminates at the One in this passage in the *Sigillus*.

Aristotelian categories by the expression *determinata*.[21] There Bruno speaks of noetic ascent towards the One as a descent in reverse. He explains how Platonists and Peripatetics, for this purpose, reduce infinite individuals to species, and these species ultimately to "determinati geni", which a certain Archytas holds to be ten. These ten are then reduced to one being.[22] The metaphysical scheme fits with that of the *Sigillus*. The number of species differ, however, and I shall return to this issue in a moment.

Under the name of Archita, the work *Decem praedicamenta*, translated by Domenico Pizzimenti, had been printed in Venice in 1561. Aquilecchia holds, however, that Bruno may not have known this work, even though he refers to it. Instead, he may have known Archytas' work through Simplicius' commentary on Aristotle's *Categories*, published in Boethius' *Opera omnia*, Basel 1570.[23] According to the report of Archytas, then, the Aristotelian doctrine of the ten categories was derived from Pythagorean thought.[24] In Renaissance thought Plato was commonly thought to be a Pythagorean. This would explain why Bruno in this passage of *De la causa* attributes this doctrine not only to Peripatetics, but also to Platonists.

Given this background we can be fairly sure that by "ten or twelve *determinata*", mentioned in the quotation from the *Sigillus* on pp. 54-55 above, Bruno means the ten Aristotelian categories, or predicaments, which Bruno speaks of as genera ("determinati geni") in *De la causa*. This usage can be explained. In Aristotle's philosophy there are ten categories.[25] In his terminology 'genus' (γένος) can also denote one of the ten categories.[26] Hence the expression *determinata* in the quotation from *Sigillus* on pp. 54-55 above may be an elliptical expression for *determinata genera*.

But why does Bruno mention "ten or twelve *determinata* [*genera*]" in the quotation from the *Sigillus* on pp. 54-55 above? Aristotle's *Categories* is, again, one possible explanation. There he divides these ten categories into two groups,

---

[21]   This source for the *Sigillus* is suggested by TIRINNANZI in BRUNO, *Le ombre delle idee*, etc., tr. N. Tirinnanzi (Milan 1997), p. 430 n. 219.

[22]   BRUNO, *Causa* v, p. 297: "Quindi i Peripatetici e Platonici, infiniti individui riducano ad una individua raggione di molte specie; innumerabili specie comprendono sotto determinati geni, quali Archita primo volse che fussero diece; determinati geni ad uno ente, una cosa". For Archita, see also BRUNO, *De compendiosa architectura* iii 7, p. 60.19-21: "Archytas Tarentinus et Gorgias Leontinus et alii denario eorum, quae praedicamenta appellantur, proposito, nihilo minora et pauciora proposuere quam Lullius."

[23]   See the note by AQUILECCHIA, in BRUNO, *Causa*, p. 377 n. 41. The crucial passage to which Aquilecchia refers, occurs in BOETHIUS, *In praedicamenta Aristotelis* i, p. 114.5-6: "Archites etiam duos composuit libros quos καθολόυς λόγους inscripsit, quorum in primo haec decem praedicamenta disposuit".

[24]   BOETHIUS, *In praedicamenta Aristotelis* i, p. 114.5-12.

[25]   ARISTOTLE, *Categories* iv 1ᵇ25-2ᵃ10. Here Aristotle mentions the following ten categories: (1) substance, (2) quantity, (3) quality, (4) relation, (5) place, (6) time, (7) position, (8) state, (9) action, (10) affection. See also ARISTOTLE, *Topica* I ix 103ᵇ20-24.

[26]   E.g. ARISTOTLE, *De anima* i 1 402ᵃ22-26.

the first consisting of just substance, and the second comprising the remaining nine, all of which are accidents. When these two groups are added to the ten, we arrive at twelve.[27] This subdivision may explain why Bruno mentions "ten or twelve" *determinata* in the above quotation. In the *Sigillus* ii 15 we find another, more plausible explanation of the "ten or twelve *determinata* [*genera*]". There Bruno states that there are ten categories, which he calls *formae generales*. In addition to the ten categories — Aristotelian categories we may assume — Bruno adds two, namely movement (*motus*) and cause (*causa*). Hence there are ten or twelve categories, depending on the inclusion of the last two categories added by Bruno.[28]

One may wonder, however, why Bruno would speak of contemplating accidents at such a high level of abstraction, moving between genera and the One. Further, even though Bruno only claims that these *determinata* are used in our abstraction from genera to the One, one may also wonder whether he also regarded these *determinata* as having ontological status. According to Aristotle, the categories not only structure reality, they are also the forms through which our thoughts can be formed, reflected in the subject-predicate structure of our language.[29] The categories thus endow our thoughts and language about the extra-mental world with the possibility of objective validity. Although this idea of Aristotle may ultimately be behind Bruno's use of the categories, their uses differ. For in the *Sigillus* and in *De la causa* Bruno does not regard the categories as intermediaries between our thoughts and language, on one hand, and the extra-mental world on the other, but as intermediaries between genera and the One, thus reflecting his concerns about a unified nature of descent and noetic ascent.[30] This is probably how Bruno understands noetic ascent as 'abstraction' through the categories, or the "ten or twelve *determinata*", as explained in the quotation on pp. 54-55 above. Such a use of categories would explain how Bruno conceives of them as a means of mediating between sensible multiplicity and the supra-intelligible One.

In the quotation from the *Sigillus* on pp. 54-55 above, Bruno also holds that this intellectual process of abstraction leads to "a supreme, analogous one of all things", that is, a form of "understanding" of the One. That is, he adds, an understanding of the first cause of the universe. This is a traditional idea found in

---

[27] ARISTOTLE, *Categories* iv-v 2ª4-2ᵇ6.

[28] BRUNO, *Sigillus* ii 15, p. 207.4-6: "Formae vero rerum generales sunt etiam duodecim: decem puta categoriae, quibus addimus L motum, M causam."

[29] ARISTOTLE, *Metaphysics* V vii 1017ª22-27.

[30] BRUNO, *Causa* v, p. 297, as quoted on p. 56 n. 22 above; *Sigillus* ii 22, pp. 213.21-214.6, as quoted on p. 55 n. 19 above. CUSANUS, *De docta ignorantia* ii 6, p. 80.1-7, as quoted on p. 144 n. 37 below, similarly speaks of ten categories inserted between the One and genera. GILES, *Super authorem De causis, Alpharabium* vii, fol. 25ᵛ, lines 33-42, as quoted on p. 144 n. 39 below, also inserts the ten categories in the order of descent, though not between the One and genera, but at the lowest ontological level, i.e. that of individuals. For a discussion of this difference between Giles and Cusanus, see pp. 144-147 below.

scholasticism, deriving from the idea of a hierarchy of causes propounded in the *Liber de causis*.[31]

(ii) Intention

The second central concept in the quotation on pp. 54-55 above is intention (*intentio*). The term *intentio* has at least two distinct meanings in Bruno's mnemonic writings. First, it is a general term denoting something like a philosophical viewpoint or understanding. Second, it is a technical term derived from a theory of intentionality in scholastic epistemology. Aquinas used the term *intentio* with several meanings, including the second of these senses.[32] He used it to denote the psychological act in the rational soul in which the attention focuses on sense data in the imagination or fantasy.[33]

Bruno defines *intentio* as "the act of the cognitive or appetitive faculty towards the [sense] object", and contrasts it with conception (*conceptio*), which is the act occurring when a faculty receives sense objects.[34] He also distinguishes primary intentions from secondary intentions. Primary intentions (*intentiones primae*) he divides into intentions of particulars and intentions of universals. Primary intentions of particulars are based on direct sense impression, for instance, the impression produced by looking at Socrates or at the sun. Primary intentions of universals are concepts ultimately based on intentions of particulars. For instance, the intention of 'animal' is based on that of men, which may, for instance, be based on the perception of Socrates. Secondary intentions (*intentiones secundae*) are concepts of concepts produced by primary intentions. An example of this could

---

[31] Cf. SPRUIT, *Il problema*, pp. 147-148, where BRUNO, *Sigillus* ii 22, p. 213.21-23 ("Sic enim per concretionem intelligibile unum et verum ad nos descendit, quemadmodum necessarium est nos ad ipsum per abstractionem ascendere") is interpreted within a Neoplatonic three world metaphysics (the sensible world, the intelligible world and the conceptual world in the human mind). Although Bruno certainly adheres to this idea elsewhere in the *Sigillus*, and indeed in other works, this seems not to be the case in the next lines, ibid., ii 22, pp. 213.23-214.6, quoted and translated on p. 55 n. 19 above. We do find a three world metaphysics in BRUNO, *Sigillus* i 16, pp. 164.27-165.7; *De umbris* §52.10-12, pp. 43-44; *Causa*, epist., p. 23; *Cabala* i, p. 69; *De compositione* dedication, I i 1, I i 5, I ii 20, pp. 89.20-90.30, 94.12-95.2, 101.4-24, 198.6-13; *Oratio valedictoria*, pp. 14.22-15.5; *Lampas* §252.[1-5], p. 1372 (= BOL, vol. 3, p. 206.14-19); *De magia naturali* §7.1-2, p. 172 (= BOL, vol. 3, p. 403.4-5); *De minimo* I 1, p. 136.21-28.

[32] For the various meanings of *intentio* in the philosophy of Aquinas, see SIMONIN, 'La notion d'*intentio* dans la philosophie de St Thomas', pp. 448-460.

[33] For this meaning of *intentio* in Aquinas, see SIMONIN, 'La notion d'*intentio* dans la philosophie de St Thomas', pp. 456-457.

[34] BRUNO, *Summa*, p. 50.19-22: "Intentio quippe est actus potentiae cognoscitivae vel appetitivae versus obiectum, conceptio vero est actus quidam informationis seu receptionis ab obiecto in potentiam". For *intentio* in Bruno's philosophy, see TOCCO, 'Le fonti', pp. 508-509; KLEIN, 'L'imagination', p. 19; SPRUIT, *Il problema*, p. 113; 'Spunti sulle fonti della psicologia bruniana', p. 206; CLUCAS, '*Amorem*', p. 7.

be 'species of animals'.[35] Aquinas had upheld a fairly similar distinction between primary and secondary intentions.[36] When Bruno uses *intentio* in the quotation on pp. 54-55 above, he may mean that intentions — primary intentions of particulars, then primary intentions of universals, then secondary intentions — lead, or are in some way related to increasing degrees of abstraction.

In relation to *intentio*, Bruno also distinguishes (a) "first and simple intellect", which, "just as a unity embracing all numbers", does not have objects outside itself, but is them itself in some way, and is therefore able to comprehend without the use of intentionality; from (b) "the rest", e.g. human intellects, which have to use intentionality, since the object is outside them. This means that the "first and simple intellect" is able to comprehend without temporal progression and without sense data, unlike other intellects.[37] The underlying idea is that Mind does not have a distinction between 'knower' and 'known'. It is that thing which is in act by thinking its thoughts. In this sense it is different from the human mind that uses discursive reason. These comments are similar to those Bruno advances in the *Sigillus* insofar as he states that noetic ascent through abstraction aims at a simultaneous understanding of all, an act in which we imitate, albeit imperfectly, the divine mind by understanding the intelligible species.[38] Our understanding of

---

[35] BRUNO, *Summa*, p. 49.8-18: "Intentionum alia prima, alia secunda. Intentio prima est quae immediate fundatur in re, et haec est duplex: particularis et universalis. Illa fundatur immediate primo, sicut intentio Socratis in Socrate, solis in sole sensibili; ista fundatur immediate secundo, sicut intentio animalis fundatur in homine, cuius intentio fundatur in Socrate. Intentio secunda est quae mediate fundatur in primis, cui per se et primo non respondet aliquid extra, sicut huic intentioni nomen, cui non respondet subiectum externum nisi nominatum, quod subinde erit hoc vel illud particulare." For primary and secondary intentions, see also BRUNO, *Theses de magia* §10.6-10, p. 330 (= *BOL*, vol. 3, p. 458.19-22). There, Bruno explicitly refers the distinction between primary and secondary intentions to Avicenna's *De sufficientia*, that is, to AVICENNA, *Metaphysica* i 2. See Bassi's note to the *Theses de magia*, p. 403. See also BRUNO, *De compositione* I i 1, p. 94.12-18. For Bruno's distinction between primary and secondary intentions, see CORSANO, *Il pensiero*, p. 99.

[36] SIMONIN, 'La notion d'*intentio* dans la philosophie de St Thomas', pp. 458-459; COLOMBO, 'Intenzionalità', col. 989.

[37] BRUNO, *Summa*, p. 113.10-22: "Intentio. Intellectus primus et simplex, qui in se ipso omnem complectitur cognitionem, sicut unitas omnem numerum, cognoscit ubique totus, sicut est ubique totus, sine distractione et applicatione; quandoquidem non habet obiectum extra se, sed, sicut dictum est, idem est obiectum et cognoscens. Ideo non intentionaliter, id est non per decursum seu influxum seu effluxum seu progressum quendam cognoscit, sed eadem absolutione cognoscit qua et est; reliqua vero quibus obiectum est externum, sive intelligentia sive ratiocinantia sive sentientia, tensione quadam seu attentione, qua nempe tendendo ad aliquid cognoscunt, informantur cognitionis propriae specie." This difference between God and human beings was underlined in AQUINAS, *Summa contra gentiles* i 55, vol. 13, p. 157.

[38] BRUNO, *Sigillus* ii 21, pp. 211.23-212.2.

these intelligible species are — like universal intentions — prompted by, though not reducible to, sensation.[39]

Up till this point in my explanation of Bruno's notion of *intentio* I have dealt with *intentio* as an intellectual response, direct or indirect, to sensation. However, Bruno also makes the important point that primary and secondary intentions are the same as *rationes*. Bruno explains *rationes* and how they relate to *intentiones* in the following passage, which describes descent from the intelligible to the sensible world:

> The species is indeed called an Idea prior to [its descent to] natural things. In natural things it is called a form or vestige of the Ideas. Posterior to natural things it is called *ratio* or *intentio*, which is distinguished into primary and secondary [intention], and which we have sometimes been accustomed to call a shadow of the Ideas.[40]

Ficino had defined reasons, *rationes*, within a Neoplatonic framework. According to him *rationes* are the rational principles in the human soul corresponding to the Ideas in the World Soul or Angelic Mind.[41] Moreover, Ficino had also used 'Ideas' and 'forms' together with 'reasons' within a metaphysical structure similar to the one Bruno employs in the quotation above.[42] Due to Bruno's identification of *intentio* with *ratio*, he could hold, in the passage quoted above and elsewhere, that the *intentio* was more than the human intellect's arrival at a logical concept. It was, in addition, an ascent to a higher reality, the realm of the Ideas.

One reason for Bruno's accommodation of the scholastic term *intentio*, for instance in the quotation on pp. 54-55 above, may well have been that the distinction between primary and secondary intentions was useful in his account of how it was possible to ascend noetically from sensible nature, known through the so-called primary intentions, to the formative principles of the universe, the Ideas, known through the secondary intentions. Sensible particulars are the point of departure of abstraction, noetic ascent, and the intellect "contracts" sensible

---

[39]　Ibid., ii 21, pp. 210.25-211.22. For Bruno's treatment of *species intelligibilis* in general, see SPRUIT, *'Species intelligibilis': from perception to knowledge*, pp. 203-213; and for *species intelligibilis* in the *Sigillus*, ibid., p. 206.

[40]　BRUNO, *De compositione* I i 1, p. 94.14-18: "Quae sane species ante naturalia appellatur idea, in naturalibus forma sive vestigium idearum, in postnaturalibus ratio seu intentio, quae in primam atque secundam distinguitur, quam nos aliquando idearum umbram consuevimus appellare." The term *intentio* in this passage is used similarly in BRUNO, *De umbris* §52.12-15, p. 44.

[41]　E.g. FICINO, *Theologia platonica* xi 4, vol. 2, p. 112.21-34; xv 16, vol. 3, p. 81.19-34. See also AUGUSTINE, *De diversis quaestionibus 83*, xlvi 2, col. 30.

[42]　For a similar use of 'Ideas', 'form' and 'reason'; see FICINO, *In epistolas duodecim Platonis*, p. 1531.23-29; *De amore* II iii, V iv, pp. 149.30-39, 185.5-7.

multiplicity through intentions.[43] Bruno takes up this point again in the *Eroici furori*, as we shall see.

Contraction in the *Eroici furori*

In the *Eroici furori* — a work discussing the idea of Neoplatonic, noetic ascent within the vernacular tradition of philosophical commentaries on love poetry — Bruno returns to the notion of intention, and I shall discuss it briefly since it sheds some light on the quotation from the *Sigillus* on pp. 54-55 above. In the *Eroici furori* he assigns to the human intellect the task of arriving at the intelligible unity of Mind.[44] This may take place when the philosopher turns away from the multitude of people and "contracts within himself", that is, withdraws in contemplation.[45] In this state "[the soul of the philosopher] contracts the divinity into itself", Tansillo proclaims, "since it is in God by means of the intention, by which it penetrates into the divine (inasmuch as it can), and since God is in the soul of the philosopher inasmuch as the human mind, once it has penetrated the divine, comes to conceive of the divine and (inasmuch as it can) to receive it and understand it in its concept [of it]."[46] In Aquinas' epistemology, too, *conceptus* is defined in conjunction with *intentio*. It is understanding, the psychological outcome of *intentio*, rather than attention. Bearing in mind that Bruno conceives

---

[43] For similar uses of *intentio*; see BRUNO, *De umbris* §§72.2-7, 84.11-12, 140.2-9, pp. 56, 63, 102; *Sigillus* ii 7, ii 11, ii 22, pp. 199.25-200.6, 203.16-26, 213.23-214.6.

[44] BRUNO, *Furori* i 3, p. 137: "La è oggetto finale, ultimo e perfettissimo; non già in questo stato dove non possemo veder Dio se non come in ombra e specchio, e però non ne può esser oggetto se non in qualche similitudine; non tale qual possa esser abstratta et acquistata da bellezza et eccellenza corporea per virtù del senso: ma qual può esser formata nella mente per virtù de l'intelletto."

[45] Ibid., ii 1, p. 315: "Se aspira al splendor alto, ritiresi quanto può all'unità, contrahasi quanto è possibile in se stesso, di sorte che non sia simile a molti, perché son molti; e non sia nemico de molti, perché son dissimili, se possibil fia serbar l'uno e l'altro bene: altrimente s'appiglie a quel che gli par megliore."

[46] Ibid., i 3, p. 137: "[anima del filosofo] contrae la divinità in sé essendo ella in Dio per la intenzione con cui penetra nella divinità (per quanto si può), et essendo Dio in ella, per quanto dopo aver penetrato viene a conciperla e (per quanto si può) a ricettarla e comprenderla nel suo concetto." For this application of 'contraction' in the *Furori*, see SARAUW, *Der Einfluss Plotins*, pp. 44-45; NELSON, *Renaissance theory of love*, p. 188. See also BRUNO, *Furori* ii 3, p. 421: "atteso che avendo contratta in sé la divinitade, è fatto divo". The concept of contraction in this noetic sense is similarly applied in Bruno's myth of Actaeon in the *Furori*. The myth recounts that Actaeon is a hunter who becomes prey of the hunt himself, killed by his own hunting dogs, thus symbolising the self-transformation, or rather self-annihilation, resulting from divine contemplation. Ibid., i 4, p. 159, Bruno states that Actaeon after he becomes a prey of the hunt himself: "s'accorse che de gli suoi cani, de gli suoi pensieri egli medesimo venea ad essere la bramata preda, perché già avendola contratta in sé, non era necessario di cercare fuor di sé la divinità". For the Actaeon myth in the *Furori*, see BEIERWALTES, 'Actaeon', pp. 345-354.

the divine as immanent in the universe, or even as the universe itself, this expression in the *Eroici furori*, "to contract the divine", may simply mean to comprehend and contemplate the infinite multiplicity of the universe within oneself.[47]

In an article published in 1916 Julie Sarauw suggested that the passage from the *Eroici furori* cited on the page above derives from Plotinus' description of mystical union with the One in *Enneads* VI vii [38] 34.8-14. Such union arises at the moment when the soul turns away from lower things and makes itself as beautiful as it can, so that it becomes like Soul. In that moment the human soul "sees it [Soul] in itself suddenly appearing", and the soul experiences union with Mind, Plotinus says.[48] This may well be Bruno's source. Elsewhere in the *Eroici furori* Bruno states that, according to Plotinus, there are three "preparations" for experiencing the divine. First, to "conform oneself" to a "divine similitude", that is, to make ourselves like the divine by turning away from perceptible things that are beneath or on the same ontological level as ourselves. Second, to apply all "intention" to the higher species. Third, to enslave all "will" and "desire" to God.[49] These three ways of preparing oneself for the divine occur, in fact, not in Plotinus but in Ficino's commentary to *Enneads* V viii [31] 10, although Bruno did not copy Ficino's comment exactly, especially not in the first preparation.[50] Sarauw did not note this, even though she based her study of Bruno and Plotinus on an edition of the Greek text of the *Enneads* accompanied by the 1580 edition of Ficino's translation and commentary.[51] Bruno did not know Greek, and on this and other occasions he clearly used Ficino's Latin translation and commentary.[52] In the

---

[47] See my discussion of Bruno's distinction between *intentio* and *conceptus* on p. 58 above.

[48] Tr. A. H. Armstrong. This is pointed out in SARAUW, *Der Einfluss Plotins*, pp. 44-45. For Ficino's Latin translation, which Bruno used, see PLOTINUS VI vii [38] 34, tr. Ficino, p. 725.38-53.

[49] BRUNO, *Furori* i 5, p. 225: "*Cicada.* In che maniera intendete che si faccia cotal conversione? *Tansillo.* Con tre preparazioni che nota il contemplativo Plotino nel libro *Della bellezza intelligibile*: de le quali 'la prima è proporsi de conformarsi d'una similitudine divina' divertendo la vista da cose che sono infra la propria perfezzione, e commune alle specie uguali et inferiori; 'secondo è l'applicarsi con tutta l'intenzione et attenzione alle specie superiori; terzo il cattivar tutta la voluntade et affetto a Dio'."

[50] FICINO, *In Plotinum* V viii [31] 11, p. 552.34-37: "[Chapter title:] Tres gradus in contemplatione divina, ac tres ad eam praeparationes. Cap. XI. [Text:] Deo fruiturus debet per communem Dei notionem atque fidem seipsum in primis divina quadam similitudine conformare: deinde tota ad Deum cogitationis intentione contendere: tertio tota Deum solum voluntate ardenter amare."

[51] Cf. SARAUW, *Der Einfluss Plotins*, p. 44, who points out PLOTINUS V viii [31] 10 as the source for the above passage in the *Furori*.

[52] SARAUW, *Der Einfluss Plotins*, p. vii, says that he used the following edition: PLOTINUS, *Opera omnia. Porphyrii Liber de vita Plotini cum Marsilii Ficini commentariis et eiusdem interpretatione castigata*, annotations to the text recorded by D. Wyttenbach, critical apparatus provided by G. H. Moser, ed. F. Creuzer, 3 vols, Oxford, 1835. The

meanwhile Bruno's use of Ficino's commentary on this point has been noted by Miguel Granada.[53]

The term 'contraction', used by Bruno in the *Eroici furori* to describe this act of intellection, does not feature in Ficino's commentary. As mentioned at the beginning of this chapter, contraction in this noetic sense was not common traditionally, certainly not as commonly as contraction in its ontological sense. There are, however, two instances where Ficino uses the term to describe some sort of noetic ascent. In the *Theologia platonica* Ficino had translated some lines from Zoroaster's *Chaldean oracles*, in which Zoroaster describes how the divinity may be "contracted" into the human soul in a mystical union, provided the soul leaves behind all bonds to the body. Zoroaster states that the soul becomes utterly intoxicated by "drinking in the divine draughts".[54] In a comment on these lines, Ficino explains that Zoroaster means to receive the *influxus* from God, transmitted by angelic minds to the human soul.[55] It is, perhaps, worth bearing in mind that this use of 'contraction' occurs in a poetic context, and for this reason it may not have the same philosophical connotations that we find elsewhere.

In a letter addressed to Lorenzo dei Medici Ficino does, however, use 'contraction' in a philosophical sense. The context is a discussion of felicity and its degrees, in particular the roles of will and intellect in the process of noetic ascent to God. Ficino distinguishes, in a traditional fashion, between an affective and an intellectual understanding of God. The former is superior to the latter, according to Ficino on this occasion. In the intellectual understanding of God, Ficino says, "we contract", that is, we limit, "His greatness [God's] according to the capacity and comprehension of our mind (*mens*)". In affective understanding, on the other hand, the human mind expands itself and thereby conforms, at least to some extent, to the immense goodness of God.[56]

---

above quotation from FICINO, *In Plotinum* V viii [31] 11, p. 552.34-37, appears in this 1835 edition of Plotinus in vol. 2, p. 1020.

[53] See note 13 by GRANADA to BRUNO, *Furori* i 5, p. 225.

[54] FICINO, *Theologia platonica* xiii 4, vol. 2, p. 237.18-20: "'Anima hominum Deum quodammodo contrahit in seipsam, quando nihil retinens mortale, tota divinis haustibus ebriatur. Tunc quoque exultat in corporis harmoniam [sic: 'harmonia'?].'" This is Ficino's translation of three lines from the Greek text of Zoroaster, *Chaldean oracles*. The Latin *contraho* is here translated from Greek verb ἄγχω, which can mean "I embrace". For Ficino's translation of these lines, see KLUTSTEIN, 'Introduction', pp. 13-14. George Gemisthos Pletho (ca. 1360- ca. 1452) had attributed the *Chaldean oracles* to Zoroaster; see BIDEZ and CUMONT, *Le mages*, vol. 2, pp. 251-260. For Zoroaster in the Renaissance, see also WALKER, *Ancient theology*, pp. 2, 11, 13, 20-21, 39, 49-50, 81, 87, 100, 103, 118, 143-144, 146. Bruno also mentioned Zoroaster as an example of the first contraction of the fifteen contractions in the *Sigillus*; see p. 8 n. 8 above.

[55] FICINO, *Theologia platonica* xiii 4, vol. 2, p. 237.20-26.

[56] FICINO, *Le lettere*, 1.115.181-185: "Superare vero eos amando gaudendoque potius quam intelligendo valemus; proinde cognoscendo Deum eius amplitudinem contrahimus ad mentis nostre capacitatem atque conceptum, amando vero mentem amplificamus ad latitudinem divine bonitatis immensam." SPRUIT, *Il problema*, p. 240, notes Ficino's use of 'contraction' here, though he does not relate it to Bruno's notion of contraction. The

Although this passage may have inspired Bruno's use of 'contraction' in his *Eroici furori*, two differences should be noticed. Even though Bruno, too, employs the distinction between affective and intellectual understanding of God in the *Eroici furori*, he does not, as Ficino does in this particular passage, conceive of them as mutually exclusive, but rather as dialectically dependent.[57] Further, whereas Ficino uses the term 'contraction' in this letter to denote a limitation of the soul's understanding of God, contrasted with the affective understanding, Bruno uses the term 'contraction' in the reverse sense, to describe the soul's assimilation to the divine — an assimilation that, ultimately, is intellectual rather than affective.

Bruno's criticism of noesis induced by melancholy: its consequences for love poetry and religion

Bruno's criticism of noetic ascent facilitated by melancholy in the second, eleventh, twelfth and fourteenth of the fifteen contractions in the *Sigillus* has ramifications in his Italian dialogues, published at London within two years of the *Sigillus*, and in his so-called *De magia naturali*, composed in Helmstedt in 1589. The most important references concerning melancholy and the fifteen contractions in the *Sigillus* occur in the *Eroici furori*.

In his *De amore*, composed between 1467 and 1469, Ficino had employed his theory of melancholy in his treatment of Neoplatonic *raptus* induced by love and poetry. Later in *De vita* he discussed melancholy at length.[58] Following Plato's *Phaedrus*, Ficino described the *furor* brought about through poetry and love as instances of Neoplatonic *raptus*.[59] On other occasions Ficino asserted that melancholy was conductive to the Platonic *furor*.[60] By the time, then, that Bruno composed his *Eroici furori* in 1584, the doctrine of melancholy had for some time been an integrated part of the tradition of philosophical commentaries on love poetry. In the *Eroici furori* Bruno writes within this tradition of philosophical

---

voluntarist view expressed by Ficino in this letter to Lorenzo dei Medici was apparently contradicted in Ficino's commentary on Plato's *Philebus*, where Ficino argued in favour of an intellectualist view; see ALLEN, 'Introduction', pp. 35-48; KRAYE, 'Moral philosophy', pp. 351-353.

[57] E.g. BRUNO, *Furori* ii 3, p. 423: "Cossì primieramente la cognizione muove l'affetto, et appresso l'affetto muove la cognizione."

[58] FICINO, *De amore* VI v, VI ix, pp. 205.20-30, 215.3-12; *De vita* i 3-6, pp. 112-122.

[59] The other forms are prophesy and mystery. The four kinds are, then, *vaticinium, mysterium, poesis, amor* (FICINO, *In Phaedrum* ii, p. 75.29 [= FICINO, *Opera*, p. 1364.8]). These four kinds are also mentioned in FICINO, *De amore* VII xiv, p. 257.2. This typology corresponds to PLATO, *Phaedrus* 265B2-5 (prophecy, mysticism, poetic frenzy and love). For these forms in Plato, see DODDS, *The Greeks and the irrational*, pp. 64-82. For these four forms in Ficino, see GENTILE, 'In margine', pp. 53-61.

[60] See pp. 91-95 below, especially p. 94 n. 28.

discussions of love, attacking the idea that melancholy is a vital element in noetic ascent.[61]

In the *Eroici furori*, as in his *Sigillus*, Bruno ironically mocks the love poet affected with melancholy.[62] The kind of frenzy which Bruno favours, he states, does not depend on the physiological state produced by melancholy. It depends instead on the cognitive faculties of the contemplating individual.[63] As in the *Sigillus*, Bruno maintains that those suffering from melancholy, that is, those who are unable to raise above the effect that excessive melancholy has on their imagination, behave dangerously and fail to ascend noetically in a true sense.[64]

It is possible to distinguish between two kinds of *furore*, Bruno states in the *Eroici furori*. One which displays "blindness, stupidity and irrational impulse", another which consists in "divine abstraction".[65] So far, Bruno seems to allude to a distinction in Ficino's *De amore* between two kinds of *furore* which are both "alienations of the mind" (*alienatio mentis*), but where one alienation is caused by human weakness (*morbus*), the other by God.[66] "Divine abstraction", as some people call it, can be divided into two kinds according to Bruno. The first turn men "void of sense and spirit [in the sense of soul] of their own" into "receptacles" for the divine "spirito e senso". The second kind of divine *furore* we find in men "naturally endowed with a lucid and intellectual spirit [again, in the sense of soul]"

---

[61] NELSON, *Renaissance theory of love*, pp. 163-233.

[62] BRUNO, *Furori* arg., i 3, pp. 5, 17-19, 123.

[63] Ibid., i 3, p. 123: "Non è furor d'atra bile che fuor di conseglio, raggione et atti di prudenza lo faccia vagare guidato dal caso e rapito dalla disordinata tempesta; ... Ma è un calor acceso dal sole intelligenziale ne l'anima et impeto divino che gl'impronta l'ali: onde più e più avvicinandosi al sole intelligenziale, rigettando la ruggine de le umane cure, dovien un oro probato e puro, ha sentimento della divina et interna armonia, concorda gli suoi pensieri e gesti con la simmetria della legge insita in tutte le cose." Bruno's criticism of physiologically induced contraction as a means of noetic ascent in the *Furori* is ignored by INGEGNO, 'Nota sul *Sigillus sigillorum* del Bruno', pp. 361-369; *Regia pazzia*, pp. 137-141, especially p. 140.

[64] Cf. BRUNO, *Furori* i 3, p. 123, cited in the note above, with BRUNO, *Sigillus* i 45, p. 189.6-14, as quoted on p. 19 n. 60 above.

[65] BRUNO, *Furori* i 3, p. 119: "sono più specie de furori, li quali tutti si riducono a doi geni: secondo che altri non mostrano che cecità, stupidità et impeto irrazionale, che tende al ferino insensato; altri consisteno in certa divina abstrazzione per cui dovegnono alcuni megliori in fatto che uomini ordinarii." For a similar division of abstraction, see also BRUNO, *Idiota triumphans* i, p. 6.19-24.

[66] FICINO, *De amore* VII iii, p. 245.10-12: "Plato noster furorem in *Phedro*, mentis alienationem definit. Alienationis autem duo genera tradit. Alteram ab humanis morbis, alteram a deo provenire existimat." Ficino refers to PLATO, *Phaedrus* 265A9-11. For the sources to this letter, see GENTILE, 'In margine', pp. 39-61. For Ficino's distinction in the *De amore* VII iii, p. 245.10-12, see also ibid., VII xii-xiii, pp. 256.19-258.10; FICINO, *In Phaedrum* ii, pp. 75.27-79.28 (= FICINO, *Opera*, p. 1364.5-47); *In Ionem*, p. 1281.40-43: "Plato noster, optime Laurenti, furorem in Phaedro, mentis alienationem definit. Al[i]enationis autem duo genera tradit. Unam ab humanis morbis, alteram a Deo provenientem." In an early letter dated December 1457, Ficino had similarly singled out *alienatio* as the meaning of *furore* in Plato; see FICINO, *De divino furore*, p. 614.1.

whose "inspired understanding" and "acute senses" turn them into "principali artefici et efficienti", i.e. men who are principles and causes of things, not into "receptacles and instruments" like the former.[67] Those who experience the former kind of divine *furore* have within them more dignity, power and efficacy, since they give room to the divine, or at least so they pretend. Those who experience the latter kind of divine *furore* are themselves more powerful and efficacious, and they are divine.[68]

The distinction in the *Eroici furori* between two kinds of "divine abstraction" — that is, between those who have an "inspired understanding" on one hand, and those who are "void of sense and reason" of their own and therefore only "receptacles", on the other — is important in relation to Bruno's notion of noetic interpretation of contraction. Abstraction is, as we have seen in the "twofold contraction" described in the *Sigillus*, a means of carrying out a descent in reverse.[69] Descent from the One to the manifold is one form of contraction, whereas abstraction, i.e. noetic ascent, is the other form of contraction from manifold towards the One.

What Bruno says about contraction as abstraction in the *Sigillus* fits well with his comments in the *Eroici furori* about "divine abstraction". First, the kind of abstraction discussed in the *Sigillus* corresponds to the form of "divine abstraction" carried out by those assigned an "inspired understanding" in the *Eroici furori*, since it is similarly based on the rational faculties.[70] Second, the "divine abstraction" of these men, Bruno adds in the *Eroici furori*, is not determined by their "black bile", i.e. melancholy, but primarily by the superiority of their rational faculties.[71] In the *Sigillus* Bruno had similarly stated that those "more noble souls" who contemplate the divine may be assisted by tempered melancholy, but that the success of their contemplation is due to their intellectual

---

[67] BRUNO, *Furori* i 3, pp. 119-121: "E questi sono de due specie perché: altri per esserno fatti stanza de dèi o spiriti divini, dicono et operano cose mirabile senza che di quelle essi o altri intendano la raggione; e tali per l'ordinario sono promossi a questo da l'esser stati prima indisciplinati et ignoranti, nelli quali come vòti di proprio spirito e senso, come in una stanza purgata, s'intrude il senso e spirito divino... Altri, per essere avezzi o abili alla contemplazione, e per aver innato un spirito lucido et intellettuale, da uno interno stimolo e fervor naturale suscitato da l'amor della divinitate, della giustizia, della veritade, della gloria, dal fuoco del desio e soffio dell'intenzione acuiscono gli sensi, e nel solfro della cogitativa facultade accendono il lume razionale con cui veggono più che ordinariamente: e questi non vegnono al fine a parlar et operar come vasi et instrumenti, ma come principali artefici et efficienti." This distinction is also made in BRUNO, *Idiota triumphans* i, pp. 6.1-7.7. For a discussion of it and its relation to the *Furori*, see INGEGNO, *Cosmologia*, pp. 192-193.

[68] BRUNO, *Furori* i 3, p. 121: "Gli primi hanno più dignità, potestà et efficacia in sé: perché hanno la divinità. Gli secondi son essi più degni, più potenti et efficaci, e son divini."

[69] BRUNO, *Sigillus* ii 22, pp. 213.21-214.6, as quoted on p. 55 n. 19 above.

[70] Cf. BRUNO, *Furori* i 3, p. 123, as quoted on p. 65 n. 63 above, with BRUNO, *Sigillus* ii 22, p. 213.21-23, as quoted on p. 58 n. 31 above.

[71] BRUNO, *Furori* i 3, p. 123, as quoted on p. 65 n. 63 above.

capacities, not to their humours alone.[72] Third, Bruno says in the *Eroici furori* that the *furore* of those adhering to reason is not "oblivion, but memory".[73] Memory was also vital to the theory of noetic ascent in the *Sigillus* as part of the *Ars reminiscendi*.[74] Fourth, in the *Sigillus* Bruno criticises the first kind of so-called "divine abstraction" among those afflicted by melancholy: such people abandon reason, becoming instead "receptacles" (used by demons and spirits). In the *Eroici furori* Bruno makes the same criticism.[75]

Both the *Sigillus* and the *Eroici furori*, then, criticise noetic ascent induced by intruding spirits or melancholy. In both instances, Bruno claims, it derives not from an active, autonomous inner experience and intellectual endeavour, but instead from extrinsic elements. This, then, is the criticism Bruno raises against the theory of noetic ascent through physiologically induced contractions in the field of love poetry. Bruno is not necessarily directing his attack against Ficino, but perhaps against those poets who pretended to employ Ficino's theory of melancholy.

The distinction between authentic human experience, on one hand, and self-suggestion which turns men into "vessels" of the divine, on the other, has some offshoots in Bruno's reflections on religion, to which I shall turn briefly. Bruno phrases his criticism against religious practices whereby men become "receptacles and instruments" of the divinity in a way that implies his disagreement with the fundamental Christian requirement that the good Christian should have faith in the Scriptures, and that he should be passive and obedient towards what is perceived as God's will. For the expression Bruno picks up on in the *Eroici furori* — religious men as passive "receptacles and instruments" — is also employed by St Paul and in the principle of *iustitia sola fide* promoted by Martin Luther (1483-1546) and Calvin.[76]

---

[72] BRUNO, *Sigillus* i 45, p. 189.6-14, as quoted on p. 19 n. 60 above.

[73] BRUNO, *Furori* i 3, p. 121: "Questi furori de quali noi raggioniamo [the divine abstraction promoted through intellectual endeavour], e che veggiamo messi in execuzione in queste sentenze, non son oblio, ma una memoria".

[74] BRUNO, *Sigillus* i 17, p. 165.11-13.

[75] Cf. BRUNO, *Furori* i 3, pp. 119-121, as quoted on p. 66 n. 67 above, with BRUNO, *Sigillus* i 45, i 46, i 48, pp. 188.20-189.14, 189.16-190.18, 191.7-21.

[76] Ad Romanos 9.20-21: "O homo, tu quis es qui respondeas Deo? Numquid dicit figmentum ei qui se finxit: Quid me fecisti sic? An non habet potestatem figulus luti ex eadem massa facere aliud quidem vas in honorem aliud vero in contumeliam?"; Ad Timotheum ii 2.20-21: "In magna autem domo non solum sunt vasa aurea et argentea, sed et lignea et fictilia: et quaedam quidem in honorem, quaedam autem in contumeliam. Si quis ergo emundaverit se ab istis, erit vas in honorem sanctificatum et utile Domino ad omne opus bonum paratum." For the use of the metaphor among Protestants, see LUTHER, *De servo arbitrio*, p. 787.13-14: "Dominus vero ... illuminet te et faciat vasculum in honorem et gloriam"; CALVIN, *Institutio religionis christianae*, III xxiii 4, col. 701: "Occurremus enim cum Paulo (Rom. 9: 20 [sic 20-21]) in hunc modum: ['Jo homo, tu quis es qui disceptes cum Deo? num figmentum dicit ei qui se finxit: cur me finxisti sic? annon habet potestatem figulus, ut ex eadem massa faciat vas aliud in honorem, aliud in contumeliam?['] Negabunt ita vere defendi Dei iustitiam, sed subterfugium captari, quale habere solent qui iusta excusatione destituuntur." For a

In the *Cabala* Bruno similarly criticises those who are passive "vessels".[77] There he attributes "santa ignoranza" and "divina asinitade" to persons who block the process of contemplation of the divinity under the pretence of religion.[78] Bruno depicts such people in the *Cabala* like those characterised as "vessels" in the *Eroici furori*, who are also called "asses", and who do not really undergo the process of *deificatio* but feign to do so.[79] An example of this in the context of religion can be found in the twelfth contraction in the *Sigillus*. There "our not very ingenious apocalyptics" are said to generate melancholic spirit inwardly, whereby they appear to others like "pious prophets and revealers". They are, in fact, "asses", like the people they convert.[80] Another example is in the fourteenth contraction, also in the *Sigillus*. There a monk is said to have increased melancholic humours in himself and thereby, in the eyes of his fellow monks, turned into a prophet and a great theologian. Bruno's drug, however, cured him and revealed him as the "ass" which he had always been.[81] These examples suggest that the theory of melancholy had become part of a religious culture detested by Bruno because it belittles the innate rational faculties in man. It is through them that the soul can communicate with the divine.

Bruno renewed his criticism of such practices in his *De magia naturali*. There he states that one kind of magic seeks to evoke "gods, demons and heroes" through "prayers, consecrations, fumigations, sacrifices, dress of certain kinds and ceremonies". This is, presumably, an allusion to Christian religious rites. In this kind of magic, Bruno continues, the practitioner turns himself into a "receptacle or instrument". This form of magic is the "magic of the desperate".[82] Bruno probably included Christian rites and practices among them.

---

discussion of Bruno's attitude towards this metaphor in Protestant doctrine, see CILIBERTO, *Giordano Bruno*, pp. 161-162; ORDINE, 'Introduction', pp. CXCIV-CXCVIII. GRANADA, 'Bruno et la *dignitas hominis*', pp. 77-80, suggests that Bruno may be thinking of Protestant doctrine in his discussion of "receptacles and instruments".

[77] BRUNO, *Cabala* declamazione, pp. 23-25.

[78] Ibid., declamazione, p. 23.

[79] For "vessels" in the *Furori*, see BRUNO, *Furori* i 3, pp. 119-121, as quoted p. 66 n. 67 above. For "asses" in the *Furori*, see ibid., i 3, p. 121: "come l'asino che porta sacramenti". For the theme of "santa ignoranza" and "divina asinitade" in the *Cabala* and other of Bruno's works, see ORDINE, *La cabala*, pp. 55-71.

[80] BRUNO, *Sigillus* i 46, pp. 189.15-190.5, as quoted on p. 20 n. 61 above.

[81] Ibid., i 48, pp. 191.24-192.5, as quoted on p. 23 n. 77 above.

[82] BRUNO, *De magia naturali* §2.17-24, p. 162 (= *BOL*, vol. 3, p. 398.8-16): "Si isti [magia] accessit cultus seu invocatio intelligentiarum et efficientum exteriorum seu superiorum, cum orationibus, consecrationibus, fumigiis, sacrificiis, certis habitibus et ceremoniis ad Deos, daemonas et heroäs; tunc vel fit ad finem contrahendi spiritus in se ipso, cuius ipse fiat vas et instrumentum, ut appareat sapiens rerum, quam tamen sapientiam facile pharmaco una cum spiritu possit evacuare — et haec est magia desperatorum". An example of such a "desperate" person being cured by a drug given by a "wise man" might be the story about the monk cured by Bruno in Brescia, reported in BRUNO, *Sigillus* i 48, pp. 191.24-192.5, as quoted on p. 23 n. 77 above.

Chapter 4

Contraction and Memory

Interpretations of Bruno's idea of memory

Plotinus' essay on matter led Bruno to assume the immanent existence of Ideas in matter. These Ideas also exist in the human memory, Bruno claims. Therefore there are two roads to the intelligible reality, due to the nature of the human soul. One consists in the contemplation and veneration of living nature, where Ideas exist intrinsically within matter. Bruno praises this approach to the divine in the *Spaccio* as a form of religion practised by the Egyptians and fated by the eternal vicissitude of things to recur again (in fact, in Bruno's philosophy). In the previous chapter we have seen how contemplation of the sensible universe is one way of approaching this intelligible reality. The other road, the theme of this chapter, consists in summoning Ideas in the soul through the inventiveness of the higher memory, as described in the mnemonic works.

We can account for this second road in three ways. First, Bruno's idea of memory in his early mnemonic works owes more to Plotinus than has hitherto been recognised. Second, even though Bruno does not link memory to contraction explicitly, his idea of noetic ascent through a "contracted similitude" of the intelligible realm is applicable to his idea of noetic ascent through memory. Finally, we must ignore Sturlese's claim that the mnemonic images in Bruno's *De umbris* are nothing but "arbitrary signs" denuded of ontological reference. Instead, I shall propose that the experimentation with mnemonic signs prescribed in Bruno's mnemonic works implies that he conceived of these images as means of noetic ascent.

Bruno mentions Plotinus in several epistemological contexts in *De umbris* and the *Sigillus*.[1] Plotinus was, Bruno says, the "prince of Platonists".[2] What was, then, Plotinus' role in relation to the idea of memory in these works? In his monumental study of Bruno's Latin works dating from 1889, Felice Tocco discussed Plotinus' presence in these two mnemonic writings of Bruno. Tocco, however, concluded that Aristotle's psychology was more influential than Plotinus' in Bruno's two works.[3] Ever since Tocco several scholars have made important observations about

---

[1]   BRUNO, *De umbris* §§54.6, 61.3, 71.2, 72.3, pp. 47, 51, 55, 56; *Sigillus* i 32, i 33, ii 3, pp. 175.22, 178.7, 196.13. The last reference concerns ontological issues. The other references concern epistemological ones.

[2]   BRUNO, *De umbris* §71.2, p. 55: "Notavit Platonicorum princeps Plotinus".

[3]   TOCCO, *Le opere*, pp. 46-48, 362-365, emphases Plotinus' importance for the idea of noetic ascent in *De umbris*, but underlines Aristotle's *De memoria et reminiscentia* and

Plotinus' contribution to Bruno's notion of memory — though without any significant revaluation of Plotinus' importance in regard to Bruno compared to that of Aristotle.[4] The most influential studies of Bruno's mnemonics after Tocco have identified Bruno's idea of memory with Aristotle's doctrine in *De memoria et reminiscentia* and the account of memory in the pseudo-Ciceronian *Ad Herennium*, or derivatives of these sources.[5] In this way Plotinus, even though Bruno praises him extravagantly several times in his epistemological theories in *De umbris* and the *Sigillus*, has been largely ignored, whereas Aristotle, whom Bruno mentions in *De umbris* rarely and in philosophically unimportant passages, has come to be seen as the main source of Bruno's mnemonics in *De umbris* and the *Sigillus*.

The interpretation that I would like to propose in this chapter is, in brief, that Plotinus' concept of memory, like his philosophy as a whole, comprised important Aristotelian traits, but that Plotinus' concept contained additional elements which also occur in Bruno's mnemonic works. The Aristotelian elements in Bruno's mnemonics derive partly from Plotinus, who incorporated elements of Aristotle's psychology, and partly from Aristotle and Aristotelian or scholastic psychology, and we cannot very often be sure which source Bruno is following. This means, in turn, that it is as untenable to identify Bruno's notion of memory with that of Plotinus exclusively, as it is to do so with that of Aristotle. Bruno draws from both sources. He does not clarify his view in a systematic manner anywhere, but uses what fits into his various philosophical aims and contexts. What I shall do is to point out where in Bruno's early mnemonic works Plotinus' theory of memory may play an unnoticed role.

First, I shall outline Plotinus' discussion of Aristotle's account of sensation and memory, pointing out where Bruno sides with Plotinus and where with Aristotle (pp. 71-73). Afterwards I shall explain Plotinus' view of memory, taking into account his doctrine that imagination and memory in the human soul are twofold. This doctrine was central to Bruno's doctrines of memory and noetic ascent (pp. 73-80). I shall then explain the role of memory in Plotinus' account of noetic

---

the pseudo-Ciceronian *Ad Herennium* as sources for the art of memory, including Bruno's (ibid., pp. 21-23).

4   DE BERNART, *Immaginazione*, pp. 22-23; STURLESE, 'Le fonti', pp. 112, 119-122; VÉDRINE, 'Image', pp. 48-49; BORSCHE, 'Denken in Bildern', pp. 95-102. Borsche makes many relevant observations concerning *phantasia* in Plotinus' and Bruno's mnemonics, which indirectly concern Plotinian components in Bruno's mnemonics.

5   TOCCO, *Le opere*, pp. 21-23; YATES, 'The Ciceronean art of memory', pp. 874-877, 901; *The art of memory*, pp. 45-50, 73-89, where Yates integrates this empirical concept of memory into her interpretation of Bruno's use of mnemonic images as magical devices; *Giordano Bruno and the Hermetic tradition*, pp. 195-199; ROSSI, *Clavis universalis*, pp. 29, 31-38; VASOLI, 'Immagini', pp. 345-346; STURLESE, 'Il *De imaginum, signorum et idearum compositione*', pp. 184-185; FELLMANN, 'Bild und Bewusstsein', pp. 23-25, 31; WILDGEN, *Das kosmische Gedächtnis*, pp. 129-132; MATTEOLI, 'L'arte della memoria nei primi scritti mnemotecnici di Bruno', p. 76 n. 5, who adheres to Yates' *Art of memory* as fundamental to Bruno's mnemonics, and ibid., pp. 86-87, maintains, though without identifying a source, that memory in Bruno's mnemonics ultimately depends on sense data as in Aristotle.

ascent and argue that this account of memory and noetic ascent may have influenced Bruno's theory of noetic ascent (pp. 80-81). Finally, I shall show how this reading fits into Bruno's original interpretation of the traditional metaphor of the Golden Chain (pp. 82-87).

Plotinus' discussion of Aristotle's doctrine on memory

Bruno draws, as mentioned above, on two main sources in his notion of memory, Neoplatonic and Aristotelian, and he manages to do so regardless of the deep philosophical differences between them on the issue of memory. Aristotle had presented a coherent theory of sensation, imagination, reasoning and memory in his *De anima* and *De memoria et reminiscentia*. In the former he had asserted that reasoning man makes use of mental images derived from sensation: "No one could ever learn or understand anything without the exercise of perception, so even when we think speculatively, we must have some mental image [φάντασμα] of which to think, for mental images [φαντάσματα] are similar to objects perceived except that they are without matter".[6] Scholastic authors used *phantasmata* as their translation of the Greek word.

This empirical theory of knowledge is the basis of the doctrine of memory presented in *De memoria et reminiscentia*. Here Aristotle connects sensation, imagination and memory as follows: "It is obvious, then, that memory belongs to that part of the soul to which imagination [φαντασία] belongs; all things which are imaginable are essentially objects of memory, and those which necessarily involve imagination are objects of memory only indirectly".[7] To the question of how we remember things that are not actually present, he answers that "it is obvious that one must consider the affection which is produced by sensation in the soul, and in that part of the body which contains the soul — the affection, the lasting state of which we call memory — as a kind of picture; for the stimulus produced impresses a sort of likeness of the precept, just as when men seal with signet rings".[8] In short, memory depends on sense data. It consists of imprints, like the imprints that seals imprint on wax.

Plotinus disagreed with Aristotle's theory of sensation and memory.[9] "We do not assert", Plotinus says, "that the impression of the sense-object enters the soul and stamps it, nor do we say that memory exists because the impression

---

[6] ARISTOTLE, *De anima* iii 8 432ª7-10, tr. W. S. Hett, Loeb ed.

[7] ARISTOTLE, *De memoria et reminiscentia* i 450ª22-25, tr. W. S. Hett, Loeb ed.

[8] Ibid., i 450ª28-32, tr. W. S. Hett.

[9] For Plotinus' doctrine of sensation, sense perception and memory, see BLUMENTHAL, *Plotinus' psychology*, pp. 70-72. For Plotinus' arguments against Aristotle's theory of memory, see ibid., pp. 80-83. For Plotinus' concept of memory, see WARREN, 'Memory in Plotinus', pp. 252-260; O'DALY, 'Memory in Plotinus and two early texts of St. Augustine', pp. 462-469; McCUMBER, 'Anamnesis as memory of intelligibles in Plotinus', pp. 160-167; GUIDELLI, 'Note sul tema della memoria nelle *Enneadi* di Plotino', pp. 75-94.

remains."[10] Sensation and hence memory are not passive reservoirs of past sense impressions, according to Plotinus, but a power of the soul characterised by its intentionality. The faculty of sight, which is independent of what is perceived, is an example of this power of the soul.[11] Plotinus produces five arguments to support his rejection of the stamp theory, a rejection which may also aim at Aristotle's interpretation of it, although Plotinus does not mention Aristotle explicitly on this occasion. First, if the soul received impressions from sense-perceptions, it would not have to use its intentionality when sensing, since the impressions would already be in the soul. Second, if the soul received impressions in sensation, how would it be possible to judge distances of objects? Third, if such impressions were impressed on the soul, and they were the basis of cognition, then how would the soul be able to judge the size of the object perceived? This leads to the fourth and most important objection, namely, that if we received impressions of the object we perceive, then we would not see the object itself, but only its impression in our mind, and the objectivity of the sensation would be doubtful. Lastly, Plotinus argues in more general terms that the stamp theory would imply that the object of perception, the impression, would not be separate from the faculty of seeing. This would make cognition impossible according to Plotinus, since that which sees and what is seen must be two separate things. The same applies to the soul and the sense impression produced by the senses. Hence Plotinus rejects the theory of the soul being stamped with sense impressions.[12]

Bruno repeats part of Plotinus' last argument almost *verbatim*, stating that we would be unable to perceive a sense-object if it was "placed" on the physical eye itself, and the soul even less so if the sense impression was stamped directly on it.[13] Verbal similarities between Bruno's and Plotinus' accounts of this idea suggest that Bruno read Plotinus rather than Ficino's commentary, since Ficino did not mention this idea in his commentary.[14] Bruno also gives an argument not advanced by Plotinus in the course of the five arguments summarised above, but which supports his rejection of the stamp theory which we also find in Aristotle.

---

[10]	PLOTINUS IV vi [41] 1.8-11, tr. A. H. Armstrong (= tr. Ficino, p. 452.29-35). Armstrong identifies ARISTOTLE, *De memoria et reminiscentia* i 450ᵃ30-32, as the doctrine here rejected; see the Loeb edition of Plotinus (Cambridge, Mass., 1966-1988), vol. 4, p. 320 n. 1. Plotinus may also, however, aim at other interpretations of the stamp theory, e.g. Stoic interpretations, as reported in DIOGENES LAERTIUS, *Lives* vii 45.

[11]	BLUMENTHAL, *Plotinus' psychology*, pp. 81-82.

[12]	For these five arguments against Aristotle's theory, see PLOTINUS IV vi [41] 1.11-40 (= tr. Ficino, pp. 452.36-453.20).

[13]	BRUNO, *Sigillus* i 28, p. 169.21-24: "Et nimirum quod experimur rem pupillae impositam non discerni, remotiorem vero posse, tanto magis ad animam est referendum, quanto ipsam plus a materiae finibus elongatam novimus." Cf. PLOTINUS IV vi [41] 1.31-36, tr. Ficino, p. 453.9-14: "Omnino vero quod fertur, non posse nos rem impositam pupillae discernere, remotam vero posse, idem quoque multoque magis est ad animam transferendum. Si enim rei vidende figuram poneremus in anima, spectaculum illud, quo insigniretur, minime cerneret."

[14]	Cf. FICINO, *In Plotinum* IV vi [41], p. 453.15: "Quintum, non discernemus rem sensui sic impositam."

"You would be mistaken in thinking," Bruno says, "that you can retain in the soul, so to speak, a sort of image of those things which sense had perceived in such a way that the soul is thereby shaped and somehow receives a vestige of the sense impression. For the *species* that next comes along to shape the soul would necessarily obliterate the preceding one. "[15]

In place of Aristotle's theory of sensation and memory Plotinus proposes that sensation is an intentional activity of the soul directed towards the object of sensation. In the case of hearing, Plotinus says: "The impression is in the air, and is a sort of articulated stroke, like letters written on the air by the maker of the sound; but the power and the substance of the soul does something like reading the impressions written on the air when they come near and reach the point at which they can be seen."[16] Just as Plotinus denies that the soul receives sense-imprints when perceiving, he denies that memory summons retained sense impressions when recollecting.[17] Plotinus argues that memory is likewise an intentional power of the soul, similar to sensation.

Bruno agrees with Plotinus that memory cannot be reduced to a passive reservoir of received sense impressions, and insists, too, that it is an intentional activity.[18] In the *Sigillus*, for instance, he states that memory does not derive from sensation or from introspection, "but from some unnamed faculty of the soul, which is used in a kind of *intentio* of, or attention to, something".[19] Bruno could use the aspect of intentionality in Plotinus' idea of memory, since it fitted into his idea of noetic ascent as a contraction of *intentiones*, and for this and perhaps other reasons, he probably accepted this aspect of Plotinus' thought.

Plotinus on the twofold memory

Plotinus' rejection of Aristotle's conception of memory should not lead one to ignore the fact that Plotinus uses a terminology about various epistemological faculties which is similar to that of Aristotle.[20] Plotinus' theory of a twofold imagination, one sensitive and one conceptual, is a case in point, which I shall deal

---

[15] BRUNO, *Sigillus* i 28, p. 170.2-6: "Temere enim eorum, quae sensus perceperat, quasi figuram quamdam opinaberis in animo servari, ut animus inde figuretur et veluti quoddam admittat impressionis vestigium; sequens enim species ad figurandum animum accedens, necessario praecedentem alteram delesset."

[16] PLOTINUS IV vi [41] 2.11-16, tr. A. H. Armstrong (= tr. Ficino, p. 453.43-50).

[17] PLOTINUS IV vi [41] 3.1-79 (= tr. Ficino, pp. 454.12-455.62).

[18] BRUNO, *De umbris* §87.8-13, p. 66.

[19] BRUNO, *Sigillus* i 28, p. 169.15-20: "Ne inquam putes per introspectum quemdam potius quam adspectum seu prospectum memoriam fieri vel comparari; effusione enim quadam provenit, qua non inquam ex oculis, sed ex innominata quadam animi facultate, quae in genere intentionis vel intendentiae cuiusdam habetur, et sepositum velutique seorsum positum intuetur."

[20] One should keep in mind, however, that Plotinus' relation to Aristotle was mediated by Alexander of Aphrodisias; see WALLIS, *Neoplatonism*, pp. 29-30.

with in this section.[21] Due to Plotinus' twofold notion of imagination, in which sensitive imagination overlaps with the Aristotelian concept of imagination, it is easy to confuse Aristotle's and Plotinus' respective theories, and it is necessary to establish the distinguishing characteristics in order to identify Bruno's sources as they are used in specific contexts.

Plotinus speaks of an image-making power (φανταστικόν) pertaining to the lower part of the soul, which is directed towards sense impressions. This image-making power corresponds partly to the Aristotelian notion of φαντασία. It is sensitive imagination. But Plotinus also speaks of an image-making power pertaining to the higher part of the soul, turned towards thoughts in Mind.[22] This is conceptual imagination, which is absent in Aristotle's psychology.[23] Whereas the image-making power in the lower part of the soul produces mental images of sense objects, the corresponding power in the higher part of the soul produces a "picture of the thought", that is, a "picture" of the Ideas contemplated in Mind. The contemplation of Ideas in Mind is not automatically apprehended in human consciousness. In order to be "remembered", the Ideas contemplated in Mind have to be articulated through "verbal expression" (λόγος), that is, a concept. That is what is meant by "a picture of the thought".[24] Plotinus explains this as follows: "The intellectual act is without parts and has not, so to speak, come out into the open, but remains unobserved within, but the verbal expression (λόγος) unfolds its content and brings it out of the intellectual act into the image-making power (φανταστικόν), and so shows the intellectual act as if in a mirror, and this is how there is apprehension and persistence and memory of it."[25] Gerard O'Daly makes the following point in relation to IV iii [27] 30.1-7: "Now if the λόγος is the vehicle of recollecting and expressing Ideas, we might reasonably infer that λόγος and remembered image are, for Plotinus, *a fortiori* essential to philosophical discourse. If we do not recall the λόγος we cannot discuss Ideas." Hence the relation of language to thought becomes a key issue in Plotinus' account of

---

21   PLOTINUS IV iii [27] 30-31 (= tr. Ficino, pp. 394.50-395.9, 395.19-50). For Plotinus' notion of imagination, see BUNDY, *The theory of imagination*, pp. 117-130, especially pp. 121-125; WARREN, 'Imagination in Plotinus', pp. 277-285; BLUMENTHAL, 'Neoplatonic interpretations of Aristotle on *phantasia*', pp. 248-249, 255.

22   PLOTINUS IV iii [27] 31.1-2, in tr. Ficino, p. 395.19-21: "Verum si imaginationis memoria est, utraque vero anima meminisse dicitur, due quedam erunt imaginandi virtutes." See also PLOTINUS IV iii [27] 29, tr. Ficino, pp. 393.59-394.36. In Aristotle the term *imaginatio*, or φαντασία, had only been used to denote a faculty inserted between sensation and intellect; see ARISTOTLE, *De memoria et reminiscentia* i 450ª22-25; *De anima* iii 8 432ª7-10. For sensitive imagination in Plotinus, see WARREN, 'Imagination in Plotinus', pp. 277-281. For conceptual imagination, see ibid., pp. 281-285. There is a discussion of conceptual imagination in its own right in PLOTINUS I iv [46] 4.1-36 (= tr. Ficino, pp. 31.65-32.46).

23   WARREN, 'Imagination in Plotinus', p. 282.

24   PLOTINUS IV iii [27] 30.1-7, tr. A. H. Armstrong (= tr. Ficino, p. 394.50-57).

25   PLOTINUS IV iii [27] 30.7-11, tr. A. H. Armstrong (= tr. Ficino, pp. 394.58-395.1). For the higher imagination, see WARREN, 'Imagination in Plotinus', pp. 281-282.

memory.[26] The function of language is, then, not to describe an empirical reality, but to summon abstract Ideas.

Implied in Plotinus' theory of conceptual imagination is his re-interpretation of Plato's theory of knowledge as recollection.[27] Plotinus does not regard the intellectual soul's memories as a recollection of prenatal knowledge, but rather as a recalling of that which the highest part of the soul knows eternally by direct intuition.[28] Contrary to Plato, Plotinus holds that that part of the human soul remains in the intelligible world, even when part of the soul is embodied in the sensible world. The problem for Plotinus is, therefore, not how to recall prenatal knowledge, but how to use this part of the soul which has never descended from the intelligible world. Human beings can do so, unless they have fallen victims of the body.[29] To do so is, Plotinus thinks, to return to our true self, to actualise it and to become what we truly are.

Plotinus' theory of memory is connected to his conception of the origin of the human soul. According to Plotinus, memory arises when a soul abandons Mind and descends. Souls animating the celestial bodies do not have memory. They do not have to exercise memory, since they are turned towards Mind in eternal and perfect contemplation.[30] (Incidentally Bruno repeats this idea.[31]) When embodied, Plotinus holds, the human soul stretches itself further downwards from Mind towards the lower ontological levels of Soul and the sensible realm. Memory, as a recollection of the intelligible world of Mind, may arise again in the human soul.[32] The human soul can thus be described as having two inclinations, one upwards towards the One and one downwards towards sensible bodies — and in this sense it is double. Plotinus underlines, however, that the soul is an indivisible unity, even though it is possible to divide it into parts for the sake of explanation.[33]

---

[26] O'DALY, 'Memory in Plotinus and two early texts of St. Augustine', p. 465.

[27] For Plato's theory of recollection, see PLATO, *Phaedo* 72E3-77A5. For Plotinus' concept of recollection, see BUNDY, *The theory of imagination*, pp. 121-122, 125-126; WARREN, 'Memory in Plotinus', pp. 256-258; McCUMBER, 'Anamnesis as memory of intelligibles in Plotinus', pp. 160-167 (qualifying Warren's interpretation of recollection in Plotinus); O'DALY, 'Memory in Plotinus and two early texts of St. Augustine', pp. 467-469; WALLIS, *Neoplatonism*, pp. 79-81; BLUMENTHAL, *Plotinus' psychology*, pp. 96-97.

[28] PLOTINUS IV iii [27] 25.10-35 (= tr. Ficino, pp. 390.36-391.7).

[29] PLOTINUS IV viii [6] 8.1-23 (= tr. Ficino, p. 476.1-38).

[30] PLOTINUS IV iv [28] 7.1-17 (= tr. Ficino, p. 401.37-62). For this theme, see WARREN, 'Memory in Plotinus', pp. 252-253; BLUMENTHAL, *Plotinus' psychology*, pp. 97-98.

[31] BRUNO, *Causa* ii, p. 125: "Questo non solo viene affirmato ne l'anima del mondo, ma anco de ciascuna stella, essendo (come il detto filosofo vòle [i.e. Plotinus, as mentioned ibid., ii, p. 123]) che tutte hanno potenza di contemplare Idio, gli principii di tutte le cose e la distribuzione de gli ordini de l'universo: e vòle che questo non accade per modo di memoria, di discorso e considerazione".

[32] PLOTINUS IV iv [28] 5.1-31 (= tr. Ficino, pp. 400.21-401.2).

[33] PLOTINUS IV ii [21] 1.1-76 (= tr. Ficino, pp. 361.31-363.25). For Plotinus' division of the soul into a rational and an irrational part, see BLUMENTHAL, *Plotinus' psychology*, p. 50. Plotinus also employed a tripartition of the soul, following a Platonic scheme

Ficino retains three important characteristics of Plotinus' theory of memory in his commentary on the *Enneads*. Ficino comments that the description of the soul being "double" is valid as a poetical description, i.e. he realises that Plotinus' distinction between the two souls is solely a way of explaining a doctrine and that the soul is a unity. One inclination of the soul, Ficino explains, is rational, i.e. the intellectual soul, the other is irrational, i.e. the sensitive soul. The former derives from the "craftsman himself of the world", by which he may mean God. The latter derives from the natural world.[34]

Second, corresponding to these two inclinations of the soul, there are two imaginative powers (*imaginationes*). One is connected with the intellectual soul, another with the sensitive soul. Intentionality (*animadversio*) is important in both of these powers.[35]

The third Plotinian characteristic in Ficino's doctrine of memory is that he identifies two memories, one superior, and one inferior.[36] Ficino explains that the inferior is bound to the senses of the body.[37] The superior, on the other hand, "at the same time comprehends signs of the intelligibles and the forms of sensible things".[38] In Ficino's translation of Plotinus the objects of the higher part of imagination, conceptual imagination, are called "concepts" (*notiones*).[39] This is no coincidence, for Plotinus explicitly connects the "image-making power" of the

---

(desiring, spirited and rational parts of the soul) as well as an Aristotelian scheme (vegetative, sensitive and intellective parts of the soul). For the faculties within these tripartitions, see ibid., pp. 21-44, 103, 135.

[34] FICINO, *In Plotinum* IV iii [27] 27, p. 392.51-65: "Opinio quasi poetica esse geminas in homine animas per substantiam inter se differentes. Rationalem quidem ab ipso mundi opifice, irrationalem vero a mundi vita." Ficino comments on PLOTINUS IV iii [27] 27.1-25 (= tr. Ficino, pp. 392.50-393.23). For Ficino's idea of the two inclinations of the soul, see KRISTELLER, *Il pensiero filosofico di Marsilio Ficino*, pp. 422-437.

[35] FICINO, *In Plotinum* IV iii [27] 31, p. 395.10-18. He comments on this idea in PLOTINUS IV iii [27] 31.1-16 (= tr. Ficino, p. 395.19-50). For Plotinus' theory of a double imagination, see WARREN, 'Imagination in Plotinus', pp. 281-285; BLUMENTHAL, 'Neoplatonic interpretations of Aristotle on *phantasia*', pp. 249, 255; *Plotinus' psychology*, pp. 94, 135-136. BLUMENTHAL, ibid., p. 99 n. 28, briefly criticises Warren, loc. cit., for not explaining the reasons for Plotinus' doctrine of two imaginations.

[36] PLOTINUS IV iii [27] 29.1-36 (= tr. Ficino, pp. 393.59-394.36). For this twofold memory in Plotinus, see BLUMENTHAL, *Plotinus' psychology*, pp. 85-86, 96-99.

[37] FICINO, *In Plotinum* IV iii [27] 31, p. 395.10-16.

[38] Ibid., IV iii [27] 31, p. 395.16-18: "Quae quidem superior [memoria], qua comprehendit intelligibilium notas simul, et sensibilium formas, declarat in nobis animal esse unum: et quando egreditur corpore, si alteram sibi educatione subegerit, vilia quidem mandat oblivioni, honestiora resumit." FICINO, *Theologia platonica* xv 16, vol. 3, p. 83.10-28, also makes a distinction between two memories, one of the senses (*sensus*) and one of the intellect (*mens*), which may reflect this distinction in Plotinus. The possible implications of this twofold notion of memory have been ignored in studies on Ficino's concept of memory. CASTELLI, 'Marsilio Ficino e i luoghi della memoria', pp. 385-386, for instance, points out Aristotle's *De memoria et reminiscentia* as Ficino's important source.

[39] PLOTINUS IV iii [27] 30.1-16 (= tr. Ficino, pp. 394.50-395.9).

higher imagination with the higher memory.[40] Higher imagination and memory are both directed towards the same kind of object, that is, concepts. When there is harmony between the two parts of the soul, Plotinus says, then the images (αἱ φαντασίαι, translated into Latin by Ficino as *imaginationes*) of the higher and the lower imagination will be experienced as one image (το φάντασμα, translated into Latin by Ficino as *phantasma*).[41] Then concept and mental image derived from sensation will become one. This particular sense of *phantasma* is distinct from the sense of the term in Aristotle's psychology, though the different senses of the same term may cause confusion.

We can summarise the findings of this section as follows. Plotinus' doctrine of a double imagination and a double memory differs from the psychology of Aristotle, and it implies that the content of imagination and memory is irreducible to sense data. Imagination and memory do use sense data, Plotinus agrees with Aristotle, but they are also, Plotinus adds, disagreeing with Aristotle, directed at the higher intelligibles. Ficino repeated Plotinus' doctrine in his Plotinus commentary, and other works besides.

Bruno's stance towards Aristotle's and Plotinus' theories of memory

Bruno had received an Aristotelian education with the Dominicans at Naples before his European *peregrinatio*. This presumably included the study of Aristotle's *De anima*, for he later taught this work for two years in Toulouse before arriving in Paris in 1582.[42] Therefore it is not surprising that on some occasions Bruno affirms the Aristotelian arguments for knowledge's, and ultimately memory's, dependency upon sense impressions, arguments which he assigns to Aristotle, or, generically, to Peripatetics.[43]

Bruno's works, however, show that he followed two, possibly three, features in Plotinus' doctrine of memory, which he knew from Ficino's Latin translation of Plotinus and from his commentary on it. First, Bruno affirms explicitly the idea of

---

[40]   PLOTINUS IV iii [27] 31.1-2 (= tr. Ficino, p. 395.19-21).

[41]   PLOTINUS IV iii [27] 31.2-20 (= tr. Ficino, p. 395.21-50). For this state of harmony in the soul, see WARREN, 'Imagination in Plotinus', p. 283. For Plotinus on the intermediary state of imagination, see ibid., p. 279; BLUMENTHAL, 'Neoplatonic interpretations of Aristotle on *phantasia*', p. 248.

[42]   SPAMPANATO, *Vita*, p. 700: "e lessi in quella città [Toulouse] doppoi, doi anni continui, il testo de Aristotile *De anima* ed altre lezioni de filosofia." For Bruno's stay in Toulouse, see AQUILECCHIA, 'Bruno, Giordano', p. 655; RICCI, *Giordano Bruno nell'Europa del cinquecento*, pp. 137-142.

[43]   E.g. BRUNO, *De compositione* dedication, p. 91.11-16: "Hoc est quod ab Aristotele relatum ab antiquis prius fuit expressum, et a neotericorum paucis capitur: 'intelligere nostrum (id est operationes nostri intellectus) aut est phantasia aut non sine phantasia', rursum: 'non intelligimus, nisi phantasmata speculemur'"; BRUNO, *Lampas* §244.1-6, p. 1230 (= *BOL*, vol. 3, p. 141.18-22). Bruno's notion of imagination is identified with his Aristotelian notion in INGEGNO, 'Nota sul *Sigillus sigillorum* del Bruno', p. 362.

two inclinations of the human soul.[44] Second, he picks up on the distinction between the rational and the irrational imaginations, citing Ficino's commentary on Plotinus' *Enneads* almost *verbatim*.[45] Plotinus embraced the idea of a twofold imagination, Bruno says explicitly.[46] On another occasion Bruno says that mental images (*phantasmata*) may summon "non-sensible forms", by which he may mean Ideas in Mind.[47] This statement may have been inspired by Plotinus' doctrine of the image-making power pertaining to the higher soul.[48] Ficino's comment about the twofold imagination of the soul has been missed in some important studies comparing Bruno's and Ficino's psychology, an omission that would explain why Bruno's adherence to a Plotinian doctrine of a twofold imagination has not been pointed out in the literature on Bruno.[49]

Does Bruno also pick up on Plotinus' doctrine of a twofold memory? Bruno was using Plotinus' theory of vision in IV vi 1, as quoted on p. 72 n. 13 above. This shows that Bruno knew IV vi 1, and therefore knew his doctrine of memory. In the *Lampas triginta statuarum*, dating from Wittenberg 1587,[50] Bruno makes a

---

[44]   BRUNO, *Sigillus* ii 5, pp. 198.17-199.1; *Furori* i 4, ii 1, pp. 189.11-19, 297.12-18; *De monade* iii, p. 356.11-27. For the first reference to the *Furori*, see SARAUW, *Der Einfluss Plotins*, pp. 36-37.

[45]   BRUNO, *Sigillus* i 32, pp. 174.22-175.3: "Duplicem subinde in nobis esse imaginationem considerato: primam quidem in anima ratiocinantem experimur, discursionis iudiciique compotem, rationique quodammodo similem; secundam vero in anima, seu vita, in nobis ratione carentem, ab hac impressam, quae quidem imaginatio non tam ratione utitur et discursione, quam fertur instinctu quodam circa corporis passiones, et tanquam communis sensus principium est sensuum reliquorum." Cf. FICINO, *In Plotinum* III vi [26], pp. 300.54-301.1: "Animadvertes iterum duplicem in nobis imaginationem: primam quidem in anima rationali discursionis et iudicii compotem, similem quodammodo rationi: secundam vero ab hac impressam in anima seu vita in nobis ratione carente, quae sane imaginatio non tam discursione utitur, quam fertur instinctu quamvis intimo: sed circa corporis passiones, quae tanquam communis sensus principium est sensuum reliquorum." CANONE, "'Phantasia' / 'imaginatio'", pp. 239-240, pointed out the similarity between these two passages in Bruno's *Sigillus* and Ficino's commentary on Plotinus' *Enneads*.

[46]   BRUNO, *Sigillus* i 32, pp. 175.13-176.1.

[47]   Ibid., i 25, p. 167.24-28: "Phantasmatum igitur (quorum speculatio necessaria fertur) concinnare species oportet, ut felix in actibus succedentium potentiarum habeare; adaptantur autem, cum tales redduntur, quae per se ipsas valeant formas non sensibiles accire." See also ibid., ii 8, p. 201.19-26, where Bruno provides an example of the cognition of intelligibilia through sensibilia perceived by *phantasmata*. For the role of *phantasmata* in Bruno's mnemonics, see SPRUIT, *Il problema*, pp. 150-154. Spruit, too, underlines the function of *phantasmata* in evoking Ideas (e.g. ibid., p. 150).

[48]   See pp. 73-77 above.

[49]   KLEIN, 'L'imagination', pp. 19-21; GARIN, '*Phantasia* e *imaginatio* fra Marsilio Ficino e Pietro Pomponazzi', pp. 350-351. KLEIN, 'L'imagination', p. 21 n. 1, mentions, however, that Ficino employed Plotinus' notion of imagination as explained in PLOTINUS IV iv [28] 13.

[50]   AQUILECCHIA, 'Bruno, Giordano', p. 660; TIRINNANZI, 'Nota ai testi', in *BOM*, p. LXXV.

statement which I am not quite sure how to interpret, but which may embrace Plotinus' theory about the double nature of memory. There Bruno says that one part of memory is a "sensitive power", "called fantasy by the Peripatetics". Another part, Bruno continues, is an "intellectual power", "which retains images perceived by reason and intellect, and which in some way is the Mind (*mens*) itself."[51] "Mind" (*mens*) is the term by which Ficino had translated Plotinus' term "νοῦς".[52] Is that what Bruno means by *mens* in this passage of his *Lampas triginta statuarum*? He may simply mean the human mind, so I cannot say definitively.

Bruno, as mentioned above, knew the *Enneads* IV vi 1 in Ficino's Latin translation.[53] On the following page in Ficino's translation, where IV vi 3 occurs, Bruno could have found Plotinus' idea that through the memory of the intellectual soul, the human soul is transformed into the intelligible world, that is, Mind. Thereby the human soul becomes itself, returning to its true, eternal and immobile self. Plotinus writes as follows:

> But, being in the middle [of the sensible and intelligible worlds], it [the soul] perceives both, and is said to think the intelligibles when it arrives at memory of them, if it comes to be near them; for it knows them by being them in a way: for it knows, not because they settle in it, but because it has them in some way and sees them and is them in a rather dim way, and becomes them more clearly out of the dimness by a kind of awakening, and passes from potentiality to actuality.[54]

---

[51] BRUNO, *Lampas* §244.1-6, p. 1230 (= *BOL*, vol. 3, p. 141.18-22): "Est memoria, utpote potentia retentiva specierum receptarum et digestarum; et haec est duplex: sensitiva specierum sensibilium, quam Peripathetici etiam phantasiam appellant, et intellectiva, quae retinet species ratione et intellectu perceptas, et quodammodo est ipsa mens." BRUNO, *Summa*, pp. 31.27-32.1, similarly explains a twofold memory. For contemplation of Ideas in Mind, see also BRUNO, *Infinito* i, p. 61: "*Filoteo*. ... Onde la verità come da un debile principio è da gli sensi in picciola parte: ma non è nelli sensi? *Elpino*. Dove dumque? *Filoteo*. Ne l'ogetto sensibile come in un specchio. Nella raggione per modo di argumentazione e discorso. Nell'intelletto per modo di principio, o di conclusione. Nella mente in propria e viva forma."

[52] The three hypostases (the One, Mind and Soul: τὸ ἕν, νοῦς, ψυκή) are described in PLOTINUS V i [10] 10.1-4. It reads in Ficino's translation, p. 491.16-21: "Iam vero demonstratum est oportere super ens esse unum, quale desiderabat ratio demonstrare, quantum scilicet de rebus talibus demonstrari possit: esse autem post ipsum unum ens atque intellectum: tertio denique loco naturam animae." These three hypostases also exist, somehow, in the human soul; see PLOTINUS V i [10] 10.5-31. In Ficino's translation, p. 491.31-35, the central lines, in which 'mens' appears, run as follows: "Est igitur nostra insuper anima divinum quiddam, alteriusque naturae, qualis est universa natura animae: perfecta vero est, quae mentem (translated from "νοῦς") habet, sed mens altera quidem in ratiocinando versatur, altera vim ratiocinandi suppeditat."

[53] See p. 72 n. 13 above.

[54] PLOTINUS IV vi [41] 3.10-16, tr. A. H. Armstrong (= tr. Ficino, p. 454.24-34). For this role of memory, see BUNDY, *The theory of imagination*, pp. 121-122, 125-126.

Bruno may be thinking of this union with Mind in his account of the double nature of memory in the *Lampas triginta statuarum*, where he says that the memory of the intellectual soul is in some way Mind itself.[55] Aristotle's doctrine on memory, unlike Plotinus', did not speak of human memory becoming identical with Mind. As already said, it is uncertain whether Bruno refers to Mind in this passage of the *Lampas triginta statuarum*. However, considering that Bruno retains two other features from Plotinus and from Ficino's commentary on it — namely the idea of the soul's two inclinations and the distinction between the rational and the irrational imaginations — we may propose that Bruno integrated in his art of memory Plotinus' subtle account of the memory of the sensitive and the intellectual soul.

The observations do not yield any definitive answer to the question about Bruno's use of Aristotelian and Plotinian doctrines of memory. They do, however, suggest that Bruno used Plotinus' doctrine of memory, and the ancillary doctrines on the soul and imagination, when they fitted into his aims. Lastly, as we shall see in the last two sections of this chapter, if we assume that Plotinus' doctrine of memory inspired, at least in part, Bruno's mnemonics, it becomes understandable why Bruno insisted that his mnemonic works concerned noetic ascent and not just retention of sense data.

Bruno's use of Plotinus' idea on noetic ascent through memory

Descent, Plotinus asserts, originates from the One, on which all being depends. Now within that structure the individual human soul has the potential to ascend noetically.[56] The form of noetic ascent which Plotinus advocates does not entail the practice of rites and sacraments traditionally associated with religion.[57] Instead, Plotinus specifies contemplation as the means of achieving mystical union with the One. Memory can be a means for such a mystical unification.

Through the memory of the intellectual soul, Plotinus claims, it is possible to reach the intelligible realm of Ideas, the Mind. Plotinus says that the soul is situated in a privileged ontological position. It is "the rational principle of all things, and the nature of soul is the last and lowest rational principle of the intelligibles and the beings in the intelligible world, but first of those in the whole world perceived by the senses."[58] His idea of human memory, especially that of the intellectual soul, is determined by this potentially elevated state of the human soul. Memory accordingly becomes a means by which the human soul gains access to the intelligible world, that is, returns to its true eternal and immobile self. Plotinus

---

[55]   BRUNO, *Lampas* §244.1-6, p. 1230 (= *BOL*, vol. 3, p. 141.18-22), as quoted on p. 79 n. 51 above.

[56]   For Plotinus' theory of noetic ascent, see ARMSTRONG, 'Plotinus', pp. 258-268; BUSSANICH, 'Mystical elements in the thought of Plotinus', pp. 5300-5328.

[57]   ARMSTRONG, 'Plotinus', pp. 259-260. For Plotinus on prayer, see RIST, *Plotinus: The road to reality*, pp. 199-212.

[58]   PLOTINUS IV vi [41] 3.6-8, tr. A. H. Armstrong (= tr. Ficino, p. 454.18-20).

explains these matters in the quotation on p. 79 above. Memory in the intellectual soul, therefore, is a form of noetic ascent, and this may be what Bruno has in mind in the *Lampas triginta statuarum*, as mentioned on p. 80 above.

In *De umbris* we find another passage which may support the possibility that Bruno integrated into his mnemonics Plotinus' idea of noetic ascent through memory. Here Bruno describes the human soul's ascent from individuals to species, and from species to one supreme genus, in much the same way as he does in the *Sigillus*.[59] The next thing he does in *De umbris* is to explain this noetic ascent by means of the hierarchy of intelligences, which leads to a supreme One, transcending the forms. Bruno drew the idea of this hierarchy from the *Liber de causis* as we shall see later.[60] Bruno asserts that even though the ancients knew that memory could proceed from many memorable species of individuals to a single species of many memorable things, they did not teach this.[61] What Bruno seems to be saying here is that his mnemonics differs from traditional forms of mnemonics — possibly those of Cicero, Quintilian and their offshoots — because it includes, in addition, a theory of noetic ascent to the One through memory. Seen from this hypothetical perspective, Bruno fuses two distinct traditions, the Neoplatonic doctrine of noetic ascent through a hierarchy of being, and the art of memory. This Neoplatonic element and his doctrine of memory derive, as we have seen, from Plotinus and Ficino.

Another aspect which corroborates Bruno's debt to Plotinus' doctrine of memory, is the role of sensibilia in Bruno's mnemonics. Their role is to gain access to the intelligible world: "Remember, therefore, that what we must examine is not those things that are in us, but the things themselves through those things which are in us. For although an image immediately manifest to the soul, we should direct our attention by looking, so to speak, not so much at it as through it."[62] Is Bruno here referring to the *phantasmata* produced by the Plotinian higher imagination, which articulate Ideas in Mind? If it is correct to read Bruno's idea of memory as at least partially derived from Plotinus', then Bruno's art of memory is not exclusively about retaining and combining retained sense experiences. It is, in addition, about the operations of the soul which summons the intelligible in the memory of the intellectual soul. This Bruno could have learnt from Plotinus' ambiguous notion of *phantasma*, which may derive from Ideas in Mind as well as from sensation, or simply be experienced unified in the harmonious soul.

---

[59] Bruno, *De umbris* §28.9-11, p. 31. Cf. Bruno, *Sigillus* ii 22, p. 213.21-27, as quoted on p. 55 n. 19 above.

[60] Bruno, *De umbris* §28.11-15, p. 31. For the relationship of this passage to the *Liber de causis*, see p. 116 n. 78 below.

[61] Bruno, *De umbris* §28.15-17, p. 31: "Porro si antiquitas novit quomodo proficiat memoria, a multis speciebus memorabilibus ad unam multorum memorabilium speciem se promovendo, ipsum certe non docuit."

[62] Bruno, *Sigillus* i 28, pp. 169.27-170.2: "Memento igitur, non ea quae sunt in nobis, sed res ipsas per ea quae sunt in nobis esse inspiciendas; quamvis enim animae praesens adsit imago, non tanquam ipsam, sed tamquam per ipsam aspicientes intendamus animo."

Bruno's treatment of the Golden Chain

Bruno's treatment of the Golden Chain in his mnemonic works supports the contention that he regards memory as a means of noetic ascent. In *De umbris* he states that "if you are able to ponder [with perhaps an obscene *double entendre*: "fondle"] that Golden Chain which is imagined to be stretched from heaven and right down to earth (just as descent from heaven is made possible through you), you will easily be able to return to heaven through an ordered [noetic] ascent."[63] He then presents a poem featuring the figures of the zodiac. This poem contains literary images and is called an 'artful connection', perhaps because the figures depicted from the zodiac are in physical contact with each other. For instance, the Ram hits Taurus with its head. Taurus, in turn, attacks the Twins, and so forth. It is a means of evoking in memory the metaphysical order, that 'Golden Chain', passing through man's soul. The 'artful connection', Bruno continues, established through the series of star constellations in the poem, greatly lightens the burden of memory.[64] Hence Bruno interprets the Golden Chain as a mnemonic device which facilitates noetic ascent.

The ultimate source of the expression 'Golden Chain' may well be the uses in Homer and the Neoplatonist Macrobius (fl. c. AD 400). Sturlese mentions the latter. But there is a more likely source, ignored by Sturlese and other Bruno scholars, namely, pseudo-Dionysius (c. AD 500), who interprets the Golden Chain as a symbol for prayer.[65] To pray, pseudo-Dionysius explains, is to climb up the Golden Chain extending from the highest heaven to earth.[66] Aquinas, Cusanus and Ficino were all familiar with this particular meaning of the Golden Chain as prayer. They all used the expression to describe some sort of noetic ascent towards

---

[63]   BRUNO, *De umbris* §34.2-7, p. 34: "Certe si ... cathenam illam auream quae e caelo fingitur ad terram usque tensa contrectare valebis, sicut e caelo per te potest factus esse descensus, facile ad caelum per ordinatum ascensum remeare valebis." See also ibid., §33.2-4, pp. 33-34.

[64]   Ibid., §34.8-10, p. 34: "Per hanc artificiosam connexionem magnum experiri possumus memoriae relevamen, quae valet etiam nullam ad invicem per se retinentia consequentiam memoriae ordinata presentare." For this role of the Golden Chain, see SPRUIT, *Il problema*, pp. 89-91. In *De compositione* Bruno adds two tables to the explanation of this poem. There the tables have twenty and twenty-four places respectively. They may have been intended to demonstrate how the poem could be used to memorise. Bruno does not explain how the poem relates to these tables; see BRUNO, *De compositione* III 6, pp. 295.8-296.4.

[65]   See Sturlese in BRUNO, *De umbris* §34.4, p. 34; STURLESE, 'Per un'interpretazione', p. 958. For the Golden Chain in Antiquity and the Middle Ages, see LOVEJOY, *The great chain*, p. 63; EDELSTEIN, 'The Golden Chain', pp. 48-66; LÉVÊQUE, *Aurea catena Homeri*.

[66]   PSEUDO-DIONYSIUS, *De nominibus divinis* iii 1, 680c (= 579a in the standard edition), in *Dionysiaca*, pp. 124-125, line A (tr. Ambrosius Traversari). For this source, see LÉVÊQUE, *Aurea catena Homeri*, pp. 44-45.

God through prayer.[67] Unlike to pseudo-Dionysius, Aquinas, Cusanus and Ficino, Bruno does not interpret the Golden Chain in his mnemonic works as a prayer through which it is possible to approach God. Nor does he say anything on this occasion about invoking the Trinity, as they had done. Nor does he identify the chain with Divine Providence, as, again, they had done. Bruno strips the metaphor of these orthodox connotations.

Instead, Bruno presents the poem featuring the figures of the zodiac. This poem is intended, he says, as a means to evoke in memory that metaphysical order — the Golden Chain — which passes through man's soul.[68] By using a poetic depiction of a chain of stars, Bruno follows, Sturlese argues, the usage of two sixteenth-century mnemonic treatises recommending readers to organise the things to be remembered in a 'chain', though not a Golden Chain.[69] In those two treatises the chain is a mnemonic device used to order mnemonic images into a series. Sturlese may be right, but there is an additional possibility, suggested by verbal similarity, that Bruno used Ficino's commentary on pseudo-Dionysius. This explains why Bruno speaks of the Golden Chain and not just the chain, as Sturlese's sources do.

In his *Explicatio* Bruno explains that the Golden Chain in *De umbris* has two related purposes, judgement, in the sense of understanding a metaphysical cause, and retention. He says about the first purpose:

In the thirteenth intention of the book *De umbris idearum* you have an explanation of the chain, which has two uses: [first,] it helps judgement itself since through this chain we know the cause of things, inasmuch as

---

[67] For the Golden Chain symbolising invocation by prayer, see AQUINAS, *In librum beati Dionysii De divinis nominibus expositio* iii 1, §§238-244, p. 76; CUSANUS, *Sermo vi*, §31.33-36, p. 115; FICINO, *In Dionysium Areopagitam De divinis nominibus* iii 1, p. 1049.10-37. BRUNO's comment on the Golden Chain in *De umbris* §34.2-7, p. 34, as quoted on p. 82 n. 63 above, resembles Ficino's commentary closely, though the verbal similarities are not conclusive. Cf. FICINO, *In Dionysium Areopagitam De divinis nominibus* iii 1, p. 1049.13-16: "Finge catenam variis contextam luminibus, quasi annulis per totum coelum diffusam, et ad terram usque porrectam, qualem Plato in decimo de Repub. fingit, qualem rursus apud Homerum, Iupiter Deos convocans per coelum proiicit, promittitque sursum se tracturum quicquid catenam apprehenderit, se vero trahi non posse deorsum." SPRUIT, *Il problema*, p. 90 n. 176, refers Bruno's comment on the Golden Chain to this passage in Ficino's commentary, and to Macrobius' Neoplatonic use. For the use of pseudo-Dionysius among Renaissance authors, see MONFASANI, 'Pseudo-Dionysius the Areopagite in mid-quatrocento Rome', pp. 189-219.

[68] BRUNO, *De umbris* §34.8-10, p. 34.

[69] ROMBERCH, *Congestorium artificiose memorie* iii 15, fol. 66ʳ: "cathenam dicimus"; SPANGENBERG, *Artificiosae memoriae libellus in usum studiosorum collectus*, sig. B4ᵛ: "De colligantia sive catena", both cited by Sturlese in BRUNO, *De umbris* §§34-35, pp. 34-35. According to Sturlese, Romberch and Spangenberg follow QUINTILIAN, *Institutio oratoria* XI ii 20, where he speaks of concatenation "like dancers hand in hand" (*chorus*).

contemplating the levels of beings in a definite order, we understand the true and distinctive essence of each thing placed, so to speak, in a centre.[70]

The Golden Chain, then, is a mnemonic device for joining entities in a scale of being, helping us to understand the "cause of things". In the *Sigillus* Bruno similarly speaks of noetic ascent as an intellectual movement upwards in a hierarchy of causes, ultimately aiming at an understanding of one single and first cause.[71] The "essence of each thing" is, Bruno says in the quotation above, "placed in a centre". Further, the scale of being set out by means of the Golden Chain, Bruno goes on in the quotation above, is continuous. He says this by speaking about the levels of being as if they are a series of interlocked rings, where the top of the relatively lower level touches the bottom of the level above it.[72]

As Bruno says in the *De umbris*, the Golden Chain is not only a means of joining entities in a scale of being. It is also a means of noetic ascent.[73] When describing return towards the One, he latches on to the image of the continuous grades of being and explains that this return takes place by means of a "contracted similitude", that is, by turning away from things on the same ontological level as ourselves and assimilating ourselves to higher ontological levels.[74] Accordingly, he says, a person who is able to conceive the "order with its levels" with his or her mind, will "contract" a "similitude" of the macrocosm, different from the one that he has by nature.[75] In the last chapter we saw how Bruno regards the contraction of *intentiones* as a means of ascending noetically. These *intentiones* he identifies with reasons (*rationes*) and shadows of Ideas (*umbrae idearum*).[76] In his last comment in *De umbris* on the Golden Chain he makes clear that the concatenation set out in

---

[70] BRUNO, *Explicatio*, p. 123.18-23: "Catenae explicationem habes in intentione decimatertia libri *De umbris idearum* [= §§34-35, pp. 34-35], quae quidem dupliciter usuvenire valet, utpote ad ipsum iudicium, cum per hanc rerum habeamus rationem, qua certa serie gradus entium contemplantes intelligamus veram distinctamque cuiusque essentiam veluti in centro quodam esse consistentem". VASOLI, 'Umanesimo e simbologia', p. 294, gives a passing commentary on this passage; CLUCAS, '*Amorem*', pp. 10-13, argues that this comment in Bruno's *Explicatio* elucidates the idea of "concatenation" in its parallel ontological, noetic and logical senses.

[71] BRUNO, *Sigillus* ii 22, pp. 213.21-214.6, as quoted on p. 55 n. 19 above.

[72] BRUNO, *Explicatio*, p. 123.23-27. In BRUNO, *De umbris* §36.4, 6, pp. 35, 36, Bruno uses the expression "rings" (*annuli*) about the scale of being set out through the Golden Chain, ibid., §§34-35, pp. 34-35.

[73] BRUNO, *De umbris* §34.2-7, p. 34.

[74] Ibid., §29.2-4, p. 32: "Ad proximius quidem superius proximum inferius per aliquos gradus contracta similitudine promovetur, quos certe gradus cum nactum fuerit omnes, iam non simile, sed idem cum illo dicendum erit." 'Similitude' is also employed in BRUNO, *Furori* i 5, p. 225, as quoted on p. 62 n. 49 above, where Bruno explains the human soul's preparations for noetic ascent.

[75] BRUNO, *De umbris* §55.9-12, p. 48: "Quem ordinem cum suis gradibus qui mente conceperit, similitudinem magni mundi contrahet aliam ab ea quam secundum naturam habet in se ipso." For this comparison, see also ibid., §30.2-5, p. 32.

[76] BRUNO, *De compositione* I i 1, p. 94.14-18, as quoted on p. 60 n. 40 above.

the Golden Chain may take place in regard to shadows of Ideas.[77] Hence there is some reason to believe that the kind of noetic interpretation of contraction dealt with in the preceding chapter — focusing on the *Sigillus* and the *Eroici furori* — is reflected in Bruno's treatment of memory in *De umbris*. If interpreted in this manner, the first purpose of the Golden Chain in *De umbris* is to facilitate contemplation leading to the soul's ascent into the intelligible realm. This interpretation agrees with Bruno's comment in *De umbris* that the reader should ascend noetically through Plotinus' "ladder" (*schala*).[78]

Read in this way, Bruno has presented a natural rather than supernatural, interpretation of the Golden Chain. He is leaving behind the idea that the Golden Chain depends on prayer to, and elevation by, God, as found in the thoughts of pseudo-Dionysius, Aquinas, Cusanus and Ficino. Instead, he is transforming it into a metaphor of a mental activity exclusively involving human faculties. Human understanding, Bruno holds, can represent the order of nature poetically by the Golden Chain, and this understanding is to be regarded, if my interpretation of Bruno's comments on the Golden Chain in the *De umbris* is correct, as a form of noetic ascent.

Bruno's original treatment of the metaphor of the Golden Chain is also in agreement with his rejection of the "magic of the desperate", the "desperate" being those who strive to invoke "gods, demons and heroes" through "prayers, consecrations, fumigations, sacrifices, dress of certain kinds and ceremonies". These "desperate" people become "receptacles and instruments" of the intruding god or demon or hero, thus appearing "wise", but only until a drug is taken and they return to their former, uninspired selves.[79] For Bruno, Christian prayer is, therefore, an example of magic of this kind.

Leaving aside this implicit polemic in Bruno's treatment of the Golden Chain, his presentation of it in *De umbris* remains problematic. He claims that the ontological structure of being and the nature of noetic ascent coincide.[80] But how does he ensure such a coincidence, if the chain is only a mnemonic device, constructed apparently without bothering about the ontological structure? Sturlese's solution, that the mnemonics of *De umbris* is reducible to a mental experimentation with letters whose relationships are "arbitrary signs" (*segni arbitrari*), does not fit Bruno's frequent assurances that ontological descent

---

[77] BRUNO, *De umbris* §36.2-5, p. 35: "Ascensus quidem qui fit per connexa atque concathenata, in proposito umbrarum idealium, non est per cathenam similibus constantem annulis, ratione quae concipitur ex proxime dictis, atque deinceps enunciandis."

[78] Ibid., §72.2-7, p. 56.

[79] BRUNO, *De magia naturali* §2.17-24, p. 162 (= *BOL*, vol. 3, p. 398.8-16), as quoted on p. 68 n. 82 above. See also the parallel criticism in the fourteenth contraction in BRUNO, *Sigillus* i 48, p. 191.17-21, described on pp. 22-23 above.

[80] BRUNO, *De umbris* §34.2-7, p. 34. For other references to Bruno's conception of the unified nature of descent and noetic ascent, see p. 1 n. 2 above.

follows the same pattern in reverse as noetic ascent.[81] Indeed Bruno states this in his *De umbris*.[82] On the other hand, as Sturlese points out, in *De umbris* Bruno underlines that the only criterion for the selection of star images is a conventional one, namely whether or not individual use of the memory system can associate personal passions to the images.[83]

However, in order to do justice to Bruno's own words about a unified nature of descent and noetic ascent, we may look out for another answer to the puzzle concerning the role of the mnemonic images in *De umbris*. Is another answer, then, to be found in Bruno's conception of memory? Memory does not depend solely on sense data, but also entails that the structure of reality is somehow present in human memory, albeit not necessarily contemplated actively. The answer, or one answer, may be here. Memory's experimentation, even with "arbitrary signs", as Sturlese calls them, may open up the contemplation of an ontological structure which, although subjectively discovered, has an independent and objective existence.[84] Such an interpretation would make Bruno's claim of a unified nature of descent and noetic ascent comprehensible.

---

[81] STURLESE, 'Introduzione', p. LXXI. STURLESE, 'Arte della natura e arte della memoria in Giordano Bruno', pp. 130-131, qualifies this view by saying that the inventions with signs in Bruno's mnemonics are not completely arbitrary, but must be ordered into a system which is an "efficacious organism" (*organismo efficace*) in a rhetorical delivery. For the inventions of such an "efficacious organism" must be able to please or impress the reader or the listener. Sturlese's general line of interpretation, denuding signs in Bruno's mnemonic works of ontological references, is followed by DAGRON, *Unité de l'être et dialectique*, p. 8 n. 2.

[82] BRUNO, *De umbris* §34.2-7, p. 34.

[83] STURLESE, 'Introduzione', p. LXXII n. 82, where Sturlese points out BRUNO, *De umbris* §164.2-9, p. 122. The same point is made in STURLESE, 'Per un'unterpretazione', p. 955. We could add in support of Sturlese's interpretation that Bruno states on one occasion that the images employed by him in *De umbris* are only intended as a proposal; see BRUNO, *De umbris* §159.4-6, p. 117; and similarly ibid., §§210.3, 222.15-19, pp. 159, 175). This weakens Yates' thesis about an astrological correspondence between star image and star. See Yates' analysis of the practice of the mnemonic images in Bruno's *De umbris*, in YATES, *Giordano Bruno and the Hermetic tradition*, pp. 195-199; *The art of memory*, pp. 199-224. For Sturlese's criticism of Yates, and her alternative analysis of the role of these mnemonic images, see STURLESE, 'Introduzione', pp. LVI-LXXIII; 'Per un'interpretazione', pp. 946-955. For further criticism of Yates' interpretation of Bruno as a Hermeticist, see WESTMAN, 'Magical reform', pp. 1-91; ROSSI, 'Hermeticism', pp. 247-273; COPENHAVER, 'Natural magic, Hermeticism, and occultism in early modern science', pp. 261-290, especially pp. 261-265, 282, 289-290. See also the criticism of Yates' conception of Pico as a magician indebted to what she conceives as Ficinian or Hermetic magic, in FARMER, 'Introductory monograph', pp. 115-132.

[84] Apart from the references in the mnemonic works already given to support this interpretation, we also find Bruno stating his belief in innate ideas corresponding to the ontological structure as it is defined through contraction; see BRUNO, *Acrotismus*, pp. 93.19-94.3: "Cum vero in sequenti parte dicit [Aristotle], innatam esse nobis viam, ex notioribus nobis, ad notiora naturae: unde ab universalibus, confusis, hoc est universis, totis, confusis, contractis, compactis, indistinctis, veluti commixtis, ad particularia,

Bruno's doctrine of noetic ascent through memory, presented in this chapter, agrees to a large extent with his account of the fifteen contractions in the *Sigillus* in the first chapter. In his account of the fifteen contractions Bruno described and criticised at considerable length noetic ascent facilitated through food and melancholy (contractions eleven, twelve and fourteen). Noetic ascent, he said in the fourteenth contraction, may be initiated by melancholy, but is not dependent on it. Likewise, Bruno dismissed the role of emotions in his account of noetic ascent (contractions five to eight). Noetic ascent through memory, which Bruno favours, clearly has nothing to do with misguided contractions of these kinds. Nor, it should be admitted, does Bruno mention noetic ascent through memory in his accounts of the first and the fifteenth contractions, in which he praises the solitary man and the contemplative philosopher respectively. His praise of these two types of men, nevertheless, conforms with his Neoplatonically inspired account of memory as a means of noetic ascent inasmuch as the activity of memory is a contemplative act, possibly also a solitary one. There are, besides, several other Neoplatonic elements in Bruno's account of the fifteen contractions. In the third contraction (*contractio horizontis in centrum*) Bruno drew on Neoplatonic sources, in particular Plotinus and the *Liber de causis*. In the theoretical account of noetic ascent introducing the fifteen contractions in the *Sigillus*, as explained on pp. 24-25 above, and in the account of noetic ascent through memory, we also find Neoplatonic sources, Plotinus again being conspicuous. Plotinus' idea of noetic ascent through the intellectual soul's memory, and indeed Bruno's familiarity with his doctrine of memory, may explain why Bruno regarded memory as a powerful means of noetic ascent, and possibly why he wrote several mnemonic treatises.

---

partes, simplicia, distincta, absoluta, pura, immixta, a consideratione videlicet et contemplatione per modum contractionis et impuritatis, ad contemplationem absoluti, solius, nudi, atque puri." Although VASOLI, 'Umanesimo e simbologia', p. 275, does not take the possibility of a Plotinian notion of memory into consideration in relation to Bruno's mnemonics, I agree, at least in principle, with him when he states about the relationship between sensible mnemonic images and the intelligible reality which they must evoke: "la mnemotecnica deve offrire il modo di apprendere in immagini intuitive anche le supreme verità sensibili e di racchiudere nei limiti dell'ordine imposto ai suoi elementi la stessa architettura schematica dell'intero universo."

PART TWO
SOURCES OF BRUNO'S CONCEPT OF
CONTRACTION

Chapter 5

Physiologically Induced Contraction

Ficino's notion of physiologically induced contraction

Bruno discusses melancholy, as we have seen in Chapters 1 and 3, as a form of physiologically induced contraction in the soul in the *Sigillus* and in the *Eroici furori*. Where does this come from? Yates and Ingegno have interpreted Ficino as a source.[1] In this chapter I shall outline Ficino's theory of physiologically induced contraction as a means of noetic ascent, and discuss Yates and Ingegno's interpretation.

The term 'contraction' occurs in a physiological sense in classical Latin. The Latin noun *contractio* derives from the verb *contraho*, ultimately deriving from the verb *traho*. It denotes a process of drawing together or compressing. In Cicero we find the physiological meaning of the term, for instance "a contraction of the nerves (of the parts of the body)" (*contractio nervorum* [*membrorum*]), or simply *contractio*, denoting a bodily contraction.[2] This meaning also occurs in Biblical Latin.[3]

In classical Latin a psychological meaning of contraction occurs, e.g. *contractio animi*, designating dejection or depression. Cicero also used 'contraction' with this last meaning.[4] Similarly he used the diminutive *contractiuncula* to denote a slight mental depression.[5] 'Contraction' or its cognates were used in this sense by different medieval authors. An example is Augustine, who, in a work about instructing pagans in Christian doctrine, advised the preacher to rid himself of gloomy moods in order to appear joyful to the audience.[6]

I shall now pass on from these uses of 'contraction' in classical Latin to another use which is far more important to my argument, namely Ficino's use of the term in one of his accounts of noetic ascent. Our starting point is the classical and medieval physiological theory of the four humours, deriving from Galen (129-199), among others. In Ficino's interpretation of it, the humour melancholy and the contraction of *spiritus* that it induced became a central theme in his conception

---

[1]   For Yates' interpretation, see the references on p. 93 n. 18 below. For Ingegno's interpretation, see the references on p. 95 n. 34 below.

[2]   For examples of this use, see CICERO, *Pro Sestio* viii 19; *De natura deorum* II lx 150; *De officiis* I xli 146.

[3]   1 Liber Samuhelis 14.19.

[4]   CICERO, *Tusculanae disputationes* I xxxvii 90; ibid., IV vi 14.

[5]   Ibid., III xxxiv 83.

[6]   AUGUSTINE, *De catechizandis rudibus liber unus* x 14, cols 321-322.

of noetic ascent. Ficino gave an original treatment of melancholy in *De vita*, finished for publication in 1489.[7] The aim of *De vita* is how to care for one's health. The first book is dedicated to the care and health of learned people; the second gives advice about how to obtain a long life; and the third is a combination of the two, about obtaining a life both healthy and long.[8] The theme of melancholy is treated in the first book (most importantly in Chapters 2-6); its celestial procurator, Saturn, is described in the third book.

In the first book of *De vita*, Ficino defines *spiritus* as an instrument for learned people's intellectual labour. *Spiritus* is "a vapour of blood — pure, subtle, hot and clear."[9] Through the blood's motion in the body, *spiritus* is distributed to the entire body, including the brain, and is used by the soul in the exercise of the interior and exterior senses.[10] As vapour from the blood, *spiritus* is a semi-corporeal and a semi-incorporeal link between soul and body.[11]

Spiritus affects the lower faculties, not the higher faculties of the soul such as *imaginatio*, *ratio* and *mens*.[12] However, *spiritus* may encourage imagination, and thereby provide an initial stimulus for discursive reasoning, which in turn may stimulate mind's non-discursive contemplation.[13] In *De vita* Ficino associates this *spiritus* of the individual with cosmic spirit (*spiritus mundi*).[14] Cosmic spirit is the fifth element, which Ficino sometimes calls aether, penetrating the entire universe. It thus provides the medium whereby the superlunary stars and planets, or more precisely their rays, influence the sublunary world,[15] and notably for present

---

[7]   On Ficino's theory of melancholy, see KLIBANSKY et al., *Saturn and melancholy*, pp. 254-274; WALKER, *Spiritual and demonic magic*, pp. 4-5; KRISTELLER, *Il pensiero filosofico di Marsilio Ficino*, pp. 225-228.

[8]   FICINO, *De vita* prooemium, lines 25-32, pp. 102-104.

[9]   Ibid., i 2.11-13, p. 110: "Instrumentum eiusmodi spiritus ipse est, qui apud medicos vapor quidam sanguinis purus, subtilis, calidus et lucidus definitur." For Ficino's notion of *spiritus*, see WALKER, *Spiritual and demonic magic*, pp. 3-6, 10, 12-13, 25-27, 38-40, 44-48, 76.

[10] FICINO, *De vita* i 2.13-15, p. 110: "Atque ab ipso cordis calore ex subtiliori sanguine procreatus volat ad cerebrum; ibique animus ipso ad sensus tam interiores quam exteriores exercendos assidue utitur." For the notion of *spiritus* employed here, see WALKER, 'The astral body', p. 120. For the inner and outer faculties of the senses, see also PARK, 'The organic soul', pp. 465-469.

[11] KLIBANSKY et al., *Saturn and melancholy*, p. 265.

[12] FICINO, *De vita* iii 22.1-44, pp. 362-364. For *imaginatio*, *ratio* and *mens* in Ficino's *De vita*, see KLIBANSKY et al., *Saturn and melancholy*, pp. 265-266. For the relationship between *imaginatio*, *ratio* and *mens* in Ficino's *Theologia platonica*, see VASOLI, 'La *ratio* nella filosofia di Marsilio Ficino', pp. 223-224.

[13] For the relationship between *imaginatio* and *spiritus*, see FICINO, *De vita* iii 22.18-31, p. 364. Similarly ibid., iii 22.4-11, p. 362 (the "vapores", mentioned ibid., iii 22.7, p. 362, can be *spiritus* as defined in the passage ibid., i 2.11-13, p. 110, as quoted on p. 92 n. 9 above). For *imaginatio* in Ficino's thought, see WALKER, *Spiritual and demonic magic*, pp. 6, 15, 21.

[14] For Ficino on *spiritus mundi*, see WALKER, *Spiritual and demonic magic*, pp. 8, 12-13, 16, 22-23, 32-34, 45, 47-48, 52-53.

[15] Ibid., pp. 12-13.

purposes, an individual's *spiritus*.[16] The superlunary aether (superlunary fire), by virtue of the celestial region's motion, mixes with the air in the sublunary region, which thereby becomes heated, making what is traditionally called sublunary fire. There is thus a continuum between superlunary fire (air warmed and mixed with aether) and air. Animals' bodies, including human bodies, produce *spiritus* partly through inhaling and purifying air, and partly from digesting food, etc.[17] This doctrine of *spiritus* provided the foundation of Ficino's idea of magic.[18] Moreover, the *spiritus* of the human body can also be exposed to the influence of certain stars by pursuing deeds governed by those stars. Contemplation, for instance, makes the soul susceptible to Saturn.[19] Lastly, each of the three faculties in the human soul — *imaginatio*, *ratio* and *mens* — can be brought in tune with the influence of various stars, and thereby aided through sympathy.[20]

This theoretical framework will help us understand Ficino's comments about contraction in other works. He uses the word in two senses. He uses it, first, in a noetic (i.e. mystical) sense. In Ficino's letter to Lorenzo dei Medici, already cited in Chapter 3, he affirms that affective understanding is superior to intellectual understanding of God. By intellectual understanding "we contract", that is, we limit, "His [God's] greatness according to the capacity and comprehension of our mind (*mens*)".[21] The second sense occurs in Ficino's account of the humours. Humours, that is, corporeal fluids, can affect *spiritus* directly and thereby indirectly affect the function of interior and exterior senses. Besides taking care of the *spiritus*, learned people should also look after their humours, Ficino says in *De vita*. Here he builds on the physiological doctrine of Hippocrates (ca. 460-370 BC) and Galen about the four humours: *sanguis* (pure blood), *phlegma* or *pituita*

---

[16]   FICINO, *De vita* iii 2.89-94, iii 22.108-115, pp. 254, 368.

[17]   Ibid., iii 3.1-42, iii 4.1-69, pp. 255-257, 259-263. For this theme, see WALKER, *Spiritual and demonic magic*, pp. 12-13.

[18]   FICINO, *De vita* iii 26.49-63, 77-84, pp. 386, 388. Yates regarded *spiritus* and cosmic spirit as fundamental to Ficino's magic, which she conceived of as inseparable from Hermeticism; see YATES, *Giordano Bruno and the Hermetic tradition*, pp. 11-83. In her interpretation of mnemonic images as magical, cosmic spirit is considered central; see YATES, *The art of memory*, pp. 155-159. For an account of the relationship between *spiritus* and cosmic spirit in Ficino's thought, see INGEGNO, *Cosmologia*, pp. 126-142. Ingegno claims, like Yates, that Bruno adopted Ficino's conception of *spiritus* and cosmic spirit and the relationship between them (ibid., pp. 160-167). COPENHAVER, 'Scholastic philosophy and Renaissance magic in the *De vita* of Marsilio Ficino', pp. 525-530, argues that Galen is the source to Ficino's idea of stones preparing the human *spiritus* for reception of celestial influence (FICINO, *De vita* iii 12.28-31, pp. 298-300 [= *Opera*, p. 547.2-5]). Yates' interpretation of Ficino's magic as founded on Hermeticism has been criticised by Copenhaver, who instead suggests scholastic and Neoplatonic sources as the theoretical backbone of Ficino's magic; see COPENHAVER, 'Renaissance magic and Neoplatonic philosophy', pp. 351-369; 'Iamblichus, Synesius and the Chaldean oracles', pp. 441-455.

[19]   FICINO, *De vita* iii 2.67-72, p. 252.

[20]   WALKER, *Spiritual and demonic magic*, pp. 14-16.

[21]   FICINO, *Le lettere*, 1.115.181-185, as quoted on p. 63 n. 56 above.

(phlegm), *cholera* (red bile, also called yellow bile), and *atra bilis* (black bile) or *melancholia*.[22] The movement of humours, which may affect the *spiritus*, is described by Ficino as a contraction. When discussing noetic ascent in his *Theologia platonica*, he presents various ways in which the mind can free itself from the body in order to ascend towards God. He asserts of one of them that it "derives from the contraction of melancholy, which separates the soul from external affairs, so that the soul is just as disengaged in a man who is awake as it normally happens at some time in a man when he is asleep."[23] Seen in isolation, this statement suggests that noetic ascent depends on the contraction of melancholic humours. However, Ficino is careful to avoid such a conclusion in *De vita*. He states that *spiritus*, which can be affected by humours, may trigger imagination and thereby indirectly the higher faculties (reason and mind), but that mind's contemplation of the divine is not reducible to the effect of *spiritus*.[24] Whether Ficino's account is consistent on this score is open to debate.

The humour melancholy was of particular interest to Ficino, since it was essential to intellectual work. According to the pseudo-Aristotelian *Problemata* "all those who have excelled in whatever faculty, have been melancholics".[25] Plato agreed, Ficino held, since he stated in the *Theaetetus* that intelligent people were prone to exuberant excitement and frenzy (*furor*).[26] Democritus (ca. 460-357 BC) also concurred, Ficino holds.[27] "Our Plato", Ficino adds, seems to have asserted in *Phaedrus* that "without madness (*furor*) one knocks at the doors of poetry in vain". Most importantly, Ficino asserts, this Platonic frenzy occurs only in melancholics.[28] Here Ficino translates the Greek word for frenzy, μανία, as *furor*. However, in the passage from the *Phaedrus*, Plato did not identify μανία with

---

[22]   For the classical doctrine of humours, see KLIBANSKY et al., *Saturn and melancholy*, pp. 3-15. For its later adaptations, see SIRAISI, *Medieval and early Renaissance medicine*, pp. 104-109.

[23]   FICINO, *Theologia platonica* xiii 2, vol. 2, p. 219.22-25: "Tertius vacationis modus fit ex melancholici humoris contractione animam ab externis negotiis sevocantis, ut anima tam cavet [or rather 'vacet' as in *Opera*, p. 294.27] homine vigilante, quam solet dormiente quandoque vacare." AGRIPPA, *De occulta philosophia* iii 55, p. 567.24-28, followed Ficino's observation. The statement of Ficino is noted by Ingegno (see references on p. 100 n. 61 below). I shall discuss Ingegno's use of this statement on pp. 100-101 below.

[24]   See pp. 91-93 above.

[25]   FICINO, *De vita* i 5.3-5, p. 116: "Quod quidem confirmat in libro *Problematum* Aristoteles, omnes enim inquit viros in quavis facultate praestantes melancholicos extitisse." For the source, see PSEUDO-ARISTOTLE, *Problemata* xxx 1 953a10-19.

[26]   FICINO, *De vita* i 5.5-7, p. 116: "Qua in re Platonicum illud quod in libro *De scientia* scribitur confirmavit, ingeniosos videlicet plurimum concitatos furiososque esse solere." Clark and Kaske cite PLATO, *Theaetetus* 144A5-B2.

[27]   FICINO, *De vita* i 5.7-8, p. 116.

[28]   Ibid., i 5.8-12, p. 116: "Quod quidem Plato noster in *Phaedro* [245A1-8] probare videtur, dicens poeticas fores frustra absque furore pulsari. Etsi divinum furorem hic forte intelligi vult, tamen neque furor eiusmodi apud physicos aliis unquam ullis praeterquam melancholicis incitatur."

melancholy. The connection between the two was probably invented by Ficino, who hoped thereby to unite the Platonic doctrine of divine inspiration with the physiological theory of the humours.[29]

Ficino mentions three physical causes for the state of *furor*, namely celestial, natural and human. At birth the celestial influence from the planets Saturn and Mercury induces a melancholic nature, since both produce something "cold and dry" in us. For those not born under these celestial circumstances, or for those wanting to enhance such a privileged birth, the two other causes — natural and human — can be supplied by intellectual labour, particularly philosophy.[30] These natural and human causes also imply, however, that the learned should take precautions not to succumb to physical pleasures that might withdraw the soul from the desired state of a tempered melancholy.[31]

Such a powerful theory of melancholy was naturally entangled with Ficino's solution to the Neoplatonic question of the relation between the 'one' and the 'many', especially his notion of noetic ascent towards unity, in which the influence of Saturn was important.[32]

Bruno's criticism of physiologically induced contraction

Bruno uses the term 'contraction' in a physiological sense, above all in the fifteen contractions of the *Sigillus*.[33] Some Bruno scholars, notably Ingegno, equate Ficino's physiological interpretation of contraction with contraction in the strictly noetic sense in Bruno's philosophy, i.e. the idea that the philosopher can ascend through the ontological hierarchy to the purely intelligible realm.[34] As we have seen, in some of Ficino's works contractions of this kind are employed to explain noetic ascent, namely through physiologically contracted humours, especially black bile, or melancholy. Bruno employs 'contraction' in this physiological sense too, but the critical question is whether or not Bruno regards such physiological contraction as sufficient to ascend noetically, and which theological framework he employs it in.

---

[29]   KLIBANSKY et al., *Saturn and melancholy*, p. 259.

[30]   FICINO, *De vita* i 4.22-48, p. 114.

[31]   Ibid., i 7, pp. 122-128.

[32]   E.g. FICINO, *Theologia platonica* xviii 5, vol. 3, pp. 196-197.

[33]   BRUNO, *Sigillus* i 45, i 46, i 48, pp. 187.15-189.14, 189.15-190.18, 191.6-192.5; *De magia naturali* §2.17-30, p. 162 (= *BOL*, vol. 3, p. 398.8-22); *De principiis* §41.1-6, p. 634 (= *BOL*, vol. 3, p. 530.5-11).

[34]   INGEGNO, *Cosmologia*, pp. 251-256, especially p. 251; *La sommersa nave*, pp. 90-91; *Regia pazzia*, pp. 133-143, especially p. 133 n. 71. Ingegno's identification is reaffirmed in MANCINI, *La sfera infinita*, p. 67 n. 152, but rejected in SPRUIT, *Il problema*, pp. 141 n. 118, 148-149. STURLESE, 'Le fonti', p. 116, follows Ingegno's general assertion that the fifteen contractions in the *Sigillus* (i 35-49) are inspired by Ficino. STURLESE, 'Le fonti', p. 144, also follows Ingegno when she points out FICINO, *Theologia platonica* xiii 2, vol. 2, p. 215.8-18, as the source for BRUNO, *Sigillus* i 45, p. 187.16-21.

In the fifteen contractions in the *Sigillus*, Bruno criticises the kind of contraction facilitated by black bile or melancholy (the second, eleventh and fourteenth). He reinforces his criticism in the fourteenth contraction, where he speaks of the intrusion of a foreign spirit, produced by an excessive concentration of melancholy. However, it should be remembered that Bruno does not mention Ficino's theory of *spiritus* or melancholy in these three contractions. He may be thinking of later adaptations of Ficino's theories of *spiritus* and melancholy or, just possibly, ones independent of Ficino.

What is, by comparison, Bruno's view of the relationship between spiritual ascent and melancholy? His treatment of contraction in this sense, as we have seen in Chapters 1 and 3, shows that, although Bruno was very critical of noetic ascent facilitated solely through melancholy, he does not entirely exclude the physiological theory from his account of noetic ascent. For, as he says in the eleventh contraction, even "more noble souls" who manage to contemplate the divine can be assisted by melancholy. However, their success is not due to their melancholy, but to their superior intellect. Similarly, those who fail to undertake such contemplation do so because of their inferior intellectual capacity. In itself melancholy is insufficient, although it can provide a starting point of contemplation if well balanced. Intellect, on the other hand, is paramount in Bruno.[35] In this way, then, the noetic and physiological meanings of contraction denote related rather than distinct concepts.

Ficino's account in *De vita* of the relationship between *spiritus*, on one hand, and the higher faculties of the soul, on the other, could be described similarly.[36] Hence Bruno's criticism may not be directed against Ficino, but against those who employed a theory of *spiritus* and melancholy like the one presented by Ficino. In particular Bruno's criticism may aim at those who had adapted Ficino's physiological theory of melancholy but ignored its philosophical setting. Ficino may even have been aware of this danger himself, for on one occasion he warns his reader, that Saturn will be "most hostile" to those charlatans who simulate a contemplative life but do not practise it.[37]

Bruno's view of balanced melancholy, as necessary but insufficient unless aided by intellectual powers, is maintained in the *Lampas triginta statuarum*. There melancholy is regarded in relation to cognition.[38] In this context Bruno does not speak explicitly about noetic ascent towards the One, but he does mention the interior and exterior faculties, all of which relate to noetic ascent as he describes it

---

[35]   BRUNO, *Sigillus* i 45, p. 189.6-14, as quoted on p. 19 n. 60 above.

[36]   See pp. 91-93 above.

[37]   FICINO, *De vita* iii 22.39-41, p. 364: "Nullis vero Saturnus est infensior quam hominibus contemplativam vitam simulantibus quidem nec agentibus."

[38]   BRUNO, *Lampas* §242.1-3, p. 1226 (= *BOL*, vol. 3, p. 140.14-16): "Igitur cognitionis ratio dependet a ratione naturalis complexionis, quae naturali et Saturniae melancholiae regulatae tribuitur." Similarly in BRUNO, *De compendiosa architectura* i 4, p. 7.13-16: "Materialis causa, quam brevibus exponam, temperatior Saturnii cuiusdam habitus extitit melancholia, in qua residens spiritus, aptius se praebet animo ad opus contemplationis instrumentum".

elsewhere. Among the faculties whose function depends on melancholy, we thus find an ordered series of faculties, namely, sensation (*sensus visus* and *sensus auditus*), imagination (*phantasia*), reason (*ratio*), intellect (*intellectus*) and mind (*mens*).[39] Bruno refers to some of these five faculties in his description of noetic ascent in the *Sigillus*, though without mentioning melancholy as starting point for their work.[40]

Reason builds, Bruno says in the *Lampas triginta statuarum*, on sensation but turns sense impressions into concepts.[41] Intellect intuits in a simple "contracted" vision what reason discerns in a fragmented way.[42] This role of intellect and its contraction is similar to Bruno's description of noetic ascent in the *Eroici furori*.[43] Mind, Bruno continues in the *Lampas triginta statuarum*, is the culmination of cognition progressing from sensation to intellect.[44] It is, he says elsewhere, an intuition like that of intellect, but unlike that of intellect it is not based on an immediate conception of reason's discursive work.[45]

From this passage in the *Lampas triginta statuarum* we may gather that Bruno — even though he does not explicitly relate these faculties to the Neoplatonic scheme of hypostases there — regards melancholy and the contractions it induces as a starting point for the human soul's ascent to Mind. Melancholy, if balanced, provides the initial impulse, which is complemented by the work of sensation, imagination, reason, intellect and mind. Here intellect's contraction of concepts is distinct from the contraction induced by melancholy, although these two senses of contraction are related, namely inasmuch as the latter may provide an initial stimulus to the former. From this distinction we can make sense of Bruno's criticism of the second, eleventh and fourteenth contractions in the *Sigillus*, since they are based exclusively on the effects of physiologically induced contractions.

The last part of soul's movement towards the One is not completed by the rational faculties, but is the One which comes to the human soul, commonly described as ecstasy. In the *Lampas triginta statuarum* Bruno also lists ecstasy as a state dependent upon the initial impulse of melancholy, adding, on this occasion, that in such a state the human being is brought out of the sense world and driven

---

[39] BRUNO, *Lampas* §243.1-19, pp. 1228-1230 (= *BOL*, vol. 3, pp. 140.24-141.17). There is a parallel description of *ratio*, *intellectus* and *mens* in BRUNO, *Summa*, p. 32.1-28.

[40] Some of these faculties are listed in BRUNO, *Sigillus* i 31, p. 172.18-23. Their respective roles in noetic ascent are described ibid., i 31-34, pp. 172.23-180.18, as described on pp. 24-25 above.

[41] BRUNO, *Lampas* §243.11-13, p. 1228 (= *BOL*, vol. 3, p. 141.9-11).

[42] Ibid., §243.14-17, p. 1230 (= *BOL*, vol. 3, p. 141.12-15): "Est intellectus, qui est vel habitus verificationum per discursum acquisitarum, vel est simplex apprehensio et aperta quaedam visio atque contracta eorum quae per rationem veluti dispersim et disgregatim coniiciuntur."

[43] See BRUNO, *Furori* i 3, p. 137, as quoted on p. 61 nn. 44 and 46 above; ibid., i 4, p. 155. Similarly in BRUNO, *Infinito* i, p. 61, as quoted on p. 79 n. 51 above.

[44] BRUNO, *Lampas* §243.18-19, p. 1230 (= *BOL*, vol. 3, p. 141.16-17).

[45] BRUNO, *Summa*, p. 32.19-28.

towards the intelligible world.[46] This description of ecstasy as a noetic ascent from the sensible world into the intelligible world resembles that of Iamblichus' contemplation in the *Eroici furori*, the possible model of the fifteen contractions.[47] However, Bruno does not use the term 'ecstasy' there.[48]

Finally, faith, understood as philosophical and not as theological faith, is also related to melancholy in the *Lampas triginta statuarum*.[49] As we have seen in Chapter 1, Bruno's preference for philosophical faith over theological faith, that is, for human experience over Scripture and revelation, is important to his conception of noetic ascent.[50] He uses the theory of melancholy and of physiologically contracted humours to subvert Christian theology. This theological framework of Bruno was foreign to Ficino's ideas of noetic ascent, since Ficino claimed that faith, in the traditional theological sense, we may assume, is a prerequisite of noetic ascent.[51]

Although, therefore, Bruno and Ficino use the theory of melancholy for quite different purposes, we may assume that Ficino, and possibly Agrippa, were among Bruno's sources for his theory of melancholy. Bruno does not acknowledge Ficino as a source in this context, but this proves little. His widespread, if unacknowledged, use of Ficino's works is well known.[52]

Interpretations of Bruno's fifteen contractions in the *Sigillus sigillorum*

Mersenne was among the first to attack Bruno's infinite and heterodox cosmology on the grounds that it led to irreligion and deism. He did so in his *L'impiété des déistes* from 1624. It is less known that in the same work Mersenne also attacked the fifteen contractions in Bruno's *Sigillus*, reporting each contraction and stating his criticism of the first five contractions in strong terms. Bruno's treatment of miracles, raptures, prophecies, revelations, faith and imagination in these five

---

[46]   BRUNO, *Lampas* §245.1-4, p. 1232 (= *BOL*, vol. 3, p. 142.3-6): "Est estasis, upote facultas ad extrahendum a sensibus, a praesentibus, et appulsus ad superiora, et continuatio quaedam rationis humanae cum intelligentia divina seu daemoniaca, sive bona sive mala illa sit." Other faculties and mental states are described ibid., §§241.1-244.11, pp. 1226-1230 (= *BOL*, vol. 3, pp. 140.4-141.27).

[47]   BRUNO, *Furori* ii 1, p. 327, as quoted on p. 14 n. 32 above.

[48]   Cf. BRUNO, *Sigillus* i 46, p. 190.3-14, where 'ecstasy' is applied in an unfavourable manner. 'Ecstasy' is not included in Bruno's description of contraction in the noetic sense: ibid., ii 22, pp. 213.21-214.6, as quoted on p. 55 n. 19 above. Ecstasy is scorned in the twelfth contraction; see ibid., i 46, pp. 189.15-190.5, as quoted on p. 20 n. 61 above.

[49]   BRUNO, *Lampas* §246.12-27, pp. 1232-1234 (*BOL*, vol. 3, p. 143.1-16). For the distinction between philosophical and theological faith, see p. 16 above.

[50]   See p. 16 above.

[51]   Cf. Ficino's reflections on faith in relation to noetic ascent in FICINO, *In Epistolas Pauli prooemium*, p. 425.29-31, as quoted on p. 22 n. 75 above.

[52]   E.g. Bruno's use of Ficino's commentary on Plotinus' theory of noetic ascent, as noted by Sturlese in relation to BRUNO, *De umbris* §72.2-7, p. 56.

contractions led Mersenne to assert that Bruno destroyed the "foundations of true religion". The ultimate reason for this, Mersenne announces, was that Bruno "did not believe at all in Christian faith, and in the divine".[53] In his attack on Bruno's doctrine, Mersenne treats Bruno in a patronising tone rather than arguing with him. That Bruno does not believe in "the divine" is obviously not true; on the contrary, although he undoubtedly conceived of it in a heretical way.

When Clemens turned to the fifteen contractions in the *Sigillus* more than two centuries later, in 1847, he reported the first, eleventh and thirteenth contraction, and translated the twelfth contraction into German.[54] He repudiated Bruno for his heterodoxy from time to time from a Christian viewpoint but he tempered his contempt on this occasion, striving to decipher the veiled terms used by Bruno. He suggested, for example, that Bruno was alluding to Francis of Assisi (1181/1182-1226) in the thirteenth contraction when he says that imagination, if stirred, can produce a bodily wound.[55] The important point is, Clemens assured his readers, that Bruno did not doubt the miraculous events recorded in these fifteen contractions. Bruno was instead questioning the love for the Saviour, which was the source and cause of the various states of contraction described in the fifteen contractions.[56]

Clemens' interpretation is unconvincing. In the fifteen contractions Bruno mentions Christ explicitly once only, comparing him with Zoroaster, Lull, Paracelsus and others who intensified their intellectual abilities through solitude. In this passage love of Christ is not indicated by Bruno as a cause of contraction.[57] Bruno may, however, be alluding to Christ in the twelfth contraction when he speaks of the "death of some Adonis", who is the object towards which the person

---

53 MERSENNE, *L'impiété des déistes* i 10, pp. 232-234: "Ce meschant homme a encore esté pire que Cardan, comme sçavent ceux qui le hantoient lors qu'il estoit à Paris, et comme tesmoigne le livre qu'il a intitlé *Sigillus sigillorum*, dans lequel il met quinze sortes de contractions à ce qu'il puisse sapper les fondements de la vraye religion: car dans la premiere il rapporte les miracles de nostre Seigneur à la qualité du lieu; les ravissemens ecstatiques des saincts en l'air à l'imagination, et à la melancholie dans la 2 espece de ses contractions; dans la troisieme, il veut que la prophetie vienne par le racourcy qu'on fait de l'horizon au centre; dans la quatriesme, il feint que les revelations arrivent par la force de la grande attention. La cinquiesme passe au delà de Cardan, qui disoit que le transport des montagnes surpassoit les forces de la nature, car il veut que cela se puisse faire par une affection de foy, ou plustost d'imagination, de presomption, et de sole creance, comme on verra si on le lit attentivement, car pour ce qui est de la foy chretstienne, et divine, il n'en croit point." Mersenne mentions, but does not criticise the remaining contractions (ibid., i 10, pp. 234-235). I am indebted to Claudio Buccolini, who, in his paper at the *Letture Bruniane* in Rome in October 1999, drew my attention to this passage of Mersenne.

54 CLEMENS, *Giordano Bruno*, pp. 175-177.

55 Ibid., p. 177. For Francis of Assisi Clemens refers to BRUNO, *Sigillus* i 47, p. 190.14-18.

56 CLEMENS, *Giordano Bruno*, p. 177: "Der Angriff ist daher lediglich gegen die Quelle und die Ursache jenes Zustandes, d. h. gegen die Liebe zu dem gekreuzigten Heilande gerichtet."

57 BRUNO, *Sigillus* i 35, pp. 180.21-181.11.

in ecstasy, caused by melancholy, directs his attention.[58] But even in this case, love of Christ — if he is indeed meant — does not cause the contraction, as Clemens claimed. Love of Christ is, instead, the desired result for those inflicting this condition upon themselves. Although Clemens' work did much in its time to reinstate Bruno as a serious philosopher, his reading forces Bruno's *Sigillus* into a Christian mould for which there is no textual basis in Bruno's works. This distortion prevented him from understanding the philosophical implications of Bruno's idea of contraction in its noetic sense.[59]

Bruno's fifteen contractions also attracted the enthusiasm of Frances Yates. Yates read Bruno from a very different viewpoint, one free of Christian prejudices. She interpreted the fifteen contractions in the *Sigillus* i 35-49 as "religious experiences", claiming that there Bruno follows and develops Agrippa's magic.[60] She referred the first contraction to Agrippa's *De occulta philosophia* iii 55, dealing with the importance of solitude to religious leaders, and the twelfth to the fifteenth contractions to *De occulta philosophia* iii 4, where Agrippa — according to her reading — distinguished religion based on divine, genuine magic from religion based on superstition. Her interpretation is suspect on two counts. First, Yates simply ignored the remaining contractions. Second, she ignored Bruno's theoretical introduction to the fifteen contractions (*Sigillus* i 31-34, as described on pp. 24-25 above). There Bruno does not adhere to Agrippa, who is not even mentioned. His source is Plotinus, whose theory of noetic ascent through the Neoplatonic order Bruno explicitly praises. Further, if we are to speak about "religious experience" in relation to the fifteen contractions, it is certainly not an "experience" based on faith, hope, fear and the intervention of supernatural beings in any Christian sense. Instead it is a "religious experience" based on the individual's rational faculties as they endeavour to comprehend unity in the intelligible realm.

Ingegno, by and large, followed Yates' interpretation. He saw Bruno's magic in opposition to the doctrines and ceremonies of Christianity, and contended that in the fifteen contractions of the *Sigillus* and in his works on magic Bruno had picked up the notion of contraction from Ficino's *Theologia platonica* xiii 2.[61] Ingegno refers to a passage from *Theologia platonica* xiii 2 in corroboration, describing how the contraction of melancholy can lead to noetic ascent. I have cited and translated the passage above.[62] The kind of contraction Ficino describes is based on a non-rational process, which, as we have seen, Bruno contrasts with

---

[58]   Ibid., i 46, p. 190.5: "alicuius Adonidis mortem". For the context, see ibid., i 46, pp. 189.16-190.14.

[59]   For Clemens' religious standing, see BLUM, 'A note on the author', in CLEMENS, *Giordano Bruno* (reprint), pp. v-vi.

[60]   YATES, *Giordano Bruno and the Hermetic tradition*, pp. 271-272; *The art of memory*, p. 253.

[61]   INGEGNO, 'Nota sul *Sigillus sigillorum* del Bruno', p. 365; *Cosmologia*, pp. 251-256; *La sommersa nave*, pp. 90-91; *Regia pazzia*, pp. 133-140, especially p. 133 n. 71. MANCINI, *La sfera infinita*, p. 67 n. 152, follows Ingegno.

[62]   FICINO, *Theologia platonica* xiii 2, vol. 2, p. 219.22-25, as quoted on p. 94 n. 23 above.

contraction produced by noetic ascent. And, as we have also seen, it is a contraction with which Ficino similarly contrasts noetic ascent, though unnoticed by Ingegno.[63] Ingegno is sensitive to Bruno's strong reservations in the fifteen contractions about noetic ascent through melancholy, but he nevertheless maintains that this passage in Ficino, *Theologia platonica* xiii 2, was the source for Bruno's idea of noetic ascent, and that what he conceived as Ficino's main problem, to balance the good and bad effects of melancholy, is central to Bruno too.[64] Hence this aspect of Bruno's *Sigillus* seemed to Ingegno to support Yates' overall thesis.

There are four problems with Ingegno's interpretation. First, even though Bruno may well have been familiar with Ficino's use of the term 'contraction' in the *Theologia platonica* xiii 2, we cannot be sure that this passage of Ficino was Bruno's only source. Ficino draws on a physiological tradition of contraction going back to Galen, and Bruno could have derived his ideas of contraction in this sense from an intermediary source. Second, Ingegno does not consider that, even though Bruno agrees that melancholy might initiate noetic ascent, it is not in itself sufficient, even if balanced, to produce noetic ascent, but must be assisted by the work of the rational faculties.[65] This oversight by Ingegno is related to a third problem with his interpretation, namely, that he does not contextualise Bruno's doctrine of melancholy within his epistemology. Fourth, Ingegno ignores the fact that Bruno's account of the fifteen contractions subverts Christian theology, and excludes, by implication, among other things, the traditional theological notion of faith. Ficino's version of noetic ascent, on the other hand, does not conflict with notions of faith.

More recently, Sturlese has reaffirmed Ingegno's interpretation of Bruno's notion of contraction. She agrees with Ingegno that the fifteen contractions in the *Sigillus* are inspired by Ficino, as Ingegno had explained, and her work on the possible sources to these fifteen contractions are accordingly coloured by this perspective.[66] She compares nine of the fifteen contractions in the *Sigillus* with passages from Ficino's *Theologia platonica* xiii 1-5, namely contractions one, two, six, eight, nine, ten, eleven, thirteen and fifteen.[67] Three of the comparisons are very compelling, since specific names and expressions are used in the same sense in the respective passages of Bruno and Ficino.[68]

In addition, however, to the criticism I have already raised in relation to Ingegno's interpretation, there are at least two problems raised by Sturlese's comparisons and by her conclusion, that the fifteen contractions of the *Sigillus*

---

[63] See my discussion of this passage on pp. 94-95 above.

[64] The ambivalence of the theory of melancholic humours is pointed out in INGEGNO, *La sommersa nave*, pp. 91-92.

[65] Cf., for instance, BRUNO, *Sigillus* i 45, p. 189.6-14, as quoted on p. 19 n. 60 above.

[66] For her agreement with Ingegno's interpretation, see STURLESE, 'Le fonti', p. 116.

[67] For her suggestions for sources to the fifteen contractions, see ibid., pp. 141-145. They are listed in the notes to the individual contractions in Chapter 1, pp. 8-23 above.

[68] STURLESE, 'Le fonti', pp. 141-142 (third contraction), 143 (ninth contraction), 145 (fifteenth contraction).

derived from *Theologia platonica* xiii 1-5. First, none of the passages from the *Theologia platonica* voice the scepticism regarding *furore* generated by melancholy which we have seen in the eleventh, the twelfth and the fourteenth of Bruno's fifteen contractions.[69] Bruno may well have used Ficino's doctrine of melancholy in Ficino's *Theologia platonica*, but if so, it is important to acknowledge that he changed many details, incorporated ideas from other sources (some of which we cannot identify) and used it for completely different purposes to Ficino. Second, even though Sturlese manages to identify a parallel use of certain names in the third contraction of the *Sigillus* and in Ficino's *Theologia platonica* xiii 2, she does not provide a comparable quotation from Ficino's *Theologia platonica* for Bruno's expression, "contraction of the horizon into the centre".[70]

As in the case of Ingegno, I think that Sturlese is correct in comparing Bruno's texts with Ficino's. But one has to ask the critical question how they used the terms in order to acknowledge potential differentiation and disagreement. The case of contraction in the physiological sense, in particular when applied to melancholy, suggests that, although Ficino and Bruno shared a terminological framework, that did not hinder them from articulating rather distinct philosophical outlooks in agreement with their theological orientations.

---

[69]   Ibid., pp. 141-145.

[70]   For her comparison of this third contraction with Ficino's *Theologia platonica*, see ibid., pp. 141-142.

Chapter 6

The Scholastic Tradition
of Contraction

The concept of contraction was widely used in scholastic theories of individuation. Hence Bruno's use of this concept within this particular philosophical field does not in itself allow us to identify his sources. There are, however, a number of external and internal relations between Bruno's philosophy, in particular his theory of individuation, and the scholastic tradition concerning the *Liber de causis*. These relations have not yet been explored in the literature on Bruno, although they may shed some light on his use of contraction as an ontological concept. In this chapter I shall outline the historical background of the *Liber de causis*, present its central ideas, and explain how the term 'contraction' was used in its scholastic commentaries. I shall suggest that this scholastic tradition may well be one of the important sources to Bruno's ontological concept of contraction.

The reception of the *Liber de causis* in the Renaissance

The *Liber de causis*, also known as the *Liber Aristotelis de expositione bonitatis purae*, is a Latin translation of an Arabic work probably composed in the ninth century.[1] The Latin translation was made in the twelfth century, possibly by Gerard of Cremona and subsequently revised by Guindisalvi.[2] The author of the *Liber de causis* draws, among other sources, on Proclus' *Elements of theology*, Plotinus' *Enneads* and the pseudo-Aristotelian *Theology*, the latter two probably in the Arabic versions.[3]

---

[1]   For the alternative title, see PATTIN, 'Introduction', pp. 91-92. For the idea that the Latin version of *Liber de causis* is translated from an Arabic version, see ibid., p. 92. For the discussion of the date of its composition, see ibid., pp. 92-93.

[2]   Ibid., pp. 98-101.

[3]   For Proclus' *Elements of theology* as a source, see COSTA, 'Le fonti e la struttura del *Liber de causis*', pp. 1-17; '"Esse quod est supra eternitatem"', pp. 47-52. For the Arabic version of Plotinus' *Enneads* as a source, see COSTA, 'Le fonti e la struttura del *Liber de causis*', pp. 17-29; '"Esse quod est supra eternitatem"', pp. 42-47. For the use of the pseudo-Aristotelian *Theology*, see COSTA, 'Le fonti e la struttura del *Liber de causis*', pp. 17-21, 24-26. For the differences between key doctrines in the metaphysics in the *Liber de causis* and those of Plotinus and Proclus respectively, see COSTA, 'Le fonti e la struttura del *Liber de causis*', pp. 30-31. For the influence of the *Liber de*

The *Liber de causis* was falsely attributed to Aristotle, among many others, until Aquinas, in his commentary to the *Liber de causis*, written in 1272, observed the borrowings from Proclus and questioned Aristotle's authorship.[4] He had been able to make this identification because he had consulted the Latin translation of Proclus' *Elements of theology* made by William of Moerbeke (ca. 1215-1286) in 1268.[5] The recognition of influences from Plotinus' *Enneads* and the *Theology* of pseudo-Aristotle, on the other hand, is much more recent and is still not clear in every detail.

In this chapter I shall not consider the sources of the *Liber de causis*. I shall instead make a few bibliographical observations regarding the reception of the work and its commentaries in the Renaissance, and introduce the philosophical doctrines in the *Liber de causis* which became central in the scholastic discussions of the theory of individuation articulated through the concept of contraction. Finally, I shall present different interpretations of contraction among scholastic commentators, and discuss the distinctive features of Giles' interpretation and their affinities with Bruno's interpretation of contraction in the ontological sense.

Both before and after Aquinas' discovery the *Liber de causis* was an important metaphysical work. In 1255 the work was even made part of the required reading for students at the University of Paris. They were obliged to devote seven weeks to a course on the *Liber de causis*.[6] The work was also an important and institutionalised text for Dominicans in the thirteenth century. Bruno, to note in passing, was a Dominican.[7] Since this Order, and the Aristotelianism which it fostered, remained very important in Renaissance philosophy, it would be interesting to know how and to what extent the *Liber de causis* continued to exert influence in this period. It may well have remained important within this Order in the fifteenth and sixteenth centuries, since Ludovico of Ferrara (d. 1496), who was Procurator of the Dominican Order from 1481 to 1484, composed a commentary on the *Liber de causis*.[8] In addition, two other members of the Dominican Order wrote commentaries on the *Liber de causis*, namely Crisostomo Javelli (1470-1538) and Michael de Asti (fl. ca. 1562).[9]

As for the *Liber de causis* and its general influence in Renaissance philosophy, we know that Cusanus as well as Cardinal Bessarion (1403-1472) both owned a

---

causis in the Arabic world, see TAYLOR, '*The Kalam fi mahd al-khair* (*Liber de causis*) in the Islamic philosophical milieu', pp. 37-52. For the influence of the Latin version of pseudo-Aristotle's *Theology* in the Renaissance, see KRAYE, 'The pseudo-Aristotelian *Theology* in sixteenth- and seventeenth-century Europe', pp. 265-286.

[4] For Aquinas' attribution, see COSTA, '"Philosophus in libro *De causis*"', pp. 611-612. For other attributions by scholastic philosophers before Aquinas, see ibid., pp. 633-644.

[5] AQUINAS, *Super Librum de causis expositio* proemium, p. 3.1-5. For Aquinas' identification of sources, see ELDERS, 'Saint Thomas d'Aquin et la métaphysique du *Liber de causis*', p. 429.

[6] ZWAENEPOEL, 'Introduction', p. 15.

[7] AQUILECCHIA, 'Bruno, Giordano', p. 654.

[8] LOHR, 'Medieval Latin Aristotle commentaries', p. 321.

[9] LOHR, *Latin Aristotle commentaries*, vol. 2, pp. 203, 22.

manuscript of the treatise, that Pico commented upon it in his *Conclusiones*, that Ficino considered it a work belonging to the Platonic tradition, and, as we shall see in the next chapter, that Cusanus' adversary, the Heidelberg professor John Wenck (d. 1460), wrote a commentary on the *Liber de causis* and referred to the *Liber de causis* in his attack on Cusanus' *De docta ignorantia*. Still other commentaries on the *Liber de causis* were written in the Renaissance.[10]

The bibliographical information provided by Taylor, Cranz, Schmitt, Lohr and Knox about the *Liber de causis* proved that the work was popular in the late Middle Ages and in the Renaissance — even after its chief source, Proclus' *Elements of theology*, had become available through various Latin and vernacular translations.[11] Taylor lists two hundred and thirty-seven Latin manuscripts of the *Liber de causis* circulating in the Middle Ages.[12] And Cranz lists fifteen publications of Gerard of Cremona's Latin translation of the *Liber de causis* among the sixteenth-century publications of Aristotle's works.[13] To this number we should add an unknown number of publications of the *Liber de causis* which appeared outside these publications of Aristotle's works. Ten of these fifteen sixteenth-century publications of Aristotle, in which the *Liber de causis* appeared, were published in or before 1576, when Bruno left the Dominican order in Naples,

---

[10] MS Cues 195 contains the *Liber de causis* on fols 1ʳ-34ᵛ. It was, in fact, Aquinas' commentary on the *Liber de causis*, see p. 141 n. 27 below. BARDENHEWER, 'Zur Geschichte der lateinischen Uebersetzung', pp. 290 n. 4, 300, claims that Bessarion's hand is detectable in a MS of the *Liber de causis*, including commentaries by Albert, Aquinas and Giles, held at the San Marco library. This MS is listed as Lat. Z. 288 (coll. 1839) in *Cento codici bessarionei*, pp. 86-87. We find explicit references to the *Liber de causis* in PICO, *Conclusiones* 6>1-10, pp. 460-464, and likewise in FICINO, *Responsio*, p. 46, line 39. For the *Liber de causis* in the works of Cusanus, Pico and Ficino, see KRISTELLER, 'Proclus as a reader', p. 196. For some references to, or paraphrases of, the *Liber de causis* up to the seventeenth century, see BARDENHEWER, 'Zur Geschichte der lateinischen Uebersetzung', pp. 204-302. The MS containing Wenck's *In Librum de causis* is held at the Stadtbibliothek in Mainz, in MS 610, fols 2ʳ-38ᵛ, as recorded in TAYLOR, 'The *Liber de causis*', p. 83. For Wenck's reference to the *Liber de causis* see p. 149 n. 68 below. Neither Bardenhewer nor Kristeller have called attention to Wenck's commentary in the above mentioned texts. Nor have they paid attention to the Renaissance commentaries; see p. 107 n. 24 below.

[11] Cf. KRISTELLER, 'Proclus as a reader', p. 196, who has asserted that "its vogue [i.e. of the *Liber de causis*] seems to have declined after Proclus's own *Elements of theology* had become known directly." Kristeller's assertion may be true, but it still needs to be pointed out that at least fifteen editions of the *Liber de causis* came out in the sixteenth century and that several commentaries were composed during the Renaissance.

[12] TAYLOR, 'The *Liber de causis*', pp. 68-80.

[13] CRANZ, *A bibliography*, p. 169. See also SCHMITT and KNOX, *Pseudo-Aristoteles latinus*, pp. 18-20.

and eight out of these ten were published in Venice.[14] The uses of the *Liber de causis* in Renaissance philosophy have not yet, however, been studied.[15]

For the Latin commentaries on the *Liber de causis* the bibliographical information is even scantier. We know that commentaries were produced by the following late thirteenth-century authors. (i) Roger Bacon (ca. 1214 - ca. 1292), who wrote his commentary between 1241 and 1245;[16] (ii) pseudo-Henry of Ghent, who wrote his commentary between 1245 and 1255;[17] (iii) Albert the Great (1193-1280) wrote a commentary on the *Liber de causis* in his *De causis et processu universitatis a prima causa*, composed between 1265 and 1272, that is, a few decades after the *Quaestiones*.[18] *De causis et processu universitatis a prima causa* is divided into two books, of which the second is a commentary on the *Liber de causis*;[19] (iv) Aquinas, who wrote his commentary in 1272;[20] (v) Siger of Brabant (ca. 1240 - ca. 1284), who wrote his commentary between 1275 and 1276;[21] and

---

[14]　CRANZ, *A bibliography*, nn. 107.755 (1507), nn. 108.193 (1550/1552), nn. 108.219 (1551), nn. 108.423 (1560), nn. 108.456 (1562), nn. 108.579 (1572), nn. 108.599 (1575), nn. 108.610 (1576).

[15]　In MAHONEY, 'Metaphysical foundations of the hierarchy of being', pp. 166-179, the *Liber de causis* is pointed out as one source to scholastic theories of hierarchies of being in the thirteenth century. But apart from a brief assertion about a reference of Agostino Nifo (1469/1470-1538) to the *Liber de causis* (ibid., p. 198), the treatise is not considered in the context of Renaissance metaphysics (ibid., pp. 186-204).

[16]　For the dating, see COSTA, '"Philosophus in libro *De causis*"', p. 614.

[17]　For the dating, see ZWAENEPOEL, 'Introduction', p. 15. This anonymous commentary attributed to pseudo-Henry, *Quaestiones in Librum de causis*, extant in one manuscript, now MS h.II.1, is held in the Real Biblioteca of El Escorial. For this MS, see ZWAENEPOEL, 'Introduction', pp. 6-7. For the attribution to pseudo-Henry, see ibid., pp. 15-19. For this commentary of pseudo-Henry, see also COSTA, '"Philosophus in libro *De causis*"', pp. 618-622. Pseduo-Henry singled out Aristotle as the author, Costa argues, because the theme of first principle in Aristotle's *Metaphysics* XII is also dealt with in the *Liber de causis*; see COSTA, '"Philosophus in libro *De causis*"', pp. 639-644. Even after Aquinas had identified Proclus' *Elements of theology* as a source, GILES, *Super authorem De causis, Alpharabium* Proaemium, Y, regarded the *Liber de causis* as a supplement to Aristotle's *Metaphysics*. For Aristotelian ideas discussed in the *Liber de causis*, see COSTA, '"Philosophus in libro *De causis*"', pp. 644-648.

[18]　For the dating, see GUAGLIARDO, 'Introduction', p. XI.

[19]　According to Pattin, Albert comments on *Liber de causis* i-v(vi) in II i, on *Liber de causis* vi(viii)-xiv(xv) in II ii, on *Liber de causis* xv(xvi)-xviii(xix) in II iii, on *Liber de causis* xix(xx)-xxiii(xxiv) in II iv, on *Liber de causis* xxiv(xxv)-xxxi(xxxii) in II v. For the division in Albert's commentary, see PATTIN, 'Introduction', pp. 122-123. Fauser lists thirty-eight manuscripts of, or extracts from, this work (FAUSER, 'Prolegomena', pp. VII-XII).

[20]　For the dating, see SAFFREY, 'Introduction', pp. XXXIII-XXXVI. Aquinas' commentary, *Super Librum de causis expositio*, is known through fifty manuscripts listed by Saffrey, of which eighteen belong to Italian libraries, including one library in Naples (ibid., pp. XL-LII). The MS in Naples is held in the Biblioteca Nazionale (ibid., pp. XLV-XLVI). Saffrey also lists one incunabulum from 1493 (ibid., p. LII).

[21]　For the dating, see WIPPEL, 'Siger of Brabant', p. 768.

(vi) Giles, who wrote his commentary between 1289 and 1291.[22] Several other commentaries were produced before 1500, some by unidentified authors.[23]

In the fifteenth and sixteenth centuries at least six commentaries were written: (i) a commentary by Wenck, as already mentioned; (ii) a commentary by Ludovico of Ferrara, also mentioned; (iii) a commentary by Jacob of Gostynin (d. 1506) dating from 1490; (iv) a commentary by Ambrogio Flandino (1462-1531); (v) a commentary by Michael de Asti (fl. ca. 1562); (vi) a commentary by Crisostomo Javelli, first printed in Lyon in 1568 and reprinted there in 1580.[24] The commentaries by Wenck, Ludovico of Ferrara, Ambrogio Flandino and Michael de Asti were not available in print in Bruno's lifetime, and he would not, in all probability, have known them. The commentary of Jacob of Gostynin, printed just once in Krakow in 1507, was far removed from Bruno's European itinerary, and it is unlikely that he would have come across it. The commentary by Javelli, on the other hand, was printed in Lyon, and Bruno might well have been familiar with it.

Which printed commentaries would Bruno have been likely to come across? Among the scholastic authors, Bruno almost certainly knew the commentaries by Albert and Aquinas from his early formation as a Dominican.[25] Albert's commentary, contained in his *De causis et processu universitatis a prima causa*,

---

22   For the dating, see PUNTA and TRIFOGLI, 'Giles of Rome', p. 77. The relatively high number of manuscripts of Giles' commentary, recorded by Taylor, suggests that Giles' commentary had also been popular before the sixteenth century: TAYLOR, 'The *Liber de causis*', p. 81, lists thirteen MSS.

23   TAYLOR, 'The *Liber de causis*', pp. 81-84.

24   For the three first commentaries, see TAYLOR, 'The *Liber de causis*', p. 83. No copies of LUDOVICO OF FERRARA, *Commentaria in Librum de causis*, are known (TAYLOR, 'The *Liber de causis*', p. 83). JACOB OF GOSTYNIN, *In Librum de causis*, is held at Krakow, Bibl. Uniwersytetu Jagiellonskiego, MS 505, fols 148-[189]. It was printed in Krakow in 1507 (TAYLOR, 'The *Liber de causis*', p. 83). AMBROGIO FLANDINO, *Annotationes in librum de causis*, is held at Mantova, MS BC G.III.10 (XVI), fols 1ʳ-267ᵛ (LOHR, *Latin Aristotle commentaries*, vol. 2, p. 149). For MICHAEL DE ASTI, *Commentarium in librum de causis*, see LOHR, *Latin Aristotle commentaries*, vol. 2, p. 22. JAVELLI, *In librum de causis. Commentarii duo*, in JAVELLI, [*Opera*]. Antoine de Harsy: Lyon, 1580, vol. 1, pp. 469b-506b. In ibid., pp. 469b-475a we find the Latin translation of the *Liber de causis*; ibid., pp. 475a-506b we find Javelli's Latin commentary on the *Liber de causis*. According to LOHR, *Latin Aristotle commentaries*, vol. 2, p. 203, this commentary was first printed in JAVELLI, [*Opera*]. Lyon 1568, vol. 1, pp. 469-506. None of these six Renaissance commentaries is included in the list of commentaries listed in PATTIN, 'Introduction', pp. 122-130.

25   For Bruno's knowledge of Albert, see FIRPO, *Processo*, pp. 193, 286; RICCI, *Giordano Bruno*, pp. 62, 72, 82, 407, 408. For the importance of Aquinas' philosophy to Bruno, see SPAMPANATO, *Vita*, pp. 651-652; FIRPO, *Processo*, pp. 16-17, 55, 57, 60, 168, 177, 178, 217, 259, 270, 272, 277, 286, 287; BLUM, *Aristoteles*, p. 100 *et passim*; PAPULI, *Qualche osservazione*, pp. 205-206, 209-210; SPRUIT, *Il problema*, pp. 26-27; RICCI, *Giordano Bruno*, pp. 41-42, 45, 69-71, 74, 75, 77-79, 145, 232, 378, 442, 513.

was printed in 1517.[26] Aquinas' commentary, *Super Librum de causis expositio*, came out in three printed editions in the sixteenth century, two printed at Venice in 1507 and 1551 respectively, and one at Rome in 1570-71.[27] Giles' commentary was printed together with the text of the *Liber de causis* in Venice in 1550, one year before one of the publications of Aquinas' commentary.[28] However, there may well exist other sixteenth-century editions of commentaries from the thirteenth century, which I am not aware of.[29] Finally, a commentary by Javelli was printed in Lyon in 1568 and reprinted there in 1580.[30] We can, however, ignore this work of Javelli in the present examination, since Javelli did not use the term 'contraction' in this commentary.[31]

If the information presented here is representative, then the sixteenth-century printed editions that Bruno would be likely to have come across would be Albert's commentary published in 1517; Aquinas' commentary — published at Venice in 1507 and 1551, and at Rome in 1570-1571; the one by Giles, published in Venice in 1550; and the one by Javelli, published in 1568 and 1580. This does not, of course, exclude the possibility that Bruno knew of one or more of the other commentaries through manuscripts or reports by intermediary authors.

How could Bruno have been introduced to the works of Giles of Rome?

Given the availability of Giles' commentary and the popularity of the *Liber de causis*, it is quite likely that Bruno read Giles' commentary. It is possible that Bruno had gained some knowledge of Giles' thought during his early education. The Augustinian Teofilo da Vairano, or Variano (d. 1578), had taught him logic the year before Bruno entered the Dominican order, when he was fourteen or fifteen years old, i.e. around 1563; and he may well have introduced Bruno to the

---

[26] ALBERT, *De causis et processu universitatis a causa prima*, in ALBERT, *[Parva naturalia]*. Heirs of Ottaviano: Venice, 1517, fols 186ʳ-230ᵛ. For Albert's *editio princeps*, printed in Venice in 1517, see FAUSER, 'Prolegomena', pp. XXIX-XXX.

[27] For the edition in Rome in 1570-1571, see FAUSER, 'Prolegomena', pp. LIII-LIV. For the two other Venice editions, see CRANZ, *A bibliography*, nn. 107.755 (1507), 108.219 (1551).

[28] For a comparison between the 1550 edition and the earlier MSS of Giles' commentary on the *Liber de causis*, see PATTIN, 'Introduction', pp. 124-125.

[29] In the catalogue at the British Library I have checked the titles indicated in the catalogue under the heading "single works", and looked through the actual editions listed in the catalogues under "Two or more works" of Roger Bacon, Siger of Brabant or Giles of Rome. I have also checked the following catalogues for fifteenth- and sixteenth-century editions: *The National Union Catalog*; *The First Printed Catalogue of the Bodleian Library 1605*; *Catalogue of Books Printed on the Continent of Europe, 1501-1600 in Cambridge Libraries*; *Verzeichnis der im deutschen Sprachbereich erschienenen Drucke des XVI. Jahrhunderts*.

[30] For bibliograhical information about Javelli's commentary, see p. 107 n. 24 above.

[31] JAVELLI, *In librum de causis. Commentarii duo*, pp. 475a-506b.

works of Giles.[32] Vairano had not only studied logic during his education as an Augustinian, which he finished in 1562, but also natural philosophy and theology. For according to the Agustinian *ratio studiorum*, which Teofilo had followed, the commentaries of Giles or of Thomas Aquinas on the *Sentences*, a collection of doctrinally central texts from the Scriptures and Church Fathers compiled by Peter Lombard (ca. 1100-1160), were to be read as part of the curriculum of theology.[33] Giles' commentaries on the *Sentences* had been published in Venice in 1482, 1492; and they were published there once again in 1521 and in 1581. Ingrid Rowland has recently argued that Teofilo da Vairano was under the influence of the Neoplatonist Giles of Viterbo (1465/69-1532).[34] This local strand of Neoplatonism, especially some of Giles of Viterbo's Neoplatonic metaphors, e.g. *vestigium* and Actaeon, probably entered Bruno's philosophy through Teofilo da Vairano.[35] In Giles of Viterbo's unfinished but widely circulated work from 1513, the *Sententiae ad mentem Platonis*, he "began to recast the western Church's standard theological textbook, Peter Lombard's twelfth-century *Sententiae*, in a spirit compatible with contemporary thought".[36] According to Rowland, in this work Giles of Viterbo borrowed formulations about the concept of *vestigium* from Giles of Rome's commentary on Peter Lombard's *Sentences*.[37]

Given this background, we can assume that the logic teacher whose private lessons Bruno attended in Naples would at least have been familiar with Giles' commentary on the *Sentences*. Unfortunately, we do not know to what extent Teofilo drew attention to Giles' ideas in his lectures on logic. But it is possible that these lectures were backed up with ontological reflections, since Aristotelian logic asserts that the subject-predicate structure of propositions in logic is isomorphic with the substance-accidents structure of things. If the young Bruno had indeed

---

32 FIRPO, *Processo*, p. 156: "Et son stato in Napoli a imparar littere de humanità, logica et dialettica sino a 14 anni; et solevo sentir le lettioni publiche d'uno che si chiamava il Sarnese, et andavo a sentir privatamente la logica da un padre augustiniano, chiamato fra Theofilo da Vairano, che dopo lesse la metafisica in Roma." See also the report dating from 7 December 1585 by Guillaume Cotin, librarian at Saint-Victor in Paris, in SPAMPANATO, *Vita*, p. 651: "Il [Bruno] dit le principal maystre qu'il ait eu en philosophie estre ...,[4] augustin, qui est trespassé." Note 4 to this sentence reads: "Il y a, à cet endroit, un blanc dans le manuscrit; il faut suppléer 'Teofilo da Vairano'" (ibid., p. 651 n. 4). For Bruno's encounter with Teofilo da Vairano, see CARELLA, 'Tra i maestri di Giordano Bruno. Nota sull'agostiniano Teofilo da Vairano', p. 64.

33 CARELLA, 'Tra i maestri di Giordano Bruno. Nota sull'agostiniano Teofilo da Vairano', p. 68: "iuxta sententiam Aegidii Romani vel sancti Thomae".

34 ROWLAND, 'Giordano Bruno and Neapolitan Neoplatonism', pp. 103-104.

35 Ibid., pp. 97-119, especially pp. 106-107, 110-119. Rowland holds that the concept of *vestigium* in Bruno's *De umbris idearum*, and the imagery for the Actaeon myth in his *Eroici furori* were coloured by Giles of Viterbo's *Sententiae ad mentem Platonis*. For the Actaeon myth in this text of Bruno, see p. 61 n. 46 above.

36 ROWLAND, 'Giordano Bruno and Neapolitan Neoplatonism', p. 105. She cites this work of Giles of Viterbo from a MS held in the Biblioteca Apostolica Vaticana; MS Vat. Lat. 6325.

37 ROWLAND, 'Giordano Bruno and Neapolitan Neoplatonism', p. 110 n. 44.

acquired some introduction to Giles' work from Vairano, this would help to explain why he might have turned to Giles' commentary on the *Liber de causis* later in his career.

Although this external link between Bruno and Giles of Rome's commentary on the *Liber de causis* is far from conclusive, it does encourage us to look out for traces of influences in Bruno's thought from Giles' commentary on the *Liber de causis*, and not only from the commentaries on the *Liber de causis* written by Albert and Aquinas.

The doctrines of the *Liber de causis* and Bruno's philosophy

(i) Primary and secondary causes

The *Liber de causis* is a short work consisting of thirty-one commented propositions, or thirty-two, depending on the division of the work. It sets out a hierarchy of being, stretching from the highest ontological level, the primary cause, to the lowest ontological level, nature. From a pedagogical point of view it must have been an exceptional introduction to metaphysics for university students and others with a reading knowledge of Latin and some interest in lofty speculation. In a fairly simple Latin and with several pedagogically useful repetitions, it introduces core notions in a metaphysical system without going into great detail. These qualities are its strength and its weakness. They are its strength insofar as its brief comments stimulate the reader to work out how the propositions could be interpreted. They are its weakness as far as its vague ideas do not leave the reader with a fully articulated and concise metaphysical system with great explanatory power.

The most important concepts in the hierarchy of being presented in the *Liber de causis* emerge through the distinction between primary and secondary causes. The First Cause is a creative cause which gives being (*esse*) to everything, whereas a secondary cause is a formal cause which, among other things, imparts motion and generation to sensibilia. The First Cause is more efficacious than the secondary cause. If a secondary cause recedes, the First Cause will subsist.[38]

The distinction between the First and the secondary causes is relevant to our examination of Bruno's unified theory of descension and ascension. The concept of contraction, in the ontological sense, emerges in the *Sigillus* when Bruno explains noetic ascent as a reversion of ontological descent. By describing the process of the former, he describes indirectly descent too. He writes of noetic ascent as follows:

> So we contract to being or essence generally, just as from the posterior to
> the prior, the effects to the causes, those the particular causes to the
> common causes, and these proximate and immediate causes to more

---

[38]   PSEUDO-ARISTOTLE, *Liber de causis* i 1-8, iv 37-38, ed. Pattin, pp. 134-135, 142.

remote and intermediate causes, and these secondary causes to first causes, and these many first causes to a single cause.[39]

This distinction between primary and secondary causes may be derived from the *Liber de causis*, but it may also be mediated through scholastic authors who applied the terms in their metaphysical accounts.[40] Whatsoever the source is to the passage in the *Sigillus*, we should notice that this hierarchy of causes is an example of a parallel descent and noetic ascent, favoured in principle by Bruno on several occasions.[41]

(ii) Hypostases and the distinction between eternity and time

Let us return to the *Liber de causis*. The First Cause is prior to eternity, since it creates eternity.[42] Being, the product of the First Cause, descends into time through the lower hypostasis dependent upon the First Cause and Mind (*intelligentia*) — Mind is dependent upon the First Cause and also timeless — namely the hypostasis Soul (*anima*).[43] The hypostasis Soul, then, exists "on the horizon of eternity from below and above time".[44]

---

[39] BRUNO, *Sigillus* ii 22, p. 214.2-6: "idque ad esse simpliciter sive essentiam contrahamus, sicut posterius in prius, effectus in causas, has partiales in communes, illasque proximas et immediatas ad remotiores atque mediatas, easque secundas ad primas, ipsasque plures ad unam." The distinction between the primary cause and secondary causes also features near the beginning of Bruno's metaphysical discussion in the second book of *De la causa*; see BRUNO, *Causa* ii, p. 101: "*Dicsono.* Credete per questo che chi conosce le cose causate e principiate, conosca la causa e principio? *Teofilo.* Non facilmente la causa prossima e principio prossimo; difficilissimamente (anco in vestigio) la causa e principio primo." See also ibid., ii, pp. 103, 111. The extreme difficulty of arriving at knowledge of the First Cause, emphasised by Bruno in the statement ibid., ii, p. 101, cited above in this note, is similarly clear in PSEUDO-ARISTOTLE, *Liber de causis* v(vi) 62, ed. Pattin, p. 149: "Et causa prima est supra res intellectibiles sempiternas et supra res destructibiles, quapropter non cadunt super eam sensus neque meditatio neque cogitatio neque intelligentia."

[40] For the distinction between primary and secondary causes, see KNUUTTILA, 'Modal logic', p. 349. For another Renaissance author who probably paraphrased PSEUDO-ARISTOTLE, *Liber de causis*, i, in these terms, see PICO, *Heptaplus* vi 4, pp. 316-318: "causa secundaria primariae obedit et adiungitur, sicut cum Deus producit aquae producunt, et hae quidem primo quia proxima sunt causa, sed non aliter quam Deo praecipiente, quia causa primaria magis influit quam secunda." The quotation and its relationship to the first paragraph in the *Liber de causis* is found in BARDENHEWER, 'Zur Geschichte der lateinischen Uebersetzung', p. 301. I cite Pico from Garin's edition.

[41] See p. 1 n. 2 above.

[42] PSEUDO-ARISTOTLE, *Liber de causis* ii 20, 23, ed. Pattin, p. 138. For this doctrine and its sources, see COSTA, "'Esse quod est supra eternitatem'", pp. 41-62.

[43] PSEUDO-ARISTOTLE, *Liber de causis* ii 25-26, ed. Pattin, p. 139.

[44] Ibid., ii 22, p. 138: "Esse vero quod est post aeternitatem et supra tempus est anima, quoniam est in horizonte aeternitatis inferius et supra tempus." For the interpretation of

Cristina d'Ancona Costa has argued that this phrase became popular in thirteenth-century philosophy. It derived, not from Proclus, but from a passage in the Arabic *Theology* of pseudo-Aristotle, in which the following formulation from Plotinus' *Enneads* is paraphrased: "Soul ... lies, so to speak, on the frontier (ἔσχατος) of the intelligible".[45] The expression used in the *Theology* of pseudo-Aristotle for 'frontier', Costa points out, is the Arabic expression *fī ufqi*, which means 'horizon'.[46] As mentioned, Bruno uses the image of 'horizon' in his accounts of noetic ascent, notably in the third contraction in the *Sigillus*. This passage in the Latin *Liber de causis* may well be among Bruno's direct or indirect sources for this analogy.[47]

A possible interpretation of Bruno's use of 'horizon' in the third contraction in the *Sigillus* might be as follows. Bruno asserts that some men are able to intuit what is going on at distant places by means of a "contraction of the horizon into the centre". 'Horizon' may, as conjectured in Chapter 1, symbolise the hypostasis Soul, as in the *Liber de causis*, and 'centre' may symbolise the hypostasis Mind in the Neoplatonic system. By a "contraction of the horizon into the centre" Bruno might, then, be describing a turning of an individual soul towards Mind, which is its 'centre', i.e. he may be describing noetic ascent, which moves or "contracts" the individual soul to Mind. When individual souls turn towards Ideas in Mind, they comprehend that on which other things at the same and lower ontological levels depend, e.g. events at distant places. Consequently, men who achieve this can intuit what is occurring at places beyond the reach of the sense organs. If this suggestion is correct, then Bruno intended to give a metaphysical explanation of a form of understanding that might otherwise be accounted for by means of supernatural interferences or miracles. An explanation of this kind agrees with Bruno's tendency in the fifteen contractions to propose natural causes for effects traditionally ascribed to supernatural ones. It would also be in line with the Neoplatonic framework in which he places the fifteen contractions when he introduces them at the *Sigillus* i 31-34, as described on pp. 24-25 above.

But let us, once again, return to the *Liber de causis*. The conception of the First Cause as the prime cause in a hierarchy of causes is probably derived from the Neoplatonic doctrine of the over-flowing of the One.[48] In the *Liber de causis*, the

---

this image by Giles, see BARDENHEWER, 'Zur Geschichte der lateinischen Uebersetzung', pp. 292-294.

[45] PLOTINUS IV iv [28] 2.16-17, tr. A. H. Armstrong. For this identification, see COSTA, 'Le fonti e la struttura del *Liber de causis*', pp. 20-21. For Aquinas' interpretation of PSEUDO-ARISTOTLE, *Liber de causis* ii 22, see ELDERS, 'Saint Thomas d'Aquin et la métaphysique du *Liber de causis*', pp. 431-432.

[46] COSTA, '"Esse quod est supra eternitatem"', pp. 58-59.

[47] For the third contraction, see pp. 10-13 above.

[48] SWEENEY, 'Doctrine of creation in *Liber de causis*', pp. 282-285; COSTA, 'Le fonti e la struttura del *Liber de causis*', pp. 36-38.

First Cause's endowment of being is explained as creation (*creatio*).[49] Pagan Neoplatonism is given creationistic connotations. However, the doctrine of creation *ex nihilo* is not mentioned explicitly. The degree to which the *Liber de causis* conforms with this doctrine depends on the interpretation of the terms 'being' (*esse*) and 'creation' (*creatio*). Beierwaltes points out that the creation in the *Liber de causis* is impersonal and independent of the free will of a creator, and that it does not take place in time. Both points conflict with the Christian doctrine of creation *ex nihilo*.[50] Finally, it is said in the *Liber de causis*, that the First Cause is pure goodness, which is ultimately received by nature.[51] This idea may derive from Neoplatonic philosophy, where the Good is identified with the One.[52]

In the *Liber de causis*, three ontological levels, or emanations, are causally dependent upon the First Cause, namely Mind (*intelligentia*), Soul (*anima*) and nature (*natura*).[53] According to Costa, this system of hypostases derives from Plotinus' metaphysics, not from that of Proclus.[54] In the *Liber de causis* Mind is an intellectual substance caused directly by the First Cause.[55] Mind then causes the Soul, which in turn causes nature.[56] Even though the First Cause is ultimately the causal origin of the sensible universe, individuation occurs only in Mind, Soul and nature, since the First Cause is pure being (*esse*), whereas Mind, Soul and nature combine form (*forma*) and being (*esse*). The combination of form and being is described with an untranslated Arabic expression, *yliathim*, designating something composed.[57] Finally, God is said to govern (*regere*) intelligences, which depend upon the First Cause.[58] Thereby Christian monotheism is reinforced. This idea presumably occurs in the Arabic original. Islam, too, is monotheistic.

---

[49] PSEUDO-ARISTOTLE, *Liber de causis* xvii(xviii) 148, ed. Pattin, p. 174: "Redeamus autem et dicamus quod ens primum est quietum et est causa causarum, et, si ipsum dat omnibus rebus ens, tunc ipsum dat eis per modum creationis."

[50] BEIERWALTES, 'Der Kommentar', p. 194. Cf. SWEENEY, 'Doctrine of creation', pp. 277-282, 289, who argues that the doctrine of creation in the *Liber de causis* conforms with the Christian doctrine of *creatio ex nihilo*.

[51] PSEUDO-ARISTOTLE, *Liber de causis* viii(ix) 79, ed. Pattin, p. 154.

[52] WALLIS, *Neoplatonism*, p. 59.

[53] For the Neoplatonic sources for these hypostases, see COSTA, 'Le fonti e la struttura del *Liber de causis*', pp. 15-17, 30-31.

[54] Ibid., pp. 15-17.

[55] PSEUDO-ARISTOTLE, *Liber de causis* viii(ix) 86, ed. Pattin, p. 156.

[56] Ibid., viii(ix) 85, p. 156. For the intermediary role of Mind and its Neoplatonic sources, see COSTA, 'La doctrine de la création "mediante intelligentia" dans le *Liber de causis* et dans ses sources', pp. 212-232. For some scholastic interpretations of the doctrine, see ibid., pp. 209-212.

[57] PSEUDO-ARISTOTLE, *Liber de causis* viii(ix) 90, ed. Pattin, p. 157: "Et intelligentia est habens *yliathim* quoniam est esse et forma et similiter anima est habens *yliathim* et natura est habens *yliathim*. Et causae quidem primae non est *yliathim*, quoniam ipsa est esse tantum." For this doctrine of *yliathim* and its sources in regard to First Cause, see COSTA, '"Cause prime non est yliathim"', pp. 327-349.

[58] PSEUDO-ARISTOTLE, *Liber de causis* xxii(xxiii) 173-174, ed. Pattin, pp. 183-184.

(iii) Substance

According to the *Liber de causis*, the hypostasis Mind is an undivided substance (*substantia*).[59] Plotinus had defined Mind similarly.[60] Mind, we are told in the *Liber de causis*, is an intelligible substance, i.e. it is not composed with matter.[61] Mind as a substance must be distinguished from composed substances (*substantiae compositae*), i.e. corporeal substances composed of matter and form. Mind is a substance beyond time, it is eternal and indestructible. Composed substances, which are dependent upon Mind, exist in time and are subjected to generation, corruption and destruction.[62] There are thus two ontological realms, one of eternity and another of time. But these two realms are connected through an intermediary, "whose substance falls under eternity and whose operation falls under time".[63] The hypostasis Soul is the intermediary which ensures the connection between the two realms, Mind and composed substances, and that is why Soul is said to exist, as already mentioned, "on the horizon of eternity from below and above time".[64]

The characteristic of Mind in the *Liber de causis* fulfils Bruno's criterion for a substance, namely, to be eternal and permanent — a criterion which Aristotle's concept of substance does not meet according to him, as we have seen in Chapter 2.[65] There is yet another similarity in the respective treatments of Mind by the author of the *Liber de causis* and Bruno. Just as the author of the *Liber de causis* describes Mind as eternal and indestructible, Bruno describes the World Soul, which disposes of Mind as a potency, in the same way in his *De la causa*, namely as "permanent and eternal".[66] However, Bruno's alternative — a universal substance with two eternal and permanent principles, matter and the World Soul, the latter being dependent upon Mind — differs from the *Liber de causis*. For in the theory of individuation of the *Liber de causis*, matter is not regarded as an

---

[59]   Ibid., vi(vii) 64, 70, ed. Pattin, pp. 149, 151.

[60]   PLOTINUS V iii [49] 5.30-39. For this notion in Plotinus, see HALFWASSEN, 'Substanz/Akzidens; I. Antikke', col. 501.

[61]   PSEUDO-ARISTOTLE, *Liber de causis* vii(viii) 73, ed. Pattin, p. 152.

[62]   Ibid., xxviii(xxix)-xxix(xxx), ed. Pattin, pp. 192-200.

[63]   Ibid., xxx(xxxi) 211, ed. Pattin, p. 199: "Necesse est igitur ut sit res alia tertia media inter utrasque [eternal and temporal realms] cuius substantia cadat sub aeternitate et ipsius actio cadat sub tempore."

[64]   Ibid., ii 22, ed. Pattin, p. 138, as quoted on p. 111 n. 44 above. In ibid., xxx(xxxi) 210-213, ed. Pattin, pp. 198-201, Soul is not identified explicitly, but Aquinas points out that this intermediary is Soul by referring to *Liber de causis* ii; see AQUINAS, *Super Librum de causis expositio* xxxi, pp. 141.20-142.5.

[65]   BRUNO, *Causa* epist., iii, pp. 17-19, 189. For Bruno's criticism of Aristotle's concept of substance, see pp. 30-34 above.

[66]   Ibid., iii, p. 189: "e veramente è cosa necessaria che come possiamo ponere un principio materiale costante et eterno, poniamo un similmente principio formale." The 'principio formale' is explained as the 'datore de le forme'; see ibid., iii, p. 189. By 'datore de le forme' Bruno refers to the World Soul; see pp. 27 n. 93, 37 n. 50 above. The hypostasis Mind is described as a power of the World Soul, see BRUNO, *Causa* ii, p. 121, as cited on p. 35 n. 38 above.

equal, co-principle together with Mind; in the *Liber de causis* matter receives according to its capacity to receive, but the active role of matter in this context is far less pronounced in the *Liber de causis* than in Bruno's theory of individuation. Nor is matter described as eternal in the *Liber de causis* as Bruno does in *De la causa*, hence describing his universal substance as having two eternal principles, the World Soul and matter.[67]

The conception of Mind as timeless and incorruptible was commonplace in Neoplatonism, hence Bruno could have picked up this idea from a variety of other Neoplatonic sources.[68] As mentioned already, Plotinus had similarly identified Mind as substance,[69] and Bruno paraphrased Plotinus' argument in favour of a substance sustaining corporal substances.[70] So Plotinus is undoubtedly an important source on this point. On the other hand, Bruno, as pointed out in Chapter 1, took over the image of the hypostasis Soul known from the *Liber de causis* ("on the horizon of eternity from below and above time"), and applied it to the hypostasis Soul as well as to the individual soul of a human being.[71] These verbal similarities suggest that Bruno was familiar with the distinction between eternity and time in the *Liber de causis*, directly or indirectly. So even though it is probably untenable to claim that Bruno's notion of substance derives from the *Liber de causis*, it is still possible that the notion of substance in the *Liber de causis* prepared him for more authentic Neoplatonic interpretations of substance.

(iv) Higher and lower intelligences

In the *Liber de causis*, the transmission of forms from Mind to nature is described in proposition ix(x). There the term 'intelligentia' is employed in two senses. First, it denotes the first emanation from the First Cause, the hypostasis Mind. Second, it is used to describe intellectual substances comprising forms, intelligences.[72] The latter are of two kinds. Some comprise "less universal forms" (*formae minus universales*) and some comprise "more universal forms" (*formae plus universales*).[73] Proposition ix(x) in the *Liber de causis* is based on proposition 177 in Proclus' *Elements of theology*. Dodds explains in relation to the latter proposition that the hierarchy of intelligences is parallel to that of genera and species. Hence, each higher intelligence contains one genus, implicitly several

---

[67] BRUNO, *Causa* iii, p. 169, as quoted on p. 33 n. 22 above.

[68] The most important source is PLOTINUS III vii [45]. For this theme, see WALLIS, *Neoplatonism*, p. 53; BEIERWALTES, 'Einleitung', pp. 9-88.

[69] PLOTINUS V iii [49] 5.30-39.

[70] BRUNO, *Causa* ii, p. 139. See AQUILECCHIA's note ibid., p. 138 n. 73.

[71] For 'horizon' applied to the human soul, see BRUNO, *De magia naturali* §16.6-10, p. 188 (= *BOL*, vol. 3, p. 409.16-20); *De immenso* i 1, p. 202.16-19. Both passages are quoted on p. 11 n. 17 above. See also BRUNO, *Furori* i 4, p. 189, as quoted on p. 11 n. 20 above. For 'horizon' applied to the hypostasis Soul, see BRUNO, *Sigillus* i 37, p. 182.20-24, as quoted on p. 10 n. 14 above.

[72] PSEUDO-ARISTOTLE, *Liber de causis* ix(x) 92, ed. Pattin, p. 158.

[73] Ibid., ix(x) 92, p. 158.

species, and each of the more numerous lower intelligences contains one species.[74] The *Liber de causis* explains that the degree of universality of forms contained in intelligences is determined by the mode of being of the various forms. The lower intelligences thus exist in a "particular mode" (*per modum particularem*), whereas the higher intelligences exist in a "universal mode" (*per modum universalem*).[75]

The intelligences comprising less universal forms, the 'inferior intelligences', are thus distinguished from those comprising more universal forms, the 'superior intelligences'. This subdivision of intelligences is ultimately determined by the ontological proximity to the First Cause. The superior intelligences are more proximate to the One (*unum*) whereas the inferior are more remote. As a consequence, superior intelligences have more unity and power than inferior intelligences, and the former are more restricted in number than the latter.[76] Ultimately the ontologically lower position of the inferior intelligences is explainable by their limited capacity to receive (*recipere*) universal forms. Due to the limited power of inferior intelligences, they have to separate and divide what they receive, and cannot, therefore, receive universal forms in their completeness.[77] In this way superior and inferior intelligences are intermediaries between unity and plurality.

Bruno refers on several occasions to this distinction between higher and lower intelligences.[78] Furthermore, as we have seen in Chapter 3, he discusses

---

[74] DODDS' note in PROCLUS, *Elements of theology*, p. 292.

[75] PSEUDO-ARISTOTLE, *Liber de causis* ix(x) 93, ed. Pattin, p. 158.

[76] Ibid., ix(x) 94-95, pp. 158-159.

[77] Ibid., ix(x) 98, p. 160. The Plotinian doctrine of reception according to the capacity of the recipient appears in PROCLUS, *Elements of theology* prop. 173, pp. 150.22-152.7. It presupposes the principle articulated ibid., prop. 177, pp. 156.1-9, 156.16-20. For this doctrine in Plotinus, see p. 38 n. 53 above.

[78] In the following passage Bruno uses the distinction between higher and lower intelligences, though he increases the number of ontological steps; see BRUNO, *De umbris* §28.9-15, p. 31: "Novit quidem et docuit antiquitas quomodo proficiat discursus hominis a multis individuis ad speciem, a multis speciebus ad unum genus ascendens; insuper quomodo infima intelligentiarum per omnes formas intelligat species distincte, inferioris distincte per plures atque multas formas ipsas omnes species concipiunt, superiores per pauciores, suprema per unam, et ipsum quod est supra omne non per formam aliquam." Forms in intelligences are also referred to ibid., §52.13, p. 44. For the higher and lower intelligences mentioned in the quotation, see PSEUDO-ARISTOTLE, *Liber de causis* ix(x) 92-94, ed. Pattin, p. 158. Sturlese may be referring inaccurately to the first passage in the *Liber de causis* in her note to *De umbris* §28.11-15, p. 31, where she gives "10(9)" instead of "9(10)". Bruno retained this notion of intelligences later in his philosophy, including this distinction between higher and lower intelligences; see BRUNO, *Causa* v, pp. 295-297; *Summa*, pp. 109.16-27, 114.27-115.4, 125.11-126.8. He rejected the popular idea of nine intelligences governing each of the respective nine spheres; see BRUNO, *Furori* arg., p. 41. For Bruno's notion of 'intelligence', see SPRUIT, *Il problema*, pp. 230-234, 300-316. SPRUIT, ibid., pp. 307 n. 106, 309 n. 113, mentions Aquinas' commentary to proposition iv and ix(x) of the *Liber de causis* as part of the background of Bruno's notion of intelligence. For Arabic sources to Bruno's notions of higher and lower intelligences, see SPRUIT, 'Motivi peripatetici', pp. 393-398.

contraction as descent and noetic ascent through genera and species in the hierarchy of being.[79] Insofar as the distinction between higher and lower intelligences in the *Liber de causis* is parallel to that between genera and species, his concept of contraction, as descent and ascent, concerns this distinction between intelligences in the *Liber de causis*.

(v) Contraction

It is precisely in relation to this proposition ix(x) in the *Liber de causis* that we find the notion of contraction, namely, in discussions of the reception of forms in inferior intelligences from superior intelligences. The term *contractio* is not employed in this or any other of the propositions of the *Liber de causis*.[80] But in proposition 177 of Proclus' *Elements of theology*, on which proposition ix(x) in the *Liber de causis* is based, the Greek equivalent of the Latin verb *contraho*, συστέλλω, occurs. In the Greek text of *Elements of theology* this Greek verb appears as a participle attributed to those Ideas which are more akin to the One, "while their number is relatively contracted" (τῷ ποσῷ συνεσταλμένα).[81] An example may clarify this language. Whereas the superior intelligence contains the Idea of trees as a genus, this Idea is implicitly present in the Ideas of specific species of trees, for example that of an oak. One superior intelligence thus indirectly comprises numerous inferior intelligences, and the superior intelligences are therefore more restricted, "contracted", with regard to number than the inferior intelligences. In Moerbeke's Latin translation of 1268, the participle in Proclus' text is translated as an adjective (*quantitate contracta*) describing the relatively limited number of forms in superior intelligences compared to the number of particular forms in inferior intelligences.[82]

In his *Quaestiones*, pseudo-Henry used 'contraction' in his commentary on the *Liber de causis*.[83] This is the earliest use of the noun contraction I have found in

---

[79] BRUNO, *Sigillus* ii 22, pp. 213.21-214.6, as quoted on p. 55 n. 19 above.

[80] Here I rely on *Liber de causis* as the text appears in Pattin's edition, including the variations indicated in the apparatus.

[81] PROCLUS, *Elements of theology* prop. 177, p. 156.7-9: "τὰ [Ideas in superior intelligences] γὰρ τῷ ἑνὶ συγγενέστερα, τῷ ποσῷ συνεσταλμένα, τῇ δυνάμει τὰ μετ' αὐτὰ ὑπεραίρει". Tr. E. R. Dodds.

[82] PROCLUS, *Elementatio theologica* prop. 177.6-9, tr. Moerbeke, p. 87: "Superiores [intellectus] quidem enim potentiis utuntur maioribus, unialiores secundis existentes; inferiores autem, multiplicati magis, minuunt potentias quas habent. Que enim uni magis congenea, quantitate contracta, potentia que post ipsa excedunt; et que ab uno remotius e converso."

[83] PSEUDO-HENRY, *Quaestiones in Librum de causis* theorema 4.28-31, qu. 25, p. 61: "Praeterea, cum dicitur quod est esse primum creatum, aut est sermo de esse universaliter sumpto, aut de esse contracto ad intelligentiam, aut aliquid aliud. Non de esse contracto, quia de isto esse dicit in commento quod nihil est latius eo, quod non est esse intelligentiae." See also ibid., theorema 4.79-81, resp. ad qu. 25, p. 63: "Ad illud quod quaeritur: aut est sermo in theoremate de esse universaliter sumpto aut contracto,

the scholastic tradition. If it is correct that this work of pseudo-Henry dates from 1245-1255, and Moerbeke's translation of *Elements of theology* from 1268, then pseudo-Henry could not have taken the term from Moerbeke's translation.[84] It may simply have been a commonly used term in theories of individuation. Be this as it may, it was not Moerbeke's Latin translation which put the term 'contraction' at the centre of the scholastic tradition revolving around the *Liber de causis*.

The concept of contraction, in its ontological sense, was used in various meanings by commentators on the *Liber de causis*. In the subsequent part of this chapter I shall describe some examples of four different meanings of ontological contraction, make some comparisons with Bruno's use of the term, and finally ask whether Giles may be among Bruno's sources.

Essence contracted into existence

(i) Pseudo-Henry

The commentary *Quaestiones in Librum de causis* attributed to pseudo-Henry, composed between 1245 and 1255, as mentioned above, is organised as a discussion of each proposition in the *Liber de causis*. The *quaestiones* raised in relation to each proposition are discussed in the scholastic fashion.[85]

Pseudo-Henry states explicitly that he prefers the theory of individuation in the *Liber de causis*, which he assumes is of Aristotelian origin, to the Platonic theory of individuation through participation in Ideas. This is because, he says, Plato's doctrine of Ideas cannot account for generation and change in nature. Generation and change could, however, be explained by the different kinds of forms that, according to "Aristotle" in the *Liber de causis*, exist in the superior and inferior intelligences.[86] Aristotle had criticised Plato on this score in the first book of his *Metaphysics*.[87] In order to justify his claim, pseudo-Henry refers to the seventh book of Aristotle's *Metaphysics*, dealing with generation, probably VII vii-ix. This

---

<ul>
<li>dicendum, ut arguitur, quod non de esse contracto sed universaliter sumpto ad quodlibet creatum."</li>
</ul>

[84] For the date of Moerbeke's translation, see SAFFREY, 'Introduction', pp. XXXIII-XXXIV. For the date of pseudo-Henry's commentary, see ZWAENEPOEL, 'Introduction', pp. 14-15.

[85] For a description of the MS, see ZWAENEPOEL, 'Introduction', pp. 7-19.

[86] PSEUDO-HENRY, *Quaestiones in Librum de causis*, theorema 3, resp. ad qu. 23.48-54, p. 59: "Sic immateriale potest transmutare materiale, ut intelligentia corpus caeli, ut anima spiritum aut proprium corpus. Loquendo de transmutatione secundo modo, sic habet veritatem et intelligitur ad litteram VIIus *Metaphysicae*. Est enim sermo ibi de generatione naturali, quam Plato dicebat esse ab Ideis, quae, secundum Aristotelem et commentum Averrois ibidem, non habent virtutem transmutandi aliquo modo materiam."

[87] ARISTOTLE, *Metaphysics* I ix 991^{a}8-991^{b}9.

and other references to Aristotle probably reflects the author's misconception that the *Liber de causis* had an Aristotelian origin.

Pseudo-Henry introduces 'contraction' in relation to the *Liber de causis*, proposition iv, entitled *Prima rerum creatarum est esse*. In *Quaestio* 24, concerning proposition iv, he asks whether being is created or not.[88] It is not, he first argues. Since being has to be being of something, it cannot be being in itself.[89] In his next *quaestio* he continues this objection, stating that being (*esse*) must be "assumed" (*sumptum*) or "contracted" (*contractum*) into Mind or some other entity.[90] In the replies to *quaestiones* 24 and 25, however, he modifies this view by distinguishing between being that is 'being universally' and being that is 'contracted' to whatever created entity.[91]

(ii) Aquinas

Aquinas' *Super Librum de causis expositio* was composed in the first half of 1272, four years after William of Moerbeke's Latin translation of Proclus' *Elementatio theologica* was finished in 1268.[92] Aquinas warns his reader in the *Prooemium* to his commentary that we find only "extracts" (*excerptus*) of Proclus' *Elements of theology* in the *Liber de causis*. The *Elements of theology*, he says, contains a much more ample and extensive exposition of the ideas propounded in the *Liber de causis*.[93] Aquinas was already familiar with the treatise when he composed his *De ente et essentia*, between 1252 and 1256, where he draws important metaphysical ideas from it and mentions it by name.[94] The philological discoveries made possible through Moerbeke's Latin translation of Proclus' *Elementatio theologica* in great measure shaped Aquinas' commentary on the *Liber de causis*.

For Aquinas the *Liber de causis* should not, as pseudo-Henry held, be harmonised with Aristotle's thought. Instead he subjects it to textual and philosophical criticism. As a result he distinguishes the ideas in the *Liber de causis* from those of Aristotle. Aquinas identified thirty-seven of the two hundred and eleven propositions in Proclus' work, often documented with quotations from Moerbeke's translation. This textual criticism is accompanied by a thorough

---

[88] PSEUDO-HENRY, *Quaestiones in Librum de causis* theorema 4.5, qu. 24, p. 60: "Et est prima quaestio utrum esse sit creatum."

[89] Ibid., theorema 4.12-13, qu. 24, p. 60: "Esse autem non est per se existens, sed in illo cuius est esse, cum sit actus entis."

[90] Ibid., theorema 4.28-31, qu. 25, p. 61, as quoted on p. 117 n. 83 above.

[91] Ibid., theorema 4.79-81, resp. ad qu. 25, p. 63, as quoted on p. 117 n. 83 above.

[92] For a general discussion of Aquinas' commentary, see SAFFREY, 'Introduction', pp. XIII-XXXVII; BEIERWALTES, 'Der Kommentar', pp. 192-215; ELDERS, 'St. Thomas d'Aquin et la métaphysique du *Liber de Causis*', pp. 429-438; LIBERA, 'Albert le Grand et Thomas d'Aquin interprètes du *Liber de Causis*', pp. 349-350, 370-373, 376-388; GUAGLIARDO, 'Introduction', pp. XIX-XXXII. For the role of the *Liber de causis* in Aquinas' works, see ELDERS, 'St. Thomas d'Aquin et la métaphysique du *Liber de Causis*', pp. 438-442.

[93] AQUINAS, *Super Librum de causis expositio* proemium, p. 3.5-10.

[94] E.g. AQUINAS, *De ente et essentia* iv, p. 32.3-4.

philosophical analysis, in which the *Liber de causis* is corrected against works by Aristotle, Augustine and pseudo-Dionysius.

Aquinas does not use the term *contractio* in the same contexts of the *Liber de causis* as pseudo-Henry, notably in relation to proposition iv, which deals with 'being'. Nor does Aquinas use the term, or its cognates, elsewhere in his commentary. This omission assumes some importance when we compare Aquinas' discussion of the philosophical themes treated by pseudo-Henry in his commentary on proposition iv of the *Liber de causis*, namely the ontological status of 'being' (*esse*). This problem has profound implications for theories concerning the relationship between God and nature and for theories of individuation. Aquinas' position differs from that of pseudo-Henry in regard to proposition iv in the *Liber de causis*, as we shall see shortly, and that may be the reason why he omitted the notion of contraction. This conjecture is supported by the fact that Aquinas was not shy of using 'contraction' in his theory of individuation in the *Summa theologiae*, written about the same time as his commentary on the *Liber de causis*.[95]

Proposition iv in the *Liber de causis* asserts that "the first of created things is being (*esse*) and there is nothing else created before it".[96] Aquinas points out that this is a rephrasing of Proclus' *Elements of theology*, proposition 138, which he cites from Moerbeke's translation.[97] In Proclus' text it is stated that "of all the deified things which participate in the divine character, the first and highest is being itself (τὸ ὄν)."[98] The words τὸ ὄν in the Greek text are ambiguous philosophically. They can be translated into the Latin infinite *esse*, 'being', thereby denoting 'being' generally. Alternatively, however, they can be translated as "existing entity" (*ens*).[99] The twelfth-century Latin translation of the *Liber de causis* made from an Arabic text uses *esse*; Moerbeke chooses *ens*.[100]

---

[95] E.g., AQUINAS, *Summa theologiae* 1a, qu. 44, art. 2, resp., vol. 4, p. 458, as quoted on p. 128 n. 144 below.

[96] PSEUDO-ARISTOTLE, *Liber de causis* iv 37, ed. Pattin, p. 142: "Prima rerum creatarum est esse et non est ante ipsum creatum aliud."

[97] AQUINAS, *Super Librum de causis expositio* iv, p. 27.11-14: "Et hanc etiam propositionem Proclus in suo libro ponit cxxxviiiam, sub his verbis: 'Omnium participantium divina proprietate et deificatorum primum est et supremum ens.'" This quotation is from PROCLUS, *Elementatio theologica* prop. 138.1-2, tr. Moerbeke, p. 69, which reads in Boese's edition: "Omnium participantium divina proprietate et edeificatorum [sic deificatorum] primum est et supremum ens." For this question of being in Aquinas' commentary, see translator's note in AQUINAS, *Commentary on the Book of causes*, p. 30 n. 12. For Aquinas' interpretation of proposition iv in the *Liber de causis* and his integration of into his philosophy, see FABRO, *Participation et causalité selon S. Thomas d'Aquin*, pp. 229-244.

[98] PROCLUS, *Elements of theology* prop. 138, p. 122.7-8.

[99] For the introduction of the term into medieval Latin, see GABRIEL, 'Sein', cols 175, 186.

[100] PSEUDO-ARISTOTLE, *Liber de causis* iv 37, ed. Pattin, p. 142, as quoted on p. 120 n. 96 above. Cf. PROCLUS, *Elementatio theologica* prop. 138.1-2, tr. Moerbeke, p. 69, as cited on p. 120 n. 97 above. For the rendering of τὸ ὄν in the *Liber de causis*, see COSTA, 'La doctrine de la création "mediante intelligentia" dans le *Liber de causis* et dans ses sources', p. 214.

In his *Liber de causis* commentary Aquinas refers to, but does not follow, Moerbeke's *ens*.[101] In this particular case he follows *Liber de causis'* *esse*. Aquinas asserts, therefore, in his commentary on proposition iv to the *Liber de causis* that "being itself came to be superior to all other created things".[102] Aquinas' comment differs from that of pseudo-Henry, as the latter formulates it on one occasion in the *Quaestiones*.[103] Being, pseudo-Henry said in his commentary on the *Liber de causis*, following broadly a Neoplatonic line, is contracted with the forms in intelligences, which in turn are contracted into created entities.[104]

"Those things that are less common" than being, Aquinas continues in his comment upon proposition iv in the *Liber de causis*, are "related to the more common [i.e. being] by means of some addition."[105] Separate substances like intelligences and souls consist of being and essence (*essentia*), and are therefore what is rendered in the Latin version of the *Liber de causis* with an Arabic expression, *yliathim*, meaning universality.[106] This denotes, according to Aquinas, entities composed of being (*esse*) and form (*forma*).[107] Aquinas explains that *yliathim* is derived from the Greek word *hyle* (ὕλη), matter, since separate substances too are composites, like corporeal substances, which are composed of form and matter.[108] However, separate substances are not composed of matter and form, but of being and form, Aquinas says.[109] His interpretation at this point is, then, governed by his refusal to attribute potentiality, and hence matter, to intelligible entities, a position which inspired his axiomatic distinction between essence and existence. Elsewhere Aquinas rejects explicitly the idea that intelligences and souls are composed of form and matter, and assigns this opinion, which he finds repugnant, to Avicebron's *Fons vitae*.[110]

---

[101] For his reference, see AQUINAS, *Super Librum de causis expositio* iv, p. 27.11-14, as quoted on p. 120 n. 97 above.

[102] AQUINAS, *Super Librum de causis expositio* iv, p. 29.3-5: "Et ex hoc concludit [i.e. the author of the *Liber de causis*] quod, propter illud quod dictum est, ipsum esse factum est superius omnibus rebus creatis." For Aquinas' own interpretation of *esse*, see GABRIEL, 'Sein', cols 189-190; TAYLOR, 'Aquinas, the *Plotiniana Arabica*', pp. 217-239.

[103] Cf. PSEUDO-HENRY, *Quaestiones in Librum de causis* theorema 4.12-13, qu. 24, p. 60, as quoted on p. 119 n. 89 above.

[104] PSEUDO-HENRY, *Quaestiones in Librum de causis*, theorema 4.79-81, resp. ad qu. 25, p. 63. See quotation on p. 117 n. 83 above.

[105] AQUINAS, *Super Librum de causis expositio* iv, p. 29.7-8: "nam ea quae sunt minus communia videntur se habere ad magis communia per modum additionis cuiusdam."

[106] PSEUDO-ARISTOTLE, *Liber de causis* viii(ix) 90, ed. Pattin, p. 157.

[107] AQUINAS, *Super Librum de causis expositio* ix, p. 64.6-15. He also proposed this interpretation, citing the *Liber de causis* viii(ix) 90, ed. Pattin, p. 157, in his *De ente et essentia* iv, pp. 31.18-32.6.

[108] For an examination of Aquinas' claim, in particular Aquinas' equation of the Arabic term *yliathim* with matter (ὕλη), see TAYLOR, 'Hylomorphic composition', pp. 506-513. For the doctrine and the sources of *yliathim* in the *Liber de causis* viii(ix), see p. 113 n. 57 above.

[109] AQUINAS, *Super Librum de causis expositio* ix, p. 64.9-13.

[110] AQUINAS, *De ente et essentia* iv, pp. 29.32-30.7.

(iii) Giles

Giles composed his *Super de causis* between 1289 and 1291, almost two decades after Aquinas had written his commentary on the *Liber de causis* in 1272.[111] Unlike pseudo-Henry's and Aquinas' commentaries on the *Liber de causis*, Giles' commentary has not yet been published in a modern critical edition. Giles was Aquinas' pupil from 1269 to 1272. He was familiar with this work of his master, whose interpretation he discussed.[112] Giles also knew of Aquinas' identifications of a substantial number of propositions from the *Liber de causis* with propositions from Moerbeke's Latin translation of Proclus' *Elements of theology*, which was probably also accessible to Giles.[113] He mentions Proclus throughout the commentary, referring in almost every proposition to propositions in the *Elements of theology*.[114]

Even though he probably knew, through Aquinas, that Aristotle was not the author of the *Liber de causis*, Giles nevertheless regarded the *Liber de causis* as a supplement to the discussion of the 'first principle' in Aristotle's *Metaphysics*.[115] Clearly, Giles did not perceive Aristotle and the Neoplatonist Proclus as irreconcilable, but he saw them as engaged in the same metaphysical discussion about the first cause and first principle of the universe, despite their different opinions and arguments.

The Venice 1550 edition of Giles' commentary, the last edition to be published, came out with an unusually detailed index running over thirty-eight pages, about a fifth of the entire volume. The index lists philosophical terms used in the work. Each term is provided with a short definition and reference to the respective propositions in Giles' commentary. The index, and in particular its form, suggests that it was used as a philosophical dictionary. The term 'contraction' is not listed separately in the index — possibly because it denotes relationships between ontological levels or ontological entities rather than the levels or entities themselves, which are listed. However, the term features frequently in his explanatory comments on the theory of individuation of the *Liber de causis*, especially in his comments on the first ten propositions.[116]

---

[111] See PUNTA and TRIFOGLI, 'Giles of Rome', p. 77.

[112] HOCEDEZ, 'Introduction', in GILES, *De esse et essentia*, pp. 46-48. For Giles' disagreement with Aquinas in regard to the *Liber de causis*, see TRAPÉ, 'Il neoplatonismo', pp. 52-54; NASH, 'Giles of Rome', pp. 81-82.

[113] For Giles as a pupil of Aquinas, see NASH, 'Giles of Rome', p. 57.

[114] For Giles' use of Proclus in his commentary on the *Liber de causis*, see ibid., pp. 81-82.

[115] GILES, *Super authorem De causis, Alpharabium* proaemium, Y. For this passage, see COSTA, 'Le fonti e la struttura del *Liber de causis*', p. 1 n. 1; TRAPÉ, 'Il neoplatonismo', p. 50.

[116] GILES, *Super authorem De causis, Alpharabium* i, ii, iv, v, vi, vii, ix, x, xiv, xviii, xxii, fols 4ᵛ (lines 25-31), 5ʳ (lines 28-31, 39-42), 8ʳ (lines 38-44), 8ᵛ (lines 9-18), 15ᵛ (lines 16-20), 16ᵛ (lines 14-18), 20ᵛ (lines 19-24, 35-42), 23ʳ (lines 10-11), 23ᵛ (lines 14-18, 23-25), 25ᵛ (lines 18-21, 34-44), 35ᵛ (lines 30-41), 36ᵛ (lines 30-36), 37ʳ (lines 32-37, 42-46), 38ᵛ (lines 38-44), 47ᵛ (lines 44-46), 62ʳ (lines 41-44), 74ʳ (lines 14-20, 28-36), 74ᵛ (lines 41-44).

Pseudo-Henry used the notion only a few times in his commentary on the *Liber de causis*. Aquinas had not used it at all in his commentary but only in contemporary or almost contemporary works. Giles, on the other hand, embraced the term and used it to explain all levels of individuation. He had also used the term in his theory of individuation in his earlier *De esse et essentia*, though less frequently but still in relation to the *Liber de causis*.[117] Of the three authors, and the *Liber de causis* itself, Giles was certainly the one who made contraction a key notion in discussions concerning the *Liber de causis*.[118] In Giles' commentary, the notion is almost exclusively employed in the ontological sense of individuation. It concerns the four ontological levels, namely God, intelligences, souls and particulars composed of matter and form. Giles also employs the term in his account of how the Neoplatonic doctrine of reception according to the capacity of the recipient should be understood on the three last mentioned ontological levels.[119]

According to the *Liber de causis*, God creates the lower levels in the hierarchy of being through intelligences, which, in turn, create Soul and nature.[120] How does Giles use contraction in his account of that hierarchy of being?

When commenting upon God, the First Cause, Giles follows Aquinas' interpretation of the *Liber de causis* and identifies Him with pure being (*esse purum*).[121] As such, God is not contracted with anything, Giles says.[122] This is in

---

[117] The notion contraction is used in GILES, *De esse et essentia* theorema 1, pp. 2.13-17, 4.1-3 and theorema 4, p. 16.1-10. He mentions the *Liber de causis* ibid., theorema 1, p. 4.11-17 and theorema 3, pp. 13.16-14.3. For the concept contraction in Giles' *De esse et essentia*, see PETERSON, 'Cardinal Cajetan and Giles of Rome', pp. 434, 437. Peterson ignores the concept contraction in Giles' commentary on the *Liber de causis*.

[118] This observation agrees with Vescovini's emphasis on Giles' role in the development of the notion contraction in Cusanus' theory of individuation in the *De docta ignorantia*. See VESCOVINI, 'Introduzione', p. 27. However, Vescovini states this point in general terms without citing specific references to 'contraction' in Giles' works.

[119] GILES, *Super authorem De causis, Alpharabium* x, fol. 37^r, lines 32-37: "Omne quod recipitur in aliquo, recipitur per modum rei recipientis. Ergo quae recipiuntur in intelligentiis inferioribus recipiuntur modo inferiori, et contracto, et particulari. Quae vero recipiuntur in superioribus, recipiuntur modo superiori, excellenti et universali. Intelligentiae ergo secundae intelligent per species inferiores, particulares, et contractas. Intelligentiae vero primae per species universaliores, et minus contractas." For the Neoplatonic sources for this doctrine, see p. 38 n. 53 above.

[120] PSEUDO-ARISTOTLE, *Liber de causis* viii(ix) 87, ed. Pattin, pp. 156-157.

[121] For God as pure being; see GILES, *Super authorem De causis, Alpharabium* ii, iv, ix, xxvi, fols 8^v (line 13), 16^v (lines 35-36, 40-42), 35^r (lines 25-26), 89^v (lines 2-3). For Giles on God as pure being in his commentary on the *Liber de causis*, see TRAPÉ, 'Il neoplatonismo', pp. 59-61; NASH, 'Giles of Rome', p. 90.

[122] GILES, *Super authorem De causis, Alpharabium* ii, fol. 8^r, lines 40-42: "Propter quod sciendum quod est dare unum verum Deum qui est ipsum esse purum non determinatum ad aliquod praedicamentum, non contractum ad aliquod genus entium." Similarly ibid., ii, iv, vi, x, fols 8^v (line 13), 16^v (lines 42-43), 23^v (lines 15-18), 36^v (lines 33-35). This usage is similar to that of AQUINAS, *Quaestiones quodlibetales* quodlibetum 3, qu. 1, art. 1, pp. 71-72; see quotation on p. 127 n. 143 below.

agreement with Aquinas' distinction between existence and essence. God is, therefore, Giles says, similar to a light source (*lux*) which is distinct from its manifestations as colours (*colores*) when contracted (*lux contracta*) into sensible particulars. Similarly, God is pure being existing above time, and He gives being to lower hypostases without being diminished Himself.[123]

(iv) Pico

In the Renaissance Pico challenged the distinction between being and essence that Aquinas proposed in his interpretation of proposition iv in the *Liber de causis*. In his *Conclusiones* Pico warns the reader that even though the author of the *Liber de causis* claims that "being, which is the first created thing, exists above Mind, you should not believe that as a hypostasis it is distinct from Mind."[124] Hereby Pico probably means, like Proclus, that the hypostasis Mind indirectly contains being, one of the three elements in the triadic subdivision of the hypostasis Mind, being-life-Intelligence.[125]

(v) Bruno

On rare occasions Bruno rejects Aquinas' distinction between existence and essence, as Pico had done. However, Bruno does not do so for the same reason as Pico, but in order to defend his conception of living matter according to which being and essence are unified, though logically distinct.[126] In the *Summa terminorum metaphysicorum* Bruno follows the expression used by the *Liber de causis* and Aquinas of God, saying that he "gives being" (*dat esse*).[127] This position suggests that Bruno maintained the scholastic idea of being, ultimately the idea of God as a transcendent entity.

---

[123] GILES, *Super authorem De causis, Alpharabium* ii, fol. 8ᵛ, lines 1-18. Ibid., ii, fol. 8ᵛ, lines 11-13: "Sicut ergo album, et universaliter color dicunt lucem contractam: propter quod lux non est color, sed super color, lux non est alba sed super alba, sic omnis perfectio infra esse videtur [i.e. the author of the *Liber de causis*] dicere quoddam contractum esse, ideo Deus est ipsum esse purum non contractum".

[124] PICO, *Conclusiones* 6>4, p. 462: "Quamvis dicat Abucaten [the assumed author of *Liber de causis*] quod esse, quod est primum creatum, est super intelligentiam, non credas tamen illud secundum hypostasim esse distinctum ab intelligentia." Pico is probably writing against PSEUDO-ARISTOTLE, *Liber de causis* iv 37-38, ed. Pattin, p. 142: "Prima rerum creatarum est esse et non est ante ipsum creatum aliud. Quod est quia esse est supra sensum et supra animam et supra intelligentiam, et non est post causam primam latius neque prius creatum ipso."

[125] Cf. PROCLUS, *Elements of theology* prop. 101, p. 90. See also Dodds' note ibid., p. 252-253.

[126] E.g. BRUNO, *De immenso* viii 9, p. 310.9: "Adde, quod est nusquam distincta essentia ab esse". To distinguish these two concepts in regard to nature, Bruno adds in this context, is to mistake a logical distinction for an ontological one (ibid., viii 9, p. 310.10-18).

[127] BRUNO, *Summa*, p. 67.3-4: "Deus ... omnibus dat esse". See also ibid., pp. 86.11-16, 99.4-6.

However, Bruno's position is not entirely consistent. In his *De la causa* he has first Teofilo claiming, much in line with the statement in his *Summa terminorum metaphysicorum*, that absolute form gives being to all things.[128] Immediately afterwards Dicson sums up the argument, saying that "forms have no being without matter".[129] In this second statement the metaphysical structure in which Bruno's thoughts about contraction develops is reversed, insofar as he does not operate with a transcendent God who gives being and forms. Instead, he places matter — that is, his unified concept of matter — at the summit of the metaphysical structure, claiming that it gives being to forms, and that it co-determines individuation together with forms (see further Chapter 2, pp. 39-47). In this respect, Bruno's stance is unique. He does not comply with scholastic metaphysics, although his own builds on its terminology. Contrary to the scholastic focus on God as a transcendent entity who gives being to forms, Bruno focuses on the ontological and theological potentialities of matter.

Superior intelligences contracted into inferior intelligences

Albert's *De causis et processu universitatis a prima causa*, composed between 1265 and 1272, is not a commentary on the *Liber de causis*. But, as the title indicates, it does deal with the theme of procession from the First Cause, and, as already said, its second book is in fact organised as a discussion of the *Liber de causis*.[130] The notion contraction appears in this context. In his *De causis et processu universitatis a prima causa*, Albert explains how the universal forms in the superior intelligences are "contracted" into the particular forms in inferior intelligences, which are ultimately contracted with matter.[131] Forms of superior intelligences and their relation to forms of inferior intelligences was, as mentioned above, the theme of proposition ix(x) in the *Liber de causis*.

Aquinas does not employ 'contraction' within a Neoplatonic framework of emanation, either in his commentary on the *Liber de causis* or in his *Summa theologiae*. Instead, Aquinas interpreted emanation within a Christian scheme of

---

[128] BRUNO, *Causa* iii, p. 189, as quoted on p. 27 n. 93 above. This position he also holds in his *Sigillus* ii 10, pp. 202.20-203.5, also quoted on p. 27 n. 93 above.

[129] BRUNO, *Causa* iii, pp. 189-191: "le forme non hanno l'essere senza la materia". See also ibid., v, p. 277.27-33. For matter as the principle of being, see BLUM, *Aristoteles*, pp. 62-66.

[130] See the reference to Pattin's explanation on p. 106 n. 19 above.

[131] ALBERT, *De causis et processu universitatis a prima causa* II ii 22, p. 116.24-33: "Et propter hoc quod intelligentiae proprinquae uni primo et puro minoris sunt quantitatis et maioris simplicitatis, propter hoc etiam sequitur, quod bonitates et formae, quae procedunt ex intelligentiis primis, procedant processione universali unita simplici. Quae cum receptae sunt in secundis, quia in secundis determinantur et contrahuntur, necesse est, quod ab ipsis procedant processione magis particulari et magis composita et contracta et magis et magis ad materiam inclinata." The term 'contraction' is also employed to describe the hierarchy of causes within this theory of procession ibid., II ii 15, II ii 16, pp. 108.73-80, 109.11-15.

creation, and interpreted the *Liber de causis* accordingly.[132] He speaks of an "emanation" from a first principle or first cause.[133] The hierarchy of being, following an ontological structure of dependency or causation, as in Albert, thus also features in Aquinas' philosophy. However, the kind of emanation Aquinas has in mind is the Christian one used among scholastics, not Plotinus'. In particular, he equates emanation with the Christian account of creation *ex nihilo*.[134] There are at least two important differences between Neoplatonic and Thomistic notions of 'emanation'. For Plotinus emanation is an eternal process.[135] Second, the Christian God cares for His Creation, whereas the creative power of the One does not care for its products.[136]

With regard to intelligences, the intermediaries between God and His Creation, Giles agrees with Aquinas that intelligences consist of being and form exclusively and individuate themselves without matter.[137] In another respect, however, Giles differs from Aquinas' terminology. He says intelligences are "contracted" from being and form and he uses the term to differentiate universal forms from particular forms, the former being "less contracted", the latter being "more contracted".[138] Giles accommodates the idea of intelligences to Aristotelian terminology by asserting that intelligences are contractions from the First Cause into genera. These genera are contracted into species, whose forms ultimately are contracted with matter in the individuation of sensible particulars.[139] Hence Giles makes use of the term 'contraction' throughout the hierarchy of being to explain the increasing multiplicity in the descending hierarchy of being.

The individuation of souls is also described by means of the term 'contraction'. Here Giles distinguishes between souls of celestial bodies, which are immaterial, and human souls, which are by nature united with material bodies. Human souls,

---

[132] AQUINAS, *Summa theologiae* 1a, qu. 45, art. 1-8, vol. 4, pp. 464-477.

[133] E.g. ibid., 1a, qu. 45, art. 1, 2 and 4, vol. 4, pp. 464, 466, 468.

[134] Ibid., 1a, qu. 45, art. 1, resp., vol. 4, p. 464: "Respondeo dicendum quod, sicut supra dictum est [ibid., qu. 44, art. 2], non solum oportet considerare emanationem alicuius entis particularis ab aliquo particulari agente, sed etiam emanationem totius entis a causa universali, quae est Deus: et hanc quidem emanationem designamus nomine 'creationis'."

[135] WALLIS, *Neoplatonism*, p. 65.

[136] For the differences between Plotinus' doctrine of emanation and Christian creation, see ibid., pp. 64-65. For a comparison between Aquinas and Bruno on this point, see GHIO, 'Causa emanativa e causa immanente', pp. 529-554.

[137] GILES, *Super authorem De causis, Alpharabium* ix, fol. 35ᵛ, lines 35-37: "Forma ergo materialis individuatur per materiam signatam in qua recipitur. Sed forma separata cuiusmodi est natura intelligentiarum individuatur se ipsa." For Giles' theory of individuation of intelligences in his commentary on the *Liber de causis*, see NASH, 'Giles of Rome', p. 90.

[138] GILES, *Super authorem De causis, Alpharabium* x, fol. 37ʳ, lines 32-37, as quoted on p. 123 n. 119 above.

[139] For contraction between genera and species, see ibid., vii, fol. 25ᵛ, lines 40-42: "Advertendum tamen quod sicut intelligentia contrahitur ad certum genus, sic contrahitur ad certam speciem, et per certam differentiam."

since they are by nature part of a composite body and soul, are finite, unlike the celestial souls or intelligences, which are not. Human souls are "contracted" with matter, i.e. the body, with which they are combined.[140]

As we have seen, Albert did not follow the use of 'contraction' which we saw in Moerbeke's Latin translation of Proclus' *Elements of theology*, namely, to describe the relatively limited number of superior intelligences compared with the more numerous inferior intelligences. Instead, he used the term to describe descent from superior to inferior intelligences. Bruno's use of 'contraction' is, in turn, distinct from that of Albert in this respect. Whereas Albert had used the concept to describe procession downwards in the hierarchy of being, from superior to inferior intelligences, Bruno uses the concept of contraction to describe ascent as well as descent, noetic ascent being an important aspect of the former.[141]

Matter contracted by form

Aquinas applies 'contraction' to substances placed lower in the hierarchy of being than simple substances, that is, corporeal hylomorphic substances. He denies that it applies to angels, which he identifies with intelligences. "Since an angel does not have a form in matter, it is not limited or contracted through any matter, like natural forms [i.e. forms in matter, also known as corporeal forms]".[142] Nor does contraction occur in God.[143] By contrast Aquinas attributes contraction to material things in the *Summa theologiae*. Aquinas thus applies the term 'contraction' to the lowest level in the hierarchy of being, the level where matter exists. He states that "matter is contracted through form into a defined species; in the same way, the substance of a given species is contracted to a delimited mode of being by an

---

[140] Ibid., v, fol. 20ᵛ, lines 35-39: "Ulterius forte dubitaret aliquis utrum animae nostrae sint compositae ex finito et infinito. Dicendum quod animae nostrae sunt perfectio materiae, et per essentiam uniuntur corporibus, ita quod ex tali anima, et corpore fit unum secundum esse, propter quod natura animarum naturarum non est infinita natura, eo modo quo est infinita natura intelligentiarum et animarum orbium, sed limitatur, et contrahitur et particulatur talis natura ratione corporis in quo recipitur."

[141] Cf. BRUNO, *Sigillus* ii 22, p. 214.6-19, as quoted on p. 26 n. 88 above.

[142] AQUINAS, *Responsio ad lectorem venetum de 36 articulis*, art. 7, p. 340: "Habet autem angelus finitam naturam secundum comparationem ad suum superius quod est Deus, qui est ens et bonum infinitum, cuius similitudo in angelo participatur finite. Cum tamen angelus non habeat formam in materia, non limitatur vel contrahitur per aliquam materiam sicut form[a]e naturales." For Aquinas' view on matter, see GILSON, *Aquinas*, pp. 29-45, 174-186.

[143] AQUINAS, *Quaestiones quodlibetales* quodlibetum 3, qu. 1, art. 1, pp. 71-72: "Cum autem Deus sit ipsum esse subsistens, manifestum est quod natura essendi convenit Deo infinite absque omni limitatione et contractione; unde eius virtus activa se extendit infinite ad totum ens, et ad omne id quod potest habere rationem entis."

accident superimposed on it, as, for instance, 'man' is contracted by 'white'."[144]
This is the standard use of the term 'contraction' in scholasticism and its offshoots.

Aquinas' use of contraction presupposes the Aristotelian conception of matter as pure potentiality, which is actualised, that is, given existence and essence, through form. Having said so, Aquinas modifies Aristotle's theory of individuation. Owens explains: "What role, then is left to form in the causing individuation? In the Aristotelian background of Aquinas, form is the cause of being. For Aristotle, this meant that the form gives being to both the matter and the composite body. For Aquinas, it meant the same, but with the proviso that an efficient cause was furnishing the influx of existence."[145] This efficient cause is, in Aquinas' thought and still according to Owens, God.[146] However, Aquinas's theory of individuation of corporeal substances differs from Aristotle's theory in another respect, namely by regarding matter as a principle of individuation at one point in the course of individuation. After God has given being, and after form has given being to matter, matter affects the individuation of a corporeal substance by its accidents, first by its quantities, then by its qualities.[147] The above quotation from Aquinas reflects this role of matter, as far as Aquinas speaks of a two-folded contraction. This role of matter in individuation is similarly reflected in Aquinas' notion of matter as extended corporeity, *materia signata*, and as such a principle of individuation.[148] So even though Aquinas follows Aristotle by attributing to form the role of giving being to matter, to "contract" matter, there are important qualifications on Aquinas' part to be aware of.

Aquinas' use of contraction presupposes the Aristotelian conception of matter as pure potentiality, which is actualised, that is, given existence and essence, through form. Bruno rejects, as we have seen in Chapter 2, the Aristotelian notion of matter, and hence the scholastic notion of 'contraction' tied to this idea. As far as Aquinas used the term 'contraction' in this manner, Bruno did not follow his usage. Admittedly, Aquinas also spoke of a two-folded contraction, but it differs from Bruno's idea of dialectical relationship between matter and form.[149] Aquinas spoke, as we have just seen, about a two-folded contraction between form, on one hand, and accidents of matter, on the other hand. Bruno did not refer to accidents

---

[144] AQUINAS, *Summa theologiae* 1a, qu. 44, art. 2, resp., vol. 4, p. 458: "Sed considerandum est quod materia per formam contrahitur ad determinatam speciem; sicut substantia alicuius speciei per accidens ei adveniens contrahitur ad determinatum modum essendi; ut homo contrahitur per album." For Aquinas' principle of individuation, see OWENS, 'Thomas Aquinas (b. ca. 1225; d. 1274)', pp. 173-194.

[145] OWENS, 'Thomas Aquinas (b. ca. 1225; d. 1274)', p. 176. For this view of Aristotle, Owens refers, p. 176 n. 19, to Aristotle, *Metaphysics* VII xvii 1041ª9-ᵇ28; VIII ii 1043ª2-26. For Aquinas' idea, Owens refers (p. 176 n. 20) to AQUINAS, *Summa theologiae* 1a, qu. 104, art. 1, ad 1m, vol. 5, p. 464.

[146] OWENS, 'Thomas Aquinas (b. ca. 1225; d. 1274)', pp. 175-176.

[147] Ibid., p. 186.

[148] WEISHEIPL, 'The concept of matter in fourteenth century science', pp. 149-153.

[149] AQUINAS, *Summa theologiae* 1a, qu. 44, art. 2, resp., vol. 4, p. 458, as quoted on p. 128 n. 144 above.

of matter, but simply to matter; and by 'form' he did not refer to form as a species, but to form as the World Soul.[150]

Hence Bruno placed the dialectical relationship between matter and form within a Neoplatonic scheme, whereas Aquinas, by and large, retained the Aristotelian one, in which matter is passive potentiality. In order to convey his attribution of active as well as passive potentiality to matter, Bruno did not follow Aquinas' usage, but may instead have turned towards a usage found in Giles, according to whom matter co-determines individuation together with form within a Neoplatonic scheme.

Matter and form contracted interdependently

With regard to corporeal entities, the lowest level, Giles follows Aquinas' usage inasmuch as Giles too speaks of matter and form being united, "contracted". Giles constantly qualifies this idea, however, by insisting that the individuation taking place through such a contraction depends upon matter (*ratione materiae*).[151] Giles therefore speaks of a "double limitation" (*duplex limitatio*) in his theory of individuation of particulars, one dependent upon form, another upon matter.[152] This double determination, as Girolamo Trapé explains, helps Giles to account for the differentiation among individuals belonging to the same species, for instance, to explain why the blades of grass differ.[153]

In the *Liber de causis* the doctrine of reception according to the capacity of the recipient is both stated generally and more specifically in relation to higher and lower intelligences.[154] The doctrine derives from Proclus' *Elements of theology*,

---

[150] BRUNO, *Causa* ii, p. 147, as quoted on p. 36 n. 48 above; *Sigillus* ii 10, ii 22, pp. 203.1-5, 213.14-214.19. In these lines in the *Sigillus* 'forma absoluta' corresponds to the World Soul; see p. 37 n. 50 above.

[151] E.g. GILES, *Super authorem De causis, Alpharabium* iv, fol. 16ᵛ, lines 32-35: "Sic albedo si esset separata esset infinita albedo, et quaelibet forma separata (secundum hunc ordinem quem videmus) de se non determinatur ad specialem modum illius formae: Sed si determinatur et contrahitur hoc est ratione materiae in qua recipitur." The same role is attributed to matter ibid., iv, ix, xxii, fols 16ᵛ (lines 29-31), 35ᵛ (lines 30-41), 74ʳ (lines 14-20). The example of contraction ibid., xxii, fol. 74ʳ, lines 14-20 is similar to one in AQUINAS, *Summa theologiae* 1a, qu. 44, art. 2 resp., vol. 4, p. 458. For Giles' view on matter as a principle of individuation, see PETERSON, 'Cardinal Cajetan and Giles of Rome', pp. 434-437; TRAPÉ, 'Il neoplatonismo', pp. 57-58.

[152] GILES, *Super authorem De causis, Alpharabium* iv, fol. 16ᵛ, lines 14-18: "Ulterius forte dubitaret aliquis, unde veniat ille modus loquendi, et quomodo sit rationabile, quod intelligentiae dicantur infinitae formae et finita entia, vel quod dicantur habere infinitam naturam et finitum esse. Dicendum quod rei creatae potest competere duplex finitas, sive duplex limitatio. Una ex parte formae, et si sit illa res materialis potest ei competere alia limitatio, et alia contractio ex parte materiae."

[153] TRAPÉ, 'Il neoplatonismo', p. 80.

[154] PSEUDO-ARISTOTLE, *Liber de causis* ix(x) 98-99, ed. Pattin, p. 160.

proposition 142,[155] which probably derives from Plotinus' *Enneads* VI iv-vi.[156] In the *Liber de causis* reception takes place according to the potency (*potentia*) of the recipient.[157] Giles uses the term *capacitas* rather than *potentia*.[158] The doctrine was phrased in the *Liber de causis* as valid for all entities, but the only ontological level to which it was applied was that of intelligences. The distinction between universal and particular forms, the *Liber de causis* says, is a result of the varying capacities of the respective intelligences to receive forms.[159] Giles reaffirms the general validity of the doctrine. But, contrary to the *Liber de causis*, he pays particular attention to the implications of this doctrine on the lowest ontological level, matter in corporeal entities.[160] Neither his emphasis upon this Neoplatonic doctrine nor its sources has been pointed out in the literature, slight as it is, on his commentary on the *Liber de causis*.[161]

Did Giles interpret the "potency" of the recipient exclusively as a passive potency, as Aquinas and Aristotle had done?[162] Giles speaks of a "double limitation" (*duplex limitatio*) for finite entities, where both form and matter determine individual substance, but he does not assign active potentiality to matter. Matter is passive, but, as such, it is accessible to, or can receive, individuating forms in different ways. Hence Giles is not claiming, as Bruno, that matter has 'active potentiality', or, as he puts it, that "one is matter, one is the potency by which all that exists, exists in act".[163] Giles' statement about a *duplex limitatio* is nevertheless of particular interest in relation to Bruno's idea of a "double contraction" (*duplex contractio*) in his *Sigillus* and *De la causa*.[164] Bruno employs

---

[155]   Ibid., Pattin's note p. 185 note 'e'.

[156]   LEE, 'The doctrine of reception', pp. 82-97.

[157]   PSEUDO-ARISTOTLE, *Liber de causis* ix(x) 98-99, xxi(xxii) 170, xxiii(xxiv) 177, ed. Pattin, pp. 160, 182, 185.

[158]   Cf., e.g., GILES, *Super authorem De causis, Alpharabium* v, fol. 20ᵛ, lines 22-24: "Unde illud esse non manet in sua plenitudine, sed contrahitur et particulatur secundum capacitatem eius in qua recipitur." See also ibid., v, fol. 20ᵛ, line 50 to fol. 21ʳ, line 3; xxii, fol. 76ᵛ, line 40 to fol. 77ʳ, line 3.

[159]   PSEUDO-ARISTOTLE, *Liber de causis* ix(x) 98, ed. Pattin, p. 160.

[160]   For the doctrine applied to the relationship between God and all, see GILES, *Super authorem De causis, Alpharabium* xxii, fol. 74ᵛ (lines 41-44). For the doctrine applied to celestial souls, see ibid., v, fol. 20ᵛ (lines 19-24). For the doctrine applied to matter, see ibid., iv, xxii, fols 16ᵛ (lines 29-35), 74ʳ (lines 14-20).

[161]   TRAPÉ, 'Il neoplatonismo', pp. 49-86; NASH, 'Giles of Rome', pp. 57-91; PETERSON, 'Cardinal Cajetan and Giles of Rome', pp. 434-437; PUNTA and TRIFOGLI, 'Giles of Rome', pp. 72-75. The presence of the doctrine is mentioned very briefly in TRAPÉ, 'Il neoplatonismo', pp. 79-80. For the sources of the Neoplatonic doctrine of reception according to the capacity of the recipient, see p. 38 n. 53 above.

[162]   ARISTOTLE, *Metaphysics* VII viii 1033ᵇ5-19; *Physics* I vii 191ᵃ5-14; AQUINAS, *Summa theologiae* 1a, qu. 44, art. 2, arg., vol. 4, p. 457.

[163]   BRUNO, *Causa* iv, p. 239, as quoted on p. 44 n. 83 above.

[164]   BRUNO, *Sigillus* ii 22, p. 214.6-19; *Causa* ii, p. 147.

the terms *limitatio* and *contractio* synonymously in his theory of individuation, so the comparison between *duplex limitatio* and *duplex contractio* is revealing.[165]

It is likely that one of Bruno's impulses for his ontological concept of contraction — characterised by an interdependency between matter and form — derives from the *Liber de causis*' Neoplatonic doctrine of reception according to the capacity of the recipient. The assumption is supported by the fact that the doctrine of reception according to the capacity of the recipient frequently appears in Bruno's Italian and early Latin works.[166] It even found its way into his account of the Egyptians' religion in the *Spaccio*. Nature is venerated as divine according to its varying capacities to receive.[167]

One may ask the further question whether Bruno's concept of contraction, related as it is to the Neoplatonic doctrine of reception according to the capacity of the recipient, derives from Giles' commentary on the *Liber de causis*.[168] Given Bruno's philosophical propensity towards hylozoism, it is not difficult to see why he might have been attracted to Giles' doctrine of contraction. By paying attention to the vocabulary through which Giles had discussed the capacity of the recipient, i.e. matter, and by emphasising this aspect, as his concept of matter encouraged him to do, the doctrine could have become a starting point for a philosophical subversion of the traditional relationship between form and matter. Given these similarities, one may ask whether Giles' commentary on the *Liber de causis* was the source to Bruno's concept of contraction.

As we have seen, Giles conceived of matter as an indeterminate potency which is the principle of individuation. Although Giles' conception of matter was distinct from earlier and contemporary scholastic interpretations, one must also admit that

---

[165] BRUNO, *De immenso* i 1, p. 205.1-4: "per naturae ergo dictamen [desiderium praesentis vitae] vult esse semper, per eam vero (quae est a contractione formae ad hanc materiam, et limitatione materiae ab hac forma) ignorantiam, vult semper esse hoc quod est". In this context Bruno compares the desire of the human soul to ascend towards the One with nature's disposition to actualise itself completely and immediately; both 'desires' suffer from complacency manifested in a satisfaction with the soul's present state. Hence both suffer from "ignorance". The human soul ignores the desire for One and nature the disposition for complete actualisation of all potentialities. It is in the latter's process of actualisation that contraction is used.

[166] See references on p. 38 n. 56 above.

[167] BRUNO, *Spaccio* iii 2, pp. 415, 427.

[168] The possibility of such an early inspiration from Giles in Bruno's *Sigillus* has not been considered in CLEMENS, *Giordano Bruno*, p. 143; MANCINI, *La sfera infinita*, p. 67; MIGNINI, 'La dottrina dell'individuo in Cusano e in Bruno', p. 348. SPRUIT, *Il problema*, pp. 27, 47 nn. 21 and 22, 109 n. 28, 111 n. 37, 144 n. 132, 283 n. 14, 307 n. 106, 309 n. 113, 313 n. 128, suggests Aquinas' commentary on the *Liber de causis* as a source for Bruno's philosophy in general, but ignores Giles' commentary. Spruit, accordingly, ignores the possibility that Giles' commentary is a source for Bruno's ontological concept of contraction; see ibid., pp. 147-149, 157-158, 203. Nor has this commentary of Giles been considered in relation to Bruno's concept of ontological contraction in other studies on this concept in Bruno's philosophy; see the references on p. 29 n. 3 above.

his interpretation was far from being the only one which endorsed matter as a principle of individuation. Avicenna and Aquinas, to mention just two philosophers, had done so too in accordance with their respective philosophies.[169] Aquinas did not use the term *duplex contractio*, as Giles and Bruno, but, as we have seen, Aquinas too regarded matter and form as co-determining principles.[170] In fact, the doctrine of matter as a principle of individuation had gained so much support in the course of the thirteenth century, that it was explicitly rejected in the Condemnation of 1277 (article 46).[171] Hence, Giles was not the only one to endorse the idea of matter as a principle of individuation. Nor was he, accordingly, the only one who emphasised what I have called a dialectical relationship between matter and form in individuation. It was essentially a scholastic doctrine. Lastly, the doctrine of reception according to the capacity of the recipient is crucial in Aquinas' doctrine of participation, wherefore Bruno could have found it there rather than in the *Liber de causis* or in Giles.[172] So even though a thorough examination of scholastic texts on individuation might show that the phrase *duplex limitatio*, or even *duplex contractio*, only occurs in Giles' texts, that would prove little, for the idea of a mutual dependency between matter and form was commonplace in scholastic theories of individuation.

Since neither the external evidence for Giles' influence on Bruno (Teofilo da Vairano's possible introduction of Giles to Bruno), nor the internal evidence (verbal similarities between Bruno's and Giles' phrases on individuation through contraction, the *duplex contractio* or the *duplex limitatio*) is conclusive, the link between Giles and Bruno concerning contraction as an ontological concept remains a plausible possibility, though one which has yet to be proved.

Conclusion

Although I have not presented any conclusive evidence in support of my suggestion about Giles' concept of contraction as a source for Bruno, and although one can argue that Bruno's theory of matter and form as co-determinating principles in individuation can be found in other scholastic sources, there are still some reasons to believe that the *Liber de causis* and its scholastic commentary tradition influenced Bruno and his theory of individuation.

First, the *Liber de causis* itself remained an important text in the Renaissance, as proved by Taylor, Schmitt, Lohr, Cranz and Knox. Not only was the *Liber de causis* available in many reprints in the sixteenth century; scholastic commentaries

---

[169] For this principle in Avicenna's theory of individuation, see BÄCK, 'The Islamic background: Avicenna (b. 980; d. 1037) and Averroes (b. 1126; d. 1198)', pp. 45-52. For the principle in Aquinas' theory of individuation, see OWENS, 'Thomas Aquinas (b. ca. 1225; d. 1274)', pp. 181-187.

[170] I have checked the Aquinas CD-ROM edited by R. Busa. Milan 1992.

[171] See article 46 in the Condemnation of 1277, cited in *Chartularium Universitatis Parisiensis*, vol. 1, p. 546, as quoted on p. 39 n. 57 above.

[172] FABRO, *Participation et causalité selon S. Thomas d'Aquin*, especially pp. 509-537.

by Albert, Aquinas and Giles were also published even as late as in the 1570s, the decade in which Bruno finished his studies at the Dominican Order in Naples. Moreover, new commentaries were composed during the Renaissance. The general Procurator of the Dominican Order from 1481 to 1484, Ludovico Ferrara, thus composed a commentary on the *Liber de causis*. So the scholastic tradition surrounding the *Liber de causis* was alive at the time of Bruno; the text itself and some of its commentaries were available, and, at least in a not too distant past, the *Liber de causis* had been taken seriously within Bruno's Order. Second, Bruno's teacher, the Augustinian Teofilo da Vairano, could have introduced Bruno, a Dominican, to the commentary on the *Liber de causis* composed by another Augustinian, Giles of Rome.

Third, Bruno's criteria for a substance — that it is permanent and eternal, i.e. not corruptible as it is in the Aristotelian concept of substance, according to Bruno — are partly fulfilled in the *Liber de causis*. There Mind is defined as an eternal and permanent substance, contrary to composed substances, which are changeable and subjected to generation and destruction. In this way the *Liber de causis* endorses the co-existence of an eternal and permanent realm (Mind) and a temporal one (composed substances in nature). A further advantage of this notion of substance was that it was open to Bruno's Neoplatonic elaborations, stimulated by other Neoplatonic sources, Plotinus, for instance.

Fourth, there are two reasons for suggesting that Bruno was deriving his ontological concept of contraction from the scholastic tradition of *Liber de causis* rather than from late medieval or Renaissance natural philosophy. One reason is philological. With one insignificant exception, the term 'contraction' was not used to describe individuation in the first four books of the Latin translation of Aristotle's *Physics*. Nor was the term used in Averroes' commentary to these books.[173] This does not exclude, of course, that the term was employed in one or more of the many commentaries on Aristotle's *libri naturales*. The other reason is philosophical. In the Aristotelian tradition of natural philosophy, important in medieval and Renaissance scholastic philosophy, the Neoplatonic doctrine of a universally animating World Soul was extrinsic.[174]

The absence of the doctrine of the World Soul in Aristotelian natural philosophy was a hindrance to Bruno's hylozoistic agenda, ultimately to his theology. This may explain Bruno's scornful comments in *De la causa* about Francisco Patrizi da Cherso (1529-1597) and his criticism of Aristotelian natural philosophy in his *Discussiones Peripateticae*, printed in Venice in 1581.[175] For

---

[173] For the exception, used to describe a relative, numerical limitation of causes, see ARISTOTLE, *De physico auditu libri octo. Cum Averrois Cordubensis in eosdem commentariis* ii, fol. 61va: "Modi autem causarum numero quidem sunt multi, in capita vero contracti et hi pauciores".

[174] ARISTOTLE had refused Plato's notion of the World Soul in his *De anima* i 3 406^{b}25-407^{b}13.

[175] BRUNO, *Causa* iii, pp. 165-167. For Bruno's report of, and criticism of, the view found in Aristotelian natural philosophy that matter is like a woman, i.e. passive, whereas form is like a man, i.e. active, see ibid., iv, pp. 219-231, 265. For the source of this

although Patrizi did raise points of criticism which we can also find in Bruno, Patrizi did not, in Bruno's view, give up his Aristotle and substitute him with a more fertile philosophy, and Bruno therefore mocked him as a sterile philosopher. Only in 1591, seven years after Bruno's rejection in *De la causa*, did Patrizi publish an alternative philosophy inspired by Neoplatonism, namely in his *De nova de universis philosophia*.[176]

Seen from this perspective, Bruno did not break with the scholastic tradition as such in his interpretation of contraction. He refused one Aristotelian strain in scholasticism, i.e. its natural philosophy; but he embraced another Neoplatonic strain in scholasticism, namely the *Liber de causis* and its several scholastic commentaries. From this perspective it becomes possible to see Bruno's interest in the more authentic Neoplatonism, transmitted by Ficino, as a natural extension of the scholastic Neoplatonism, which he, with all probability, had known from his formative years in Naples. For these reasons I think it is reasonable to maintain that the *Liber de causis* and its commentaries formed an important background for Bruno's ontological concept of contraction, and to suggest Giles' commentary as a possible source for this concept of Bruno.

---

simile, see ARISTOTLE, *Physics* I ix 192ª13-25. This image was also conveyed in the Latin translation of Aristotle accompanied by Averroes' commentary; see, for instance, ARISTOTLE, *De physico auditu libri octo. Cum Averrois Cordubensis in eosdem commentariis* i, fols 45ᵛᵇ-46ᵐ. For Bruno's relationship to Patrizi, see TOCCO, *Le fonti*, pp. 35-37; AQUILECCHIA, 'Ramo, Patrizi e Telesio nella prospettiva di Giordano Bruno', pp. 32-35. For the criticism of Aristotle's natural philosophy in Patrizi's *Discussiones Peripatetica*, see DEITZ, "Falsissima est ergo haec de triplici substantia Aristotelis doctrina'", pp. 227-245.

[176] For a brief exposition of the metaphysics of this work, see DEITZ, "Falsissima est ergo haec de triplici substantia Aristotelis doctrina'", pp. 246-247.

Chapter 7

Cusanus and the Scholastic Tradition of Contraction

Interpretations of the relationship between Cusanus and Bruno

In the preceding chapter I have examined the scholastic tradition of contraction as it appears in commentaries to the *Liber de causis*, and argued that this scholastic tradition, including Giles' commentary, was an important background for Bruno's ontological concept of contraction. There is, however, another possibility, Cusanus. Is it possible that Bruno's concept of contraction owes more to him than to this scholastic tradition? At first glance it seems very likely that Cusanus was Bruno's source given that Bruno definitely knew Cusanus' works or some of them. Here I shall examine the possibility that Bruno drew his concept of contraction from Cusanus.

Much attention has been dedicated to Cusanus' influence on Bruno among Bruno scholars. In this chapter, I shall examine Cusanus from two angles. First, I shall outline previous interpretations of the relationship between Cusanus and Bruno. Second, I shall examine previous interpretations, remarkably few, of Cusanus' approach to scholastic notions of contraction, especially as it features in commentaries on the *Liber de causis*.

In Bruno's Italian dialogues, published during 1584 and 1585, Cusanus' influence is most evident in his cosmology and metaphysics. This was recognised almost immediately. Seventeenth-century thinkers recognised Cusanus' influence on Bruno's cosmology. In his *Apologia pro Galileo*, published in 1622, Tommaso Campanella (1568-1639) underlined the impact of Cusanus' cosmological ideas on Bruno's cosmological works.[1] The cosmological element in Bruno's philosophy was noticed again two years later, in 1624, when Mersenne attacked Bruno's heterodox cosmology on the grounds that it led to irreligion and deism.[2]

---

[1]   CAMPANELLA, *Apologia pro Galileo* ii, pp. 9-10: "Item doctissimus cardinalis Cusanus hanc sententiam amplexus est, et alios soles, aliosque in firmamento stellato circumgyrantes planetas, agnovit. Et quidam Nolanus, et alii, quos haeresis nominare non permittit, hanc sententiam tuentur. Sed in hoc condemnati non sunt tanquam haeretici; nec qui catholici, a librorum editione prohibiti fuerunt." See also ibid., iv, p. 52: "Et cardinalis Cusanus et Keplerus et Nolanus et alii dixere idem ante Galileum." For Campanella on Bruno, see RICCI, *La fortuna*, pp. 83, 109-110.

[2]   We find an explicit criticism of Bruno's infinite cosmology in MERSENNE, *L'impiété des déistes* ii 17, pp. 326-342. Mersenne also criticises Bruno's notion of *anima mundi* as

Mersenne and Campanella were writing in a century when new philosophical ideas, especially cosmological ones, were developing rapidly. This consideration may to some extent explain why Bruno's adaptation of Cusanus' cosmological ideas has been studied. Emile Namer underlined this focus on the cosmological element in Bruno's philosophy when he said of Bruno's cosmological insight that it "was so profound and so all-encompassing that it permitted Kepler and Galileo to orientate their researches and their telescopes, that it furnished Newton with the indispensable framework for a principle of inertia, namely, an infinite universe, without centre or privileged direction".[3]

These claims are arguable. In particular, they ignore the metaphysical and theological principles underlying Bruno's cosmological ideas, principles which were largely foreign to the mechanical world view emerging during the seventeenth century. This is true of the notion of contraction. Key Cusanian metaphysical notions, such as the coincidence of opposites, and the closely related pairs of opposites, *maximum-minimum*, *complicatio-explicatio*, in some instances provided the speculative premises of Bruno's cosmological conclusions.

It is possible to distinguish three major interpretations of the relationship between Cusanus and Bruno. First, there are studies focusing chiefly on the cosmology and metaphysics in the three Italian dialogues written between 1584 and 1585, *La cena*, *De la causa* and *De l'infinito*, as well as in some later works. This is the most common interpretation. Such studies do not take into consideration the earlier Latin mnemonic writings published in 1582 and 1583, in particular *De umbris* and the *Sigillus*.[4] The reception of Bruno in the first part of the seventeenth

---

leading to magic and cabala (ibid., ii 19, pp. 358-361; the "Il" ibid., p. 358 refers to Bruno). For Mersenne's criticism of Bruno, see RICCI, *La fortuna*, pp. 86-89.

[3] NAMER, *Giordano Bruno*, p. 42: "Son intuition [Bruno's] fut si profonde et si vaste, qu'elle permit à Képler et à Galilée d'orienter leurs recherches et leurs lunettes et qu'elle fournit à Newton le cadre indispensable au principe d'inertie, nous voulons dire un univers infini, n'ayant ni centre ni direction privilégiée." For the reception of Bruno's cosmological ideas, see RICCI, *La fortuna*, pp. 79-110.

[4] TOCCO, *Le opere*, pp. 139-141, 162-164, 353-354; *Le fonti*, pp. 585-612; OVERBACH, *Der Intuitionsbegriff*, pp. 95-153; CASSIRER, *Individuum*, pp. 49, 74; MAHNKE, *Unendliche Sphäere*, pp. 48-59; CORSANO, *Il pensiero*, pp. 115, 119-120, 153-154, 166, 169; HEIMSOETH, 'Giordano Bruno', pp. 400-407; BADALONI, *La filosofia*, pp. 53, 65-74, 85-91, 174, 327-328; *Tra cosmologia ed etica*, pp. 57-66; KOYRÉ, *From the closed world*, pp. 6, 14, 18-19, 40-44; HUBER, *Einheit*, pp. 34-36; BLUMENBERG, *Aspekte*, pp. 125-126, 128-130, 133-134, 138-140, 146, 149, 150-151, 158-159; VÉDRINE, *La conception*, pp. 8-9, 59, 62, 70-76, 128-132, 151, 154, 165-170, 191-194, 198-199, 220-223, 246, 250, 330, 334; 'L'influence', pp. 211-212 *et passim*; 'Image', pp. 50-51; PAPI, *Antropolgia*, pp. 24-33, 52-53; GARIN, *Rinascite e rivoluzioni*, pp. 257-281; GRUNEWALD, *Die Religionsphilosophie*, p. 18; STERN, *Giordano Bruno — Vision einer Weltsicht*, pp. 40-43, 54, 56-57, 62; BLUM, *Aristoteles*, pp. 69 n. 109, 92; BEIERWALTES, 'Absolute identity', pp. 88-90; MEIER-OESER, *Die Präsenz*, pp. 231-281; CILIBERTO, *Giordano Bruno*, pp. 60-61, 214; CALCAGNO, *Giordano Bruno*, pp. 29-33; GATTI, *Renaissance science*, pp. 113, 118-120, 122, 126, 132, 155-156, 158, 192; BÖNKER-

century may partly explain this. It is also, of course, a reflection of the simple fact that it is in these cosmological writings that we find solid evidence of Cusanus' influence.

Second, there is a group of studies also dealing with Cusanus' role in Bruno's early Latin mnemonic works.[5] Sturlese's studies belong in this group. She has argued convincingly that in Bruno's *De umbris* we find him paraphrasing Cusanus' metaphysical principle of the coincidence of opposites. Bruno illustrated this principle with a woodcut taken directly from Cusanus' *De beryllo*.[6] Sturlese concluded that Bruno knew Cusanus' works by 1582, and that he had read the 1514 or 1565 edition of Cusanus.[7] However, none of these studies on Bruno's mnemonics by Sturlese or others has examined the possible influence of Cusanus on Bruno in regard to the notion of contraction as a theory of individuation.

Third, three studies analyse Bruno's ontological notion of contraction as it appears in his *Sigillus* and in his *De la causa*. In Clemens' study of 1847, Cusanus' notion of contraction is compared with that of Bruno as formulated in his *Sigillus* and *De la causa*. Clemens identifies Cusanus' *De docta ignorantia* as the source.[8] Although Clemens' interpretation had the merit of taking Bruno seriously as a philosopher at a time when he was dismissed as an insubstantial and heretical thinker, it was, nevertheless, strongly imbued with Christian prejudices. He refused to see Bruno's adaptation of Cusanus' notion of contraction as anything other than a theory of individuation in matter, in particular in his *De la causa* and the *Sigillus*.[9] And Clemens did not recognise that Bruno's interpretation of contraction was original. For this reason Clemens also ignored the radical difference between the views of Cusanus and Bruno. Instead, Clemens held that Bruno gave a "less penetrating treatment" of the notion than Cusanus had done.[10] Moreover, Clemens failed to see how Bruno linked this ontological contraction to a noetic one, ultimately leading to Bruno's unorthodox solution to the problem of the soul's return to the One. Clemens concludes that Bruno's "apostasy" from Christianity,

---

VALLON, 'La matematica', pp. 67-78; RICCI, *Giordano Bruno*, pp. 257, 259, 286-288, 290-291, 297, 446, 476.

[5]   INGEGNO, *Cosmologia*, pp. 73, 75; DE BERNART, *Immaginazione*, pp. 33-37; MADDAMMA, 'Introduzione', pp. 8-9.

[6]   STURLESE, 'Niccolò Cusano', pp. 955-958.

[7]   Ibid., pp. 957-958.

[8]   CLEMENS, *Giordano Bruno*, p. 143.

[9]   For contraction ("Zusammenziehung" or "Einschränkung" in Clemens' German translations) in Cusanus' *De docta ignorantia*, see ibid., pp. 74-80. For Cusanus' notion of contraction in Bruno's idea of contraction, see ibid., p. 143. For Bruno's *Sigillus* as an example, see ibid., p. 9. For other instances in Bruno's works, see ibid., pp. 17-18.

[10]   Ibid., p. 143: "Ferner die hiermit zusammenhängende Ableitung der Materie und ihrer durch die Einschränkung (*contractio*) bestimmten Verschiedenheit, welche überaus bedeutende Lehre von Bruno jedoch keine so tief eindringende Behandlung, als von Cusa, erfuhr, noch erfahren konnte, weil er ihr keinen Grund anzuweisen wusste". Clemens was a Catholic who regarded Cusanus as the height of sound Catholic philosophy; see BLUM, 'Note on the author', in CLEMENS, *Giordano Bruno* (reprint), p. VIII.

and his "hate" of Christianity, i.e. Bruno's unorthodox idea of God and man's relation to the divine, was simply caused by a "psychological" defect in his mind.[11]

More recently Mancini has affirmed the validity of Clemens' study.[12] In his study of contraction, Mancini focuses on the same sources as Clemens did, i.e. Cusanus' *De docta ignorantia* on the one hand, and Bruno's *Sigillus* and *De la causa*, on the other, maintaining that this work of Cusanus was the source for Bruno's concept of contraction.[13] A third study, by Mignini, also very recent, advanced a similar reading of Bruno's notion of contraction in *De la causa*.[14] Like Clemens, Mancini and Mignini do not explore the differences between Cusanus' and Bruno's treatments of the concept of contraction. And, also like Clemens, they do not take into consideration the scholastic tradition of contraction in the commentaries on the *Liber de causis*.

Bruno's explicit references to Cusanus

The chief problem for any investigation of Cusanus' influence on Bruno's idea of contraction is that Bruno never attributes this idea explicitly to Cusanus.[15] This has not been taken into account in the studies of Clemens, Mancini and Mignini. In fact, Bruno does not mention Cusanus at all in any work published before *La cena*, written in the early part of 1584 and published later the same year.[16] How, then, do we know that Bruno is adapting Cusanus' idea of contraction? How can we know that this idea does not derive from some other source, possibly common to Cusanus and Bruno?

What conclusions about Bruno's use of Cusanus can then be drawn from Bruno's explicit references to Cusanus? First, from the cosmological dialogues we can say definitely that Bruno knew Cusanus' major work, *De docta ignorantia*.[17]

---

[11] CLEMENS, *Giordano Bruno*, p. 169: "Ich werde daher ohne Scheu, mit Zugrundelegung der in Bruno's Schriften selbst enthaltenen Angaben, die Ursachen des Abfalls des Philosophen vom Christenthume und seines bittern Hasses gegen dasselbe psychologish zu ermitteln versuchen, und lege nur Widerspruch gegen die Absicht ein, mich zum Sittenrichter über Schuld oder Unschuld desselben aufwerfen zu wollen."

[12] MANCINI, *La sfera infinita*, p. 245 n. 2.

[13] Ibid., pp. 67-71, 146-147.

[14] MIGNINI, 'La dottrina dell'individuo in Cusano e in Bruno', p. 348.

[15] The identifications examined in relation to this point are mainly, though not exclusively, based on the citations (the *testimonia*) by Hoffmann and Klibansky in their edition of CUSANUS, *De docta ignorantia*, p. 177. Hoffmann and Klibansky omitted Bruno's reference to Cusanus in BRUNO, *Spaccio* (iii 2, p. 379), *De lampade combinatoria* (praefatio, p. 234.6-9), *Oratio valedictoria* (p. 17.2-7), and *Adversus mathematicos* (p. 60.12). The *Indice* by LEFONS includes these additional references, as well as those mentioned by Hoffmann and Klibansky.

[16] AQUILECCHIA, 'Bruno, Giordano', p. 657. See also the discussion of the date of publication of *La cena* by KNOX, 'An arm and a leg', pp. 166-176.

[17] BRUNO, *Cena* iii, p. 133 states that Cusanus, because of the second book of his *De docta ignorantia*, CUSANUS, *De docta ignorantia* ii 12, p. 103.13-14, is among a series of

Furthermore, Bruno's reference in his *Spaccio* to the problem of the quadrature of the circle suggests that he probably used the 1565 edition of Cusanus, the only fifteenth- or sixteenth-century edition of Cusanus' works in which both *De quadratura circuli* and *De docta ignorantia* appeared together.[18]

Now let us turn to the ideas which Bruno picked up from Cusanus. Both references to Cusanus in *La cena* concern astronomical issues, that is, Cusanus' comments on the movement of the earth and the heterogeneous nature of the sun. In *De l'infinito* Bruno also draws on two of Cusanus' cosmological statements in *De docta ignorantia*, namely the possibility that other worlds are inhabited and the nature of light surrounding planets. The reference in the intervening dialogue, *De la causa*, concerns a metaphysical rather than cosmological idea, namely, that of the coincidence of opposites.[19] Bruno returns to the mathematical illustration of this idea, the infinite circle being equivalent to an infinite straight line, in the *Adversus mathematicos*.[20] Bruno also used the doctrine of the coincidence of

---

philosophers who hold, like Copernicus, that the sun moves. For Cusanus on this point, see KOYRÉ, *From the closed world*, pp. 14-16. Moreover, Cusanus' doctrine on the dissimilar parts of the sun, explained in the *De docta ignorantia*, is reported by BRUNO, *Cena* iii, pp. 155-157. This derives from CUSANUS, *De docta ignorantia* ii 12, p. 105.3-16. Again, the *Infinito* is indebted to the *De docta ignorantia* in regard to the question of the habitability of the various worlds in the universe; see BRUNO, *Infinito* epist., p. 25, and compare CUSANUS, *De docta ignorantia* ii 12, pp. 107.7-108.4. In the same context Bruno discusses the nature of light; see BRUNO, *Infinito* iii, pp. 195-197, paraphrasing CUSANUS, *De docta ignorantia* ii 12, p. 105.8-16. See also Bruno's dismissive comment on Cusanus' *De docta ignorantia* in BRUNO, *Infinito* iii, p. 197.

[18] Bruno mentions Cusanus in BRUNO, *Spaccio* iii 2, p. 379, and deals with the mathematical problem ibid., iii 2, pp. 379-387. Cusanus' *De quadratura circuli* was not printed in the Strasbourg 1490 and Paris 1514 and Cortemaggiore 1520 editions. Apart from the Basel 1565 edition, these three editions are the only fifteenth- and sixteenth-century editions held at the British Library. The British Library does not hold a separate fifteenth- or sixteenth-century edition of Cusanus' *De quadratura circuli*. The latter does appear, however, in the Basel 1565 edition (pp. 1091-1101). I have also checked the following catalogues for fifteenth- and sixteenth-century editions of collected works of Cusanus and *De quadratura circuli*: *The National Union Catalog*; *Catalogue Général des Livres Imprimés de la Bibliothèque Nationale*; and the *Verzeichnis der im deutschen Sprachbereich erschienenen Drucke des XVI. Jahrhunderts*. In addition to British Library editions mentioned above, these catalogues mention that *De quadratura circuli* was printed together with Johann Mueller's *De triangulis omnimodis libri quinque* (Nuremberg: J. Petrejus, 1533). Cusanus' *De quadratura circuli* was not included in his *Opuscula theologia et mathematica* (Martin Flach: Strasbourg, c. 1500), which is identical with the 1490 edition mentioned above. Bruno could have learned of *De quadratura circuli* through intermediary reports. Therefore we cannot conclude definitively from the inclusion of *De quadratura circuli* in the 1565 edition that Bruno used this 1565 edition of Cusanus. For Bruno's use of Nicholas of Cusa's ideas on the quadrature of the circle, see AQUILECCHIA, 'Giordano Bruno e la matematica', pp. 155-157.

[19] BRUNO, *Causa* v, pp. 299-301.

[20] BRUNO, *Adversus mathematicos*, p. 59.23-25.

opposites in *De umbris*. There he is probably alluding to Cusanus' *De beryllo*, though without mentioning Cusanus explicitly.[21] Bruno returned to the principle of coincidence of opposites in the *Spaccio*, where he applied it to the field of ethics.[22] Apart from his disagreement with Cusanus in *De immenso* concerning the problem of whether or not the earth is a fiery star like the sun, the references in the later Latin works are either tangential to Bruno's philosophy, or they simply praise Cusanus in general terms, either as an esoteric philosopher inaccessible to ordinary philosophers and theologians, or for his anticipation of Copernicus' ideas.[23]

There are, however, two passages, one in the *Infinito* and another in the *Oratio valedictoria*, in which Bruno tempers his admiration for Cusanus. In the former he complains that Cusanus did not rid himself of all the errors he had imbibed from traditional philosophy and theology.[24] In the second passage he presents Cusanus as a representative of an ecclesiastical establishment that he despised: "Good God, in what respect is Aristotle comparable to this Nicholas of Cusa, who is greater than Aristotle in proportion to the degree he is accessible to very few? About his mind, I would declare that I recognised Nicholas' mind to be not just equal to, but far superior to Pythagoras', were I not deterred from doing so by Nicholas' priestly garb."[25]

Among all these explicit references, the only one of potential importance in relation to Bruno's concept of contraction as a theory of individuation is his explicit attribution to Cusanus in *De la causa* of the principle of coincidence of opposites. Bruno employs this principle in *De la causa* in his description of contraction in its ontological sense, as has already been explained in Chapter 2. The origin and subsistence of the universe is characterised by a coincidence of opposites, Bruno holds on the basis of Cusanus' principle. However, there is at least one important difference between their application of this idea. For, as already said in Chapter 2, whereas Bruno identifies infinite and animate matter as the object of this coincidence, Cusanus identifies God as this object.[26] Of course, one can argue that Bruno, like Cusanus, holds that God is characterised by a

---

<ol>
<li value="21"> STURLESE, 'Niccolò Cusano', pp. 953-957. Cf. BRUNO, *De umbris* §§52.16-53.14, pp. 44-45, with CUSANUS, *De beryllo* §§8.13-10.22, pp. 11-13.</li>
<li value="22"> BRUNO, *Spaccio* i 1, pp. 57-59.</li>
<li value="23"> BRUNO refers to Cusanus in *De immenso* iii 9, pp. 381.25-382.3. The disagreement is stated ibid., iv 8, pp. 45.17-46.19. See also Bruno's praise of Cusanus in BRUNO, *De lampade combinatoria* praefatio, p. 234.6-9.</li>
<li value="24"> BRUNO, *Infinito* iii, p. 197.</li>
<li value="25"> BRUNO, *Oratio valedictoria*, p. 17.2-7: "Deus bone, ubi illi Cusano adsimilandus [Aristotle], qui quanto maior est, tanto paucioribus est accessibilis? Huius ingenium si presbyteralis amictus non interturbasset, non Pythagorico par, sed Pythagorico longe superius agnoscerem, profiterer."</li>
<li value="26"> The first principle is formally described as a coincidence of act and potency in BRUNO, *Causa* iii, p. 205. Compare the description of matter ibid., iv, pp. 243-245. For Bruno's application of the principle of coinciding opposites, see also pp. 47-49 above. My distinction between Cusanus' and Bruno's respective application of the principle of coincidence of opposites concurs with MORAN, 'Pantheism', pp. 144-145.</li>
</ol>

coincidence of opposites, but then it should be added that whereas 'God' means the universe itself to Bruno, the word means a transcendent entity to Cusanus.

Even though Bruno uses Cusanus' idea of coincidence of opposites, we cannot on that basis infer that he also borrowed Cusanus' idea of contraction, although Bruno must have been familiar with Cusanus' interpretation of contraction through his reading of Cusanus' *De docta ignorantia*. One reason for being cautious in this respect is that Bruno applies his sources freely — his application of Cusanus' principle of the coinciding opposites to his pantheism is one example. Another reason is that Bruno, though he knew Cusanus' comments on contraction in the *De docta ignorantia*, rejected the metaphysical structure to which Cusanus applied the concept, and therefore also Cusanus' interpretation of the concept itself. Finally, Bruno could have picked up his version of contraction from other sources in the scholastic tradition of the *Liber de causis*. In the subsequent section I shall examine Cusanus' concept of contraction as it emerges in his *De docta ignorantia*, and then compare it with Bruno's interpretation.

Cusanus and the scholastic tradition of contraction

Cusanus was in possession of a manuscript, now MS Cues 195, containing four texts. The first is a work that the MS calls *Liber de causis* (fols 1^r-34^v). The MS does not give an author's name. From the *incipit* and *explicit* one can deduce that this work is Aquinas' commentary on the *Liber de causis*.[27] Cusanus' possession of Aquinas' commentary on the *Liber de causis* has been noted by several scholars, and the importance of the *Liber de causis* to Cusanus' ontology has also been pointed out.[28] However, the possible influence of the work and its scholastic commentaries on Cusanus' thought has never been examined in detail.[29] Second

---

[27]   The *incipit* of AQUINAS, *Super Librum de causis expositio* in MS Cues 195, fol. 1ra, reads: "Sicut philosophus [Aristotle] dicit decimo ethicorum [*Nicomachean ethics* X vii 1177^{a}12-18] ultima felicitas hominis consistit in optima hominis operatione, que est supreme potentie scilicet intellectus, respectum optimi intelligibilis"; the *explicit* on fol. 34vb reads: "non participat unitatem ab aliquo alio et huius quidem probatio inducitur que premissa est. Et sic finitur liber de causis. Sint deo gratie omnipotenti qui est prima omnium causa". The *incipit* and *explicit* correspond to p. 1.4-6 and p. 145.17-21 of Saffrey's edition, with a few unimportant differences of wording and word order. Cusanus, like Bruno, was well versed in Aristotelian philosophy. He came across it in his formative years during his studies in Padova (VANSTEENBERGHE, *Le Cardinal*, p. 12) and in Cologne (ibid., p. 15).

[28]   For Cusanus' possession of the MS Cues 195, see KRISTELLER, 'Proclus as a reader', p. 196 n. 26; BEIERWALTES, 'Der Kommentar', p. 201. For the overall importance of the *Liber de causis* to Cusanus' ontology, in particular in relation to *De docta ignorantia*, see FLASCH, *Nikolaus von Kues*, pp. 144-145, 578; HAUBST, 'Albert, wie Cusanus ihn sah', pp. 167, 170-171, 172. See the references to the *Liber de causis* listed in the indexes of authors in CUSANUS, *De docta ignorantia*, p. 168; *De coniecturis*, p. 240.

[29]   The *Liber de causis* does not feature in the titles listed in the bibliographical surveys published in *MFCG*, 1 (1960 [cited from the 2nd ed. 1968]), pp. 99-123; 3 (1963), pp.

in MS Cues 195 comes Moerbeke's Latin translation of Proclus' work, the *Elementatio theologica* (fols 34^v-66^v), with Cusanus' marginal notes.[30] Third is Giles' *Tractatus de esse et essentia* (fols 67^r-105^v).[31] Finally there is a rather short text by Petrus Philargi, also called Peter of Candia (anti-pope Alexander V, 1409-1410), entitled *Libellus de terminis theologicalibus* (fols 106^r-110^r). How and when was the manuscript acquired? When did Cusanus study it? What did he make of the doctrines he found in the *Liber de causis*? Which commentators did he know of? How did they influence his ideas of the *Liber de causis*? We shall have to leave these problems aside, and focus on Cusanus' treatment of contraction in his account of individuation, and, as far as possible, establish his position in the scholastic tradition of contraction.

In *De docta ignorantia* from 1440, Cusanus employs 'contraction' as part of his theory of individuation.[32] In the second book Cusanus explains that an

---

224-237; 6 (1967), pp. 179-202; 10 (1973), pp. 209-234; 15 (1982), pp. 121-147. Nor does it feature in the bibliography complied by Vescovini in CUSANUS, *La dotta ignoranza*, pp. 49-56. HOPKINS, *Metaphysics of contraction*, pp. 97-112, and his 'Introduction', in CUSANUS, *On learned ignorance*, pp. 1-43, does not mention the *Liber de causis*.

[30] The *incipit* of PROCLUS, *Elementatio theologica*, tr. Moerbeke, in MS Cues 195, fol. 34vb, reads "Omnis multitudo participat aliqualiter uno. Si enim nullatenus participaret neque totum unum esset, neque unum quidquam multorum ex quibus multitudo"; the *explicit* on 66vb reads: "Si autem transitive ex semper intelligente. Et quandoque intelligente una substantia erit. Sed impossibile. Hec enim semper different ut ostensum est. Cum hoc quod et inconveniens est [ed. Boese: 'esset'] anime supremum quod perfectum [ed. Boese: 'supremum semper perfectum'] ens non obtinere alias potentias et illa perfecta facere. Omnis ergo Anima parcialis tota descendit." The *incipit* and *explicit* correspond to prop. 1.1-3, p. 3, and prop. 211.7-11, p. 103, of Boese's edition. Cusanus annotated the text. For Cusanus' marginal notes, see *Cusanus-Texte. III. Marginalien. 2. Proclus latinus* (ed. Senger), pp. 18-19, 111-121.

[31] The *Tractatus de esse et essentia* in MS Cues 195 is GILES, *Theoremata de esse et essentia*. The *incipit* in the MS, fol. 67ra, reads: "Omne esse vel est purum per se existens et infinitum vel est participatum in aliquo receptum et limitatum. Volentes de esse tractatum componere ne laboremus in equivoco distinguemus duplex esse"; the *explicit* reads on fol. 105va: "ad genus substantie quod de huiusmodi esse directe nec substantia que est genus nec substantia que est analogum predicatur. Et hec de essentia et de esse dicta sufficiant. Laus igitur sit ipsi deo in quo est omne esse qui est trinus et unus in secula seculorum benedictus Amen" The *incipit* and *explicit* correspond to p. 1.2-5 and p. 159.2-7 of Hocedez' edition, with minor differences.

[32] For the concept of contraction in *De docta ignorantia*, see LOHR, 'Metaphysics', pp. 551, 555; VESCOVINI, 'Introduzione', pp. 26-29; 'Temi ermetico-neoplatonici', pp. 128-130; INGEGNO, *Regia pazzia*, pp. 116-133; HOPKINS, *Metaphysics of contraction*, pp. 97-112; BEIERWALTES, '"Primum est dives per se"', pp. 168-169; STURLESE, 'Niccolò Cusano', p. 963; COUNET, *Mathématiques et dialectique chez Nicolas de Cuse*, pp. 128, 187-188, 190, 220-222. The only studies explaining the sources for contraction in Cusanus historically are the two by Vescovini mentioned in this note. She mentions the school of Albert including Dietrich, Duns Scotus (1265-1308), Giles and others, though without providing references.

absolute unity is made manifold through an individuation, that is, a contraction, into individuals through four interrelated unities:

> And in this way we find that there are three universal unities gradually descending to the particular in which they are contracted, so that they may be the particular in act. The first absolute unity enfolds everything in an absolute manner, the first contracted unity enfolds everything in a contracted manner. Their [hierarchical] order entails, however, that the absolute unity should be considered to enfold, as it were, the first contracted unity, so that it enfolds everything else by means of the latter [i.e. by means of the contracted unity]; that the first contracted unity should be considered to enfold the second contracted unity and, by means of the latter, the third contracted unity; that the second contracted unity should be considered to enfold the third contracted unity, which is the last universal unity, and the fourth unity [counting inclusively from absolute unity] from the first, so that, by means of the third contraction, the first unity may arrive at the particular. And so we see how the totality of things is contracted through three steps into this and that particular.[33]

Here Cusanus describes a series of ontological enfoldings (*complicationes*), actualised through four 'unities', ultimately leading to the individuation of particulars. How does Cusanus explain these unities?

He offers first a mathematical interpretation. The first unity is the absolute unity, which is one; the second unity is the plurality of the universe, 'unfolded' from the first absolute unity. This second unity is tenfold, Cusanus continues, since it comprises the ten predicaments. It is, therefore, a tenfold contraction of the first absolute unity.[34] The ten predicaments may be the ten categories which Aristotle

---

[33] CUSANUS, *De docta ignorantia* ii 6, p. 79.19-28: "Et ita reperimus tres universales unitates gradualiter descendentes ad particulare, in quo contrahuntur, ut sint actu ipsum. Prima absoluta unitas omnia complicat absolute, prima contracta omnia contracte. Sed ordo habet, ut absoluta unitas videatur quasi primam contractam complicare, ut per eius medium alia omnia; et contracta prima videatur secundam contractam complicare, et eius medio tertiam contractam; et secunda contracta tertiam contractam, quae est ultima universalis unitas et quarta a prima, ut eius medio in particulare deveniat. Et sic videmus, quomodo universum per gradus tres in quolibet particulari contrahitur." 'Ordo' corresponds presumably to 'τάξις', which in Greek Neoplatonism means a series of hierarchically related entities. The Greek term is used in PROCLUS, *Elements of theology* props 21, 125, 132, pp. 24.5, 110.29, 116.28. On these occasions Moerbeke uses 'ordo' in his translation; see PROCLUS, *Elementatio theologica* props 21.5, 125.1, 132.1, tr. Moerbeke, pp. 14, 63, 66. See also DODDS' explanation of 'τάξις' in PROCLUS, *Elements of theology*, pp. 208-209, 267, 270. 'Ordo' is used similarly in another account of contraction, namely in DIETRICH, *De animatione caeli* iv, §3, pp. 15-16.

[34] CUSANUS, *De docta ignorantia* ii 6, p. 79.10. Here Cusanus refers to his *De coniecturis* for further clarification. According to the editors, Hoffmann and Klibansky, Cusanus

held we can predicate of nature (substance, quantity, quality, relation, position, time, being-in-a-position, having, doing, being-affected).[35] The third unity is symbolised by the square of ten, that is, one hundred. Finally, the fourth unity is symbolised by one thousand, which is the cube of ten.[36]

Having provided this mathematical interpretation of contraction, Cusanus adds a second explanation which is more in tune with Aristotelian metaphysics. Without assigning each of these unites explicitly to any of the following notions, he says that the universe is like an ontological hierarchy departing from the "ten most general concepts", which are contracted into genera, species and, finally, individuals, which are absolute unity in act.[37] What are these "most general concepts"? Are they Aristotle's ten categories, also discussed on pp. 55-58 above, the ontological counterpart to the above mentioned ten predicates? Aristotle had listed ten universals, or categories, in his *Categories*, claiming that, on a logical level, nine of them constitute the range of possible predicates of substances (again, substance being one category), and, on an ontological level, that they delineate the possible modes of being of substances.[38] The ten categories thus provide, in Aristotle's thought, a correspondence between language and reality.

At this point it should be mentioned that Giles had provided terminology which Cusanus may have used in his explanatory comment. Giles had stated that intelligences are contracted into "certain predicates". Intelligences exist contractedly in genera, which in turn exist contractedly in species, and which are ultimately individuated in the "ten predicates", that is, we may assume, the traditional ten categories or predicaments. We detect these ten predicaments directly. By contrast we detect the species and genera indirectly, by contemplating nature in its sensible manifestations.[39] Intelligence is intermediary between God,

---

refers to *De coniecturis* i 7 (especially §§27.17-28.16, pp. 34-35), where he also provides an epistemological account on the basis of the same series of numbers.

[35]   ARISTOTLE, *Categories* iv 1^{b}25-2^{a}4.

[36]   CUSANUS, *De docta ignorantia* ii 6, p. 79.10-18.

[37]   Ibid., ii 6, p. 80.1-7: "Est igitur universum quasi decem generalissimorum universitas, et deinde genera, deinde species. Et ita universalia sunt illa secundum gradus suos, quae ordine quodam naturae gradatim ante rem, quae actu ipsa contrahit, existunt. Et quoniam universum est contractum, tunc non reperitur nisi in generibus explicatum, et genera non reperiuntur nisi in speciebus; individua vero sunt actu, in quibus sunt contracte universa."

[38]   ARISTOTLE, *Categories* iv 1^{b}25-2^{a}10.

[39]   GILES, *Super authorem De causis, Alpharabium* vii, fol. 25^v, lines 33-42: "Ideo forte Auctor primam causam quasi solum negative describit. Sed de intelligentia non sic dicendum est[.] Nam cum intelligentia recedat a simplicitate primi, et non habeat esse in sua infinitate: sed habeat specialem modum essendi, de necessitate contrahitur ad praedicamentum determinatum. Distinguendo ergo Ens, solum in decem praedicamenta, ita quod substantia non sit nisi unum genus, et unum praedicamentum, et quia intelligentia secundum suam quiditatem contrahitur ad determinatum genus ad quod contrahitur. Et cum intelligentia ipsa sit quaedam res per se existens scire possumus, quod contrahitur ad praedicamentum substantiae. Advertendum tamen quod sicut

pure act or the First Cause, on one hand, and corporeal substances combined of matter and form, on the other hand. Giles also applies contraction to describe the relation between the forms in intelligences and matter.[40] There is, however, a difference between Giles and Cusanus. In the above mentioned explanation of *De docta ignorantia* ii 6, Cusanus locates the ten categories between the first unity and genera.[41] Giles, on the other hand, locates them on the lowest ontological level, i.e. that of individuals. This difference becomes less marked when we consider Cusanus' immediate qualification, namely, that the universe is actualised, "unfolded" (*explicatum*), implying that the ten categories only exist in genera, which only exist in species, which, ultimately, only exist in individuals.[42] In this way, the ten categories are also located on the lowest ontological level in Cusanus, as in Giles. On pp. 147-148 below, we shall return to Cusanus' idea of *explicatio*. Another difference between Cusanus and Giles is that the latter is reluctant to describe, as Cusanus does, the relation between God and the next lower ontological level as a contraction. God gives being, Giles declares, but is not itself contracted to anything.[43] A further difference between Giles' and Cusanus' uses of the term 'contraction' in their respective accounts of procession from God is that Giles does not speak of the several ontological levels as unities.

Giles' use of the concept of contraction as a theory of individuation has never been considered as a possible source for Cusanus' concept of contraction.[44] Was he

---

intelligentia contrahitur ad certum genus, sic contrahitur ad certam speciem, et per certam differentiam."

[40] E.g. GILES, *Super authorem De causis, Alpharabium* vii, fol. 25ᵛ, lines 40-42, as quoted on p. 126 n. 139 above.

[41] CUSANUS, *De docta ignorantia* ii 6, p. 80.1-2, as quoted on p. 144 n. 37 above.

[42] Ibid., ii 6, p. 80.1-7, as quoted on p. 144 n. 37 above.

[43] GILES, *Super authorem De causis, Alpharabium* ii, fol. 8ʳ, lines 40-42, as quoted on p. 123 n. 122 above.

[44] HAUBST, *Das Bild des Einen und Dreieinen Gottes in der Welt nach Nikolaus von Kues*, pp. 124-129. Haubst, ibid., p. 125, identifies two meanings of contraction in Cusanus' thought. First, creation is a contracted being, God being non-contracted. Second, within Creation, form and matter are contracted. Haubst, ibid., p. 125 n. 65, cites the following three sources for Cusanus' two meanings: (a) LULL, MS Cues 83: *Ex libro de forma Dei*, fols 96ᵛ-97ʳ, at fol. 96ᵛ, lines 57-58: "generalia contracta in elementis" (= ed. Roth, p. 48, line 13), and at fol. 97ʳ, lines 1-3 (= ed. Roth, p. 48, lines 31-38): "Decem praedicamenta sunt communia ad elementa et ad elementata. Principia enim innata constituunt substantiam communem a qua exeunt per accidens communis qualitas quantitas et cetera. Ipsa autem substantia est contracta in celo primo, secundario in elementis, tertio in elementatis et sicud subtantia est contracta tripliciter sic similiter praedicamenta accidencium sunt contracta tripliciter. Aliter non esset ordo formatus neque motus"; (b) DUNS SCOTUS, *De primo principio* iv, conclusio 8: "igitur est unum ex eis sicut ex contrahente et contracto, actu et potentia"; and, most importantly, (c) AQUINAS, *Summa theologiae* 1a, qu. 7, art. 2. Haubst is referring to ibid., 1a, qu. 7, art. 2, resp., vol. 4, p. 74: "Si autem sint aliquae formae creatae non receptae in materia, sed per se subsistentes, ut quidam de angelis opinantur, erunt quidem infinitae secundum quid, inquantum huiusmodi formae non terminantur neque contrahuntur per aliquam materiam: sed quia forma creata sic subsistens habet esse, et non est suum esse, necesse

Cusanus' source? There are significant differences between Giles' and Cusanus' interpretations of contraction, and, as pointed out above, Cusanus could also have derived the concept from his own manuscript, MS Cues 83, containing excerpts from Lull's *Liber de forma dei* or from other scholastic sources besides Giles. The notion contraction was probably a commonly used concept in the philosophical and theological tradition in which Cusanus found himself. This granted, Giles may be among those scholastic philosophers who presented 'contraction' in a way that appealed to Cusanus.

Cusanus' interpretation of contraction does not, unlike Giles', revolve around the Neoplatonic doctrine of reception according to the capacity of the recipient. Giles used contraction to explain that individuation not only depends on form, but also on the matter individuated by form. Cusanus touches briefly on this idea in his *De docta ignorantia*, though without mentioning 'contraction' or its cognates. But Cusanus does not use the occasion to emphasise the role of the recipient.[45] He speaks, instead, of matter as the passive potentiality, as a *possibilitas*, receiving forms.[46] This is also significantly different from Bruno's idea of contraction, in which matter is assigned active potentiality, implying a dialectical relationship

---

est quod ipsum eius esse sit receptum et contractum ad determinatam naturam. Unde non potest esse infinitum simpliciter." As regards Duns Scotus, Haubst seems to cite the wrong place. The quotation occurs in chapter 4, though not in conclusio 8 as Haubst says, but in conclusio 9 (DUNS SCOTUS, *De primo principio* iv, conclusio 9, p. 118). Moreover, even though the correspondence of "contrahente" with "actu", and "contracto" with "pontentia" does not conflict with Cusanus' use of the notion contraction in his *De docta ignorantia* ii 6, p. 79.19-28, it does not explain the interrelation of four unities through contraction in CUSANUS, *De docta ignorantia* ii 6, p. 79.19-28. For the concept of contraction as a theory of individuation in Duns Scotus' philosophy, see WOLTER, 'John Duns Scotus (b. ca. 1265; d. 1308)', pp. 276, 285, 287, 289. Other authors who have ignored Giles as a possible source for Cusanus include HOPKINS, *Nicholas of Cusa's metaphysics of contraction*, pp. 97-112; MORAN, 'Pantheism', pp. 146-152; LEINKAUF, 'Die Bestimmung des Einzelseienden durch die Begriffe *contractio*, *singularitas* und *aequalitas* bei Nicolaus Cusanus', pp. 185-195. My interpretation agrees with VESCOVINI, 'Introduzione', pp. 26-27, who states briefly that Giles' notion of contraction is particularly important to the second book in Cusanus' *De docta ignorantia*, though without providing any further explanation or references. In an earlier article Vescovini had suggested that contraction in *De docta ignorantia* derived from the school of Albert and was available in Dietrich's and in Duns Scotus' works. See VESCOVINI, 'Temi ermetico-neoplatonici', p. 129.

[45] CUSANUS, *De docta ignorantia* ii 2, p. 68.23-30: "Communicat enim piisimus (this form is attested in classical Latin: see Lewis and Short and *Oxford Latin Dictionary*, s.v. 'pius') Deus esse omnibus eo modo, quo percipi potest. Cum igitur Deus absque diversitate et invidia communicet et recipiatur, ita quod aliter et alterius contingentia recipi non sinat, quiescit omne esse creatum in sua perfectione, quam habet ab esse divino liberaliter, nullum aliud creatum esse appetens tamquam perfectius, sed ipsum, quod habet a maximo, praediligens quasi quoddam divinum munus, hoc incorruptibiliter perfici et conservari optans."

[46] E.g. ibid., ii 7, ii 8, pp. 83.7, 85.5-8, 89.22-25.

between matter and form. This crucial difference between Cusanus' and Bruno's respective interpretations of contraction has been ignored in Bruno studies.[47]

Cusanus explains that universals in the genera and species exist *ante rem*, that is, they are ontologically prior to sensible particulars.[48] Above these unities ontologically is the absolute universal, which is God, the first unity.[49] Within this hierarchy Cusanus follows Aristotelian doctrine, maintaining that the universals are actualised in individuals.[50] The universals thus actualised have a potential existence prior to their contraction into individuals.[51] God, the first unity, is conceived of as having existence independently from that of individuals.[52]

How are we to understand the procession from absolute unity through *complicatio-explicatio*, described in Cusanus' *De docta ignorantia* ii 6?[53] From time to time Cusanus uses the term 'emanation' about the procession from God to particulars.[54] This suggests that he adheres to the Neoplatonic idea of the One and its emanation. But Cusanus does not associate the term 'emanation' with 'intelligible matter', 'abiding-procession-return' and other authentic Neoplatonic concepts.[55] For Cusanus, like Aquinas, emanation primarily denotes a hierarchy of being in which there is a smooth gradation from the highest ontological level (God) to the lowest (Creation).

There is, however, one crucial difference between Cusanus' idea of emanation and that of Aquinas. Cusanus does not follow the example of *Liber de causis* or scholastic philosophers, like Aquinas and Giles, in his account of descending ontological dependencies. According to the *Liber de causis* and scholastic sources, God creates intelligences, which, in turn, create the hypostasis Soul, which finally creates nature.[56] Cusanus objects to this theory of ontological succession that the emanation producing the universe must have taken place through a "simple emanation".[57] This is so, he argues from a logical point of view, for if the parts of the universe were not created together with the universe itself, that is, without separate stages of ontological dependency, then the universe as a whole would lack unity and perfection. Intelligences, therefore, were not created first, then Soul, and

---

[47] CLEMENS, *Giordano Bruno*, p. 143; MANCINI, *La sfera infinita*, p. 67; MIGNINI, 'La dottrina dell'individuo in Cusano e in Bruno', p. 348.

[48] CUSANUS, *De docta ignorantia* ii 6, p. 80.1-7, as quoted on p. 144 n. 37 above.

[49] Ibid., ii 6, p. 80.23-24.

[50] Ibid., ii 6, p. 80.8-10.

[51] Ibid., ii 6, p. 80.11-15.

[52] See also ibid., ii 2, p. 65.13-16. On this separation between God and the universe, articulated in Cusanus' interpretation of *contractio*, see BEIERWALTES, '"Primum est dives per se"', pp. 168-169.

[53] CUSANUS, *De docta ignorantia* ii 6, p. 79.19-28, as quoted on p. 143 n. 33 above.

[54] Ibid., ii 4, p. 74.25-28: "Quoniam vero dictum est universum esse principium contractum tantum atque in hoc maximum, patet, quomodo per simplicem emanationem maximi contracti a maximo absoluto totum universum prodiit in esse."

[55] For 'intelligible matter', see p. 41 n. 66 above. As regards the doctrine 'abiding-procession-return', see WALLIS, *Neoplatonism*, pp. 66, 106, 132-133.

[56] PSEUDO-ARISTOTLE, *Liber de causis* viii(ix) 82-87, ed. Pattin, pp. 155-157.

[57] CUSANUS, *De docta ignorantia* ii 4, p. 74.26-27: "per simplicem emanationem".

then nature, as "Avicenna and other philosophers hold".[58] These "other philosophers" may well include the author of *Liber de causis* (in particular its proposition viii(ix) 87), Aquinas, Giles and probably many other scholastic philosophers.[59]

The tensions between the scholastic tradition of contraction and Cusanus emerge in Cusanus' objection. He took on the terminology provided by the scholastic tradition of contraction, but he rejected the ontological separation between God and the Creation introduced through the idea of intelligences and Soul as intermediaries. In his theory of causation, which revises scholastic doctrine, Cusanus adheres to the traditional idea of God as pure act. But he regards God as one single cause whose effect is unitary, and adequately described through the binary concepts *complicatio-explicatio*, and *maximum-minimum*. The first pair was widely used in twelfth-century Platonism, whereas the latter had been assigned to the idea of ontological contraction and to Proclus' idea of individuation by Giles, among others.[60]

Cusanus' criticism of the ontology accompanying the scholastic tradition of the *Liber de causis* is detectable in his well-known polemics with Wenck in the decade

---

[58]   Ibid., ii 4, pp. 74.28-75.4: "Omnia autem entia, quae sunt partes universi, sine quibus universum — cum sit contractum — unum, totum et perfectum esse non posset, simul cum universo in esse prodierunt, et non prius intelligentia, deinde anima nobilis, deinde natura, ut voluit Avicenna et alii philosophii."

[59]   PSEUDO-ARISTOTLE, *Liber de causis* viii(ix) 87, ed. Pattin, pp. 156-157: "Et causa quidem prima non est intelligentia neque anima neque natura, immo est supra [Pattin adds: 'intelligentiam et'] animam et naturam, quoniam est creans omnes res. Verumtamen est creans intelligentiam absque medio et creans animam et naturam et reliquas res, mediante intelligentia." My contention that Cusanus aims, among others, at the author of *Liber de causis* with his words "other philosophers", agrees with Senger's note to this phrase of Cusanus. See Senger's note in CUSANUS, *De docta ignorantia*, Book II, Latin text with German tr., eds E. Hoffmann, P. Wilpert and K. Bormann, tr. P. Wilpert, notes by H. G. Senger, 3rd ed. F. Meiner: Hamburg, 1999, p. 35 n. 49. There, Senger conjectures that Cusanus, with the expression "other philosophers", refers to PROCLUS, *Elementatio theologica* prop. 129, tr. Moerbeke, p. 65, and PSEUDO-ARISTOTLE, *Liber de causis* loc. cit. These references are also cited in the apparatus to the 1932 Klibansky and Hoffmann edition, p. 75. In addition, Klibansky and Hoffmann cite MACROBIUS, *Commentarium in somnium Scipionis* i 14.6-8; PROCLUS, *Elementatio theologica* prop. 111, ed. Creuzer-Dübner, Paris 1855; PSEUDO-ARISTOTLE, *Liber de causis* §3, ed. Bardenhewer, p. 166 [= PSEUDO-ARISTOTLE, *Liber de causis* iii 32-36, ed. Pattin, pp. 140-141].

[60]   For the terms *explicatio-complicatio*, see GREGORY, 'The Platonic inheritance', p. 71 n. 52; COUNET, *Mathématiques et dialectique chez Nicolas de Cuse*, pp. 80-84. Giles makes the connection between *contractio* and *maximum* in GILES, *De esse et essentia* theorema 4, p. 16.1-10, of which line 5-10 reads: "et quia omne participatum est esse limitatum et contractum et non habet rationem omnis esse, ab esse puro per se existenti et infinito in quo reservatur omnis ratio essendi et quod est maxime tale, fluit et causatur omne esse participatum quod respectu esse primi est esse secundum quid et contractum."

following the composition of *De docta ignorantia*.[61] Between 1442 and 1443 Wenck wrote *De ignota litteratura* in response to this work of Cusanus.[62] Cusanus wrote a reply to Wenck's accusations in 1449 in the *Apologia doctae ignorantiae*, which was printed together with *De docta ignorantia* in three editions of Cusanus' works in the fifteenth and sixteenth centuries.[63]

To Wenck there is one important consequence of Cusanus' idea of emanation from God, which is of interest to our study, namely that "everything", i.e. the Creation, still according to Wenck's interpretation of *De docta ignorantia*, "coincides with God".[64] This was, effectively, an accusation of pantheism. In his *Apologia* Cusanus rejects Wenck's reading.[65] Irrespective of the merits of Cusanus' defence, Wenck's criticism is valuable to us because it focuses attention on Cusanus' terminology when he says that the universe is "enfolded" in the Absolute Maximum, God, and that nature is "contracted" and "unfolded" from him.[66]

Seen against the background of the scholastic tradition of the *Liber de causis*, particularly Aquinas' interpretation of it, it is possible to see what made Wenck voice these criticisms. When Cusanus presents Wenck as an interlocutor in his *Apologia*, he makes Wenck state that God gives being to everything, and is "not contracted".[67] Here Cusanus portrays his adversary as an exponent of the scholastic tradition of the *Liber de causis*, according to which God had been described as that which "gives being", and according to which — following Aquinas and Giles — God was not contracted into his Creation.[68] This polemic with Wenck certainly

---

[61]　On this debate, see VANSTEENBERGHE, 'Introduction', pp. 1-18; HAUBST, 'Nikolaus von Kues und Johannes Wenck, neue Erörterung und Nachträge', pp. 81-88; FLASCH, *Nikolaus von Kues*, pp. 181-194; HOPKINS, 'Introduction', pp. 3-18; GIACON, 'Il *De ignota litteratura* di Giovanni Wenck', pp. 63-72; CRANZ, *Nicholas of Cusa*, pp. 5-6, 26-27; COUNET, *Mathématiques et dialectique chez Nicolas de Cuse*, pp. 67-72.

[62]　FLASCH, *Nikolaus von Kues*, p. 184.

[63]　Ibid., p. 185. Cusanus' *Apologia* came out in his collected works: CUSANUS, *Opera* (Strassburg, 1490?), fols 206ʳ-212ᵛ; *Opera* (Paris, 1514), vol. 1, fols 34ᵛ-41ʳ; *Opera omnia* (Basel, 1565), pp. 63-75.

[64]　WENCK, *De ignota litteratura*, p. 24.19: "Omnia cum Deo coincidunt."

[65]　CUSANUS, *Apologia*, pp. 22.10-23.14.

[66]　WENCK, *De ignota litteratura*, p. 26.27-30: "Haec maximitas absoluta omnia habet in se, et ipsa est in omnibus, quia sua universitate omnia complectitur, quemadmodum natura, quae est contracta, est quasi explicatio omnium quae per motum fiunt." For contraction, see also ibid., pp. 36.20-29, 37.14-34.

[67]　CUSANUS, *Apologia*, p. 8.16-19: "'Unde nec Deus est hoc aut illud, nec caelum nec terra, sed dans esse omnibus, ut ipse sit proprie forma omnis formae, et omnis forma, quae non est Deus, non sit proprie forma, quia formata ab ipsa incontracta et absoluta forma.'"

[68]　PSEUDO-ARISTOTLE, *Liber de causis* i 1-8, iv 37, ed. Pattin, pp. 134-35, 142. On God as not contracted, see AQUINAS, *Quaestiones quodlibetales* quodlibetum 3, qu. 1, art. 1, pp. 71-72, as quoted on p. 127 n. 143 above; GILES, *Super authorem De causis*, *Alpharabium* ii, fol. 8ʳ, lines 40-42, as quoted on p. 123 n. 122 above. In his attack on Cusanus' *De docta ignorantia* Wenck criticises Cusanus' alleged view on being and corrects Cusanus with the *Liber de causis*; see WENCK, *De ignota litteratura*, p. 34.12-

shows that the notion of contraction was at the centre of a vast philosophical and theological problem: how to consider God as the cause of all things, but nevertheless distinct from his effects.[69]

Cusanus' contribution to Bruno's concept of contraction

What was, then, Cusanus' contribution to Bruno's concept of contraction? Bruno seems to have developed his fundamental idea of contraction as a theory of individuation between 1582 and 1584, that is, between his *De umbris* and his *Sigillus* and *De la causa*. In the first mentioned work he uses Cusanus' mathematical illustrations of God as a coincidence of opposites, and of procession from God, and it would be reasonable to expect Bruno to draw on Cusanus' version of ontological contraction too in this work.[70] Bruno does speak of contraction in the ontological sense in *De umbris*, but in such a way that it is difficult to pin down a source.[71]

There may, however, be at least one allusion to Cusanus' concept of contraction. In *De umbris* Bruno distances himself from "common philosophy", that is, predominantly Aristotelian and scholastic philosophy, in which the "efficient principle" is "contracted" into "this" or "that" entity. Instead, he prefers the philosophy of the "eloquent laymen" in which the efficient principle is "intrinsic" — intrinsic, we may assume, to nature — and is sometimes "contracted" into "all" entities, sometimes into "single" entities.[72] In *De la causa*

15: "Et valde claudicat huius conclusionis probatio, quod Deus sit cui esse quodlibet quod est[,] est esse [omne id quod est]; cum etiam secundum auctorem Causarum, prima causa sit in quolibet praeterquam quod alicui misceatur." (The comma in the first brackets has been inserted by me; the words in the second pair by Hopkins.) Wenck aims at the following words in CUSANUS, *De docta ignorantia* i 23, p. 46.22-23: "Unde Parmenides subtilissime considerans aiebat Deum esse, cui esse quodlibet, quod est, est esse omne id, quod est." That Wenck refers to the author of the *Liber de causis* when he speaks of "auctor Causarum" has been noted by Hopkins in WENCK, *De ignota litteratura*, p. 34 n. 135. There Hopkins refers Wenck's comment, cited in this note, to PSEUDO-ARISTOTLE, *Liber de causis* §19, ed. Bardenhewer, p. 181.7-8: "Causa prima regit res creatas omnes praeter quod commisceatur cum eis." This passage is identical in Pattin's edition (PSEUDO-ARISTOTLE, *Liber de causis* xix(xx) 155, p. 177). As already pointed out on p. 105 n. 10 above, Wenck composed a commentary on the *Liber de causis*. Since it was almost definitely unknown to Bruno, and since Wenck does not explicitly relate the *Liber de causis* to Cusanus' use of contraction in his *De ignota litteratura*, I shall not discuss it further.

69   For this problem, see ROLLS, *God and the world*.

70   STURLESE, 'Nicolò Cusano', pp. 955-958.

71   BRUNO, *De umbris* §§29.2-4, 63.2-6, 92.12-17, 94.2-9, 234.14-17, pp. 32, 52, 69, 69-70, 193.

72   Ibid., §94.2-9, pp. 69-70: "Propterea intelligas nos minime alligatos esse communi philosophiae, cum naturae nomen materiae, formaeque adstrinxerit, sed et cum efficiens intrinsecum principium recognoverit, sive sit omnibus commune, sive ad hoc

Bruno identifies the efficient cause of the universe with Mind, acting through the World Soul, which is the formal principle of the universal substance.[73] This efficient cause is probably what he means by efficient principle in *De umbris*. In support of this assumption we can add that in *De la causa* Bruno also defined the World Soul as intrinsic to the universe (*artefice interno*), just as he determines the "efficient principle" in *De umbris* as intrinsic.[74]

The idea of the efficient principle, in Cusanus' terminology the Absolute Maximum, being contracted into all particulars, can be found in *De docta ignorantia* ii 6, as already shown.[75] However, there Cusanus does not speak of the Absolute Maximum, as an efficient principle, being "intrinsic", as Bruno does on this occasion in *De umbris*. The idea of the Absolute Maximum being contracted into all also features in *De docta ignorantia* ii 5, where Anaxagoras' dictum *Quodlibet in quolibet* is incorporated into Cusanus' theory of individuation.[76] Bruno may allude to this Neoplatonic doctrine of all-in-all very opaquely in his *De umbris*. He certainly adopts it in later works, but no elaborate adaptation of Cusanus' metaphysics of contraction occurs in this early work.[77]

This exceptional statement about ontological contraction in *De umbris* does not appear in a fully elaborated theory of individuation. Whether it is indebted to Cusanus is not clear. If we make the assumption that it is, we should also acknowledge that the brief statement in *De umbris* differs from Cusanus' interpretation of contraction in at least two respects. First, as said, in the key passage from *De docta ignorantia* ii 6, quoted on p. 143 above, Cusanus does not speak of the Absolute Maximum as an intrinsic cause, as Bruno does in *De umbris*. Second, the contraction actualised by matter — one part of the so-called double contraction which Bruno describes in the two later works, the *Sigillus* and *De la causa* — is absent in this passage of *De umbris*.

The second point raises the question of whether Bruno was inconsistent or whether he changed, or developed, his thoughts about contraction between *De*

---

suppositum, vel ad illud fuerit contractum. Unde libentius idiotas loquentes audimus, dum naturam istius hominis cum illius hominis natura comparant: non enim ut universale logicum, vel ad eius similitudinem licet apprehendere naturam, sed ut physicum, quod est tum in omnibus, tum ad singula contractum." For a discussion of this passage, see BLUM, *Aristoteles*, p. 58. For the "eloquent layman", see Sturlese's note to BRUNO, *De umbris* §94.6, p. 70, in which she refers to CUSANUS, *De visione dei* ix, §35, p. 154: "Si igitur humanitatem, quae est simplex et una in omnibus hominibus, respexero, reperio ipsam in omnibus et singulis hominibus ... Unde haec natura humanitatis quae est contracta".

[73] BRUNO, *Causa* ii, p. 113, as quoted on p. 35 n. 38 above.

[74] Ibid., ii, p. 117.

[75] CUSANUS, *De docta ignorantia* ii 6, p. 79.19-28, as quoted on p. 143 n. 33 above.

[76] Ibid., ii 5, pp. 76.1-78.29. For the Neoplatonic origin of the doctrine 'all in all', see WALLIS, *Neoplatonism*, pp. 54-55.

[77] For the doctrine 'all in all' in Bruno's philosophy, see BRUNO, *Causa* ii, p. 135; *Infinito* i, pp. 85, 101; *Furori* arg., ii 2, pp. 15, 389; *Lampas* §64.1-4, p. 1020 (= *BOL*, vol. 3, p. 42.22-24); *Sigillus* ii 3, p. 196.15-19; *De immenso* v 9, pp. 146.1-149.12. For the doctrine 'all in all' in Bruno, see SPRUIT, *Il problema*, p. 144.

umbris, published in 1582, and the *Sigillus* and *De la causa*, published over the following two years. I believe the latter is the case. The affinities between contraction in the relevant passage in *De umbris* and contraction in Cusanus' *De docta ignorantia* ii 6 could then be read as an indication of Bruno's admiration for Cusanus' polemics against Aristotelian and scholastic philosophy — though without implying that Bruno shared Cusanus' interpretation of contraction.[78]

The main source for Bruno's concept of contraction was not, however, Cusanus, despite his several references to him. For Bruno upheld an interpretation of contraction involving a dialectical relationship between matter and form, which is absent in Cusanus' *De docta ignorantia*, the key work for Cusanus' idea of contraction. Giles, on the other hand, had proposed such a dialectical interpretation of contraction through his emphasis on the Neoplatonic doctrine of reception according to the capacity of the recipient, i.e. matter. Bruno revised the idea of matter through his reading of Plotinus' *Enneads* II iv, conflating intelligible and corporeal matter and emphasising the active potentiality of matter. Bruno incorporated Cusanus' principle of coincidence of opposites into this idea of matter. On the basis of an interpretation of contraction as the one found in Giles and Bruno's own interpretation of Plotinus' notion of matter, Bruno could give a pantheistic account of the relationship between unity and multiplicity which was distinct from the Christian version Cusanus had presented in his *De docta ignorantia*.

Cusanus' Christology

Cusanus not only drew on the scholastic tradition of contraction in his theory of individuation, he also accommodated it to his theology. Having distinguished between God, the Absolute Maximum, and the universe, the contracted maximum, in the first two parts of *De docta ignorantia*, Cusanus sets out in the third and last part of the work to solve the question of how the Creation returns to unity with its creator.

Cusanus makes it clear that it must be some sort of being which, unified with the Absolute Maximum, is eventually capable of providing such a return to union with the creator, and he states that such an entity "would have to be a contracted maximum, that is, God and creature, the absolute and the contracted, and this by a contraction which could only subsist in itself in the subsistence of the Absolute Maximum."[79] Moreover, he maintains that only a hypostatic union of God and a creature of this kind can ensure a form of contraction which unites the Absolute Maximum and the universe.[80]

---

[78] Cf. STURLESE, 'Nicolò Cusano', pp. 954-958; 'Per un'interpretazione', pp. 961-962.

[79] CUSANUS, *De docta ignorantia* iii 2, p. 124.14-17: "sed necessario foret maximum contractum, hoc est Deus et creatura, absolutum et contractum, contractione, quae in se subsistere non posset nisi in absoluta maximitate subsistente."

[80] Ibid., iii 2, p. 125.15-17.

The creature suitable to be elevated to a union with the Absolute Maximum must neither be an inferior nor a superior being, i.e. it must not be totally deprived of intelligence, as an animal, on the one hand, nor a pure intelligence, as an angel, on the other hand.[81] Man, Cusanus writes, is such a being which is "raised above all the works of God and placed little lower than the angels", since he is endowed with both intellectual and sensible natures. He continues: "Hence this nature is one that would, if united with the Absolute Maximum, be the universe's fullness of perfections of all and everything, so that in this very humanity all things would reach their highest level."[82] Consequently, and precisely because of man's reason, Cusanus extols "the ancients" who called man a "microcosm" or "*parvus mundus*".[83] It is not man as a whole to whom this elevated role pertains, only man as intellect, since intellect abstracts from the sense world and differs from the sensitive part of man.[84]

From these lines one might believe that Cusanus holds every human being to be a mediator between God and the universe, at least in potential form. Nevertheless, neither the human race, nor any other species or genus in the universe, can actually receive the Absolute Maximum. If so, then the species or genus in question would potentially become everything which the Absolute Maximum is, which is impossible. Hence the union of the Absolute Maximum and universe cannot be found in a created being in the universe. Nor, on the other hand, can it be the Absolute Maximum, God, itself, since it has limits. The only logical possibility, Cusanus concludes, is a being who owes its subsistence to God and is God in some way, and who at the same time is a contracted being.[85]

Although the species human being in itself cannot be the hypostatic union, this species, due to its intellect, still shares more with the Absolute Maximum than any other created beings in the universe.[86] Therefore the hypostatic union must be found within this species, and not, for instance, within those of dogs or plants.[87] Moreover, it must be one man possessing all perfections.[88] This being is the Son of

---

[81] Ibid., iii 3, pp. 125.24-126.7.

[82] Ibid., iii 3, pp. 126.29-127.6: "Humana vero natura est illa, quae est supra omnia Dei opera elevata et paulo minus angelis minorata, intellectualem et sensibilem naturam complicans ac universa intra se constringens, ut microcosmos aut parvus mundus a veteribus rationabiliter vocitetur. Hinc ipsa est illa, quae si elevata fuerit in unionem maximitatis, plenitudo omnium perfectionum universi et singulorum existeret, ita ut in ipsa humanitate omnia supremum gradum adipiscerentur."

[83] Ibid., iii 3, p. 127.2-3. For this theme in Cusanus' thought, see DUPRÉ, 'Der Mensch als Mikrokosmos im Denken des Nikolaus von Kues', pp. 68-87. For Bruno's use of the metaphor of man as a microcosm, see SPRUIT, *Il problema*, pp. 85 n. 164, 105; GRANADA, 'Bruno e la *dignitas hominis*', pp. 66-82.

[84] CUSANUS, *De docta ignorantia* iii 4, p. 131.14-27.

[85] Ibid., iii 2, p. 125.3-17.

[86] Ibid., iii 3, pp. 125.24-127.6, especially pp. 126.29-127.6.

[87] Ibid., iii 3, p. 128.6-10.

[88] Ibid., iii 3, p. 127.7-13.

God, Jesus Christ.[89] Even though Christ is of human origin, and as such belongs to the species of human beings, this is not what qualifies him as a hypostatic union. It is, instead, that the perfection of all things exists in Christ. Christ is the Son of God and as such identical to the Word of God, by which all things come into being.[90] No other human being can claim such a status.[91]

Through this metaphysical explanation of Christ, Cusanus achieves two things at once. First, he renders Christ a privileged entity who fits into his metaphysics of contraction. By doing so, Cusanus also makes his philosophy compatible with Christian doctrine. Second, Cusanus assigns to Christ an intermediary role, which we find in pagan Neoplatonism in relation to the One. Through the Son, every single created thing in the universe returns to the Absolute Maximum. "Through Him who is the contracted maximum, all things would proceed into a contracted being from the Absolute Maximum, and by His mediation would revert to the [Absolute Maximum], having, as it were, emanation as their origin and return as their end."[92]

The 'return' in question may be ambiguous. It is phrased in a way which is similar to Proclus' pagan idea that everything emanated from the One returns to the One.[93] The idea is not, of course, restricted to Proclus. It is fundamental to all Neoplatonism. Cusanus' 'return' is also, however, stated in a less heterodox way, to mean that, through the redemption of Christ, our souls will return to Heaven after death.[94] Whatever the meaning, this return is distinct from noetic ascent, a Neoplatonic return, in Bruno's thought.

These Christological ideas in Cusanus' idea of contraction were not to Bruno's taste.

---

[89]   Ibid., iii prologus, iii 3, iii 4, pp. 118.2-9, 127.7-128.10, 129.15-132.27. For Cusanus on Christ as a contraction from absolute maximum, see INGEGNO, *Regia pazzia*, pp. 126-128, 132-133.

[90]   CUSANUS, *De docta ignorantia* iii 3, pp. 127.3-6, 128.1-10.

[91]   Cf. LAZZARINI, 'Contrazione e incontrazione', where Cusanus' careful requirements to this hypostatic union are ignored. Lazzarini thus claims that, according to Cusanus, the individual human being has the potential to mediate between the sensible universe and God (p. 314). Christ, he adds, is "il grande mediatore" (ibid., p. 315). Although the title of this article by Lazzarini promises some clarification of contraction in Cusanus' Christology, the author only once (p. 313 n. 8) addresses the concept of contraction directly as it is used in Cusanus' *De docta ignorantia*, citing CUSANUS, *De docta ignorantia* iii 1, probably p. 120.4-6, where it is said that genera and species only exist "contractedly" in individuals. Otherwise Lazzarini does not explain the concept as it appears in this work of Cusanus with regard to human beings or to Christ.

[92]   CUSANUS, *De docta ignorantia* iii 3, p. 127.17-21: "per quem cuncta initium contractionis atque finem reciperent, ut per ipsum, qui est maximum contractum, a maximo absoluto omnia in esse contractionis prodirent et in absolutum per medium eiusdem redirent, tamquam per principium emanationis et per finem reductionis."

[93]   PROCLUS, *Elements of theology* prop. 21, p. 24.

[94]   CUSANUS, *De docta ignorantia* iii 4, pp. 129.23-130.17.

Bruno's criticism of orthodox Christology

To a heterodox philosopher like Bruno the challenge was to put forward his arguments for his philosophical beliefs, but to do so without running the risk of being charged with heresy by the Inquisition. None of the explicit references to Christ in Bruno's Italian and Latin works have heretical implications.[95] He does, however, on several occasions, allude to Christ and in such a way that it is difficult to avoid drawing the conclusion that he denied Christ's divinity and hence rejected Christian theology.[96]

One example of this is a passage in the *Spaccio* where Bruno calls Centaur, half man, half horse, "a person who is made of two natures", and a "hypostatic union".[97] The last predicate is normally reserved for Christ in orthodox theology. Is there more than scorn in these words of Bruno? Very probably there is. Bruno adds that Isis and Jove have noted that "for man to be divine it is fitting that he have something of a beast in him".[98] Elsewhere in the *Spaccio* Bruno associates Isis with the cult of the Egyptians, in which living nature, especially beasts, are regarded as divinely animated and worshipped as divine.[99] For Bruno, then, the Centaur symbolises his view that a true religion should venerate God in things, that matter was alive and that it produced from within itself animals, including human beings. As he says in the *Cabala*, what distinguished humans from supposedly lower forms of life was not their souls but their bodies.[100] The opposition to Cusanus' Christology — where the notion of contraction and the

---

[95] Christ is mentioned by name in the following places without attributing to him heretic predicates: BRUNO, *Candelaio* v 17, v 23, pp. 349, 393; *Sigillus* i 35, p. 181.5-7; *Lampas* §322.12-16, p. 1316 (= *BOL*, vol. 3, p. 183.20-24); *De lampade combinatoria* praefatio, p. 240.1-10; *De magia mathematica* §2.27-30, p. 10 (= *BOL*, vol. 3, p. 495.16-20); *Summa*, p. 16.13-18; *De principiis* §§90.1-3, 99.7-8, pp. 698-700, 710-712 (= *BOL*, vol. 3, pp. 560.16-18, 566.7-15); *De monade* vii, xi, pp. 427.23-428.1, 464.21-24.

[96] E.g. BRUNO, *Sigillus* i 46, p. 190.5, where Bruno mentions the worshipping of "Adonidis mors", i.e. Christ on the Cross; BRUNO, *Spaccio* iii 3, p. 461, where Bruno depicts Orion, urinating in heaven with fear, an allusion to Christ's walking on water. An anonymous reader noted in this second passage that Bruno here identified Orion with Christ; see ibid., iii 3, p. 460 n. 4.

[97] BRUNO, *Spaccio* iii 3, p. 495: "in cui [i.e., Centaur] una persona è fatta di due nature: e due sustanze concorreno in una ipostatica unione?" A contemporary reader commented in the margin "Rursus in Christum sub persona centauri sicut supra sub Orione" (ibid., iii 3, p. 494 n. 54). For Centaur, see my article, 'Bruno's *Spaccio* and Hyginus' *Poetica astronomica*', pp. 72-73, and GATTI, 'L'idea di riforma', p. 70.

[98] BRUNO, *Spaccio* iii 3, p. 495: "In fine (sia stato detto quantosivoglia da Iside, Giove et altri dell'eccellenza de l'esser bestia, e che a l'uomo per esser divino gli conviene aver de la bestia, e quando appetisce mostrarsi altamente divo, faccia conto di farsi vedere in tal misura bestia)".

[99] Bruno associates Iside with the cult of the Egyptians ibid., iii 2, pp. 417, 425, 445. And he describes the Egyptians' cult of living nature ibid., iii 2, pp. 415-417, 425, 431-435, 445-447.

[100] For Centaur, see ibid., iii 3, pp. 497-499.

terms 'hypostatic union', or 'union' are interpreted in agreement with orthodox Christianity — could not be starker.[101]

---

[101] For 'hypostatic union' or 'union' in this sense, cf. CUSANUS, *De docta ignorantia* iii 3, pp. 126.24-28, 127.3-6, 127.13-16, 128.2-6, 129.3-7.

Conclusion

Bruno applied the concept of contraction in a variety of meanings, among which two interpretations, one ontological and the other noetic, are central to his philosophy. The concept was used by Bruno to explain how multiplicity originates from unity, and how the human soul could ascend from multiplicity to unity.

Scholastic philosophers had used the concept of contraction to explain how the sensible universe was derived from a first cause and principle, identified as God, through a series of causes. Bruno used these sources and their interpretation for the same purpose. Among all of these authors, including Bruno, the notion of contraction remained more or less the same, accounting for the dependencies of inferior on superior being. What did change dramatically between scholastic authors, on the one hand, and Bruno, on the other, was the metaphysical structure and the "theology" in which the concept was employed.

Bruno's idiosyncratic concept of matter is the key to his metaphysics. It was primarily due to this interpretation of matter that he was able to transplant the scholastic use of contraction from a transcendent metaphysics into an immanent metaphysics. By assigning to matter active as well as passive potentiality, the causal dependencies in his metaphysical architecture differed completely compared with his scholastic predecessors. For Bruno, matter was no longer a passive recipient of causes. It was, instead, a co-determining principle together with the formal principle. Accordingly, Bruno redefined contraction, so that he could explain his theory of matter and form. In this way contraction became a key concept in his metaphysics.

Through the Neoplatonic doctrine of reception according to the capacity of the recipient, transmitted to Bruno through the *Liber de causis*, scholastic philosophers, among these Giles of Rome, had stressed the theoretical possibility of a dialectical relationship between matter and form. Giles had thus spoken of a "double determination" (*duplex limitatio*). This may have been one source for Bruno's expression "double contraction" (*duplex contractio*). As already mentioned, the theoretical possibility of a dialectical relationship between matter and form was widespread in scholastic theories of individuation, so even though it featured in the *Liber de causis*, and in particular in Giles' interpretation of it, we cannot be sure that the *Liber de causis*, or indeed Giles' commentary on it, were privileged sources to Bruno in this respect.

Giles did certainly not pursue the hylozoistic possibilities of this interpretation of matter and form, as Bruno would later do. He retained the Aristotelian conception of matter as passive potentiality. It was, instead, Bruno who formulated a theory of matter as both passive and active potentiality, inspired by philosophers like David of Dinant and Avicebron. Although Bruno may have borrowed Giles' idea of contraction through matter as well as form, Bruno's notion of matter did not derive from Giles, but from his interpretation of Plotinus' theory of intelligible and corporeal matter. Having arrived at this notion of matter through Plotinus, he employed the term 'contraction' within a metaphysical structure that suited his pantheistic inclinations.

Through the *Liber de causis* and its scholastic commentaries Neoplatonic doctrines had been part of scholastic philosophy from the twelfth century. Several references to the *Liber de causis* in Renaissance philosophy suggest that it continued to exert influence well into the sixteenth century. Ficino's Latin translation of Plotinus' *Enneads* may not have been as revolutionary to Bruno's metaphysics as has been assumed, since Bruno could have been introduced to, or at least been prepared for, Plotinus' and Proclus' systems of hypostases through the *Liber de causis*, where they are presented in a way that makes them sound more creationistic than in Plotinus' and Proclus' authentic philosophies. In the *Eroici furori*, for example, Bruno uses the expression 'horizon' to denote the hypostasis Soul. Sarauw refers the passage in the *Eroici furori* to Plotinus' *Enneads*. However, in Ficino's translation of the lines in question, 'horizon' is not used. But in the *Liber de causis* 'horizon' symbolises the hypostasis Soul.[1]

This coincidence means, on one hand, that what has been perceived as genuinely Plotinian contributions to Bruno's theory of hypostases may in fact originate from the *Liber de causis*, and, on the other hand, that in some cases it is probably impossible to determine which source is used. However, Ficino's translation of, and commentary on, Plotinus undoubtedly supplied Bruno with a notion of matter absent from scholastic interpretations of Neoplatonism derived from the *Liber de causis*. Bruno blended this scholastic theory of individuation through contraction with a Plotinian or Ficinian account of spiritual and corporeal matter and thereby produced his own idiosyncratic theory of matter.

Besides the tradition of the *Liber de causis* another source was significant to Bruno's use of the notion contraction, namely Cusanus. Cusanus probably picked up the notion from the scholastic tradition of which Giles had been part, but subjected the concept to his Neoplatonic idea of procession from unity to plurality. Moreover, Cusanus' metaphysics and theology are not heterodox and therefore contraction does not, as it does in Bruno, appear in a heterodox metaphysics.

As we have seen in Chapter 7, Bruno did not believe in Christ. Bruno's critical considerations about Christ are reflected in his use of the term 'contraction' in the *Spaccio*. There we encounter this notion in the ontological sense, describing the relation between the divine and human. The divine, Bruno states immediately before Asclepius' lament, cannot be experienced directly by human beings. It is accessible to him only inasmuch as it is contracted in living nature.[2] Asclepius' lament may be read as a literary device, exhorting the reader to venerate the divine

---

[1]   See p. 11 n. 20 above.

[2]   BRUNO, *Spaccio* iii 2, p. 427. For the passage, see INGEGNO, *Regia pazzia*, pp. 136-137. However, Ingegno's reading of this page in the *Spaccio* is coloured by his basic interpretation of contraction in the noetic sense as inspired by Ficino and his theory of a cosmologically structured descent and ascent; see ibid., pp. 133-134.

in this way.[3] In the *Spaccio*, Bruno foretells that the ancient Egyptian wisdom, of which Asclepius was part, will flourish in the future, when the wheel of vicissitude has turned again, implying that nature is experienced, and venerated, as God in things.[4] The concept of contraction — both as a theory of individuation and as a means of the contemplative philosopher's noetic ascent — helps us understand the philosophy underlying these views.

---

[3] For Asclepius in the *Spaccio*, see my article 'Bruno's *Spaccio* and Hyginus' *Poetica astronomica*', pp. 71-72. Cf. YATES, *Giordano Bruno and the Hermetic tradition*, pp. 211-215; D'AMICO, *Giordano Bruno*, pp. 257-260.

[4] BRUNO, *Spaccio* iii 2, p. 417.

Bibliography

Manuscripts

Bernkastel a./Mosel, Hospital zu Cues, MS 83, 325 fols.
Bernkastel a./Mosel, Hospital zu Cues, MS 195, 110 fols.

Primary sources

AGRIPPA OF NETTESHEIM. *De occulta philosophia*, ed. V. Perrone Compagni. E. J. Brill: Leiden, New York and Cologne, 1992. (*Studies in the history of Christian thought*, vol. 48.)

ALBERT THE GREAT. *Opera omnia*, eds B. Geyer et al., vol. 1-. Aschendorff: Münster i. W., 1951-.

— *De causis et processu universitatis a prima causa*, ed. W. Fauser, in Albert the Great, *Opera omnia*, vol. 17, pt 2.

AQUINAS. See THOMAS AQUINAS.

ARISTOTLE, *De physico auditu libri octo. Cum Averrois Cordubensis in eosdem commentariis*, in *Aristotelis opera cum Averrois commentariis*, 12 vols in 14 parts. Junctas: Venice, 1562-1574. Anastatic reprint: Minerva: Frankfurt, 1962, vol. 4.

PSEUDO-ARISTOTLE. *Liber de causis*, ed. A. Pattin, in A. Pattin, 'Le *Liber de causis*. Édition établie à l'aide de 90 manuscripts avec introduction et notes': *Tijdschrift voor filosofie*, vol. 28, 1966, pp. 134-203. Cited as PSEUDO-ARISTOTLE, *Liber de causis*.

— *Liber de causis*, ed. O. Bardenhewer, in O. Bardenhewer, *Die pseudo-aristotelische Schrift 'Ueber das reine Gute' bekannt unter dem Namen* Liber de causis. Herder'sche Verlagshandlung: Freiburg, 1882.

— *Problemata*, ed. P. Louis, in Aristotle, *Problèmes*, 3 vols. Les Belles Lettres: Paris, 1994.

AUGUSTINE. *De catechizandis rudibus liber unus*, in *PL*, vol. 40, cols 309-348.

— *De diversis quaestionibus 83*, in *PL*, vol. 40, cols 11-102.

AVERROES. *Sermo de substantia orbis*, Hebrew and English text, ed., tr. and comm. A. Hyman. The Medieval Academy of America: Cambridge, Mass. and Jerusalem, 1986. (*Medieval academy books*, vol. 96.)

BACON, R. *Quaestiones supra Librum de causis*, in Bacon, *Opera hactenus inedita*, ed. R. Steele, 16 fascicules. Oxford: Clarendon Press, 1905-40, fasc. 12.

BOETHIUS, *In praedicamenta Aristotelis*, in Boethius, *Opera omnia*. Sebastian Henricpetri: Basel, 1570. Pp. 112-214.

BRUNO, G. *De compendiosa architectura artis Lullii*, in *BOL*, vol. 2, pt 2, pp. 1-65.

— *Articuli centum et sexaginta adversus huius tempestatis mathematicos atque philosophos*, in *BOL*, vol. 1, pt 3, pp. 1-118. Cited as Bruno, *Adversus mathematicos*.

— *Cabala del cavallo pegaseo con l'aggiunta dell'asino cillenico*, in *BOeuC*, vol. 6.

— *Camoeracensis Acrotismus seu rationes articulorum physicorum adversus peripateticos Parisiis propositorum*, in *BOL*, vol. 1, pt 1, pp. 53-190. Cited as Bruno, *Acrotismus*.

— *Candelaio*, in *BOeuC*, vol. 1.

— *Cantus circaeus ad eam memoriae praxim ordinatus quam ipse Iudiciariam appellat*, in *BOL*, vol. 1, pt 1, pp. 179-257.

— *De la causa, principio et uno*, in *BOeuC*, vol. 3.

— *La cena de le ceneri*, in *BOeuC*, vol. 2.

— *De gli eroici furori*, in *BOeuC*, vol. 7.

— *Idiota triumphans seu de Mordentio inter geometras deo, dialogus*, in Bruno, *Due dialoghi sconosciuti e due dialoghi noti*, ed. G. Aquilecchia. Edizioni di storia e letteratura: Rome, 1957. Pp. 1-17. (*Storia e letteratura. Raccolta di studi e testi*, vol. 63.)

— *De imaginum, signorum et idearum compositione ad omnia inventionum, dispositionum et memoriae genera*, in *BOL*, vol. 2, pt 3, pp. 85-322. Cited as Bruno, *De compositione*.

— *De immenso et innumerabilibus seu de universo et mundis*, in *BOL*, vol. 1, pt 2, pp. 191-398.

— *De l'infinito, universo e mondi*, in *BOeuC*, vol. 4.

— *De lampade combinatoria lulliana*, in *BOL*, vol. 2, pt 2, pp. 225-327.

— *Lampas triginta statuarum*, in *BOM*, pp. 927-1590.

— *Libri physicorum aristotelis explanati*, in *BOL*, vol. 3, pp. 261-393.

— *[De magia mathematica]*, in *BOM*, pp. 3-158.

— *[De magia naturali]*, in *BOM*, pp. 159-320 [= *De magia* in *BOL*, vol. 3, pp. 492-506].

— *De monade numero et figura, secretioris nempe physicae, mathematicae et metaphysicae elementa*, in *BOL*, vol. 1, pt 2, pp. 319-484.

— *Oratio valedictoria*, in *BOL*, vol. 1, pt 1, pp. 1-25.

— *De progressu et lampade venatoria logicorum. Ad prompte atque copiose de quocumque proposito problemate disputandum*, in *BOL*, vol. 2, pt 3, pp. 1-84. Cited as Bruno, *De lampade venatoria*.

— *De rerum principiis et elementis et causis*, in *BOM*, pp. 585-759.

— *Sigillus sigillorum ad omnes animi dispositiones comparandas habitusque perficiendos adcommodatus*, in *BOL*, vol. 2, pt 2, pp. 161-217.

— *Spaccio de la bestia trionfante*, in *BOeuC*, vol. 5.

— *Summa terminorum metaphysicorum*, in *BOL*, vol. 1, pt 4, pp. 1-128.

— *[Theses de magia]*, in *BOM*, pp. 321-412.

— *Triginta sigilli*, in *BOL*, vol. 2, pt 2, pp. 79-120.

— *Triginta sigillorum explicatio*, in *BOL*, vol. 2, pt 2, pp. 121-160. Cited as Bruno, *Explicatio*.

— *De triplici minimo et mensura ad trium speculativarum scientiarum et multarum activarum artium principia*, in *BOL*, vol. 1, pt 3, pp. 119-361. Cited as Bruno, *De minimo*.

— *De umbris idearum*, ed. R. Sturlese. L. S. Olschki: Florence, 1991. (Bruno, *Le opere latine*, vol. 1.)

— *De vinculis in genere*, in *BOM*, pp. 413-584.

CALVIN, J. *Institutio religionis christianae*, eds G. Baum, E. Cunitz and E. Reuss, 2 vols. Schwetschke: Brunswick, 1869.

CAMPANELLA, T. *Apologia pro Galileo*. G. Tambach: Frankfurt, 1622.

Chartularium Universitatis Parisiensis, 4 vols, eds H. Denifle and E. Chatelain. Delalain: Paris, 1889-1897.

CUSANUS. See NICHOLAS OF CUSA.

DAVID OF DINANT, *Quaternulorum fragmenta*, ed. M. Kurdzialek, in *Studia Mediewistyczne*, vol. 3 (1963). Panstwowe Wydawnictwo Naukowe: Warsaw, 1963.

DIACETTO, F. C. DA. *I tre libri d'amore*. G. Giolito: Venice, 1561.

DIETRICH OF FREIBERG. *De animatione caeli*, ed. L. Sturlese, in Dietrich, *Opera omnia*, general ed. K. Flasch, eds B. Mojsisch, R. Imbach, L. Sturlese, M. R. Pagnoni-Sturlese et al., 4 vols. F. Meiner: Hamburg, 1977-1985. Vol. 3, pp. 1-46.

PSEUDO-DIONYSIUS THE AREOPAGITE. *De divinis nominibus*, in *Dionysiaca*, ed. P. Chevallier, 2 vols with continuous pagination. D. de Brouwer: Bruges, Paris, 1937-1950.

DUNS SCOTUS. *De primo principio*, ed. and tr. E. Roche. Nauwelaerts: Louvain, 1949. (*Franciscan Institute Publications. Philosophy series*, vol. 5.)

FICINO, M. *Opera*, 2 vols with continuous pagination. S. Henricpetri: Basel, 1576. (Anastatic reprint: ed. S. Toussaint, 2 vols. Phénix Éditions: Paris, 2000.)

— *Commentarium in Convivium Platonis, de amore*, in Ficino, *Commentaire sur le Banquet de Platon*, Latin and French text, ed., tr. and intro. R. Marcel. Les Belles Lettres: Paris, 1956. Cited as Ficino, *De amore*.

— *In Dionysium Areopagitam De divinis nominibus*, in Ficino, *Opera*, pp. 1024-1128. Cited as Ficino, *In De divinis nominibus*.

— *De divino furore*, in Ficino, *Opera*, pp. 612-615.

— *In Epistolas D. Pauli, ascensus ad tertium coelum, ad Paulum intelligendum*, in Ficino, *Opera*, pp. 425-472.

— *In epistolas duodecim Platonis*, in Ficino, *Opera*, pp. 1530-1536.

— *Le lettere*, vol. 1, ed. S. Gentile. L. S. Olschki: Florence, 1990.

— *El libro dell'amore*, ed. S. Niccoli. L. S. Olschki: Florence, 1987. (*Istituto Nazionale di Studi sul Rinascimento. Studi e Testi*, vol. 16.)

— *Liber de lumine*, in Ficino, *Opera*, pp. 976-986.

— *In Phaedrum*, in M. J. B. Allen, *Marsilio Ficino and the Phaedran Charioteer*, ed. and tr. M. J. B. Allen. University of California Press: Berkeley, Los Angeles and London, 1981. Pp. 73-129.

— *In Platonis Ionem, vel de furore poetico*, in Ficino, *Opera*, pp. 1281-1284.

— *In Plotinum*. See Plotinus, *Operum philosophicorum omnium libri LIV*.

— *Responsio petenti Platonicam instructionem et librorum numerum*, in Klibansky, *The continuity of the Platonic tradition during the Middle Ages. Outline of a corpus Platonicum medii aevi*. Warburg Institute: Glückstadt and Hamburg, 1939. Pp. 45-47.

— *Theologia platonica de immortalitate animorum ad Laurentium Medicem virum magnanimum*, in Ficino, *Théologie platonicienne de l'immortalité des âmes au magnanime Laurent de Médicis*, Latin and French text, ed., French tr. and intro. R. Marcel, 3 vols. Les Belles Lettres: Paris, 1964-70. (*Les classiques de l'humanisme.*)

— *In Timaeum commentarium*, in Ficino, *Opera*, pp. 1438-1484.

— *De vita*, in Ficino, *Three books on life*, eds and tr. C. V. Kaske and J. R. Clark. Center for Medieval and Early Renaissance Studies: State University of New York at Binghamton: Binghamton, New York, 1989. (*Medieval & Renaissance texts & studies*, vol. 57, The Renaissance Society of America, *Renaissance Texts Series*, vol. 11.)

GILES OF ROME. *Opus super authorem De causis, Alpharabium*. J. Zoppino and P. dei Nicolini da Sabbio: Venice, 1550.

— *Theoremata de esse et essentia*, ed. and intro. E. Hocedez. Museum Lessianum: Louvain, 1930. (*Museum Lessianum-section philosophique*, vol. 12.) Cited as Giles, *De esse et essentia*.

— *Tractatus de esse et essentia*: MS Cues 195, fols 67^r-105^v.

PSEUDO-HENRY OF GHENT. *Les* Quaestiones in Librum de causis *attribuées à Henri De Grand*, ed. J. P. Zwaenepoel. Publications universitaires: Louvain and Paris, 1974. (*Philosophes médiévaux*, vol. 15.) Cited as pseudo-Henry, *Quaestiones in Librum de causis*.

IAMBLICHUS. *De mysteriis Aegyptorum, Chaldaeorum, Assyriorum*, together with works by other authors, all in Latin by M. Ficino. A. Manuzio: Venice, 1497, fols a2^r-f1^r.

— *De mysteriis Aegyptorum*, ed. E. des Places, Les Belles Lettres: Paris, 1989.

JAVELLI, C. *In librum de causis. Commentarii duo*, in JAVELLI, [*Opera*]. Antoine de Harsy: Lyon, 1580, vol. 1, pp. 469b-506b.

LANDINO, C. *Disputationes camaldulenses*, ed. P. Lohe. Sansoni: Florence, 1980. (*Istituto Nazionale di Studi sul Rinascimento. Studi e Testi*, vol. 6.)

LOYOLA, ST IGNATIUS. *Exercicios espirituales*, in Loyola, *The spiritual exercises*, Spanish and English text, ed. and tr. J. Rickaby, 2nd ed. Burns Oates and Washbourne LTD: London, 1923.

LULL, R. *Lectura artis*, ed. J. G. Estelrich, in Lull, *Opera latina*. 22 vols. Brepols: Turnhout, 1959-. Vol. 20, pp. 335-438. (*Corpus Christianorum. Continuatio mediaevalis*, vol. 113.)

— *Ex libro de forma Dei*: MS Cues 83, fols 96^r-97^r.

— *Ex libro de forma Dei*: (MS Cues 83), in U. Roth, *Cusanus-Texte. III. Marginalien. 4. Raimundus Lullus. Die Exzerptensamlung aus Schriften des Raimundus Lullus im Codex Cusanus 83*, ed. U. Roth. C. Universitätsverlag C.

Winter: Heidelberg, 1999. (*Schriften der Philosophisch-historischen Klasse der Heidelberger Akademie der Wissenschaften*, vol. 13.) Cited as ed. Roth.

LUTHER, M. *De servo arbitrio*, ed. U. Freitag, in *Martin Luthers Werke. Kritische Gesamtausgabe*, vol. 1-. H. Böhlaus: Weimar, 1883-. Vol. 18, pp. 551-787.

MERSENNE, M. *L'impiété des déistes* etc., 2 vols. Billaine: Paris, 1624.

NICHOLAS OF CUSA [NICOLAUS KHRYPFFS]. *[Opera]*. M. Flach?: Strasbourg, 1490?

— *[Opera]*, ed. and with a prefatory epistle by J. le Fèvre, 3 vols. J. Badius: Paris, 1514.

— *[Collections]*. B. M. Dulcibellus: Cortemaggiore, 1520?

— *Opera*, H. Petri: Basel, 1565.

— *Apologia doctae ignorantiae discipuli ad discipulum*, ed. R. Klibansy, in *COO*, vol. 2.

— *De beryllo*, eds J. G. Senger and C. Bormann, in *COO*, vol. 11, pt 1.

— *Compendium*, eds B. Decker and C. Bormann, in *COO*, vol. 11, pt 3.

— *De coniecturis*, eds J. Koch and C. Bormann, in *COO*, vol. 3.

— *De docta ignorantia*, eds E. Hoffmann and R. Klibansky, in *COO*, vol. 1.

— *La dotta ignoranza*, Italian tr. with intro. and notes by G. F. Vescovini, 2nd ed. Città nuova: Rome, 1998. (*Fonti cristiane per il terzo millennio*, vol. 7.)

— *On learned ignorance: A translation and an appraisal of* De docta ignorantia, tr. and intro. J. Hopkins. Banning Press: Minneapolis, 1985.

— *Sermo VI*, eds R. Haubst, M. Bodewig, W. Krämer and H. Pauli, in *COO*, vol. 16, pp. 99-118.

— *De visione Dei*, ed. A. D. Riemann, in *COO*, vol. 6.

PICO DELLA MIRANDOLA, GIOVANNI. *De hominis dignitate, Heptaplus, De ente et uno, e scritti vari*, ed. E. Garin. Vallecchi: Florence, 1942. (*Edizione nazionale dei classici del pensiero italiano*, vol. 1.) Cited as Pico, *Scritti vari*.

— *Commento dello illustrissimo signor conte Joanni Pico Mirandolano sopra una canzona de amore composta da Girolamo Benivieni cittadino fiorentino secondo la mente et opinione de' platonici*, in Pico, *Scritti vari*, pp. 443-581. Cited as Pico, *Commento*.

— *Conclusiones sive theses DCCCC*, ed., tr. and comm. S. A. Farmer, in Farmer, *Syncretism in the West: Pico's 900 theses (1486). The evolution of traditional religious and philosophical systems*. Centre for Medieval & Early Renaissance Studies: Tempe, Arizona: 1998. (*Medieval & Renaissance texts & studies*, vol. 167.) Pico's text (pp. 181-535) is cited as Pico, *Conclusiones*.

— *Heptaplus. De septiformi sex dierum geneseos enarratione ad Laurentium Medicem*, in Pico, *Scritti vari*, pp.167-385.

PLATO, *Timaeus*, Latin tr. and comm. Calcidius, ed. J. H. Waszink. 2 vols. Warburg Institute and E. J. Brill: London and Leiden, 1962 and 1975. (*Corpus Platonicorum Medii Aevi. Plato latinus*, vol. 4.)

PLOTINUS. *[Opera]*, tr. and comm. M. Ficino. A. Miscomini: Florence, 1492.

— *Operum philosophicorum omnium libri LIV in sex enneades distributi*, Greek and Latin text, ed., tr. and comm. M. Ficino. P. Perna: Basel, 1580. Translation cited as tr. Ficino.

— *Opera*, eds P. Henry and H.-R. Schwyzer, 3 vols. Clarendon: Oxford, 1964-1982. Cited as Plotinus.

— *Les deux matières. [Ennéade II.4]*. Greek and French text, ed. P. Henry and H.-R. Schwyzer, tr., intro. and comm. J.-M. Narbonne. J. Vrin: Paris, 1993. Pp. 11-270. (*Histoire des doctrines de l'antiquité classique*, vol. 17.)

PROCLUS. *Elementatio theologica*, tr. William of Moerbeke, ed. H. Boese. Leuven University Press: Leuven, 1987. (*Ancient and medieval philosophy*, vol. 5.)

— *Elementatio theologica*: MS Cues 195, fols 34^v-66^v.

— *The elements of theology*, ed. and tr. E. R. Dodds, 2nd ed. Clarendon Press: Oxford, 1963.

ROMBERCH, J. [Host de Romberch, J.] *Congestorium artificiose memorie*. M. Sessa: Venice, 1533.

SPANGENBERG, J. *Artificiosae memoriae libellus in usum studiosorum collectus*. P. Seitz: Wittenberg, 1570.

THOMAS AQUINAS. *Opera omnia*, vol. 1-. Rome, 1882-.

— *De ente et essentia*, in Aquinas, *De ente et essentia*, intro. and notes by M.-D. Roland-Gosselin. J. Vrin: Paris, 1948. (*Bibliothèque thomiste*, vol. 8.)

— *In librum beati Dionysii De divinis nominibus expositio*, ed. C. Pera, intro. P. Caramello, with a doctrinal synthesis by C. Mazzantini. Marietti: Turin, Rome, 1950.

— *Super Librum de causis expositio*, ed. and intro. H. D. Saffrey. Nauwelaerts: Louvain, 1954. (*Textus philosophici Friburgenses*, vol. 4.)

— *Liber de causis*: MS Cues 195, fols 1^r-34^v.

— *Commentary on the Book of causes*, tr. and notes by V. A. Guagliardo, C. R. Hess and R. C. Taylor, intro. V. A. Guagliardo. Catholic University of America Press: Washington, D. C., 1996.

— *Quaestiones quodlibetales*, ed. and intro. R. P. Mandonnet. Lethielleux: Paris, 1926.

— *Responsio ad lectorem venetum de 36 articulis*, in Aquinas, *Opera omnia*, vol. 42, pp. 337-346.

— *Summa theologiae*, in Aquinas, *Opera omnia*, vols 4-12.

— *Summa contra gentiles*, in Aquinas, *Opera omnia*, vols 13-15.

WENCK, J. *De ignota litteratura*, in J. Hopkins, *Nicholas of Cusa's debate with John Wenck*, pp. 95-118. Hopkins has provided the page and line numbers of the 1910-edition by Vansteenberghe, to which I also refer.

Secondary sources

ALLEN, M. J. B. 'Introduction', in Ficino, *The Philebus commentary*, Latin and English text, ed., tr. and notes by M. J. B. Allen. University of California Press: Berkeley, 1975. (*Center for Medieval and Renaissance Studies*, vol. 9.) Pp. 1-58.

D'AMICO, M. *Giordano Bruno. Avventure e misteri del grande mago nell'Europa del cinquecento*. Piemme: Casale Monferrato, 2000.

AQUILECCHIA, G. 'Lo stampatore londinese di Giordano Bruno e altre note per l'edizione della *Cena*', in Aquilecchia, *Schede bruniane (1950-1991)*. Vecchiarelli: Rome, 1993. Pp. 157-207. (*Memoria bibliografica*, vol. 18.) Originally published in *Studi di filologia italiana*, vol. 7 (1960), pp. 101-162.

— 'Ancora su Giordano Bruno ad Oxford (in margine ad una recente segnalazione)': *Studi secenteschi*, vol. 4 (1963), pp. 3-13.

— 'Bruno, Giordano', in *Dizionario bibliografico degli italiani*, vol. 1-. Istituto della enciclopedia italiana: Rome, 1960-. Vol. 14, pp. 654-665.

— 'Introduzione', in Bruno, *De la causa, principio et uno*. Einaudi: Turin, 1973. Pp. XI-XLVIII. (*Nuova raccolta di classici italiani annotati*, vol. 8.)

— 'Ramo, Patrizi e Telesio nella prospettiva di Giordano Bruno', *Discorsi. Richerche di storia della filosofia*, vol. 9 (1989), pp. 27-40.

— 'Bruno e la matematica a lui contemporanea in margine al *De minimo*', *GCFI*, vol. 69 (1990), pp. 151–159.

ARMSTRONG, A. H. *The architecture of the intelligible universe in the philosophy of Plotinus. An analytical and historical study.* Cambridge University Press: Cambridge, 1940. (*Cambridge classical studies*, vol. 6.) Cited as Armstrong, *Intelligible universe.*

— 'Plotinus', in *CHLGEMP*, pp. 193-268.

BÄCK, A. 'The Islamic background: Avicenna (b. 980; d. 1037) and Averroes (b. 1126; d. 1198)', in *Individuation in scholasticism. The later Middle Ages and the Counter-Reformation 1150-1650*, pp. 39-67.

BADALONI, N. *La filosofia di Giordano Bruno*. Parenti: Florence, 1955.

— *Giordano Bruno. Tra cosmologia ed etica.* De Donato: Rome and Bari, 1988. (*Saggi*, vol. 6.) Cited as Badaloni, *Tra cosmologia ed etica.*

BARDENHEWER, O. 'Zur Geschichte der lateinischen Uebersetzung'. See pseudo-Aristotle, *Liber de causis*, ed. O. Bardenhewer, pp. 204-302.

BASSI, S. 'Editoria e filosofia nella seconda metà del '500: Giordano Bruno e i tipografi londinesi': *Rinascimento*, 2nd series, vol. 37 (1997), pp. 437-458.

BAUR, L. *Cusanus-Texte. III. Marginalien. 1. Nicolaus Cusanus und ps. Dionysius im Lichte der Zitate und Randbemerkungen des Cusanus.* C. Winter's Universitätsbuchhandlung: Heidelberg, 1941. (*Sitzungberichte der Heidelberger Akademie der Wissenschaften. Philosophisch-historische Klasse*, 4, 1940/41.

BEIERWALTES, W. 'Der Kommentar zum *Liber de causis* als neuplatonisches Element in der Philosophie des Thomas von Aquin', *Philosophische Rundschau*, 11. Jahrgang, Heft 3/4 (1964), pp. 192-215.

— 'Deus oppositio oppositorum (Nicolaus Cusanus, *De visione dei* XIII)', *Salzburger Jahrbuch für Philosophie*, vol. 8 (1964), pp. 175-185.

— 'Actaeon. Zu einem mythologischen Symbol Giordano Brunos', *Zeitschrift für philosophische Forschung*, vol. 32 (1978), pp. 345–354.

— 'Absolute identity: Neoplatonic implications in Schelling's "Bruno"', *Contemporary German philosophy*, vol. 2 (1983), pp. 73–99.

— '"Primum est dives per se". Meister Eckhart und der *Liber de causis*', in *On Proclus and his influence in medieval philosophy*, eds E. P. Bos and P. A.

Meijer. E. J. Brill: Leiden, etc., 1992. Pp. 141-169. (*Philosophia antiqua*, vol. 53.)

— 'Einleitung', in Plotinus, *Über Ewigkeit und Zeit (Enneade III 7)*, tr., intro. and commentary by W. Beierwaltes. Vittorio Klostermann: Frankfurt am Main, 1995, pp. 9-88.

BERNART, L. DE. *Immaginazione e scienza in Giordano Bruno. L'infinito nelle forme dell'esperienza*. ETS: Pisa, 1986.

BERTAUD, E. 'Discipline', in *DS*, vol. 3, cols 1302-1311.

BIDEZ, J. and CUMONT, F., *Les mages hellénisés. Zoroastre Ostanès et Hystaspe d'après la tradition grecque*, 2 vols. Les Belles Lettres: Paris, 1938. .

BLOOS, L. *Probleme der Stoischen Physik*. H. Buske: Hamburg, 1973. (*Hamburger Studien zur Philosophie*, vol. 4.)

BLUM, P. R. *Aristoteles bei Giordano Bruno*. W. Fink: Munich, 1980. (*Die Geistesgeschichte und ihre Methoden. Quellen und Forschungen*, vol. 9.)

BLUMENBERG, H. *Aspekte der Epochenschwelle: Cusaner und Nolaner*. Suhrkamp: Frankfurt am Main, 1976. (*Suhrkamp Taschenbuch. Wissenschaft*, vol. 174.) This edition is a revised version of part four in Blumenberg, *Die Legitimität der Neuzeit*. (Suhrkamp: Frankfurt am Main, 1966). I cite the 1976 edition.

BLUMENTHAL, H. J. 'Did Plotinus believe in Ideas of individuals?': *Phronesis*, vol. 11 (1966), pp. 61-80. (Reprinted in Blumenthal, *Soul and intellect*, pp. 61-80.)

— *Plotinus' psychology. His doctrines of the embodied soul*. M. Nijhoff: The Hague, 1971.

— 'Soul, World-Soul and individual soul in Plotinus', in *Le Néoplatonisme, colloques internationaux du CNRS*. Paris, 1971. Pp. 55-63. (Reprinted in Blumenthal, *Soul and intellect*, pp. 55-63.)

— *Nous* and Soul in Plotinus: some problems of demarcation', in *Plotino e il Neoplatonismo in Oriente e in Occidente*. Accademia Nazionale dei Lincei: Rome, 1974. Pp. 203-219.

— 'Neoplatonic interpretations of Aristotle on *phantasia*', *Review of metaphysics*, vol. 31 (1977), pp. 242-256.

— *Soul and intellect. Studies in Plotinus and later Neoplatonism*. Ashgate: Hampshire, 1993.

BÖNKER-VALLON, A. *Metaphysik und Mathematik bei Giordano Bruno*. Akademie Verlag: Berlin, 1995.

— 'Giordano Bruno e la matematica', *Rinascimento*, 2nd series, vol. 39 (1999), pp. 67-93. Cited as Bönker-Vallon, 'La matematica'.

BORSCHE, T. 'Denken in Bildern. *Phantasia* in der Erkenntnislehre des Giordano Bruno', in *Giordano Bruno. Tragik eines Unzeitgemässen*, eds W. Hirdt and R. Baum. Stauffenburg: Tübingen, 1993. Pp. 93-106. (*Romanica et comparatistica. Sprach- und literaturwissenschaftlichen Studien*, vol. 20.)

BROWN, S. F. 'Henry of Ghent (b. ca. 1217; d. 1293)', in *Individuation in scholasticism. The later Middle Ages and the Counter-Reformation 1150-1650*, pp. 195-219.

BRUNNER, F. 'La doctrine de la matière chez Avicébron', *Revue de théologie et de philosophie*, vol. 6 (1956), pp. 261-279. Cited as Brunner, 'Matière chez Avicébron'.

BUCCOLINI, C. '*Contractiones* in Bruno: potenza dell'individuo e grazia divina nell'interpretazione di Mersenne', *B&C*, 2000, pt 2, pp. 503-531.

BUNDY, M. W. *The theory of imagination in classical and mediaeval thought.* University of Illinois Press: Urbana, 1927. *University of Illinois studies in language and literature*, vol. 12, nos. 2-3.

BUSSANICH, J. 'Mystical elements in the thought of Plotinus', in *Aufstieg und Niedergang der römischen Welt. Geschichte und Kultur Roms im Spiegel der neueren Forschung*, eds W. Haase and H. Temporini. W. de Gruyter: Berlin and New York, 1972-. Teil II: *Principat*, vol. XXXVI 7, pp. 5300-5330.

CALCAGNO, A. *Giordano Bruno and the logic of coincidence. Unity and multiplicity in the philosophical thought of Giordano Bruno.* P. Lang: New York, 1998. (*Renaissance and baroque: Studies and texts*, vol. 23.)

CANONE, E. "*Phantasia*' / '*imaginatio*' come problema terminologico nella lessicografia filosofica tra sei-settecento', in '*Phantasia*'-'*imaginatio*'. *Quinto colloquio internazionale. Roma, 9-11 gennaio 1986*, eds M. Fattori and M. Bianchi. Edizioni dell'Ateneo: Rome, 1988. Pp. 221-257. (*Lessico intellettuale europeo*, vol. 46.)

— *Il dorso e il grembo dell'eterno. Percorsi della filosofia di Giordano Bruno.* Istituti editoriali e poligrafici internazionali: Pisa and Rome, 2003. (*Bruniana & Campanelliana, supplementi.*)

CARELLA, C. 'Tra i maestri di Giordano Bruno. Nota sull'agostiniano Teofilo da Vairano', *B&C*, 1995, pts 1-2, pp. 63-82.

CASSIRER, E. *Individuum und Kosmos in der Philosophie der Renaissance.* B. G. Teubner: Berlin and Leipzig, 1927. (*Studien der Bibliothek Warburg*, vol. 10.)

CASTELLI, P. 'Marsilio Ficino e i luoghi della memoria', in *Marsilio Ficino e il ritorno di Platone. Studi e documenti*, 2 vols, ed. G. C. Garfagnini. L. S. Olschki: Florence, 1986. Vol. 2, pp. 383-395. (*Istituto nazionale di studi sul rinascimento. Studi e testi*, vol. 15.)

CATANA, L. 'Bruno's *Spaccio* and Hyginus' *Poetica astronomica*', *B&C*, 2000, pt 1, pp. 57-77.

Cento codici bessarionei. Catalogo di mostra, compiled by T. G. Leporace and E. Mioni. San Giorgio Maggiore: Venice, 1968.

CELENZA, C. S. 'Pythagoras in the Renaissance: The case of Marsilio Ficino', *Renaissance quarterly*, vol. 52 (1999), pp. 667-711.

— *Piety and Pythagoras in Renaissance Florence. The 'symbolum nesianum'.* Brill: Leiden, etc., 2001. (*Studies in the history of Christian thought*, vol. 101.)

CHASTEL, A. *Art et humanisme a Florence au temps de Laurent de Magnifique. Études sur la renaissance et l'humanisme platonicien.* Presses Universitaires de France: Paris, 1959. (*Publications de l'Institut d'art et d'archéologie de l'Université de Paris*, vol. 4.)

CILIBERTO, M. *La ruota del tempo. Interpretazione di Giordano Bruno.* Riuniti: Rome, 1986.

— *Giordano Bruno*. Laterza: Bari, 1992.

— 'Introduction'. See Bruno, *De la causa, principio et uno*, pp. IX-LI.

CLEMENS, F. J. *Giordano Bruno und Nicolaus von Cusa. Eine philosophische Abhandlung*. Wittman: Bonn, 1847. (Anastatic reprint: with a note on the author by P. R. Blum. Thoemmes Press: Bristol, 2000.)

CLUCAS, S. '*In campo fantastico*: Alexander Dicson, Walter Warner and Brunian mnemonics', in *Giordano Bruno 1583–1585. The English experience / L'esperienza inglese*, eds M. Ciliberto and N. Mann. L. S. Olschki: Florence, 1997. Pp. 37-59.

— '*Simulacra et signacula*: the composition of images, signs and Ideas in Brunian mnemonics', unpublished paper held at the *Einsteinforum* at the conference *Frances A. Yates: Ihr Werk im Kontext der Renaissance- und Erinnerungsforschung*, Berlin, March 8th-10th 1998.

— '*Amorem, artem, magiam, mathesim*. Brunian images and the domestication of the soul': *Zeitsprünge. Forschungen zur frühen Neuzeit*, Band 3, 1999, Heft 1/2, pp. 5-24.

COLOMBO, A. 'Intenzionalità', in *Enciclopedia filosofica*, 2nd ed., 6 vols. Sansoni: Florence, 1968-1969, vol. 3, cols 989-993.

COPENHAVER, B. P. 'Scholastic philosophy and Renaissance magic in the *De vita* of Marsilio Ficino': *Renaissance quarterly*, vol. 37 (1984), pp. 523-554.

— 'Renaissance magic and Neoplatonic philosophy: *Ennead* 4.3-5 in Ficino's *De vita coelitus comparanda*', in *Marsilio Ficino e il ritorno di Platone: studi e documenti*, ed. G. C. Garfagnini, 2 vols. L. S. Olschki: Florence, 1986. Vol. 2, pp. 351-369.

— 'Iamblichus, Synesius and the Chaldean oracles in Marsilio Ficino's *De vita libri tres*: Hermetic magic or Neoplatonic magic?', in *Supplementum festivum: Studies in the honor of Paul Oskar Kristeller*, pp. 441-455.

— 'Natural magic, Hermeticism and occultism in early modern science', in *Reappraisals of the scientific revolution*, eds R. S. Westmann and D. Lindberg. Cambridge University Press: Cambridge etc., 1990. Pp. 261-301.

CORRIGAN, K. 'Is there more than one generation of matter in the *Enneads*?': *Phronesis*, vol. 31 (1986), pp. 167-181.

— 'On the generation of matter in the *Enneads*. A reply': *Dionysius*, vol. 12 (1988), pp. 17-24.

CORSANO, A. *Il pensiero di Giordano Bruno nel suo svolgimento storico*. Sansoni: Florence, 1940.

— 'Arte e natura nella speculazione pedagogica del Bruno', in *Medioevo e rinascimento. Studi in onore di Bruno Nardi*, pp. 115–126.

COSTA, C. D'A. 'Le fonti e la struttura del *Liber de causis*': *Medioevo. Rivista di storia della filosofia medievale*, vol. 15 (1989), pp. 1-38.

— '"Cause prime non est yliathim". *Liber de causis*, prop. 8[9]: le fonti e la dottrina': *Documenti e studi sulla tradizione filosofica medievale*, vol. 1 (1990), pp. 327-351.

— '"Philosophus in libro *De causis*". La recezione del *Liber de causis* come opera aristotelica nei commenti di Ruggero Bacone, dello ps. Enrico di Gand e dello ps. Adamo di Bocfeld': *Documenti e studi sulla tradizione filosofica medievale*, vol. 2 (1991), pp. 611-649.

— '"Esse quod est supra eternitatem". La cause première, l'être et l'eternité dans le *Liber de causis* et dans ses sources': *Archives d'histoire doctrinale et littéraire du Moyen Âge*, vol. 59 (1992), pp. 41-62.

— 'La doctrine de la création "mediante intelligentia" dans le *Liber de causis*': *Revue des sciences philosophiques et théologiques*, vol. 76 (1992), pp. 209-233.

COUNET, J.-M. *Mathématiques et dialectique chez Nicolas de Cuse*. J. Vrin: Paris, 2000. (*Études de philosophie médiévale*, vol. 80.)

CRANZ, F. E. *A bibliography of Aristotle editions 1501-1600*. 2nd ed. with addenda and revisions by C. B. Schmitt. V. Koerner: Baden-Baden, 1984. (*Bibliotheca bibliographica aureliana*, vol. 38.)

— *Nicholas of Cusa and the Renaissance*, eds T. M. Izbicki and G. Christianson. Aldershot: Ashgate, 2000.

DAGRON, T. *Unité de l'être et dialectique. L'idée de philosophie naturelle chez Giordano Bruno*. Vrin: Paris, 1999. (*De Pétrarque à Descartes*, vol. 66.)

DEITZ, L. '"Falsissima est ergo haec de triplici substantia Aristotelis doctrina". A sixteenth-century critic of Aristotle — Francesco Patrizi da Cherso on privation, form and matter': *Early science and medicine. A journal for the study of science, technology and medicine in the pre-modern period*, vol. 2 (1997), pp. 227-250.

DODDS, E. R. *The Greeks and the irrational*. University of California Press: Berkeley and Los Angeles, 1951. (*Sather Classical Lecturers*, vol. 25.)

DUPRÉ, W. 'Der Mensch als Mikrokosmos im Denken des Nikolaus von Kues', in *MFCG*, vol. 13 (1978), pp. 68-87.

EDELSTEIN, L. 'The Golden Chain of Homer', in *Studies in intellectual history*, eds G. Boas et al. Johns Hopkins University Press: New York, 1953. Pp. 48-66.

ELDERS, L. 'Saint Thomas d'Aquin et la métaphysique du *Liber de causis*': *Revue Thomiste*, vol. 89 (1989), pp. 427-442.

FABRO, C. *Participation et causalité selon S. Thomas d'Aquin*. Publications universitaires de Loyvain and Béatrice-Nauwelaerts: Louvain and Paris, 1961. (*Chaire Carndial Mercier*, vol. 2.)

FARMER, S. A. 'Introductory monograph'. See Pico, *Conclusiones sive theses DCCCC*.

FAUSER, W. 'Prolegomena'. See Albert the Great, *De causis et processu universitatis a prima causa*, pp. V-XXXII.

FELLMANN, F. 'Bild und Bewusstsein bei Giordano Bruno', in *Die Frankfurter Schriften Giordano Brunos und ihre Voraussetzungen*, eds K. Heipcke, W. Neuser and E. Wicke. VHC: Weinheim, 1991. Pp. 17-36.

FIRPO, L. *Il processo di Giordano Bruno*, ed. D. Quaglioni. Salerno: Rome, 1993.

FLASCH, K. *Nikolaus von Kues. Geschichte einer Entwicklung. Vorlesungen zur Einführung in seine Philosophie*. V. Klostermann: Frankfurt am Main, 1998.

FUEHRER, M. L. 'The principle of *contractio* in Nicholas of Cusa's philosophical view of man': *The Downside review*, vol. 93 (1975), pp. 289-296.

GABRIEL, G. 'Sein; Seiendes', in *Historisches Wörterbuch der Philosophie*, general ed. J. Ritter. Vol. 1-. Wissenschaftliche Buchgesellschaft: Darmstadt, 1971-, vol. 7, cols 170-234.

GARIN, E. 'Cusano e i platonici italiani del quattrocento', in *Nicolò da Cusa. Relazioni tenute al convegno interuniversitario di Bressanone nel 1960.* Sansoni: Florence, 1962. Pp. 75-100. (*Pubblicazioni della facoltà di magistero dell'università di Padova*, vol. 4.)

— *Rinascite e rivoluzioni. Movimenti culturali dal XIV al XVIII secolo.* Laterza: Bari, 1975. (*Biblioteca di cultura moderna*, vol. 782.)

— '*Phantasia* e *imaginatio* fra Marsilio Ficino e Pietro Pomponazzi': *GCFI*, vol. 64 (1985), pp. 349-361.

GATTI, H. 'L'idea di riforma nei dialoghi italiani di Giordano Bruno': *NRL*, vol. 2 (1996), pp. 61–81.

— *Giordano Bruno and Renaissance science.* Cornell University Press: Ithaca and London, 1999.

GENTILE, S., NICCOLI, S. and VITI, P., eds. *Marsilio Ficino e il ritorno di Platone. Mostra di manoscritti, stampe e documenti, 17 maggio-16 giugno 1984. Catalogo*, with an introductory note by E. Garin. Le Lettere: Florence, 1984.

GENTILE, S. 'In margine all'epistola *De divino furore* di Marsilio Ficino': *Rinascimento*, vol. 23 (1983), pp. 33-77.

GERSH, S. E. ΚΙΝΗΣΙΣ ΑΚΙΝΗΤΟΣ. *A study of spiritual motion in the philosophy of Proclus.* E. J. Brill: Leiden, 1973. (*Philosophia antiqua*, vol. 26.)

GHIO, M. 'Causa emanativa e causa immanente: S. Tommaso e G. Bruno': *Filosofia*, vol. 30 (1979), pp. 529-554.

GIACON, C. 'Il *De ignota litteratura* di Giovanni Wenck', in *Nicolò da Cusa. Relazioni tenute al convegno interuniversitario di Bressanone nel 1960.* Sansoni: Florence, 1962. Pp. 63-74. (Pubblicazioni della facoltà di magistero dell'università di Padova, vol. 4.)

GILSON, É. *The Christian philosophy of St Thomas Aquinas.* Notre Dame Press: Notre Dame, Ind., 1956. Cited as Gilson, *Aquinas*.

Giordano Bruno: Philosopher of the Renaissance, ed. H. Gatti. Ashgate: Aldershot, 2002.

GRAESER, A. *Plotinus and the Stoics.* E. J. Brill: Leiden, 1972. (*Philosophia antiqua*, vol. 22.)

GRAFTON, A. 'The availability of ancient works', in *CHRP*, pp. 767-791.

GRANADA, M. A. 'Giordano Bruno et la *dignitas hominis*: Présence et modification d'un motif du Platonisme de la Renaissance': *NRL*, vol. 1 (1993), pp. 35-89.

— 'Giordano Bruno y la stoa: ¿una presencia no reconocida de motivos estoicos?': *NRL*, vol. 1 (1994), pp. 123-151.

GREGORY, T. 'The Platonic inheritance', in *A history of twelfth-century Western philosophy*, pp. 54-80.

GRUNEWALD, H. *Die Religionsphilosophie des Nikolaus Cusanus und die Konzeption einer Religionsphilosophie bei Giordano Bruno.* 2nd ed. Gerstenberg: Hildesheim, 1977. (*Studia irenica*, vol. 13.)

GUAGLIARDO, V. A. 'Introduction'. See Thomas Aquinas, *Commentary on the Book of causes*, pp. IX-XXXII.

GUIDELLI, C. 'Note sul tema della memoria nelle *Enneadi* di Plotino': *Elenchos. Rivista di studi sul pensiero antico*, year 9, fasc. 1 (1988), pp. 75-94.

GUTHRIE, W. K. C. *A history of Greek philosophy*, 6 vols. Cambridge University Press: Cambridge, etc., 1962-1981.

HADOT, P. *Plotinus, or the simplicity of vision*, tr. M. Chase, intro. by A. I. Davidson. University of Chicago Press: Chicago and London, 1993.

HAHM, D. E. *The origins of Stoic cosmology*. Ohio State University Press: Ohio, 1977.

HALFWASSEN, J. 'Substanz/Akzidens; I. Antikke': *Historisches Wörterbuch der Philosophie*, general ed. J. Ritter. Vol. 1-. Wissenschaftliche Buchgesellschaft: Darmstadt, 1971-. Vol. 10, cols 495-507.

HANKINS, J. *Plato in the Italian Renaissance*, 2 vols with continuous pagination. E. J. Brill: Leiden, etc., 1990. (*Columbia Studies in the Classical Tradition*, vol. 17.)

— 'Pico della Mirandola, Giovanni (1463-94)', in *REP*, vol. 7, pp. 386-392.

HAUBST, R. *Das Bild des Einen und Dreieinen Gottes in der Welt nach Nikolaus von Kues*. Paulinus: Trier, 1952. (*Trierer theologische Studien*, vol. 4.)

— 'Nikolaus von Kues und Johannes Wenck. Neue Erörterung und Nachträge': *Römische Quartalschrift für christliche Altertumskunde und Kirchengeschichte*, vol. 53 (1958), pp. 81-88.

— 'Albert, wie Cusanus ihn sah', in *Albertus Magnus - Doctor universalis 1280/1980*, eds G. Meyer and A. Zimmermann. Matthias-Grünewald: Mainz, 1980. Pp. 167-194. (*Walberberger Studien. Philosophisch-Theologische Hochschule der Dominikaner*, vol. 6.)

HEIMSOETH, H. 'Giordano Bruno und die deutsche Philosophie': *Blätter für die deutsche Philosophie*, vol. 15 (1941), pp. 396-433.

A history of twelfth-century Western philosophy, ed. P. Dronke. Cambridge University Press: Cambridge, 1988.

HOPKINS, J. *Nicholas of Cusa's metaphysics of contraction*. Banning: Minneapolis, 1983.

— *Nicholas of Cusa's debate with John Wenck. A translation and an appraisal of De ignota litteratura and Apologia doctae ignorantiae* [1981]. 3rd ed. Banning Press: Minneapolis, 1988.

— 'Introduction'. See Hopkins, *Nicholas of Cusa's debate with John Wenck*, pp. 3-18.

HUBER, K. *Einheit und Vielheit in Denken und Sprache Giordano Brunos*. Winterthur: Schellenberg, 1965.

HYMAN, A. 'Introduction'. See Averroes, *Sermo de substantia orbis*.

Indice dei nomi, dei luoghi e delle cose notevoli nelle opere latine di Giordano Bruno, compiled by C. Lefons. L. S. Olschki: Florence, 1998. (*Istituto nazionale di studi sul Rinascimento. Quaderni di* Rinascimento, vol. 38.)

Individuation in scholasticism. The later Middle Ages and the Counter-Reformation 1150-1650, ed. J. E. Gracia. State University of New York Press: Albany, 1994.

INGEGNO, A. 'Il primo Bruno e l'influenza di Marsilio Ficino': *RCSF*, vol. 23 (1968), pp. 149–170.

— 'Nota sul *Sigillus sigillorum* del Bruno', in *Studi in onore di Antonio Corsano*. Lacaita: Manduria, 1970. Pp. 361-369.

— *Cosmologia e filosofia nel pensiero di Giordano Bruno*. La nuova Italia: Florence, 1978.

— *La sommersa nave della religione. Studio sulla polemica anticristiana del Bruno*. Bibliopolis: Naples, 1985.

— *Regia pazzia. Bruno lettore di Calvino*. QuattroVenti: Urbino, 1987. (*Lo studiolo*.)

IPARRAGUIRRE, I. 'I. Vie et oeuvres', in 'Ignace de Loyola', in *DS*, vol. 7, pt 2, cols 1267-1277.

KLEIN, R. 'L'imagination comme vêtement de l'âme chez Marsile Ficin et Giordano Bruno': *Revue de métaphysique et de morale*, vol. 61 (1956), pp. 18–39.

KLIBANSKY, R. *'The continuity of the Platonic tradition during the Middle Ages' with a new preface and four supplementary chapters together with 'Plato's Parmenides in the Middle Ages and the Renaissance' with a new introductory preface*. Kraus International Publications: Munich, 1981.

KLIBANSKY, R., PANOFSKY, E. and SAXL, F. *Saturn and melancholy. Studies in the history of natural philosophy, religion and art*. Nelson: London, 1964.

KLUTSTEIN, I. 'Introduction', in Klutstein, *Marsilio Ficino et la theologie ancienne. Oracles Chaldaïques, Hymnes orphiques, Hymnes de Proclus*. L. S. Olschki: Florence, 1987. (*Istituto Nazionale di Studi sul Rinascimento. Quaderni di* Rinascimento, vol. 5.)

KNOX, D. *Pseudo-Aristoteles latinus*. See SCHMITT, C. B., and KNOX, D. *Pseudo-Aristoteles latinus*.

— 'Ficino, Copernicus and Bruno on the motion of the earth': *B&C*, 1999, pt 2, pp. 333-366.

— 'An arm and a leg: Giordano Bruno and Alessandro Citolini in Elizabethan London', in *Reflexivity. Critical themes in the Italian cultural tradition*, eds P. Shaw and J. Took. Longo: Ravenna, 2000. Pp. 161-176.

KNUUTTILA, S. 'Modal logic', in *CHLMP*, pp. 342-357.

KODERA, S. 'Narcissus, divine gazes and bloody mirrors: The concept of matter in Ficino', in *Marsilio Ficino, his theology, his philosophy, his legacy*, eds M. J. B. Allen, V. Rees and M. Davies. Brill: Leiden, 2002. Pp. 285-306.

KOYRÉ, A. *From the closed world to the infinite universe*. Harper: New York, 1958.

KRAYE, J. 'The pseudo-Aristotelian *Theology* in sixteenth- and seventeenth-century Europe', in *Pseudo-Aristotle in the Middle Ages: The Theology and other texts*, eds J. Kraye, W. F. Ryan and C. B. Schmitt. The Warburg Institute: London, 1986. Pp. 265-286. (*Warburg Institute Surveys and Texts*, vol. 11.)

— 'Moral philosophy', in *CHRP*, pp. 303-386.

KREMER, K. 'Die *creatio* nach Thomas von Aquin und dem *Liber de causis*', in *Ekklesia. Festschrift für Bishof Dr Matthias Wehr*. Paulinus: Trier, 1962. Pp. 321-344.

KRISTELLER, P. O. *Il pensiero filosofico di Marsilio Ficino*, 2nd ed. with enlarged bibliography. Le lettere: Florence, 1988. (An Italian translation of Kristeller, *Die Philosophie des Marsilio Ficino*. V. Klostermann: Frankfurt am Main, 1972.)

— 'Proclus as a reader of Plato and Plotinus, and his influence in the Middle Ages and in the Renaissance', in *Proclus. — Lecteur et interprète des anciens*. C.N.R.S.: Paris, 1987. Pp. 191-211.

LAPIDGE, M. 'Stoic cosmology', in *The Stoics*, ed. J. M. Rist. University of California Press: Berkeley etc., 1978. Pp. 161-185.

— 'The Stoic inheritance', in *A history of twelfth-century Western philosophy*, pp. 81-112.

LAZZARINI, R. 'Contrazione e incontrazione nell'individuo umano', in *Nicolò Cusano agli inizi del mondo moderno*, pp. 309-316.

LEE, J. S. 'The doctrine of reception according to the capacity of the recipient in *Ennead* VI.4-5': *Dionysius*, vol. 3 (1979), pp. 79-97.

LEINKAUF, T. 'Die Bestimmung des Einzelseienden durch die Begriffe *contractio*, *singularitas* und *aequalitas* bei Nicolaus Cusanus': *Archiv für Begriffsgeschichte*, vol. 37 (1994), pp. 180-211.

LÉVÊQUE, P. *Aurea catena Homeri. Une étude sur l'allégorie grecque*. Les Belles Lettres: Paris, 1959. (*Annales littéraires de l'Université de Besançon*, vol. 27.)

LIBERA, A. DE. 'Albert le Grand et Thomas d'Aquin interprètes du *Liber de causis*': *Revue des sciences philosophiques et théologiques*, vol. 74 (1990), pp. 347-378.

— 'Albert le Grand et le Platonisme. De la doctrine des idées à la théorie des trois états de l'universel', in *On Proclus and his influence in medieval philosophy*, eds E. P. Bos and P. A. Meijer. E. J. Brill: Leiden, 1992. Pp. 89-119. (*Philosophia antiqua*, vol. 53.)

LOHR, C. H. 'Medieval Latin Aristotle commentaries, Authors: Johannes de Kanthi—Myngodus': *Traditio*, vol. 27 (1971), pp. 251-351.

— *Latin Aristotle commentaries*, 3 vols. Leo S. Olschki: Florence, 1988.

— 'Metaphysics', in *CHRP*, pp. 535-638.

LOVEJOY, A. O. *The great chain of being. A study of the history of an idea*. Harvard University Press: Cambridge, Mass., 1936. (Reprinted: Lovejoy, *The great chain of being. A study of the history of an idea*. Harvard University Press: Cambridge, Mass., 1948.)

MACCAGNOLO, E. 'David of Dinant and the beginnings of Aristotelianism in Paris', in *A history of twelfth-century Western philosophy*, pp. 429-442.

MADDAMMA, M. 'Introduzione', in Bruno, *L'arte della memoria. Le ombre delle idee*, tr. M. Maddamma. Mimesis: Milan, 1996. Pp. 7-18.

MAHNKE, D. *Unendliche Sphäre und Allmittelpunkt. Beiträge zur Genealogie der mathematischen Mystik*. M. Niemeyer: Halle and Saale, 1937. (*Deutsche Vierteljahrsschrift für Literaturwissenchaft und Geistesgeschichte*, vol. 23.)

MAHONEY, E. P. 'Metaphysical foundations of the hierarchy of being according to some late-medieval and Renaissance philosophers', in *Philosophies of existence, ancient and medieval*, ed. P. Morewedge. Fordham University Press: New York, 1982.

— 'Reverberations of the Condemnation of 1277 in later medieval and Renaissance philosophy', in *Nach der Verurteilung von 1277. Philosophie und Theologie an der Univerität von Paris im letzten Viertel des 13. Jahrhunderts. Studien und Texte*, eds J. A. Aertsen, K. Emery, Jr., and A. Speer. Walter de Gruyter: Berlin, New York, 2001. (*Miscellanea Mediaevalia*, vol. 28.) Pp. 902-930.

MANCINI, S. *La sfera infinita. Identità e differenza nel pensiero di Giordano Bruno*. Mimesis: Milan, 2000.

MARENBON, J. *Later medieval philosophy*. Cambridge: Cambridge University Press, 1987.

MARX, J. *Verzeichnis der Handschriften-Samlung des Hospitals zu Cues bei Bernkastel a./Mosel*, compiled by J. Marx. Schaar & Dathe: Trier, 1905. (Reprinted: Cusanus-Gesellschaft: Bernkastel-Kues, 1976.)

MATTEOLI, M. 'L'arte della memoria nei primi scritti mnemotecnici di Bruno': *Rinascimento*, 2nd series, vol. 40 (2000), pp. 75-121.

MCCUMBER, J. 'Anamnesis as memory of intelligibles in Plotinus': *Archiv für Geschichte der Philosophie*, vol. 60 (1978), pp. 160-167.

MCMULLIN, E. 'Bruno and Copernicus': *Isis*, vol. 78 (1978), pp. 55–74.

Medioevo e rinascimento. Studi in onore di Bruno Nardi, 2 vols with continuous pagination. C. C. Sansoni: Florence, 1955. (*Pubblicazioni dell'Istituto di Filosofia dell'Università di Roma*, vols 1-2.)

MEIER-OESER, S. *Die Präsenz des Vergessenen. Zur Rezeption der Philosophie des Nicolaus Cusanus vom 15. bis zum 18. Jahrhundert*. Aschendorff: Münster, 1989. (*Buchreihe der Cusanus-Gesellschaft*, vol. 10.)

MERCATI, A. *Il sommario del processo di Giordano Bruno con appendice di documenti sull'eresia e l'inquisizione a Modena nel secolo xvi*. Biblioteca Apostolica Vaticana: Vatican City, 1942. (*Studi e testi*, vol. 101.)

MICHEL, P.–H. 'Renaissance cosmologies': *Diogenes*, vol. 18 (1957), pp. 93–107.

MIGNINI, F. 'La dottrina dell'individuo in Cusano e in Bruno': *B&C*, 2000, pt 2, pp. 325-349.

MONFASANI, J. 'Pseudo-Dionysius the Areopagite in mid-quatrocento Rome', in *Supplementum festivum: Studies in honor of Paul Oskar Kristeller*, pp. 189-219.

MORAN, D. 'Pantheism from John Scottus Eriugena to Nicholas of Cusa', in *American Catholic philosophical quarterly*, vol. 64 (1990), pp. 131-152.

MOREAU, J. *L'âme du monde de Platon aux stoïciens*. Les Belles Lettres: Paris, 1939.

NAMER, E. *Giordano Bruno ou l'univers infini comme fondement de la philosophie moderne*. Seghers: Paris, 1966. (*Philosophes de tous les temps*, vol. 31.)

NARBONNE, J.-M. 'Plotin et le problème de la génération de la matière; à propos d'un article récent': *Dionysius*, vol. 11 (1987), pp. 3-31.

— See Plotinus, *Les deux matières*.

NARDI, B. 'La dottrina d'Alberto Magno sull'*inchoatio formae*', in Nardi, *Studi di filosofia medievale*. Edizioni di storia e letteratura: Rome, 1960. Pp. 69-101.

NASH, P. W. 'Giles of Rome on Boethius' "Diversum est esse et id quod est"': *Mediaeval studies*, vol. 12 (1950), pp. 57-91.

NELSON, J. C. *Renaissance theory of love. The context of Giordano Bruno's* Eroici furori. Columbia University Press: New York and London, 1958.

Nicolò Cusano agli inizi del mondo moderno. Atti del congresso internazionale in occasione del quinto centenario della morte di Nicolò Cusano. Bressanone, 6-10 settembre 1964. C. C. Sansoni: Florence, 1970. (*Pubblicazioni della facoltà di magistero dell'Università di Padova*, vol. 12.)

NIKULIN, D. 'Intelligible matter in Plotinus': *Dionysius*, vol. 16 (1998), pp. 85-113.

O'BRIEN, D. 'Plotinus on evil. A study of matter and the soul in Plotinus' conception of human evil': *The Downside review*, vol. 87 (1969), pp. 68-110.

— 'Plotinus and the Gnostics on the generation of matter', in *Neoplatonism and early Christian thought. Essays in honour of A. H. Armstrong*, eds H. J. Blumenthal and R. A. Markus. Variorum: London, 1981. Pp. 108-123.

— 'J.-M. Narbonne on Plotinus and the generation of matter: two corrections': *Dionysius*, vol. 12 (1988), pp. 25-26.

— *Plotinus on the origin of matter. An exercise in the interpretation of the Enneads*. Bibliopolis: Naples, 1991. (*Elenchos*, vol. 22.)

— *Théodicée plotinienne. Théodicée gnostique*. E. J. Brill: Leiden, etc., 1993. (*Philosophia antiqua*, vol. 57.)

— 'Plotinus on matter and evil', in *The Cambridge companion to Plotinus*, ed. L. P. Gerson. Cambridge University Press: Cambridge, 1996. Pp. 171-195.

O'DALY, G. 'Memory in Plotinus and two early texts of St Augustine': *Texte und Untersuchungen*, vol. 117 (= *Studia patristica*, vol. 14), ed. E. A. Livingstone (Berlin, 1976), pp. 461-469. (Reprinted in O'Daly, *Platonism. Pagan and Christian. Studies in Plotinus and Augustine*. Ashgate: Aldershot, 2001. Pp. 461-469.)

O'MEARA, D. J. *Structures hiérarchiques dans la pensée de Plotin: Étude historique et interprétative*. E. J. Brill: Leiden, 1975. (*Philosophia antiqua*, vol. 27.)

— *Pythagoras revived: Mathematics and philosophy in late Antiquity*. Clarendon: Oxford, 1989.

— *Plotinus. An introduction to the Enneads*. Clarendon Press: Oxford, 1993.

ORDINE, N. *La cabala dell'asino. Asinità e conoscenza in Giordano Bruno*. Liguori: Naples, 1987. (*Teorie & oggetti*, vol. 29.)

— 'Introduction'. See Bruno, *Lo spaccio de la bestia trionfante*, pp. IX-CCVI.

OVERBACH, C. *Der Intuitionsbegriff bei Nikolaus Cusanus und seine Auswirkung bei Giordano Bruno*. Inaugural-Dissertation zur Erlangung der Doktorwürde genehmigt von der Philosophischen Fakultät der Rheinischen Friedrich-Wilhelms-Universität zu Bonn. Vorgelegt am 12. Mai 1920.

OWENS, J. 'Thomas Aquinas (b. ca. 1225; d. 1274)' in *Individuation in scholasticism. The later Middle Ages and the Counter-Reformation 1150-1650*, pp. 173-194.

— *The doctrine of being in the Aristotelian 'Metaphysics': A study in the Greek background of medieval thought*, preface by E. Gilson, 2nd ed. Pontifical Institute of Mediaeval Studies: Toronto, 1963.

PAGEL, W. 'Giordano Bruno: the philosophy of circles and the circular movement of the blood': *Journal of the history of medicine*, vol. 6 (1951), pp. 116-124.

PANOFSKY, E. *Studies in iconology. Humanistic themes in the arts of the Renaissance*. Oxford University Press: Oxford, 1939.

PAPI, F. *Antropologia e civiltà nel pensiero di Giordano Bruno*. La Nuova Italia: Florence, 1968. (*Pubblicazioni della facoltà di lettere e filosofia dell'università di Milano*, vol. 46.)

PAPULI, G. 'Qualche osservazione su Giordano Bruno e l'aristotelismo': *Quaderno filosofico*, vol. 10-11 (1984), pp. 201-228.

PARK, K. 'The organic soul', in *CHRP*, pp. 464-484.

PATTIN, A. 'Introduction'. See pseudo-Aristotle, *Liber de causis*, ed. A. Pattin, pp. 90-134.

PETERSON, L. 'Cardinal Cajetan (Thomas De Vio) (b. 1468; d. 1534) and Giles of Rome (b. ca. 1243/47; d. 1316)', in *Individuation in scholasticism. The later Middle Ages and the Counter-Reformation 1150-1650*, pp. 431-455.

PUNTA, F. DEL, and TRIFOGLI, C. 'Giles of Rome', in *REP*, vol. 4, pp. 72-78.

RICCI, S. *La fortuna del pensiero di Giordano Bruno 1600-1750*. Le Lettere: Florence, 1990. (*Giornale critico della filosofia italiana. Quaderni*, vol. 1.)

— *Giordano Bruno nell'Europa del cinquecento*. Salerno: Rome, 2000. (*Profili*, vol. 26.)

RIST, J. M. 'Plotinus on matter and evil': *Phronesis*, vol. 6 (1961), pp. 154-166.

— 'The indefinite dyad and intelligible matter in Plotinus': *The classical quarterly*, vol. 12 (1962), pp. 99-107.

— *Plotinus: The road to reality*. Cambridge University Press: Cambridge, 1967.

ROLLS, J. J. *God and the world: Some interpretations of the 'transcendental' analogy of being in Western theology from the thirteenth to the sixteenth centuries*. PhD dissertation, Warburg Institute, University of London, 1999.

DE ROSA, G. *Il concetto di 'immaginazione' nel pensiero di Giordano Bruno*. La città del sole: Naples, 1997.

ROSSI, P. 'Studi sul lullismo e sull'arte della memoria nel Rinascimento. I teatri del mondo e il lullismo di Giordano Bruno': *RCSF*, vol. 14 (1959), pp. 29-60.

— 'Hermeticism, rationality and the scientific revolution', in *Reason, experiment, and mysticism in the scientific revolution*, eds M. L. R. Bonelli and W. R. Shea. Science History Publications: New York, 1975. Pp. 247-273.

— *Clavis universalis. Arti della memoria e logica combinatoria da Lullo a Leibniz.* 2nd rev. ed. Il Mulino: Bologna, 1983. (*Saggi*, vol. 244).

ROTH, U. *Cusanus-Texte. III. Marginalien. 4. Raimundus Lullus. Die Exzerptensamlung aus Schriften des Raimundus Lullus im Codex Cusanus 83*, ed. U. Roth. C. Universitätsverlag C. Winter: Heidelberg, 1999. (*Schriften der Philosophisch-historischen Klasse der Heidelberger Akademie der Wissenschaften*, vol. 13.)

ROWLAND, I. D.'Giordano Bruno and Neapolitan Neoplatonism', in *Giordano Bruno: Philosopher of the Renaissance*, pp. 97-119.

SAFFREY, H. D. 'Introduction'. See Aquinas, *Super Librum de causis expositio*, pp. XIII-LXXIII.

SALVESTRINI, V. *Bibliografia di Giordano Bruno (1582-1950)*, 2nd rev. ed., ed. L. Firpo. Sansoni Antiquariato: Florence, 1958. (*Biblioteca bibliografica italica*, vol. 12.)

SAMBURSKY, S. *Physics of the Stoics*. Routledge and Kegan Paul: London, 1959.

SANTINELLO, G. 'Il neoplatonismo di Nicolò Cusano', in *Il neoplatonismo nel rinascimento*, ed. P. Prini. Paoletti: Florence, 1993. Pp. 103-115.

SARAUW, J. *Der Einfluss Plotins auf Giordano Brunos* Degli eroici furori. *(Ein Beitrag zur Philosophie der Renaissance.)* Norske: Borna and Leipzig, 1916.

SCHEUERMANN-PEILICKE, W. *Licht und Liebe. Lichtmetapher und Metaphysik bei Marsilio Ficino*. G. Olms: Hildesheim and New York, 2000. (*Studien und Materialen zur Geschichte der Philosophie*, vol. 57.)

SCHMITT, C. B. *Aristotle and the Renaissance*. Harvard University Press: Cambridge, Mass. and London, 1983. (*Martin Classical Lectures*, vol. 27).

SCHMITT, C. B., and KNOX, D. *Pseudo-Aristoteles latinus. A guide to Latin works falsely attributed to Aristotle before 1500*. The Warburg Institute: London, 1985. (*Warburg Institute Surveys and Texts*, vol. 12.)

SCHWYZER, H.-R. 'Zu Plotins Deutung der sogenannten platonischen Materie', in *Zetesis. Album amicorum door vrienden en collega's aangeboden aan Prof. Dr. E. de Strycker. Gewoon Hoogleraar aan de Universitaire Faculteiten Sint-Ignatius te Antwerpen ter gelegenheid van zijn vijfenzestigste verjaardag.* De Nederlandsche Boekhandel: Antwerpen and Utrecht, 1973. Pp. 266-280.

SENGER, H. G. *Cusanus-Texte. III. Marginalien. 2. Proclus latinus. Die Exzerpte und Randnoten des Nikolaus von Kues zu den lateinischen Übersetzungen der Proclus-Schriften 2.1* Theologia Platonis, Elementatio theologica, ed. and comm. H. G. Senger. C. Winter: Heidelberg, 1986. (*Abhandlungen der Heidelberger Akademie der Wissenschaften. Philosophisch-historische Klasse*, 1986, 2. Abhandlung.)

SIMONIN, H. D. 'La notion d'*intentio* dans la philosophie de St Thomas': *Revue des sciences philosophiques et théologiques*, vol. 19 (1930), pp. 445-463.

SINNIGE, T. G. 'Metaphysical and personal religion in Plotinus', in *Kephalaion. Studies in Greek philosophy and its continuation offered to Professor C. J. de Vogel*, eds J. Mansfeld and L. M. de Rijk. Van Gorcum: Assen, 1975. Pp. 147-154.

SIRAISI, N. G. *Medieval and early Renaissance medicine: An introduction to knowledge and practice.* Chicago University Press: Chicago, 1990.

SPAMPANATO, V. *Vita di G. Bruno con documenti editi e inediti.* 2 vols with continuous pagination. G. Principato: Messina, 1921. (*Studi filosofici*, vol. 10.)

SPRUIT, L. '*Magia: socia naturae.* Questioni teoriche nelle opere magiche di Giordano Bruno': *Il centauro*, vols 17-18 (1986), pp. 146-169.

— *Il problema della conoscenza in Giordano Bruno.* Bibliopolis: Naples, 1988. (*Saggi bibliopolis*, vol. 29.)

— 'Motivi peripatetici nella gnoseologia bruniana dei dialoghi italiani': *Verifiche*, year 18, nr 4 (1989), pp. 367-399.

— '*Species intelligibilis': from perception to knowledge*, 2 vols. E. J. Brill: Leiden, New York and Cologne, 1994-95.

— 'Spunti sulle fonti della psicologia bruniana': *NRL*, vol. 2 (1994), pp. 205-207.

— 'Giordano Bruno and astrology', in *Giordano Bruno: Philosopher of the Renaissance*, ed. Hillary Gatti. Ashgate: Aldershot, 2002, pp. 229-249.

STERN, F. B. *Giordano Bruno — Vision einer Weltsicht.* A. Hain: Meisenheim am Glan, 1977.

STURLESE, R. *Bibliografia, censimento e storia delle antiche stampe di Giordano Bruno.* L. S. Olschki: Florence, 1987. (*Istituto nazionale di studi sul rinascimento. Quaderni di* Rinascimento, vol. 6.)

— 'Il *De imaginum, signorum et idearum compositione* di Giordano Bruno ed il significato filosofico dell'arte della memoria': *GCFI*, vol. 69 (1990), pp. 182–203.

— 'Introduzione'. See Bruno, *De umbris idearum*, pp. IX-LXXVII.

— 'L'arte della memoria tra Bruno e Leibniz. Gli scritti di mnemotecnica del medico paracelsiano Adam Bruxius': *GCFI*, vol. 70 (1991), pp. 379–408.

— 'Niccolò Cusano e gli inizi della speculazione del Bruno', in *Historia philosophiae medii aevi. Studien zur Geschichte der Philosophie des Mittelalters. Festschrift für K. Flasch*, eds B. Mojsisch and O. Pluta, 2 vols with continuous pagination. B. R. Grüner: Amsterdam and Philadelphia, 1991. Pp. 953-966.

— 'Per un'interpretazione del *De umbris idearum* di Giordano Bruno': *Annali della Scuola Normale Superiore di Pisa*, 3rd series, vol. 22 (1992), pp. 943–968.

— 'Giordano Brunos Gedächtniskunst und das Geheimnis der Schatten der Ideen', in *Giordano Bruno. Tragik eines Unzeitgemässen*, ed. W. Hirdt. Stauffenburg: Tübingen, 1993. Pp. 69-91. (*Romanica et comparatistica. Sprach- und literaturwissenschaftliche Studien*, vol. 20.)

— '"Averroè quantumque arabo et ignorante di lingua greca..." Note sull'averroismo di Giordano Bruno', in *Averroismus im Mittelalter und in der Renaissance*, eds F. Niewöhner and L. Sturlese. Spur: Zurich, 1994. Pp. 319–350. This article was first published in *GCFI*, vol. 12, 1992, pp. 248–275. I cite the publication from 1994 as Sturlese, '"Averroè quantumque arbo"'.

— 'Le fonti del *Sigillus sigillorum* del Bruno, ossia: il confronto con Ficino a Oxford sull'anima umana': *NRL*, vol. 2 (1994), pp. 89–167.

— 'Arte della natura e arte della memoria in Giordano Bruno': *Rinascimento*, 2nd series, vol. 40 (2000), pp. 123-141.

Supplementum festivum: Studies in the honor of Paul Oskar Kristeller, eds J. Hankins, J. Monfasani, F. Purnell, Jr. Centre for Medieval and Renaissance Studies, State University of New York at Binghamton: Binghamton, New York, 1987. (*Medieval and Renaissance studies*, vol. 49.)

SWEENEY, L. 'Doctrine of creation in *Liber de causis*', in *An Étienne Gilson tribute*, ed. C. J. O'Neil. Marquette University Press: Milwaukee, 1959. Pp. 274-289.

TAYLOR, R. C. 'St Thomas and the *Liber de causis* on the hylomorphic composition of separate substances': *Mediaeval studies*, vol. 41 (1979), pp. 506-513.

— 'The *Liber de causis*: A preliminary list of extant manuscripts': *Bulletin de la philosophie médiévale*, vol. 25 (1983), pp. 63-84.

— 'The *Kalam fī mahd al-khair* (*Liber de causis*) in the Islamic philosophical milieu', in *Pseudo-Aristotle in the Middle Ages: The Theology and other texts*, eds J. Kraye, W. F. Ryan and C. B. Schmitt. The Warburg Institute: London, 1986. Pp. 37-52. (*Warburg Institute Surveys and Texts*, vol. 11.)

— 'Aquinas, the *Plotiniana Arabica*, and the metaphysics of being and actuality': *Journal of the history of ideas*, vol. 59 (1998), pp. 217-239.

THÉRY, G. *Autour de décret de 1210: I. David de Dinant. Étude sur son panthéisme matérialiste*. Kain: Le Saulchoir, 1925. (*Bibliothèque thomiste*, vol. 6.)

TIRINNANZI, N. '*Ars* e *phantasia* in Giordano Bruno': *Esercizi filosofici*, vol. 1 (1992), pp. 109–131.

TOCCO, F. *Le opere latine di Giordano Bruno esposte e confrontate con le italiane*. Le Monnier: Florence, 1889.

— *Le fonti più recenti della filosofia del Bruno*, in *Rendiconti della R. Accademia dei Lincei. Classe di scienze morali, storiche e filologiche*, vol. 1, 1892, pp. 503-622.

TORRELL, J.-P. *Saint Thomas Aquinas. The person and his work*. The Catholic University of America Press: Washington, D. C., 1996. (Translated by R. Royal from the French version: *L'initiation à Saint Thomas d'Aquin: Sa personne et son oeuvre*. Editions Universitaires Fribourg Suisse: Paris, 1993.)

TRAPÉ, G. 'Il neoplatonismo di Egidio Romano nel commento al *De causis*': *Aquinas*, vol. 9 (1966), pp. 49-86.

VANSTEENBERGHE, E. 'Introduction', in Vansteenberghe, 'Le *De ignota litteratura* de Jean Wenck de Herrenberg contre Nicolas de Cuse': *Beiträge zur Geschichte der Philosophie des Mittelalters*, Band 8, Heft 6 (1910), pp. 1-18.

— *Autour de la Docte ignorance. Une controverse sur la théologie mystique au XVe siècle*: Aschendorff: Münster i. W., 1915. (*Beiträge zur Geschichte der Philosophie des Mittelalters*, Band 14, Heft 2-4.)

— *Le Cardinal Nicolas de Cues (1401-1464). L'action - la pensée*. H. Champion: Paris, 1920. (*Bibliothèque du XVe siècle*, vol. 24.) (Reprint: Slatkine Preprints: Geneva, 1974.)

VASOLI, C. 'Umanesimo e simbologia nei primi scritti lulliani e mnemotecnici del Bruno', in *Umanesimo e simbolismo. Atti del IV convegno internazionale di studi umanistici*, ed. E. Castelli. Padova, 1958. Pp. 251-304.

— 'Immagini e simboli nei primi scritti lulliani e mnemotecnici del Bruno', in Vasoli, *Studi sulla cultura del rinascimento*. Lacaita: Manduria, 1968. Pp. 345–426. (*Biblioteca di studi moderni*, vol. 5.)

— 'Considerazioni sul *De raptu Pauli* di Marsilio Ficino', in *Concordia discors. Studi su Niccolò Cusano e l'umanesimo europeo offerti a Giovanni Santinello*, ed. G. Piaia. Antenore: Padova, 1993. Pp. 377-404. (*Medioevo e umanesimo*, vol. 84.)

— 'La *ratio* nella filosofia di Marsilio Ficino', in *Ratio. VII colloquio internazionale, Roma, 9-11 gennaio 1992*, eds M. Fattori and M. L. Bianchi. L. S. Olschki: Florence, 1994. Pp. 219-237. (*Lessico intellettuale europeo*, vol. 61.)

VÉDRINE, H. *La conception de la nature chez Giordano Bruno*. J. Vrin: Paris, 1967. (*De Pétrarque a Descartes*, vol. 14.)

— 'L'influence de Nicolas de Cues sur Giordano Bruno', in *Nicolò Cusano agli inizi del mondo moderno*, pp. 211-223.

— 'Image et imagination chez Bruno', in *Il neoplatonismo nel rinascimento*, ed. P. Prini. Paoletti: Florence, 1993. Pp. 45–52.

VESCOVINI, G. F. 'Introduzione', in Nicholas of Cusa, *La dotta ignoranza*, pp. 5-35.

— 'Temi ermetico-neoplatonici de *La dotta ignoranza* di Nicola Cusano', in *Il neoplatonismo nel rinascimento*, ed. P. Prini. Paoletti: Florence, 1993. Pp. 117-132.

VITALE, E. 'Sul concetto di materia nella *Theologia platonica* di Marsilio Ficino': *Rinascimento*, 2nd series, vol. 39 (1999), pp. 337-369.

WAGNER, M. F. 'Plotinus' idealism and the problem of matter in *Enneads* vi.4 & 5': *Dionysius*, vol. 10 (1986), pp. 57-83.

WALKER, D. P. 'The astral body in Renaissance medicine': *JWCI*, vol. 21 (1958), pp. 119-133.

— *Spiritual and demonic magic from Ficino to Campanella*. Warburg Institute: London, 1958. (*Studies of the Warburg Institute*, vol. 22.)

— *The ancient theology. Studies in Christian Platonism from the fifteenth to the eighteenth century*. Duckworth: London, 1972.

WALLIS, R. T. *Neoplatonism*. Duckworth: London, 1972. 2nd ed. with a foreword and bibliography by L. P. Gerson. Bristol Classical Press: London, 1995.

WARREN, E. W. 'Memory in Plotinus': *The classical quarterly*, vol. 59 (1965), pp. 252-260.

— 'Imagination in Plotinus': *The classical quarterly*, vol. 60 (1966), pp. 277-285.

WATTS, P. M. *Nicolaus Cusanus. A fifteenth-century vision of man*. E. J. Brill: Leiden, 1982. (*Studies in the history of Christian thought*, vol. 30.)

WEISHEIPL, J. A. *Friar Thomas d'Aquino. His life, thought, and work*. Doubleday & Company: New York, 1974.

— 'The concept of matter in fourteenth century science', in *The concept of matter in Greek and Medieval philosophy*, ed. E. McMullin. Notre Dame University Press: Notre Dame, Ind., 1965, pp. 147-169.

WESTMAN, R. S. 'Magical reform and astronomical reform. The Yates thesis reconsidered', in *Hermeticism and the scientific revolution*, eds R. S. Westman and J. E. McGuire, University of California: Los Angeles, 1977. Pp. 1–91.

WILDGEN, W. *Das kosmische Gedächtnis. Kosmologie, Semiotik und Gedächtnistheorie im Werke Giordano Brunos (1548-1600)*. P. Lang: New York etc., 1998. (*Philosophie und Geschichte der Wissenschaften. Studien und Quellen*, vol. 38.)

WIND, E. *Pagan mysteries in the Renaissance*. 2nd ed. Faber and Faber: London 1958.

WIPPEL, J. F. 'Essence and existence', in *CHLMP*, pp. 285-410.

— 'Siger of Brabant', in *REP*, vol. 8, pp. 764-768.

WITTMANN, M. 'Giordano Brunos Beziehungen zu Avencebrol': *Archiv für Geschichte der Philosophie*, vol. 13 (1900), pp. 147-152.

— *Die Stellung des h. Thomas von Aquin zu Avencebrol*, eds C. Baeumker and G. F. von Hertling. Aschendorff: Münster i. W., 1900. Pp. 1-79. (*Beiträge zur Geschichte der Philosophie des Mittelalters. Texte und Untersuchungen*, Band 3, Heft 3.)

WOLTER, A. B. 'John Duns Scotus (b. ca. 1265; d. 1308)', in *Individuation in scholasticism. The later Middle Ages and the Counter-Reformation 1150-1650*, ed. J. E. Gracia. State University of New York Press: Albany, 1994. Pp. 271-298.

YATES, F. A. 'The Ciceronian art of memory', in *Medioevo e rinascimento. Studi in onore di Bruno Nardi*, pp. 871–903.

— *Giordano Bruno and the Hermetic tradition*. Routledge and Kegan Paul: London, 1964.

— *The art of memory*. Routledge and Kegan Paul: London, 1966.

ZWAENEPOEL, J. P. 'Introduction'. See Albert the Great, *Quaestiones in Librum de causis*, pp. 7-21.

Index of Primary Sources

Actus apostolorum

9.1-12: p. 21 n. 69
22.5-16: p. 21 n. 69
26.12-18: p. 21 n. 69

2 Ad Corinthios

12.1-4: p. 21 n. 69

Secundum Mattheum

21.21-22: p. 14 n. 34

Ad Romanos

9.20-21: p. 67 n. 76

1 Liber Samuhelis

14.19: p. 91 n. 3

Ad Timotheum

ii 2.20-21: p. 67 n. 76

BOETHIUS, ANICIUS MANLIUS SEVERINUS

In praedicamenta Aristotelis, in
Boethius, *Opera omnia*, Basel 1570

i, p. 114.5-6: p. 56 n. 23
i, p. 114.5-12: p. 56 n. 24

BRUNO, GIORDANO

*De compendiosa architectura artis
Lullii*, eds F. Tocco and H. Vitelli, in
BOL, vol. 2, pt 2

i 4, p. 7.13-16: p. 96 n. 38
iii 7, p. 60.19-21: p. 56 n. 22

*Articuli centum et sexaginta
adversus huius tempestatis
mathematicos atque philosophos*,
eds F. Tocco and H. Vitelli, in *BOL*,
vol. 1, pt 3

p. 59.23-25: p. 139 n. 20
p. 60.12: p. 138 n. 15

*La cabala del cavallo pegaseo con
l'aggiunta dell'asino cillenico*, ed.
G. Aquilecchia, in *BOeuC*, vol. 6

declamazione, p. 23: p. 68 n. 78
declamazione, pp. 23-25: p. 68 n. 77
i, p. 69: p. 58 n. 31
ii, pp. 95-97: p. 29 n. 2

*Camoeracensis Acrotismus seu
rationes articulorum physicorum
adversus peripateticos Parisiis
propositorum*, ed. F. Fiorentino, in
BOL, vol. 1, pt 1

pp. 68.27-69.5: p. 12 n. 24
pp. 93.19-94.3: pp. 29 n. 1, 86 n. 84
pp. 94.18-95.3: p. 29 n. 1
pp. 148.19-149.3: p. 29 n. 1
p. 177.10-12: p. 33 n. 23

Candelaio, ed. G. Aquilecchia, in
BOeuC, vol. 1

v 17, p. 349: p. 155 n. 95
v 23, p. 393: p. 155 n. 95

*Cantus Circaeus ad eam memoriae
praxim ordinatus quam ipse
Iudiciariam appellat*, eds V.
Imbriani and C. M. Tallarigo in
BOL, vol. 1, pt 1

iii 1, p. 235.25-27: p. 54 n. 18

De la causa, principio et uno, ed. G.
Aquilecchia, in *BOeuC*, vol. 3

epist., p. 13: pp. 33 n. 23, 37 n. 50
epist., p. 15: p. 36 n. 48
epist., p. 17: pp. 35 n. 35, 39 n. 59,
    42 n. 72
epist., pp. 17-19: pp. 32 n. 18, 114 n.
    65
epist., p. 21: p. 29 n. 1
epist., p. 23: pp. 34 n. 27, 58 n. 31
ii, p. 101: p. 111 n. 39

v, p. 361: p. 47 n. 99

De lampade combinatoria lulliana,
eds F. Tocco and H. Vitelli, in *BOL*,
vol. 2, pt 2

praefatio, p. 234.6-9: pp. 138 n. 15,
140 n. 23
praefatio, p. 240.1-10: p. 155 n. 95
I ix, p. 280.20-25: p. 50 n. 3

Lampas triginta statuarum, ed. N.
Tirinnanzi, in *BOM*; = *BOL*, vol. 3,
indicated in brackets

§64.1-4, p. 1020 (p. 42.22-24): p.
151 n. 77
§64.14-23, p. 1022 (p. 43.7-15): p.
54 n. 18
§74.1-16, pp. 1036-1038 (p. 50.4-
19): p. 13 n. 27
§§241.1-244.11, pp. 1226-1230 (pp.
140.4-141.27): p. 98 n. 46
§242.1-3, p. 1226 (p. 140.14-16): p.
96 n. 38
§243.1-19, pp. 1228-1230 (pp.
140.24-141.17): p. 97 n. 39
§243.11-13, p. 1228 (p. 141.9-11): p.
97 n. 41
§243.14-17, p. 1230 (p. 141.12-15):
pp. 50 n. 1, 97 n. 42
§243.18-19, p. 1230 (p. 141.16-17):
p. 97 n. 44
§244.1-6, p. 1230 (p. 141.18-22): pp.
77 n. 43, 79 n. 51, 80 n. 55
§245.1-4, p. 1232 (p. 142.3-6): p. 98
n. 46
§246.12-27, pp. 1232-1234 (p.
143.1-16): pp. 16 n. 41, 98 n. 49
§252.[1-5], p. 1372 (p. 206.14-19):
p. 58 n. 31
§322.12-16, p. 1316 (p. 183.20-24):
p. 155 n. 95
§408.10-18, pp. 1434-1436 (pp.
238.19-239.1): p. 52 n. 9
§408.13-23, pp. 1434-1436 (pp.
238.22-239.6): p. 29 n. 2
§419.15-22, p. 1452 (p. 245.16-24):
p. 29 n. 1

*Libri physicorum aristotelis
explanati*, in *BOL*, vol. 3

p. 381.22: p. 21 n. 67

De magia mathematica, ed. N.
Tirinnanzi, in *BOM*; = *BOL*, vol. 3,
indicated in brackets

§2.27-30, p. 10 (p. 495.16-20): p.
155 n. 95

De magia naturali, ed. S. Bassi, in
BOM; = *De magia*, in *BOL*, vol. 3,
indicated in brackets

§2.17-24, p. 162 (p. 398.8-16): pp.
68 n. 82, 85 n. 79
§2.17-30, p. 162 (p. 398.8-22): p. 95
n. 33
§6.1-23, pp. 168-170 (pp. 401.25-
402.21): p. 1 n. 2
§7.1-2, p. 172 (p. 403.4-5): p. 58 n.
31
§16.6-7, p. 188 (p. 409.16-17): p. 10
n. 15
§16.6-10, p. 188 (p. 409.16-20): pp.
11 n. 17, 50 n. 1, 115 n. 71

*De monade numero et figura,
secretioris nempe physicae,
mathematicae et metaphysicae
elementa*, ed. F. Fiorentino, in *BOL*,
vol. 1, pt 2

iii, p. 356.11-27: p. 78 n. 44
iii, p. 356.20-27: p. 50 n. 1
v, p. 387.20: p. 20 n. 64
vii, pp. 427.23-428.1: p. 155 n. 95
xi, p. 464.21-24: p. 155 n. 95

Oratio valedictoria, ed. F.
Fiorentino, in *BOL*, vol. 1, pt 1

pp. 14.22-15.5: p. 58 n. 31
p. 17.2-7: pp. 138 n. 15, 140 n. 25

*De progressu et lampade venatoria
logicorum. Ad prompte atque
copiose de quocumque proposito*

Theoremata de esse et essentia, ed. E. Hocedez

Tractatus de esse et esentia, in MS Cues 195

PSEUDO-HENRY OF GHENT

Quaestiones in Librum de causis, ed. J. P. Zwaenepoel

HOMER

Iliad, ed. A. T. Murray, rev. ed. W. F. Wyatt

IAMBLICHUS

De mysteriis Aegyptorum, Chaldaeorum, Assyriorum, ed. and tr. M. Ficino, Venice 1497

De mysteriis Aegyptorum, ed. des Places

JAVELLI

In librum de causis. Commentarii duo, in JAVELLI, [*Opera*], Lyon 1580

LANDINO, CRISTOFORO

Disputationes camaldulenses, ed. P. Lohe

LOYOLA, ST IGNATIUS

LULL, RAYMOND

LUTHER, MARTIN

MACROBIUS

MERSENNE, MARIN

NICHOLAS OF CUSA

Index of Names